Take your kids travelling! Take them no⌐
Children grow up fast and you'll
better, more rewarding oppc
their lives, minds and souls – or you
a family holiday. It doesn't matter wh
off work and take them for a day trip tⱺ
or rent out the house and embark on a ι ⌐onth
odyssey across Europe. From bucket-and-ꜱpade to
epic escapade, family holidays create memories that
will live with you long after your children have grown
up. They provide quality time away from the rush and
stress of everyday life; they are precious, hard-earned
and over all-too-quickly. Yes, they can also be pricey
and hard work – and occasionally they might not go
to plan. But they are always money well spent, and
even the bad bits inspire priceless family jokes in
years to come. So, ignore all those miserable types
who pour scorn on this indispensable part of life –
whose blinkered, joyless view of family holidays never
sees beyond travel sickness or stroppy teenagers.
Travelling with kids is about making compromises
to meet everyone's needs. It's about sharing and
bonding as a family unit. It's the immeasurable
pleasure and satisfaction of showing your children
just how amazing the world is; of seeing their faces
light up at things you might otherwise have taken for
granted. Family holidays allow you to take stock of
life and appreciate what's really important. So seize
them. Travel with your kids. Do it this year and every
year you can.

Award-winning writer
and photographer
William Gray is the
author of Footprint's
Travel with Kids, voted
Guidebook of the Year
2008 by the British Guild
of Travel Writers, as well
as *Britain with Kids* and
Cornwall with Kids.

Buggy-friendly *piazza*.

About the book

Europe with Kids is split into two main sections. The first, **Essentials**, deals with basics, like what to pack and how to get around. The bulk of the book, however, is dedicated to destinations. Each country or regional chapter is divided into five parts. An introduction sets the scene with a map and several family-friendly highlights. Next is **Kids' stuff** – packed with ideas, resources and activities to get children interested in each destination, whether it's books to read, games to play or traditional meals to try at home – while **Tots to teens** provides a holiday planner for various age groups. This is followed by the main part of each chapter – a detailed look at the family-holiday potential of key locations. **Grown-ups' stuff** rounds things off with essential information on travel nitty-gritty, as well as some suggestions for 'family favourite' accommodation.

Europe with Kids is designed to be both inspirational and informative. You will find plenty of advice, encouragement and reassurance to plan a lifetime of holidays throughout Europe. You won't find exhaustive directories of family-friendly hotels and restaurants or laborious lists of tourist information centres. Nor will you find every region in Europe featured. Those that have been selected, however, reflect a mixture of the most popular, unusual and exciting destinations to take your kids.

Ages

Individual development varies greatly from child to child, but as a guide the following age categories are used throughout *Europe with Kids*:

Babies
(0-18 months)
Wonderfully portable, either in a stroller, papoose or backpack; may still be breastfed or require baby food; unable to communicate when things are wrong except through the obvious medium of bawling.

Toddlers/pre-school
(18 months-4 years)
Terrifyingly mobile, with issues of balance and fearlessness demanding constant surveillance; able to communicate more articulately when unwell or unsure about something.

Kids/school age
(4-12 years)
Insatiable thirst for just about everything; able to interact with other children and respond with sensitivity to certain issues; game for most activities but many may require adult supervision.

Teenagers
(13 years+)
Keen to be independent; prone to moody moments when everything seems boring, but can also be great 'adult' travel companions.

It is up to parents to individually assess whether the information given in *Europe with Kids* is suitable or appropriate for their children. While the author and publisher have made every effort to ensure accuracy with subjects such as activities, accommodation and food, they cannot be held responsible for any loss, injury or illness resulting from advice or information given in this book.

3   Introduction
5   About the book
8   Essentials

22 Britain
26   Kids' stuff
28   Tots to teens
30   London
32   Southeast England
33   East Anglia
34   Southwest England
36   Central England
38   North England
40   Wales
42   Scotland
44   Grown-ups' stuff

48 Ireland
52   Kids' stuff
54   Tots to teens
56   Dublin
58   East Coast
60   Northern Ireland
62   The Southeast
64   The Northwest
66   The West
68   Shannon
70   The Southwest
72   Grown-ups' stuff

76 France
80   Kids' stuff
82   Tots to teens
84   Paris
90   Northern France
92   Southwest France
94   Loire Valley
96   French Alps
100 South of France
103 Corsica
104 Grown-ups' stuff

110 Spain & Portugal
114 Kids' stuff
116 Tots to teens
118 Central Spain
120 Northern Spain
122 Catalonia
126 Andalucía
128 Balearic Islands
130 Canary Islands
134 Portugal
138 Grown-ups' stuff

Contents

146 Italy

150	Kids' stuff
152	Tots to teens
154	Rome
158	Tuscany
162	Venice
166	The Lakes
168	Umbria & Le Marche
170	Puglia
172	Bay of Naples
174	Sicily
175	Sardinia
176	Grown-ups' stuff

182 Central Europe

186	Kids' stuff
188	Tots to teens
190	Low Countries
194	Germany
198	Switzerland
200	Austria
202	Grown-ups' stuff

206 Greece & Turkey

210	Kids' stuff
212	Tots to teens
214	Athens
218	The Peloponnese
219	Halkidikí
222	Greek islands
226	Crete
228	Cyprus
230	Istanbul
232	Turkish coast
236	Grown-ups' stuff

242 Eastern Europe

246	Kids' stuff
248	Tots to teens
250	Czech Republic
252	Poland
253	Slovakia
253	Hungary
254	Romania
255	Bulgaria
256	Slovenia
258	Croatia
260	Grown-ups' stuff

264 Scandinavia

268	Kids' stuff
270	Tots to teens
274	Denmark
278	Sweden
282	Norway
286	Finland
290	Iceland
294	Grown-ups' stuff

300 Index
304 Credits

Inside front cover

School holidays
Store directory
Airlines A-Z
Five ways to save money
Festivals & events

Contents

10 Travel through the ages

12 Tour operators

14 What to take

16 How to get there

18 Where to stay

20 What to eat & drink

Gelato stall, Italy.

Essentials

Essentials Travel through the ages

It's hardly surprising that more parents shun holidays when their children are aged between one and four than at any other time. Not only do practicalities, like flying, become fraught with stress and logistical nightmares, but you are constantly striving to reduce the impact of your little darlings on other, often unsympathetic, travellers. That, combined with the general fatigue that stalks new parents, does little to set the wheels of family travel in motion.

We've all been there: sleep deprived, irritable, barely capable of summoning the energy (or baby paraphernalia) for a trip to the shops, let alone a holiday. However, there are several good reasons why it's never too early to start travelling with kids: babies are easy to transport in strollers, backpacks or papooses; they can't dictate where you go or what you do (so make the most of it while it lasts); in most countries locals will make a big fuss of them which is a great morale boost for weary new parents; babies often go free (the older children get, the more expensive they become, and travel is no exception); there are plenty of innovative baby travel products designed to make life easier; and choose the right hotel or resort and you get some well-deserved pampering.

Onwards, upwards and falling over
With toddlerdom come new challenges. Many parents claim this to be the most demanding time to travel with children. Health and safety is not exactly foremost in the minds of these mini-explorers and you need to be particularly wary of unfenced swimming pools and balconies with squeeze-through railings. If there's one thing that makes travel with toddlers easier it's their increasing ability to talk – even if it's just to tell you they are about to be sick.

The 'why, what, when, how' years
By the time they reach school age, kids are a real pleasure to travel with. There is something wonderfully refreshing about their innocent and undisguised joy over experiencing even the most mundane aspects of travel. For example, no other age group is particularly bothered about watching the laborious task of weighing and labelling

luggage at an airport check-in desk – but to a six-year-old boy it is an utterly transfixing event, punctuated by inconceivable weights, whirring sticker-producing machines and mysterious conveyor belts that whisk suitcases through trapdoors. Even airline food trays instigate goggle-eyed wonder and at least five minutes of vocal hyperactivity. School-age children are also at that stage when they can tell you what they like and dislike, which can either be a blessing or a curse when it comes to holiday planning. Be prepared, too, for endless questions as they grapple to comprehend new experiences, cultures and issues.

Call it educational
A whole generation of globetrotting backpackers from the 1980s and 1990s now have young families. Rather than shred their passports and settle for the odd week with the grandparents, they also want adventure and unusual places – everything, in fact that they had before, except with youngsters in tow. Eagerly meeting this demand are several adventure tour operators with dedicated family programmes offering everything from sea kayaking in Croatia to mountain biking in the Pyrenees. Europe has become an enormous adventure playground where kids can sample tamed-down versions of all the things that got their parents whooping it up 20 years earlier. The thrills and spills may be the lure of these trips, but school-age children will also absorb a huge amount of educational value from them. They'll expand their palettes as well as their minds and they will probably pick up a new skill or two, whether it's how to speak a few words of Spanish or haggle in a Turkish bazaar. Usually, the minimum age for family adventure trips is around

five or six, but you can also find tours suitable for children as young as two. Others, meanwhile, are reserved exclusively for teenagers.

The main advantage of booking an organized trip instead of going independent is peace of mind – all travel arrangements are made for you, while the itinerary is intrinsically family friendly. You will also be with like-minded parents, many of whom are facing the same challenges of raising children. The kids in the group will quickly bond and find new playmates, while the guide will provide added 'family value'. This last point, however, is worth researching carefully. Find out if the guide on your trip is a parent or has experience of communicating with children (as a teacher for example). A good guide will not only make the effort to gain the children's confidence, but will also ensure that mealtimes, talks and activities are tailored to meet their ages. If kids are happy and engaged, their parents will be happy and relaxed. It could be something as simple as turning a traditional city tour (fractious children, fretting parents) into a treasure hunt (focused children, stress-free parents).

Tuning in to teenagers

It's easy to tarnish all teenagers as moody, sullen, bored and generally peeved that you've dragged them away on holiday with you. But this hackneyed image is perhaps a little unfair. Teenagers not only make stimulating travel companions (able to tackle physical and intellectual challenges on a par with adults), but they also simplify travel logistics by being able to stay up late or be flexible with meals. Just remember to cater for their specific needs, whether it's a few shopping trips, some extreme adrenaline abuse, somewhere to meet socially with youngsters of their own age or a session at an internet café so they can catch up on gossip with their mates back home. Teenagers also like some personal space, so try to take this into account when planning accommodation.

The magic formula

For most families, getting holidays right is about making compromises. You won't necessarily please everyone all the time, but you can ensure that all ages have at least something going for them. Ten things that should definitely go into the 'holiday equation' are:

Water Whether it's the sea, a lake or a swimming pool, most children (and plenty of adults) consider swimming an intrinsic part of every holiday.

Food Don't skip the local flavours entirely, but always ensure there's at least something on the menu that kids know and like.

Friends Opportunities for interacting with other children of their own age is particularly important for teenagers and, whatever your views on them, organized kids' clubs are usually a big hit with children and allow parents some much needed adult time.

Gear Plan and pack with military precision to ensure you've got everything you need, especially if you are travelling with a baby.

Versatility Research your destination, accommodation and activities carefully to make sure they meet the needs and ages of everyone in the family.

Challenges Banish boredom by ensuring there are plenty of new experiences and adventures available for both you and your children.

Money Don't feel you have to spend a fortune to have a memorable family holiday.

Attitude Children quickly pick up on stress or anxiety, so try to stay relaxed, particularly during long journeys.

Expectations Keep them realistic; remember that what you might find interesting might bore your children senseless. Don't chastise them for ignoring the architecture in Venice's Piazza San Marco in favour of feeding the pigeons.

Fun What it's all about. Travelling with kids might not always be easy, but try to keep the stressful (or downright miserable) moments in perspective. You'll laugh about them in years to come.

Essentials Tour operators

Abercrombie & Kent
abercrombiekent.com
Long-established luxury holiday operator with escorted and tailor-made family holidays throughout Europe.

The Adventure Company
adventurecompany.co.uk
Leading specialist in worldwide family adventures with over 60 holidays on offer, including departures for single-parent families, as well as those with infants and teenagers. Centre-based adventures also available.

The Backroads
backroads.com
US-based operator offering family adventures worldwide, including European options in Croatia, France, Italy, Spain and Switzerland.

Canvas Holidays
canvasholidays.co.uk
Family camping holidays in France, Italy, Croatia, Spain, Switzerland, Austria, Germany and Holland, with self-catering accommodation to suit all budgets.

Center Parcs
centerparcs.com
A selection of 20 holiday villages in the UK, Netherlands, Belgium, Germany and France renowned for their extensive range of sports and leisure activities, plus numerous restaurants, bars, retail outlets and spa facilities.

Club Med
clubmed.com
Worldwide collection of all-inclusive holiday resorts, including several in the Mediterranean. Packages include flights, transfers, accommodation, full board (including drinks with lunch and dinner), open bar and snacks, sports activities with equipment and tuition, Club Med Baby Welcome for babies, Mini Club Med for children aged four to 10 and Club Med Passworld for teenagers.

Crystal Holidays
crystalholidays.co.uk
Skiing holidays throughout Europe, with a wide choice of family resorts and accommodation, kids-travel-free offers, private nannies, children's meals, evening clubs, plus pre-bookable extras such as baby-packs.

Discover the World
discover-the-world.co.uk
Specialist travel programmes to northern Europe with several family offerings, including Iceland fly-drives.

Esprit Holidays
esprit-holidays.co.uk
Family specialist in skiing and alpine summer holidays. Renowned childcare programme includes nurseries, babysitting, children's ski classes and activity clubs. Also arranges visits to Santa in Lapland.

Eurocamp
eurocamp.co.uk
Over 150 holiday parks in 12 European countries, including France, Spain, Italy, Germany, Switzerland, Austria and Croatia.

Explore Worldwide
explore.co.uk
Pioneers of small-group adventure holidays with 50 trips for families, including those with teenage children only.

Exodus
exodus.co.uk
A wide range of family adventure holidays, including small group departures, individual family trips and centre-based activity holidays.

Families Worldwide
familiesworldwide.co.uk
Experts in family holidays, with escorted adventure holidays and tailor-made itineraries suitable for children as young as two. European destinations include Austria, Bulgaria, Croatia, Cyprus, Finland, Greece, Italy, Romania, Slovakia, Slovenia, Spain and Turkey.

Imaginative Traveller
imaginative-traveller.com
Adventure trips to Turkey, the Pyrenees and Croatia for families with children aged six and over.

Inntravel
inntravel.co.uk
Gentle activity holidays in Austria, France, Italy, Norway, Portugal, Spain and Switzerland. Choose from hotel-to-hotel walking, cycling and family villas and cottages.

KE Adventure Travel
keadventure.com
Small selection of mainly mountain-based family activity holidays in Sweden, Turkey, Bulgaria and France.

Keycamp
keycamp.ie
Mobile home holidays in around 100 campsites throughout France, Spain, Italy, Austria, Switzerland and Croatia.

Mark Warner
markwarner.co.uk
Long-established ski and beach resort operator with comprehensive kids' facilities. Flights, transfers, meals, sailing, tennis, childcare and an Indy Club for teenagers are all part of the package.

Neilson Active Holidays
neilson.co.uk
Activity spcialist, offering a wide choice of European ski resorts and several options for a sailing holiday (flotilla, bareboat charter, training courses etc), as well as beach breaks in Greece and Turkey.

Powder Byrne
powderbyrne.co.uk
A selection of the best hotels and luxury resorts around the Mediterranean, plus top ski resorts in the Alps. Free Scallywags Kids' Clubs and excellent childcare.

Scott Dunn
scottdunn.com
Worldwide tailor-made holidays, including luxury Alpine ski chalets, Mediterranean family villas with chefs and nannies and hotels with children's clubs.

Siblu
siblu.com
Holiday parks in France, Italy and Spain offering free kids' clubs and a range of sports facilities and restaurants.

Group travel

The pros...

✅ You're with like-minded families who share similar interests in travel.

✅ Children have instant holiday pals.

✅ Trips usually have a good balance of activities and time out.

✅ Everything is organized for you, from transport to activities – and you know it's all going to be child-friendly.

✅ You know exactly how much you will spend and what you are going to get.

✅ Guide provides expert knowledge, as well as local support if things go wrong.

✅ You can explore countries that you wouldn't consider visiting independently.

✅ Children in a group are more likely to feel motivated to try adventurous things.

✅ There are trips to suit all ages, from toddlers to teenagers.

... and cons

❌ Perfect families with angelic children make you feel inadequate and tense.

❌ Personality clashes lead to awkward situations in the confines of a group.

❌ Pressure to adapt your routines to fit into other families' rules for bedtime, meals etc.

❌ Schedules can be restricting; no time to linger in a place you particularly like or lie low for a day or two if children are ill.

❌ You may well spend more than by travelling independently.

❌ Some guides pitch talks and briefings way above children's heads.

❌ You might still feel out of your comfort zone, even in a group.

❌ Frustrations may arise if some children can't keep up with the others.

❌ Some groups may have an uneven balance of ages, such as a lone teenager with half a dozen five- and six-year-olds.

Essentials What to take

It's a wonderful concept isn't it? Pack everything you think you're going to need for your holiday, then reduce it by half. The 'travel light' mantra of globetrotting gurus might suit backpackers with their handkerchief-sized super-absorbent towels and erratic rotation of underwear, but it's not always an easy, or necessarily desirable, option for families. Obviously, excessive luggage is a stress you can do without. However, whether you skimp on things or take enough in the way of clothes, equipment, toys and supplies can be the difference between making travel with kids enjoyable or just bearable.

Documents

Many countries, including the UK, USA and Australia, require children to have their own passport (for the UK Passport Service visit ukpa. gov.uk). Apply for these at least two months in advance of your departure date. Brace yourself for some fun and games when trying to get a legal passport photograph of your fidgety baby or toddler. It must be a sharp, shadowless photograph – no grins, no dummies, no fingers up noses and no evidence that mum is supporting baby's head. Forget photo booths – you'll spend a fortune trying to get an acceptable image and the experience might put you off family travel for life. A professional photographer at a studio will have lots of tricks for getting the perfect shot.

In addition to passports, make sure you have adequate family travel insurance, certificates of any medical prescriptions that may need to be shown at immigration or customs controls, a print-out of your itinerary and e-tickets (more likely nowadays than flight, rail or ferry tickets) and contact details while away. Take two copies of everything, stash one set in your hand luggage and leave the other with a friend or relative at home.

Packing

What you take will depend on several factors, such as the age of your children, the type of trip (city break, beach holiday etc), the likely climate and whether you're going to fly somewhere or pile everything into the car and drive.

The amount of gear you take is adversely proportional to the size of your child. Essentials for travelling with babies can include nappies,

umpteen changes of clothes, feeding equipment, stroller, favourite toys, travel cot, bedding, portable highchair and car seat. For toddlers you'll still need a stroller, car seat, toys and travel potty. Once kids reach four or five, they will probably want to pack their own small daypack with a few games, some activity pads and colouring pencils, a soft toy and some sweets. Teenagers meanwhile are often content with a book or magazine, an MP3 player or games console, a supply of spare batteries and a 'do not disturb' sign.

When children (especially girls) reach a

⊗ Baby comes too

➤➤ Reusable cloth nappies are easy to pack, environmentally friendly and can double up as towels. Coping with supply and demand, however, won't fit every parent's notion of what constitutes a holiday. If taking disposable nappies, be aware that your preferred brand may not be available. One option is to stuff a holdall full of nappies and check it in – they're light, so your luggage allowance won't be affected.
➤➤ Consider taking your own travel cot for extra familiarity. Many models are lightweight and fold away neatly and compactly. They also make excellent 'holding pens' while you check out a new room for potential hazards.
➤➤ Pack a raincover, sunshade and insect net for your buggy, a non-slip bath mat for the hotel tub, sun protectors for car windows, a waterproof undersheet for small children and a stair gate if staying in two-storey accommodation.
➤➤ If renting a car, consider taking your own child seat. The ones provided by the rental company may not meet the safety standards you're used to. Use a luggage-wrapping service at the airport to protect the seat in transit.

certain age, they take a determined – though not always realistic – interest in what clothes to pack. Diplomacy and supreme negotiating skills are required by parents to ensure that half your luggage isn't filled with a dozen varieties of sandals and a summer dress for each day you're away. Generally, though, clothes need to be lightweight, casual, durable, compatible with each other and easy to wash and dry.

Once you've finished deliberating over what to take you need to decide how you're going to carry it. A suitcase or holdall is fine – you can find things quickly and easily – but make sure it has wheels for those inevitable airport situations when you need to simultaneously carry a tired child and shift heavy luggage. A medium-sized case for each member of the family can be more practical than one or two colossal ones. It gives children independence, they can find their own things without turning out everyone else's and, if you're not sharing the same room in a hotel, it saves a lot of running back and forth along the corridors.

Hand luggage

Pack spare clothes and other essentials (such as wet wipes, nappies and favourite toys) in your hand luggage in case your suitcases get lost, the flight is delayed or cancelled, or you discover that your child is airsick. Remember that strict airport security measures restrict the quantities of liquids (including drinks, syrups, creams, lotions, oils, sprays and pastes) that can be carried in cabin baggage. You can carry small quantities of liquids, but only in separate containers that must not exceed 100 ml and are clearly visible in a single, transparent, re-sealable plastic bag (about the size of a small freezer bag) ready for inspection by airport security staff. Medical equipment, such as inhalers for asthma sufferers, are permitted. Prescribed medicines, accompanied by relevant documentation, may also be allowed in quantities over the 100 ml limit, but you should check with your airline beforehand.

Boredom busters

Whether it's a rainy day, a long car journey or a delayed flight, there will be occasions during every family holiday when children – from tots to teens – simply need to have some time out and occupy themselves quietly. You can encourage these all-too-ephemeral moments by packing a few books, games, toys and activities.

Babies and toddlers need familiar, comforting playthings which smell and feel like home. But, given the chance, they will also find endless fascination with new and exciting objects like telephones, sugar sachets and mini bars in hotel rooms or brochure stands, fire extinguishers and waste bins with revolving lids at airports. It doesn't always work, but try diverting their attention with a surprise toy or two.

Left to their own devices, school-age children will stuff a fairly random array of their favourite nick-nacks into their hand luggage and, while Barbie, a few Hot Wheels cars, a Nintendo DS and a bag of Haribos could well be in there, you might want to make a few additional suggestions.

For girls, a Polly Pocket doll set takes up little space and can be totally absorbing. Boys can play Top Trumps card games with each other or simply study the statistics on their own. Activity books with quizzes, stickers and colouring pages are a must, as are pads (with a mixture of ruled and plain paper) and plenty of colouring pens and pencils. Sometimes the simplest games, such as Shut the Box, can become utterly addictive.

One of the best ways to keep boredom at bay is to encourage children to keep a journal of their travels. Make it as fun and interactive as possible. Pack scissors and glue stick so they can cut and paste postcards, tickets and other souvenirs into their literary masterpiece. An envelope stuck to the inside back cover can be used to store other treasures. Offer cues ('Three things I spotted on the journey...') or use the playback function on digital cameras to help prompt kids when they complain that they can't think of anything to write.

Essentials How to get there

Experienced travellers will often tell you that it's the 'journey' not the 'getting there' that really matters; that travel is enriched by taking your time on the road, meeting people and having chance encounters. Suggest this to most parents, however, and they will either stare at you blankly, laugh out loud or start twitching uncontrollably. Whether it's the memory of dealing with a screaming baby on a flight, bickering siblings on an interminable car journey or a moping teenager who didn't want to come in the first place, every parent has good reason for treating family journeys with trepidation.

Flight plan

» Consider carefully whether there is a viable, more environmentally friendly alternative to flying.
» Budget for children under two paying 10% of the adult fare, but remember that they have to sit on your lap.
» Check whether you can take your stroller to the boarding gate and where it will be available again after landing.
» Take all baby essentials in your hand luggage.
» Pack a supply of healthy snacks.
» Don't forget to take a few sachets of Calpol (infants' paracetamol).
» Remember cups with non-spill lids for toddlers.
» Have a few boiled sweets handy to help ears pop during the final descent.
» Pack a familiar pillow or soft toy to comfort and help children sleep.
» Get to the airport in plenty of time so you're not stuck at the back of a huge check-in queue.
» Fit reins on toddlers to give them freedom, safely.
» Find out if there's a children's play area.
» Before boarding, always check the floor where you've been sitting – a favourite teddy or toy is bound to have been dropped there.
» Ensure your children drink little and often to ward off dehydration.
» If the cabin's dry air causes discomfort to your child's nose or lips, try getting them to breathe through a handkerchief soaked in a little water.
» Bring lots of toys, books and snacks to distract and amuse toddlers and babies.
» Take kids to the toilet well before the seatbelt signs come on for the final descent.
» Respect the comfort of other passengers by dealing firmly with unacceptable behaviour

(such as children kicking the seat in front), but be prepared for some people to give you the 'raised eyebrow' treatment merely at the sight of your little darlings.
» Remember, the more you tell kids not to press the hostess call button the more they will do it.

The long & whining road

It's not surprising that so many families opt for self-drive holidays, either renting a car or taking their own. With the freedom of the open road you can travel when you want and for as long as you want. You can schedule regular breaks at parks, beaches and other recreational areas to let children burn off energy. You can tweak your itinerary as you go along, there's more space for luggage and you can even time drives to coincide with when your baby or toddler normally has a daytime nap. Sounds like a piece of cake. So what's the catch?

Boredom. Close confinement. Sibling squabbles. Stress from coping with traffic. Stress from getting lost. Stress from rushing to catch the ferry. These, and a dozen other factors conspire to drive you to distraction.

In order to endure long car journeys with the kids, the first thing you need is peace of mind. Make absolutely certain, especially when renting a car, that your children will be safe. Engage child locks on the rear doors and windows, fit blinds to windows if you are travelling in a hot and sunny country and give rented child seats a thorough going-over to make sure that harnesses, buckles and head supports are not damaged in any way

If your children are old enough, get them to help you research the route and pick a few options for rest breaks and side trips. Giving kids joint ownership of the drive plan offers them an incentive to look forward to journey highlights rather than lapsing into 'moan mode'.

Make sure you've packed a good supply of snacks and drinks (see page 20). Bring along colouring pads, pencils, magnetic board games, reading books, activity books, card games… anything really that doesn't involve tiny pieces that are constantly going to end up dropped, out-of-reach, on the floor. A map is a great idea for children who want to trace the route.

Upping the technology stakes slightly, audio books are often a good means of calming a back-seat fracas or eking out another quiet hour on the road. Hand-held games systems, from the likes of Nintendo and Sony PSP, are guaranteed to absorb most kids, although you may find they pass the entire journey with barely a glance at the passing scenery. When it comes to in-car-entertainment, few things receive such universal approval from children and adults alike than a DVD player.

Coaching pros & cons

Logistically, you need to treat coach travel rather like flying – you're stuck in a confined cabin with limited legroom and your luggage is stowed out of reach in the hold. Luxury services will have an onboard toilet, TV screen and hostess service, but rarely approaching the standards you find on airlines. Rest stops may be sporadic and too short-lived and unlike flying, of course, coach travel is slower and prone to traffic jams.

Any advantages? Well, there's no doubt that coach travel is better for both your bank balance and the environment compared to flying. You also get to see more than just clouds out of the windows. And you can often step off a coach right into the heart of your destination, rather than going through the rigmarole of baggage claim and airport transfers following a flight. Coach travel also gives your itinerary huge flexibility. For example, Eurolines (eurolines.com) covers over 30 coach companies serving some 500 destinations.

On track with trains

There's no denying it: rail travel is definitely more family friendly than going by coach. Not only do you get more legroom and often a table where kids can spread out their scribble pads and pens, but you can also get up and stretch your legs and visit the buffet car for a snack or meal. Trains are faster, more frequent and basically just a lot more exciting than coaches – particularly overnight sleeper services where kids love the idea of nesting in a couchette.

That's not to say train operators exactly go off the rails with making families welcome. Eurostar and French TGV trains have 'family-friendly' coaches with baby-changing facilities – but that's about it. And don't forget that train travel with kids is not without its fair share of stressful 'crunch points' – the most notorious, of course, being the short stop at your final station when you have approximately 13 seconds to disgorge luggage, infants, baby stroller and other belongings onto the platform before the train leaves again.

And, yes, there are plenty of trains serving Paris (and even Disneyland Paris), but what about your holiday park in Provence or Brittany? To reach that you'll need to pile everyone and everything into a taxi at the train station.

Undeterred? Then check out The Man in Seat 61 (seat61.com), a superb online resource with detailed information, schedules, fares and advice for rail travel anywhere in Europe.

Making waves

Ferries pop up in a lot of holiday itineraries whether it's nipping across the Channel from England to France or splashing out on a Mediterranean cruise. Not surprisingly, kids love them. There's space to move around, different decks to explore, horizons to scan and shops to peruse… some ferries even have soft play areas and games rooms, while several cruise lines have children's clubs for different age groups, as well as facilities such as babysitting.

Essentials Where to stay

Family-friendly. Just rolls off the tongue, doesn't it? But it's a phrase that's used all to glibly by hotels, resorts and campsites keen to tap into this lucrative market. Just because they've plonked a plastic slide in the garden and scribbled chicken nuggets on the menu doesn't mean they're going to go out of their way to welcome kids or make your stay as comfortable as possible. Look beyond the superficial stuff and find out exactly what facilities are available for families.

Assess so-called 'family accommodation' on whether it includes any of the following:
» Family rooms, interconnecting rooms or suites.
» Children's menus and meal times.
» Supervised childcare.
» Babysitting or baby listening.
» Family activities or kids' clubs.
» Dedicated play areas for children.
» Cots, high chairs and other baby gear.
» Family pricing or discounts for children.
» Safety issues, such as proximity to busy roads and whether swimming pools are fenced off.

Hotel heaven & havoc
Remember those halcyon holidays before you had kids when you would casually check into your hotel room, test how bouncy the beds were, fling open the balcony doors and treat yourself to a welcome bottle of wine from the mini bar? Well, with kids yapping excitedly at your heels you will be trying, mostly in vain, to stop them doing all those things. That wonderful moment of arrival, when the holiday really starts, is a super-exuberant time when kids find joy and wonder in even the smallest things. "Wow, look mum, you've got a chocolate on your pillow – and have you seen the cool view of the building site!"

Another difference you will notice is that hotel rooms shrink once you have children. Squeeze a travel cot and a child's bed into your average double room and the floor space is reduced to roughly the area of a bath mat. Getting from one side of the room to the other is like negotiating a soft-play area – and that, of course, is exactly how your kids treat it. Then there's the en suite where the hotel staff have thoughtfully gift-wrapped all sorts of goodies for children to open – from

shower caps and sewing kits to little tubes of toothpaste. And when they tire of ransacking the mini milk pots on the complimentary coffee-making tray, there are always the long hotel corridors – ideal for running relay races.

Perhaps it's not surprising that a lot families tend to use their hotel room as a kind of base camp – a technical necessity where you sleep, wash and store your clothes, but spend as little time as possible. Of course, budget permitting, you can find sensational apartments, suites and even family chalets within the grounds of a large resort. It's probably safe to say, though, that your hotel room is unlikely to feature in your holiday snaps, but at least you've got everything you need onsite – from restaurants, room service and babysitting to swimming pool, games room and someone making your beds.

Villas, cottages & apartments
With space to spread out, villas and other self-catering accommodation offer a home-from-home atmosphere where you have flexibility and independence to maintain meal- and bedtime routines, do the cooking, load the dishwasher, lay the table… A big advantage over hotels and resorts is that you don't need to worry about disturbing other guests. Villas can also offer better value than hotels or resorts, particularly if you upsize to a bigger property and share with friends or another family. Similarly, you may find it cheaper to book a self-catering apartment for a city break.

Fun on the farm
You should check whether any age restrictions apply, but in general most farmstays are ideal for families. Children will love feeding the animals,

collecting eggs or even helping out in the kitchen. Needless to say, on a working farm, you must be aware of your children's safety at all times – including any potential allergic reactions they may have in response to contact with animals. You usually sleep in a self-contained cottage or in the farmhouse itself. As you'd expect, most meals are based on fresh, produce and include homemade breads, cakes and soups, as well as homegrown fruit and veg. It's up to you if you want to help out on the farm. Nobody is going to drag you out of bed at dawn to muck out the cowshed or round up the sheep. If you simply want to relax and restrict your farm activities to occasionally patting the border collie then that's fine. Farm tours are often available, while some farmstays offer activities like fishing, hiking, mountain biking or horse riding.

Camping

There are two types of family camping – the DIY version where dad spends most of day one grappling with multi-jointed tent poles and fiddling with an obstinate gas stove, and organized camping where you simply drive up to a ready-pitched family tent, usually on a site that has excellent facilities, such as a swimming pool and supermarket. Both are essential experiences for all families – you need to try one to appreciate the other. If you are planning on going-it-alone, make sure you are properly kitted out and try a dummy run in the back garden before setting off on something more epic. As a general rule of thumb, buy a tent that's one size up from the one you think you'll need – the extra space will always come in handy for storage and wet days.

For families that like the idea of camping but don't want to forsake life's little luxuries, there are several companies offering tipi or yurt holidays with cosy stoves, real beds and lots of plump cushions. In Britain, Feather Down Farms (featherdown.co.uk) offers pampered camping on working organic farms.

Holiday parks are popular throughout Europe and give you the option of staying in well-furnished static caravans. These have a galley kitchen and lounge area with mod cons such as LCD television, DVD player, microwave and fridge-freezer. Again, it's worth upgrading if you can – a double bed might sound fine until you discover that it's in a room the size of a double bed.

Motorhomes

There's no better way to roam than in a motorhome. Not only do they offer flexibility and self-sufficiency, but most models offer levels of comfort undreamt of in the days of the old VW camper van. Whereas your typical VW, with its pop-up roof and flatulent exhaust, might have had little more than two berths and a camping stove, modern motorhomes boast two or three double beds, fridge-freezer, microwave, four-ring cooker, DVD player, flat-screen TV, shower and toilet.

For kids, the idea that you can have bedroom, kitchen, playroom and car rolled into one is almost too exciting to comprehend. But motorhomes also have lots of practical advantages. For example, you can stick your children in seats 6 m away from the driver's cab, so that you don't have to hear them whingeing on long journeys. And when it rains, you can keep warm and dry inside the van while you rustle up a meal. Best of all, you can explore large swathes of country without having to lug suitcases in and out of hotels all the time. You only have to unpack once. And you only have to get used to one bed. Don't forget, though, that you have to make that bed. Literally. Your motorhome may have had the latest in TV technology, but when it came to beds, it might not be cutting-edge. More like "cut your bleedin' fingers off", in fact, as you struggle each evening with sliding plywood shelves, hinged legs and stow-away tables to build your beds. Once the bases are constructed, the real fun starts when you attempt to piece together 17 random-sized seat cushions into something vaguely resembling a mattress.

Essentials What to eat & drink

It's a perfectly natural reaction. You arrive at your holiday destination, dump the luggage, check out the pool and then enter the intriguing, but slightly disconcerting, world of local restaurant menus and foreign supermarkets. Is that spicy? Does it come with chips? Which one is skimmed milk? Will that cheese be too strong? Will I be handed a packet of frozen fish fingers when what I thought I'd asked for was a box of ice-lollies? Some things look perfectly familiar, while others leave you flummoxed. But don't worry – culinary culture shock isn't terminal. No matter where you are there is always something to eat, no matter how fussy you or your children are.

Breastfeeding

Breastfed babies, of course, have no qualms about coping with foreign food. They have a familiar, convenient, safe and nutritious source of nourishment wherever they go. Breastfeeding mothers, however, do need to ensure that they drink lots of fluid, eat well and keep relaxed. If you are discreet, breastfeeding is acceptable in most countries. Consider packing a nursing shawl for modesty.

Bottle-feeding

Don't assume that your preferred brand of milk formula will be available in the country you are visiting. If possible take enough with you from home. Remember that you will need to use purified, bottled or boiled water to make up the formula and that it needs to be kept refrigerated if not used within 24 hours. Sterilization is also crucial. Either invest in a compact travel sterilizer or use boiling water or sterilizing tablets.

In-flight food & drink

It's a good idea to feed babies on take-off and landing to reduce the discomfort caused by changes in cabin pressure. Make sure toddlers have non-spill cups to sip on and give older children sweets to suck. Remember that most flight attendants are pre-programmed to fill cups right up to the rim. To avoid inevitable spills, bring your own bottles or cups to decant drinks into. Don't assume baby food will be available – again, the best strategy is to bring your own. Plastic bibs with scooped rims along the bottom are useful for catching fallout – particularly if your baby is sick.

Travel snacks

Having a stash of goodies to nibble on is all part of the fun of travel if you're a child – and they can be a godsend if you're delayed. Leave it to them, however, and they'll stuff their hand luggage with nothing but crisps, chocolate bars, chewing gum and lurid-coloured chews encrusted with sherbet. You don't want to be a complete kill-joy (the odd packet of crisps and a chocolate bar is fine), but nor do you want your children going balmy on a 'sugar high' while you're stuck in a car or queuing at customs. Healthy travel snacks that you can buy straight off the supermarket shelf include cereal bars, string cheese, small boxes of raisins and individual (low sugar) boxes of cereal. And, of

DIY snacks

Trail mix Combine raisins, Cheerios, dried apricot, cranberries and pineapple, banana chips and yoghurt-coated raisins in a mixing bowl. A handful of Smarties or M&Ms isn't going to harm anyone, but only add nuts if your children are over five. Give everything a good stir, then make up individual portions in small freezer bags.

Dippers Add a scoop of peanut butter, hummus or whatever savoury dip appeals to your children to a small plastic food container. Clean and slice small pieces of celery, carrot, apple and cucumber and plant them in the dip. Add a lid and keep refrigerated until you are ready to go.

Cheese and crackers Use a cookie cutter to stamp out fun-shaped slices of cheese. Pop them in a food storage container along with a few crackers and some grapes sliced lengthways. Kids will love crafting their own cracker creations.

course, nothing beats a fresh apple or orange for healthy food on-the-go. With a little more time and effort you can help children prepare their own tasty, unprocessed travel snacks (see box).

Fussy feeders

Although some kids have more adventurous palates abroad than at home, others can be frustratingly inflexible when it comes to food. They'll consume Cheddar by the wagonload, but run a mile from a French fondue. The tomato sauce won't be the same as it is back home and the milk will taste funny. So, how do you deal with a fussy feeder on holiday? Try this list for starters:

▸ Self-catering gives you the flexibility to prepare food you like, when you like.

▸ International resorts, hotels and restaurants offer a wide selection of meals, including several that your children are bound to be familiar with.

▸ Fine for an occasional treat, fast-food outlets can be found everywhere nowadays.

▸ Take staples with you, such as soup powders, pasta and cereals – but remember that you won't be allowed to take fresh produce across some international borders.

▸ Make mealtimes enjoyable and relaxed by picking restaurants with stunning views, play areas or aquariums. The novelty of room service may also get kids in the mood for eating.

▸ Don't fill children up on juice, milk, fizzy drinks or even water just before a meal.

▸ Ask for smaller portions in restaurants and let children take their time over eating.

▸ Keep mealtime routines as regular as possible.

▸ Get them involved – kids tend to eat up if they can serve themselves at buffets or help prepare the meal.

▸ Seeing other children eating well on a group trip might be an incentive for your picky feeder.

▸ Do not force your child to eat. Be sensitive to the fact that travel can naturally affect appetites and unsettle stomachs.

▸ Take some children's multi-vitamins.

❝❞ For a moment I thought we might actually be barred from the restaurant. The head waiter glanced at our toddler twins, then fixed me with an abhorrent look as if I was trying to bring a pair of rabid, mange-ridden dogs to dinner. Earlier, we'd had the 'raised eyebrow' treatment in an art gallery and narrowly escaped eviction from the cathedral cloisters when the twins discovered its potential for echoes.

More than anything, the city break embodies those heady days of pre-parenthood when, as a carefree couple, you could nip off to Paris with nothing more than an overnight bag and a pair of theatre tickets. You could dawdle over lunch, go shopping and take in an art gallery. With youngsters in tow it can become more like a city breakdown.

One city that did go down well with our kids was Naples. Pushing a double buggy around the cobbled backstreets was pure hell. For some reason, though, Neapolitans have a soft spot for twin babies. "Gemelli, belissimo!" people would cry as they spontaneously grabbed Joe and Ellie by the cheeks before delving into the nearest *paticceria* to emerge with fistfuls of cakes. My wife, Sally, and I would then watch, bemused, as our children were force-fed chunks of *sfogliatelle* and other traditional pastries. I'm not sure whether Joe and Ellie absorbed anything of particular artistic or historical value during that city break – but they certainly never went hungry.

The beach beckons – Rhossili on the Gower Peninsula.

Britain

Contents

25 **Introduction**

26 **Kids' stuff**

28 **Tots to teens**

30 **London**

32 **Southeast England**
32 Isle of Wight
32 New Forest

33 **East Anglia**
33 North Norfolk Coast

34 **Southwest England**
34 Devon
34 Jurassic Coast
35 Bath, Bristol & Somerset
35 Cornwall

36 **Central England**
36 East Midlands
36 West Midlands
37 Cotswolds

38 **North England**
38 Manchester
38 Liverpool
38 Blackpool
38 Yorkshire
39 The Northeast
39 Lake District

40 **Wales**
40 Cardiff
40 Gower Peninsula
40 Snowdonia
41 Pembrokeshire

42 **Scotland**
42 Edinburgh
43 Glasgow
43 Highlands & Islands

44 **Grown-ups' stuff**

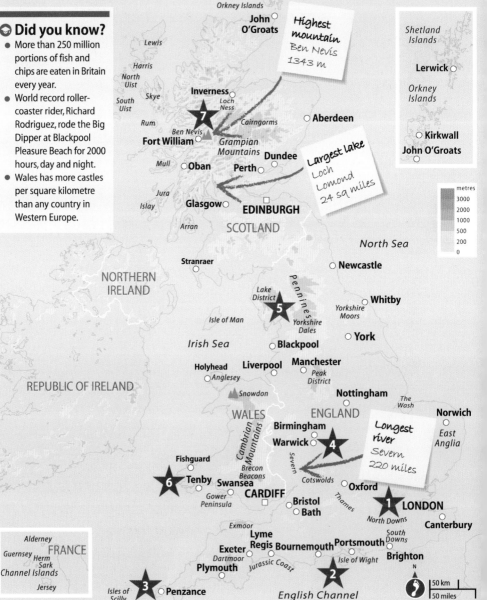

Orkney Islands

John O'Groats

Highest mountain Ben Nevis 1343 m

Shetland Islands

Lewis

Harris

North Uist

South Uist

Skye

Rum

Mull

Jura

Islay

Arran

Inverness

Loch Ness

Cairngorms

Ben Nevis

Fort William

Grampian Mountains

Oban

Perth

Glasgow

EDINBURGH

SCOTLAND

Aberdeen

Kirkwall

Lerwick

Orkney Islands

John O'Groats

Dundee

Largest lake Loch Lomond 24 sq miles

metres
3000
2000
1000
500
200
0

North Sea

Stranraer

Newcastle

NORTHERN IRELAND

Lake District

Pennines

Whitby

Yorkshire Moors

Isle of Man

Yorkshire Dales

York

Irish Sea

Blackpool

Holyhead

Anglesey

Liverpool

Manchester

Peak District

REPUBLIC OF IRELAND

Snowdon

Nottingham

The Wash

WALES

ENGLAND

Norwich

Cambrian Mountains

Birmingham

Warwick

Severn

Longest river Severn 220 miles

East Anglia

Fishguard

Brecon Beacons

Cotswolds

Oxford

Tenby

Swansea

CARDIFF

Gower Peninsula

Bristol

Bath

Thames

LONDON

North Downs

Canterbury

Exmoor

Lyme Regis

Bournemouth

Portsmouth

South Downs

Exeter

Dartmoor

Isle of Wight

Brighton

Plymouth

Jurassic Coast

N

Alderney

Guernsey

Herm

Sark

Channel Islands

Jersey

FRANCE

Isles of Scilly

Penzance

English Channel

50 km
50 miles

Introduction

Take a spin on the London Eye
▸▸ London, page 30

Hunt for dinosaurs
▸▸ Isle of Wight, page 32

Find the perfect surf beach
▸▸ Cornwall, page 35

Explore a medieval castle
▸▸ Warwickshire, page 36

Take a hike and paddle a canoe
▸▸ Lake District, page 39

Spot seals, seabirds and whales
▸▸ Pembrokeshire, page 41

Tour the Highlands & Islands
▸▸ Scotland, page 43

Many visitors to Britain (and quite a few of its residents) love to have a good moan about the weather and how expensive everything is. The fact remains, though, that these islands are not only incredibly beautiful, but they also squeeze more child-friendly beaches, cities and family attractions into one small, accessible region than anywhere in the world. Admittedly, the weather can be temperamental (or downright frustrating) at times, and there's no denying that a British family holiday sometimes requires a fair degree of stoicism – but it doesn't rain constantly. In any case, Britain is a great family holiday destination whatever the weather. Kids can have just as much fun exploring rock pools and building sandcastles on a wind-strafed Cornish beach during winter as they can surfing on one during a summer heatwave. As for the cost issue, some of the best family holiday highlights in Britain don't cost a penny – cycling in Pembrokeshire or the Isle of Wight, visiting London's Science or Natural History Museum and finding the perfect picnic spot in the Lake District or Cotswolds to name just a few.

Britain Kids' stuff

Books to read

Katie Morag's Island Stories
Red Fox, 2003
A small Hebridean community seen through the eyes of a child. Katie Morag always seems to be in some sort of bother, but her family and the friendly islanders manage to keep her out of serious trouble. Ages 4-8

The Mousehole Cat
Walker Books, 1993
A brave fisherman and his cat battle through a storm to bring food to the children of a Cornish village. Written by Antonia Barber with award-winning illustrations from Nicola Bayley. Ages 4+

Five on a Treasure Island
Hodder Children's Books, 2001
Meet Julian, Dick, Anne, George and Timmy the dog in their first adventure. There's a shipwreck off Kirrin Island, but where is the treasure? The five go on the trail, but they're not alone. Ages 6+

Friend or Foe
Mammoth, 2001
Set during the Second World War, London is under the Blitz and two friends, David and Tucky have been evacuated to the countryside where they are faced with a terrible dilemma when they witness a German plane crash on the moors. Ages 10+

Anyone for quidditch?
Alnwick Castle in Northumberland.

Harry spotter

You don't need a broomstick or magic wand to visit several of the places featured in the Harry Potter movies. Platform 9¾, the mystifying departure point for the Hogwarts Express steam train, was filmed at Platform 4 of London's King's Cross Station. Harry and his fellow wannabe-wizards disembark at Hogsmeade Station which is none other than Goathland, a village in the Yorkshire Moors, while Glenfinnan Viaduct in the Scottish Highlands featured in a spectacular action sequence in the *Chamber of Secrets*. The interior of the Hogwarts School of Witchcraft and Wizardry is based on several locations, including Lacock Abbey in Wiltshire, Gloucester Cathedral and Oxford University's Bodleian Library and the Great Hall at Christ Church. Alnwick Castle in Northumberland, meanwhile, will always be remembered as the setting for broomstick lessons and quidditch matches.

Thrill rides

Park	Ride	Thrills & spills	Wow factor	Minimum height
Alton Towers	Air	Float, swoop, soar, dive and feel like you're flying.	●●●●	140 cm
	Nemesis	Experience G-force greater than a space shuttle take-off.	●●●●●	140 cm
	Oblivion	More bonkers than a bungee – plunge 61 m into the abyss.	●●●●	140 cm
	Rita	She's the Queen of Speed, reaching 95 kph in 2½ seconds.	●●●●●	140 cm
Blackpool Pleasure Beach	Ice blast	Get catapulted at 129 kph up a vertical 64-m tower.	●●●●	132 cm
	Infusion	Suspended coaster, five loops, water features.	●●●●●	132 cm
	Pepsi Max Big One	World's tallest (72 m) and fastest (140 kph) coaster.	●●●●●	132 cm
Chessington World of Adventures	Dragon's Fury	A fiery family spinning roller coaster.	●●●	120 cm
	Rameses Revenge	Monster machine that lowers you head-first over water fountains.	●●●●●	140 cm
	Tomb Blaster	Battle with mummies to beat the curse of the tomb.	●●	110 cm
	Vampire	Fly over Transylvanian treetops on a bloodcurdling coaster.	●●●	110 cm
Drayton Manor	Apocalypse	The world's first stand-up tower drop (drop 54 m at 4 Gs).	●●●●●	140 cm
	Shockwave	Europe's only stand-up roller coaster.	●●●●●	140 cm
	Stormforce10	Plunge backwards down a 9-m water drop.	●●●●	120 cm
Legoland Windsor	Jungle Coaster	Legoland's fastest (60 kph) with a hair-raising 16m drop.	●●●	110 cm
	Viking's River Splash	Surge downstream in a fantasy Viking World.	●●	110 cm
Thorpe Park	Colossus	Swirl and corkscrew around a thundering steel track.	●●●●	140 cm
	Detonator	Get fired to ground level from a height of 30 m at 75 kph.	●●●●	130 cm
	Saw	The world's first ever horror movie-themed roller coaster.	●●●●●	140 cm
	Stealth	0-130 kph in less than two seconds, and heights of 62 m.	●●●●●	140 cm
	Tidal Wave	Climb to 26 m then get soaked as you splash down to earth.	●●●●	120 cm

Taste of Wales bara brith

What you need
- 110 g sultanas
- 110 g raisins soaked overnight in 150 ml cold tea
- 110 g Demerara sugar
- 1 tbsp coarse cut marmalade
- 1 beaten egg
- 1 tsp mixed spice
- 220 g self-raising flour

What to do
- Mix all the ingredients together.
- Put the mixture into a greased loaf tin.
- Bake at 160-170°C for one hour.
- Leave to cool for 20 minutes before turning out onto a wire tray.
- Cut into slices.
- Butter before serving.

Britain Tots to teens

Family travel in Britain is pure child's play. Nothing could be simpler. There are activities and attractions to suit every age; getting around is generally straightforward, and accommodation covers the whole gamut from campsites to luxury hotels.

Babies

The climate is gentle, baby supplies are easily found, many places are buggy-friendly and, no matter where you go, you'll usually find at least one café with highchairs or a hotel that provides cots. Seaside holidays are the natural choice – you can plonk tiny tots on the beach, swoosh them through the shallows and wheel them to sleep along the prom. The Marine Conservation Society publishes the *Good Beach Guide* (goodbeachguide.co.uk).

Toddlers/pre-school

More fun, but also more fraught, beach holidays with toddlers demand eagle-eyed surveillance by parents to ensure safety. City breaks can also work well with this age range – parks usually have excellent playgrounds, while zoos and aquariums are always a hit. They are still too young to get much out of the major theme parks, although Legoland (legoland.co.uk) in Windsor will appeal, as will the countless farm parks.

Kids/school age

Beach safety is even more paramount with this fearless age group. However, with expert tuition at surf schools, activity centres and riding stables, kids can safely start learning all kinds of new skills. They are also at an age when camping, hiking and cycling holidays start to sound feasible. As for exercising their minds, Britain is chock-a-block with interactive science museums, mysterious castles and well-interpreted nature reserves. Organizations like the National Trust (nationaltrust.org), RSPB (rspb.org.uk) and The Wildlife Trusts (wildlifetrusts.org) arrange numerous child-friendly events throughout the year.

Teenagers

You really need a surf school, sailing club or some other kind of extra incentive to keep teens keen on the beach. Sandcastles and rock pools just won't do it for them. Try giving them a taste of freedom at summer camps operated by Camp Beaumont (campbeaumont.co.uk) and

Beaches like Cornwall's Whitesand Bay are lifeguard-patrolled during summer.

PGL (pgl.co.uk) where they'll not only try out cool new activities but also meet lots of people their own age. City breaks will also strike a cord with teenagers, particularly in places like London, Glasgow and Manchester, where you can combine sightseeing with great shopping and popular culture. For adventure and adrenaline, hit the theme park trail, challenge them to climb a Munro in the Scottish Highlands or paddle a sea kayak off the Pembrokeshire coast.

❝❞ We love going to London. Don't underestimate the pleasures of simply travelling around – double-decker buses, tubes and taxis were all a rich source of entertainment for our three- and five-year-old. *Alison Rippon*

Special needs

Holiday Care (holidaycare. org.uk) has information on accommodation, attractions and activity holidays for people with all kinds of disability, while Door to Door (dptac.gov.uk) offers advice about travelling. Disability Now (disabilitynow.org.uk/ directory) lists accessible places to stay, while Vitalise (vitalise. org.uk) has five centres where disabled people and their carers can enjoy themed weeks.

Single parents

Single Parents UK (singleparents. org.uk) lists organizations offering holidays for single-parent families. Single Parent Fun (singleparentfun.com) is an excellent community site, while Acorn Adventure (acornadventure.co.uk) operates holidays in the Lake District.

Buggy walks

Totnes to Dartington Riverside Path, Devon
This level 4-km walk follows the River Dart from Totnes Bridge to the Cider Press Centre in Dartington where you'll find a toy shop and child-friendly café.

Cotswold Water Park, Gloucestershire
A 4-km walk encircles two lakes, taking in a visitor centre, lakeside café, wood sculpture trail and two adventure playgrounds.

Durham City and riverbanks
Stroll down South Bailey towards Prebend's Bridge, admire the cathedral, then take the woodland path back towards the city centre.

St Ouen's Bay, Jersey.

Channel islands

Nestled in the bay of St Malo off the French coast and over 110 km from mainland Britain, the two largest Channel Islands, Jersey and Guernsey, are prime family holiday territory. Their wide, sandy beaches and crystal clear seas are legendary, but there are also plenty of other attractions to inspire kids of all ages. The best family beaches on Jersey (jersey.com) include Green Island (a south-facing sun trap), La Rocque (with its Rock Pool Discovery Club), St Brelades Bay (where children age six and above can learn to windsurf or canoe) and St Ouen's Bay (a paradise for surfers). Away from the beach, be sure to visit Jersey's famous animal sanctuary, Durrell Wildlife (durrellwildlife.org) and the hands-on Maritime Museum in St Helier. There's also a medieval castle to explore, not to mention a couple of action-packed adventure parks: aMaizing Maze (jerseyleisure.com) and Living Legend (jerseylivinglegend.co.je).

On Guernsey (visitguernsey.com), two of the best beaches for families are Pembroke Bay, a golden arc of sand that gently shelves into the sea, and Vazon, a hotspot for all kinds of watersports. Guarding the entrance to St Peter Port, Castle Hornet is a must-see, while cycling on Guernsey is a real delight for families, thanks to the six 'Gentle and Rolling' routes around the island. Perhaps most exciting of all, however, is how easy it is to visit the nearby islands of Herm, Sark and Alderney – all linked by ferry for carefree island hopping in the English Channel.

London Cool Britannia

It's big, busy and bewildering (not to mention being one of the world's most expensive cities), but there's no denying the fact that kids love London. Just being there, in the thick of it, crawling along congested streets in a double-decker bus or rising above it all on the London Eye, gives children a huge thrill. And that's before you've hit any of the attractions. You can tailor a day out in London to suit all ages, whether it's a London Zoo/Hamleys double-whammy for six year olds or a teenage pilgrimage to the shops along Oxford Street. Whatever you decide to do, resist the temptation to cram too much into a single day. London with kids is best in small, bite-size chunks. You can always come back for more.

Two-day action plan

Day one: The South Bank
The London Eye (ba-londoneye.com) is not only a fun (30-minute) ride, but it's also the best way for kids to grasp the scale of London and pinpoint a few landmarks. As the big wheel spins them 135 m above the Thames, they'll be able to see everything from the Houses of Parliament to Wembley Stadium. Back at ground level, take a river cruise for a different perspective

◉ Inside info

of capital attractions like St Paul's Cathedral (stpauls.co.uk), *HMS Belfast* (hmsbelfast.iwm.org.uk), the Tower of London (hrp.org.uk) and Tower Bridge. However, if that sounds like too much sightseeing for one day, focus instead on other South Bank highlights. The London Aquarium (londonaquarium.co.uk) recreates a watery world of rushing streams, coral reefs, mangrove swamps and teeming rock pools. You can stroke rays in the touch pool and watch a piranha feeding-frenzy, but it's the sharks in the huge Pacific tank that are the show-stealers. The National Theatre (nationaltheatre.org.uk) hosts a free outdoor summer festival between July and September called Watch this Space, featuring all kinds of live performances, from circus acts to music and dance. The Tate Modern (tate.org.uk) has holiday activities for families, while the Unicorn Theatre (unicorntheatre.com) presents acts specifically

for children. Altogether less refined, the London Dungeon (thedungeons.com) 'gorifies' the capital's less salubrious past with vivid portrayals of torture, plague and the Great Fire of London. There are even thrill rides like Extremis – Drop Ride to Doom, a simulated hanging for anyone over 120 cm tall. Located on Lambeth Road, the Imperial War Museum (iwm.org.uk) takes a more dignified approach to history with its impressive displays of weaponry and sobering insights into the world wars. Steer younger children towards the Home Front exhibit where they'll be intrigued by concepts like rationing.

Day two: Classic sights
Start at Trafalgar Square where Nelson's Column rises above a swirling torrent of taxis and buses. Flanking the famous plaza are three arty attractions. The National Gallery (nationalgallery.org.uk) offers talks and workshops for families,

The London Eye and County Hall (home to the London Aquarium).

Museums of fun

British Museum (thebritishmuseum.ac.uk) Don't drift aimlessly through this vast cultural and historical treasure house – your kids will wilt. Instead, make use of the excellent children's programme – six museum trails, family activity backpacks, workshops, storytelling, plus an audio tour where you can join Stephen Fry on a quest for bodies, beasts and board games. If you see just one thing, make sure it's the Egyptian mummies in Rooms 62-63.

Covent Garden (covent-garden.co.uk) Cool cafés, street performers and plenty of shops make Covent Garden a guaranteed hit with teenagers. The London Transport Museum (ltmuseum.co.uk) has a learning zone, 'driver's-eye' simulators and a play area for under-fives.

Greenwich Take a boat trip from central London with Thames Cruises (thamescruises.com) to reach this World Heritage Site, dominated by Sir Christopher Wren's Old Royal Naval College (greenwichfoundation. org.uk). Damaged by fire in 2007, the glorious 19th-century tea clipper, *Cutty Sark* (cuttysark.org.uk) is undergoing restoration. In the meantime, set a course for the National Maritime Museum (nmm.ac.uk) for a hefty horde of seafaring treasures or, if time is of the essence, head to the Royal Observatory (rog.nmm.ac.uk) which has a spectacular new planetarium – not to mention zero degrees longitude at the famous Meridian Line.

Natural History Museum (nhm.ac.uk) A skeleton of Diplodocus has long reigned supreme in the Central Hall of this magnificent museum – although it has to be said that kids usually get more of a buzz from the new-fangled animatronic T Rex in the dinosaur gallery. Other highlights include Creepy Crawlies, Ecology, the Mammal Hall and earthquake simulator. Explorer Backpacks, complete with pith helmets, binoculars and drawing materials, are available for under-sevens, while Discovery Guides containing activities linked to the national curriculum can be purchased for children aged four to 16. Don't miss the Darwin Centre, the museum's new state-of-the-art science and collections facility.

Science Museum (sciencemuseum.org.uk) London's best museum for hands-on fiddling and twiddling, the Science Museum has play zones targeting different age groups. The Garden helps three to six year olds experiment with water, light and sound, the Pattern Pod engages five to eight year olds, while the Launch Pad is the museum's largest and most popular interactive gallery for school-age kids. Teenagers will find the latest science news at Antenna, while Energy challenges seven to 14 year olds to investigate energy demands for the future. There are also motion simulators, daily science shows and an IMAX cinema.

Victoria & Albert Museum (vam.ac.uk) The V&A has excellent family facilities, including a treasure trail which takes you through exhibits on Asia and the Middle East in search of objects for the perfect picnic party. Activity backpacks on themes such as Chinese treasures, glass and fancy furnishings are also available for children aged five to 12. Don't miss the Activity Cart (Sundays and holidays) – a roving art and craft trolley, suitable for children aged three and over.

as well as a choice of two paper trails – one on a Chinese Zodiac theme, the other in pursuit of 'winged things'. The National Portrait Gallery (npg.org.uk) provides activity rucksacks containing jigsaws, dressing-up gear and other goodies to stimulate four- to 12-year-olds in the Tudor, Victorian and 20th Century Galleries. However, if it's good old-fashioned brass rubbing that gets your creative juices flowing, head to St Martin-in-the-Fields (stmartin-in-the-fields.org). Grab a snack lunch at the café in the crypt, before strolling down The Mall, nipping into St James's Park (royalparks. org.uk) to see wildlife officers feeding the pelicans (daily at 1430). Continue to Buckingham Palace (royal.gov.uk) to wave at the queen, and then take a bus to Knightsbridge where the Food Halls of Harrods (harrods. com) should distract kids for at least a few minutes before they drag you to the toys on the fourth floor.

Southeast England The Wight stuff

Family attractions in Southeast England include everything from theme parks and castles to traditional seaside resorts like Brighton, Eastbourne and Hastings. However, if you have to pick just one place to take the kids, it has to be the Isle of Wight with its beaches, coastal walks, cycling tracks and watersports. Take the ferry from Portsmouth and you can easily add on a visit to the historic dockyard to see the *Mary Rose* and *HMS Victory*. Another great option for active families, the New Forest has miles of cycle tracks and several riding stables, while the North and South Downs offer plenty in the way of gentle walks.

Bodiam Castle.

Isle of Wight

A mecca for 'yachties', the Isle of Wight is the perfect place to hone your sailing skills. X-Isle Sports (x-is.co.uk) offers courses in sailing, surfing, kitesurfing, windsurfing, wakeboarding and waterskiing. There are also several excellent locations for kayaking, including the sheltered beaches of Ryde and Puckpool. Wight Ventures (wight-ventures.co.uk) will deliver rental bikes to your hotel and kit you out with helmets, water bottles and maps. An easy route to start with follows the disused railway line from Yarmouth to Freshwater Bay, a good spot for swimming. To any dinosaur fanatics in the family, the Isle of Wight will seem more like a pilgrimage than a holiday – nowhere else in Europe is more important for dinosaur remains. At the Dinosaur Isle (dinosaurisle.com) museum you're whisked back in time to the Cretaceous when the Isle of Wight was prowled by the predatory *Neovenator salerii*, as well as giant lumbering sauropods and armour-plated ankylosaurs. New discoveries are made all the time – try your luck by joining one of the museum's fossil walks.

New Forest

Once a popular hunting ground for Norman kings, William the Conqueror's 'new' forest is home to peacefully grazing herds of fallow deer and New Forest ponies. For your best chance of spotting wildlife, explore the forest (one of the few ancient oak woods left in England) on foot, bicycle or horseback. Try Country Lanes Cycle Centre (countrylanes.co.uk) and New Park Manor Equestrian Centre (newparkmanorhotel. co.uk) – both in Brockenhurst. Nestled on the banks of the Beaulieu River, Buckler's Hard (bucklershard.co.uk) provides a fascinating glimpse into past, when the New Forest supplied mighty oaks for Nelson's fleet.

Beaches & castles

In Kent, Walpole Bay has a tidal swimming pool, while West Wittering on the Sussex coast has a Blue Flag sandy beach. With babies or toddlers in tow, follow the 2-km buggy-friendly path alongside the River Cuckmere in the Seven Sisters Country Park (sevensisters.org. uk). Bristling with turrets and surrounded by a wide moat, Bodiam Castle (nationaltrust. org.uk) in Sussex is a medieval masterpiece. Leeds Castle (leeds-castle.com) is equally impressive, while Canterbury Cathedral (canterbury-cathedral.org) is famed for its stained glass windows.

⊙ Inside info

▶▶ Top attractions include Legoland (legoland.co.uk), Marwell Zoo (marwell.org), Portsmouth Historic Dockyard (historicdockyard.co.uk) and Thorpe Park (thorpepark.com).
▶▶ For further information, log on to visitsoutheastengland.com, Isle of Wight Tourism (islandbreaks. co.uk) and New Forest Tourism (thenewforest.co.uk).

East Anglia A wild & windy shore

Bulging out between the Thames Estuary and the Wash, East Anglia may be flat, but it's far from featureless. You can hire a boat to explore the 200 km of reed-fringed waterways in the Norfolk Broads or punt along the River Cam beneath the Bridge of Sighs in the magnificent university town of Cambridge. From bustling resorts, like Great Yarmouth and Southwold, to the medieval city of Norwich, this under-rated corner of Britain has lots to offer families. Pick of the crop, however, has to be Norfolk's north coast, where your kids will rediscover the pure and simple joys of kite flying, beachcombing and crabbing.

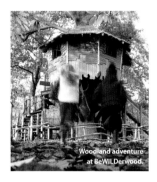
Woodland adventure at BeWILDerwood.

North Norfolk Coast

Driving north from King's Lynn, you pass Snettisham Park (snettishampark.co.uk) which has a deer safari, adventure playgrounds and children's farm, and Caley Mill (norfolk-lavender.co.uk) which is perfectly purple during July and August when the lavender fields are in bloom. Soon after, you reach Hunstanton, a traditional Victorian seaside resort with pier, amusement arcades and pony rides on the beach. Kids will love the seal-watching trips operated by Searles Sea Tours (seatours. co.uk) in the amphibious Wash Monster which is equally at home trundling across the sand flats as it is bobbing in the sea beneath Hunstanton's striped cliffs. If it's raining, seek refuge at the Sea Life Sanctuary (sealsanctuary.co.uk) which rescues injured marine mammals found along the coast and also has displays featuring penguins and otters.

Follow the coastal A149

road to Holme-next-the-Sea where a boardwalk through the dunes provides easy buggy access to the beach. Nearby is Titchwell Marsh Nature Reserve (rspb.org.uk) where top summer ticks include avocets and marsh harriers. Three pushchair-friendly nature trails explore fen and meadow habitats where, if you're lucky, you may glimpse bearded tits, water voles or the elusive bittern.

Continuing east to Brancaster, you may well find a long stretch of beach to yourself. It's a great spot to launch a kite, but not so good for swimming due to the strong tidal currents.

Beyond Burnham lies Holkham Hall (holkham.co.uk), set in a magnificent landscaped park with access to a nature reserve and a beautiful 6-km swathe of golden sands. Just east of Holkham, Wells-next-the-Sea is an old fishing port with a quay that's just the job for crabbing.

A thriving port in the 13th century, Blakeney Marshes is

now all silt and seals – you can see both in abundance with Bean's Boats (beanboattrips. co.uk). Nearby, Cley Windmill (which can put you up for the night) overlooks the Cley Marshes where you have another chance to bag a bittern. Continue on towards Salthouse for sublime seafood at Cookie's Crab Shop before reaching Sheringham and Cromer –both of which have sand at low tide, pebbles at high tide – and everything in between, from crazy golf to fish and chips.

⊙ Inside info

▸▸ Top attractions include BeWILDerwood (bewilderwood. co.uk) and Woburn Safari Park (woburnsafari.co.uk).
▸▸ The Coasthopper Bus (norfolk. gov.uk) operates between Kings Lynn and Sheringham, connecting with the Bittern Line (bitternline. com) train to Norwich.
▸▸ The North Norfolk Railway (nnrailway.co.uk) runs 9 km from Sheringham to Holt.
▸▸ For further information, log on to visiteastofengland.com.

Southwest England A shore thing

Brace yourself Brixham; look out Lyme Regis! When the summer holidays arrive, the Southwest receives a flood of families in search of quintessential British seaside. You can almost smell the factor 40 and hear the rattle of spades against buckets. Cornwall, Devon and Dorset are fringed by some of the world's most child-friendly beaches, offering everything from surf, rock pools and unrivalled sandcastle potential to great-value resorts and copious rainy-day attractions.

Net gains – rock-pooling at Sennen Cove.

Devon

Linking the resort towns of Torquay, Paignton and Brixham, the English Riviera (englishriviera.co.uk) is packed with family appeal, from sandy beaches and steam-train rides to days out at Paignton Zoo (paigntonzoo.org.uk) and Quaywest Water Park (quaywest. co.uk). Head south along the coast and you reach the South Hams (somewhere-special. co.uk), an irresistible blend of glorious beaches, intriguing inlets and rolling countryside. Lying at its heart, Kingsbridge and Salcombe offer traditional seaside treats like crabbing and boat trips, while Dartmouth has its superb castle (english-heritage.org.uk) jutting out into the Dart estuary. The beaches of the South Hams, meanwhile, are heaven on earth for kids. From east to west, take your pick from Blackpool Sands (sheltered, safe and simply idyllic), Slapton Sands (good for skimming stones), Millbay (across the estuary from Salcombe, fine sand, good for paddling), Soar Mill Cove (golden sands, streams to dam, caves to explore), Hope Cove (calm waters, small harbour at one end), Thurlestone (great rock pools, plus sand), Bantham (vast swathes of sand, shallow tidal lagoons, good surf) and Bigbury-on-Sea (natural paddling pools, rock pools, views of Burgh Island).

Just when you've set your mind on the South Hams, North Devon drops a bucket-load of golden sand and surf potential on your best-laid plans. Woolacombe Bay is the region's undisputed beach beauty, while other top surf spots include Saunton Sands and Croyde. Just inland you can saddle up at the Exmoor Pony Centre (exmoorponies.co.uk) or, if the weather turns nasty, bolt for The Milky Way (themilkyway. co.uk) – a farm and space-themed adventure park rolled into one.

◉ Inside info

>> Avoid travelling on Saturday mornings during the height of the holiday season.

>> Beware the weaver fish, a spiny rascal that burrows in sand between high and low tide – wear jelly shoes or wetsuit booties.

>> The weather is notoriously fickle – misty on the north coast, sunny on the south and vice versa – so be prepared to follow the sun.

>> For further information, log on to visitsouthwest.co.uk.

Jurassic Coast

Lyme Regis is an official gateway to the Jurassic Coast (jurassiccoast. com), a World Heritage Site that places a 150-km stretch of shoreline between Swanage and Exmouth alongside the Grand Canyon in terms of natural importance. Lyme Fossil Shop is a good place to begin your fossil foray. Its shelves are festooned with plate-sized ammonites and fossilized dinosaur poo. At the Philpot Museum (lymeregismuseum.co.uk) you can find out about Lyme's most famous fossil-hunter, Mary Anning, while the nearby Charmouth Heritage Coast Centre (charmouth.org) organizes guided fossil hunting tours where experts transform pebbly beaches into prehistoric graveyards. Hotspots include Monmouth Beach (Lyme Regis) for giant ammonites; Black Ven and Church Cliffs (between Lyme Regis and Charmouth) for ammonites, ichthyosaurs and plesiosaurs; Lulworth and Portland for fragments of fossil forest, and Purbeck for dinosaur footprints.

Wade to go – St Michael's Mount.

On Dartmoor, hike to one of the famous granite tors, picnic beside rushing streams at Dartmeet, ride the South Devon Railway (southdevonrailway.org) from Buckfastleigh to Totnes or feed lambs at Pennywell Farm (pennywellfarm.co.uk).

Bath, Bristol & Somerset

The pleasures of Bath range from boating on the River Avon (bathboating.co.uk) to exploring the magnificent Roman Baths (romanbaths.co.uk) where kids can 'meet the Romans' courtesy of a special audio tour.

In Bristol, head for the harbour where the vast propeller and rudder of the dry-docked *SS Great Britain* (ssgreatbritain. org) will astound kids. Explore-at-Bristol (at-bristol.org.uk) is a hands-on science museum, while highlights at Bristol Zoo (bristolzoo.org.uk) include the Monkey Jungle, Seal & Penguin Coasts and Explorers' Creek where you can feed parrots.

In Somerset, traditional seaside fun is just a donkey ride away at Minehead, Burnham-on-Sea, Weston-super-Mare and Clevedon. At Wookey Hole Caves (wookey.co.uk) children can search for a witch that was turned to stone, while the Fleet Air Arm Museum (fleetairarm. com) is packed with planes – including Concorde – and features a simulated journey to the flight deck of *HMS Ark Royal*.

Kids' top 10 Cornwall

❶ **Dig** the beach, any beach – make a miniature St Michael's Mount, scoop out a network of canals, build a sandy dam to hold back the tide, excavate a paddling pool.

❷ **Venture** into the tropics at the Eden Project (edenproject.com), Cornwall's essential day out. Find out where sugar, chocolate and vanilla come from, play drums and make crafts in the Jungle Town and operate the biggest nutcracker you've ever seen. If you thought plants were boring, think again.

❸ **Discover** how a marine rescue centre works at Gweek's National Seal Sanctuary (sealsanctuary.co.uk) – home to seals, otters and sea lions.

❹ **Explore** the sandy snugs, rocky islets and turquoise waters of Kynance Cove (nationaltrust.org.uk) – a real smugglers' haunt if ever there was one.

❺ **Learn** to surf at Whitesands Bay, a golden crescent at Sennen with a cool surf school (sennensurfingcentre.com), rock pools near the lifeboat ramp, acres of sand at low tide for beach cricket and great fish and chips from the café on the waterfront.

❻ **Dangle** your legs over a harbour wall, a crab line in one hand, a Cornish vanilla ice cream (with Cadbury's Flake) in the other.

❼ **Plan** an adventure to St Michael's Mount (stmichaelsmount.co.uk), the legendary home of the giant, Cormoran; walk across at low tide or take the boat.

❽ **Cycle** the 9-km stretch of the Camel Trail between Wadebridge and Padstow alongside the estuary; it's flat, easy and there's lots to see.

❾ **Catch** mackerel on a fishing trip from Padstow harbour (padstowboattrips.com).

❿ **Play** beach games, from hopscotch to stony knickers (the first to complete a designated course without losing stones or knickers wins).

If it's raining, top attractions include Crealy Great Adventure Park (crealy. co.uk), Tate St Ives (tate.org.uk/stives), Falmouth's National Maritime Museum (nmmc.co.uk), the stately home of Lanhydrock (nationaltrust. org.uk), Newquay's Blue Reef Aquarium (bluereefaquarium.co.uk) and Newquay Zoo (newquayzoo.org.uk).

Central England Historic heartlands

With its honeystone market towns and rolling hills peppered with sheep, nowhere does traditional England better than the Cotswolds – the region that inspired a million jigsaw puzzles. Elsewhere, you will find a veritable encyclopaedia of historical sites, from ancient Stonehenge and medieval Warwick Castle to the birthplaces of Shakespeare, the Industrial Revolution and, most significantly to children, the Cadbury Creme Egg.

Zebras at the Cotswold Wildlife Park.

East Midlands

Derbyshire Designated Britain's first national park in 1951, the heather-clad moors and wooded valleys of the Peak District are ideal stomping territory for active families. Two of the most popular attractions include riding the cable cars at the Heights of Abraham (heights-of-abraham.co.uk) and the trams at Crich Tramway Village (tramway.co.uk) – both near Matlock. For a forest-themed free-for-all, kids can go nuts at Conkers (visitconkers.

⦿ Inside info

▸▸ Child-friendly highlights in Oxford include Pitt Rivers Museum (prm.ox.ac.uk) or the interactive Science Oxford Hands-On (oxtrust.org.uk/handson).
▸▸ One of the region's best cycle tracks, the 21-km Tissington Trail follows the old Buxton-to-Ashbourne railway line in the heart of the Peak District.
▸▸ Longleat (longleat.co.uk) is renowned for its drive-through safari park, but also boasts the perplexing Hedge Maze.
▸▸ For further information, log on to visittheheart.co.uk and enjoyenglandseastmidlands.com.

com) with its assault course, nature trails and playgrounds.
Leicestershire Famous for its primate collection, Twycross Zoo (twycrosszoo.com) has everything from chimps and bonobos to gibbons and gorillas, while the National Space Centre (spacecentre.co.uk) challenges visitors to undertake a simulated 3D mission in Human Spaceflight: Lunar Base 2025.
Nottinghamshire With its family nature trails, cycling and horse riding opportunities, the historic royal hunting patch of Sherwood Forest (sherwoodforest.org.uk) is a great place to set free your 'inner Robin Hood'. Designed for under-10s, Sundown Adventure Park (sundownadventureland.co.uk) has gentle rides and story-book-themed attractions.

West Midlands

Birmingham Hands up who likes chocolate? Cadbury World (cadburyworld.co.uk) takes you on a mouth-watering journey through the origins and production of the sweet sensation and even goes

interactive with Purple Planet where you can chase a Cadbury Creme Egg, grow your own Cocoa beans and experience chocolate rain. Birmingham's science museum, ThinkTank (thinktank.ac), has over 200 hands-on displays, plus a planetarium and IMAX cinema.
Shropshire With no fewer than 10 museums and an iron bridge (albeit the world's first) as its star attraction, you might be put off taking kids to the Ironbridge Gorge Museums (ironbridge.org.uk). Don't be. There's nothing remotely rusty about this World Heritage Site commemorating the Industrial Revolution. At Blists Hill Victorian Town costumed actors evoke a bygone era when steam engines and horses powered industry, while at the Enginuity centre children can scheme away at their own technological innovations.
Staffordshire Taking kids to The Wedgwood Visitor Centre (wedgwood.com) might seem like, well, taking a bull into a china shop, but not only will they be fascinated by the factory tour, they'll also get a shot at the potter's wheel. For a different

Ilam Park in the Peak District.

kind of spin, Drayton Manor (draytonmanor.co.uk) and Alton Towers (altontowers.com) are two of Britain's most popular theme parks – see page 27 to see how their rides compare with the likes of Blackpool Pleasure Beach and Thorpe Park.

Warwickshire The Shakespeare Birthplace Trust (shakespeare.org.uk) manages five properties in Stratford-upon-Avon, all linked to the life of the great bard. Two of the most interesting for children are Shakespeare's Birthplace in Henley Street and Mary Arden's where you can experience what life was like in a 16th-century farmhouse. For a history lesson with more oomph, Warwick Castle (warwick-castle.co.uk) delivers with a passion. Kids can lay siege to haunted towers, torture chambers and medieval banqueting halls, but it's the legendary activities they'll remember most. Jousting, archery and falconry are held throughout summer, while winter sees a skating rink installed at the 11th-century fort.

Worcestershire Chuffing 26 km between Kidderminster and Bridgnorth, the Severn Valley Railway (svr.co.uk) is a must for all Thomas and Hornby fans, while the West Midland Safari Park (wmsp.co.uk) will appeal to the wild-at-heart with its drive-through safari (spot the white lions) and daredevil amusement park.

Woods & water

In the beautiful Forest of Dean (visitforestofdean.co.uk) you can cycle and canoe, or take to the trees at Go Ape! (goape.co.uk), a high-wire adventure with a minimum age of 10. For more sedate forest rambles, try the Dean Forest Railway (deanforestrailway.co.uk) or the Dean Heritage Centre (deanheritagemuseum.com) which has a forester's cottage and woodland trails. At Slimbridge Wetland Centre (wwt.org.uk) in the Severn Vale, you can feed geese (above), take a 4WD safari through a nature reserve and spot kingfishers from a hide.

Kids' top 10
Cotswolds

❶ Fill a long weekend or more at the Cotswold Water Park (waterpark.org) with everything from sailing, canoeing, raft-building and aerial adventures to birdwatching, angling, horse riding and water skiing.

❷ Burn off some energy in the 850-ha park and pleasure gardens of Blenheim Palace (blenheimpalace.com) which has a maze, butterfly house and adventure playground.

❸ Spot wolves, rhinos, zebras and lions at the Cotswold Wildlife Park (cotswoldwildlifepark.co.uk) – and don't miss the meerkats, penguins and otters in the walled garden.

❹ Play hide-and-seek at Hidcote Manor Gardens (nationaltrust.org.uk) where neatly clipped yew hedges partition the estate into countless outdoor rooms.

❺ Feed the trout at Bibury (biburytroutfarm.co.uk).

❻ Explore the weird and wonderful collection of artefacts, from musical instruments to Samurai armour, at Snowshill Manor (nationaltrust.org.uk).

❼ Cycle between chocolate-box villages like the Slaughters, Winchcombe, Northleach, Bibury and Burford on a self-guided tour with Cotswold Country Cycles (cotswoldcountrycycles.com).

❽ Hike part of the Cotswold Way (nationaltrail.co.uk/cotswold), a 160-km walking trail between Chipping Campden and Bath.

❾ Spend all your pocket money at the toyshop in Bourton-on-the-Water, and then beg to be taken to Birdland (birdland.co.uk).

❿ Sample scones with strawberry jam and clotted cream at Badgers Hall Tearoom (badgershall.com) in Chipping Campden.

North England City sights & wild places

If you feel your warm-weather instincts tugging you southwards, dig your heels in and spare a thought for North England. The Great British family holiday was practically invented in the seaside resort of Blackpool, but the region's appeal goes way beyond donkey rides and pleasure parks. Let your kids' imaginations run riot through Roman ruins, Norman castles and cutting-edge science centres; free their spirits in wild places like the Lake District and Yorkshire Moors, and fill their days (even the rainy ones) with attractions ranging from Beatrix Potter to The Beatles.

National Railway Museum, York.

Manchester

Footie fans will make a bee-line for Old Trafford where the Manchester United Museum and Stadium Tour (manutd.com) takes you into the hallowed heart of the world's most popular football team (controversial, but true). You can strut down the player's tunnel, admire the trophy cabinet and sit at the dressing-room peg of your favourite player. For fancy footwork on the high street, Manchester's shops will satisfy all fashion fans, while the city's mighty industrial heritage is celebrated at the Museum of Science and Industry (msim.org. uk). For family-friendly culture in Manchester, you can't beat the galleries and theatres of The Lowry (thelowry.com).

Liverpool

Not to be outdone by its Mancunian rivals, Liverpool FC has the Anfield Experience (www.liverpoolfc.tv), but there's another attraction in Merseyside's great city that

overshadows even football. Your kids may never have heard of The Beatles, but that's no reason why you shouldn't at least attempt to improve their music tastes. Think of it as part of their education. Of the many 'Fab Four' tours and attractions, your best bet with kids is The Beatles Story (beatlesstory.com) at Albert Dock. From rocking the world to exploring new ones, Spaceport (spaceport.org.uk) at Seacombe on the Wirral (ride the Mersey ferry to get there) takes you on a virtual journey through space. The nearby Blue Planet Aquarium (blueplanetaquarium. com) offers Bubblemaker diving courses for children aged eight to 15 – but you need to be at least 18 before they let you into the shark tank. If you continue south on the M53, you'll reach Chester Zoo (chesterzoo.org. uk). Family highlights north of Liverpool include the beaches, dunes and red squirrel reserve at Formby Point and Splash World (splashworldsouthport. com), a water park at Southport with slides, fountains and a lazy river ride.

Blackpool

Dating from the 18th century, Britain's archetypal seaside resort is still a big crowd-puller – thanks in no small part to Blackpool Pleasure Beach (blackpoolpleasurebeach.com). England's thrill-city-central has over 125 rides and attractions, ranging from the 140-kph Pepsi Max Big One roller coaster to ice-skating, bingo and dodgems. There's also a water park (sandcastle-waterworld.co.uk) and aquarium (sealifeeurope. com). For nostalgia mixed with fun, don't miss Blackpool Tower (blackpooltower.co.uk) where ballroom dancing, circus shows and one of Europe's largest indoor adventure playgrounds will further conspire to keep you off the beach.

Yorkshire

There's plenty to interest kids in York. Start with York Minster (yorkminster.org), England's largest medieval cathedral. Check out the Great East Window (a tennis-court-sized stained-glass marvel) before climbing the Central Tower for some gargoyle spotting. Back at street level, the National Railway Museum (nrm.org.uk) boasts the world's finest collection of trains, including the record breaking *Mallard* and a replica of Stephenson's *Rocket*, while the Jorvik Viking Centre (jorvik-viking-centre.co.uk) features a ride which weaves through a diorama of houses, backyards and market stalls – complete with authentic 'Viking' aromas of manure, fish and roasting boar.

The North York Moors National Park (moors.uk.net) offers a wonderful mixture of coast, forest and moorland. A single day could easily be divided between rock-pooling at Robin Hood's Bay and a picnic at Danby in the Esk Valley; you

⊙ **Inside** info

»» Most of Manchester's galleries and museums are free to enter.
»» For further information on the region's cities, log on to visitmanchester.com, visitliverpool.com, visityork.org, and blackpooltourism.com.
»» The York Pass (yorkpass.com) provides entry to 28 attractions.
»» The Hadrian's Wall Bus leaves Newcastle at 0940, arriving at Housesteads at 1106; you can take bicycles on the bus and pedal sections of Hadrian's Cycleway.
»» For further information, log on to northeastengland.co.uk, englandsnorthwest.com and newcastlegateshead.com.

could hike in Dalby Forest, or ride the North Yorkshire Moors Railway (nymr.co.uk) between Pickering and Whitby.

Further south, Bempton Cliffs (rspb.org.uk) are smothered with gannets, guillemots and puffins between April and August. Other attractions in the region include The Deep (thedeep.co.uk), an impressive aquarium near Hull, and the superb children's science museum, Eureka! (eureka.org.uk) in Halifax.

The Northeast

In Newcastle, younger children will enjoy Seven Stories (sevenstories.org.uk), the Centre for Children's Books, while the high-tech Centre for Life (life.org.uk) should appeal to most ages. The best day out from Newcastle is to explore Hadrian's Wall (hadrians-wall.org) – a 117-km long Roman fortification snaking between Wallsend and Bowness on the Solway Firth.

Further north, the spectacular Northumberland coast has long sandy beaches and a string of forts, including Bamburgh Castle (bamburghcastle.com) and Holy Island's Lindisfarne Castle (nationaltrust.org.uk). Slightly inland, Alnwick Castle (alnwickcastle.com) starred in the first two Harry Potter films, while the Farne Islands (accessible from Seahouses) are teeming with seabirds and seals.

Tarn Hows.

Kids' top 10
Lake District

❶ **Conquer** Mont 1. Learn how to rock-climb and abseil with Climb365 (climb365.net).
❷ Sail a yacht on Lake Windermere with Outrun Sailing (outrunsailing.co.uk).
❸ Visit Peter Rabbit and friends at the World of Beatrix Potter (hop-skip-jump.com).
❹ Cruise the lakes with Windermere Lake Cruises (windermere-lakecruises.co.uk).
❺ Ride a steam train on the Haverthwaite Railway (lakesiderailway.co.uk).
❻ Wander 'lonely as a cloud' around Grasmere before visiting William Wordsworth's house, Dove Cottage (wordsworth.org.uk).
❼ Lose yourself in the maze and see the owls at Muncaster Castle (muncaster.co.uk).
❽ Find the perfect skimming stone at Buttermere or Coniston.
❾ Picnic at Tarn Hows and then walk the buggy-friendly circuit around the lake.
❿ Conquer Scafell Pike, the highest mountain in England at 978 m, or take on the challenge of a wilderness bushcraft course with Woodsmoke (woodsmoke.uk.com).

»» For further information, log on to lake-district.gov.uk.

Wales The green heart of a red dragon

Snowdonia's Mawddach Trail.

Wales is a little beauty – squat, rugged, full of character and brilliant round the edges, just like a Welsh rugby scrum half. 'An area the size of Wales' is often banded around when comparing anything from US national parks to rainforest deforestation, but take a closer look at this 20,779-sq-km country and you will find plenty to shout about in its own right. Not only is Wales king of Britain's castles, but it also has some of the finest and cleanest beaches, great surf, wildlife-rich islands and rugged mountains – all in an area roughly the size of Massachusetts.

Cardiff

Children will be impressed by the Roof Garden and elaborate Banqueting Hall in quirky Cardiff Castle (cardiffcastle.com), but it's Cardiff Bay (cardiffbay.co.uk) where they'll have most fun, from delving into the cafés and shops at Mermaid Quay to exploring the science centre, Techniquest (techniquest.org). About 6 km west of the city, the open-air museum of St Fagans (museumwales.ac.uk) evokes 500 years of Welsh heritage with historic buildings and crafts.

Gower Peninsula

Like the more westerly peninsulas of Pembrokeshire

◉ Inside info

» The Freedom of Wales Flexi Pass (walesflexipass.co.uk) provides unlimited access to mainline train services and most buses.
» There are 14 steam and narrow gauge railways in Wales (greatlittletrainsofwales.co.uk).
» For further information log on to visitwales.co.uk.

(see opposite), the 30-km-long Gower is a magnet to beach lovers. Caswell Beach has excellent facilities and is a good place to learn how to surf, while Rhossili is the ultimate run-wild-and-free beach where you can play cricket, fly a kite, build a sandy rampart against the tide and scrawl your name in house-size letters. For a gentle blend of rural museum, farm animals, play areas and craft activities, visit the Gower Heritage Centre (gowerheritagecentre.co.uk); for boat trips in search of seals and dolphins, contact Gower Coast Adventures (gowercoastadventures.co.uk).

Snowdonia

It's a five-hour slog up and down Snowdon, the 1085-m highpoint of Snowdonia National Park (snowdonia-npa.gov.uk), but families with younger children can still get spectacular views by taking the rack-and-pinion Snowdon Mountain Railway (snowdonrailway.co.uk) from Llanberis. Located in the south of the park, the Mawddach

Trail is an excellent choice for families. Starting at Dolgellau, the 14-km traffic-free route follows the beautiful Mawddach Estuary to Barmouth and can either be walked or cycled. The pretty riverside town of Betws-y-Coed is another popular walking base, while the narrow-gauge Ffestiniog Railway (festrail.co.uk) takes you on a 22 km steam train journey between Blaenau Ffestiniog and Porthmadog. For beaches, head west along the Llyn Peninsula to Whistling Sands (Porth Oer), a sandy gem with great rock pools and a café.

Castles

You're never far from a great castle in Wales – and they're all just as castles should be, with rounded towers, arrow slits, drawbridges and moats. One of the most formidable is Beaumaris Castle on Anglesey, although kids will be just as happy to storm the ramparts of Caernarfon, Conwy and Harlech in North Wales, and Caerphilly, Kidwelly and Pembroke in South and mid-Wales.

Pembrokeshire highlights

Best beaches Choose from over 50 sandy beaches, including Blue Flag beauties like Whitesands. The best all-round family beaches (with lifeguards, lots to do and no dogs allowed) are Amroth, Saundersfoot, all of Tenby's beaches, Dale, Broad Haven and Whitesands. Dale, Broad Haven and Tenby North have canoes and boats for hire, while Barfundle and Aber Mawr are idyllic beaches for picnics. For surf, head to Whitesands, Marloes, Manorbier, Broad Haven, Caerfai, Newgale and, for strong swimmers only, Freshwater West. Hire boards from Haven Sports (havensports.co.uk) and West Wales Wind Surf and Sailing (surfdale.co.uk).

Best boat trips Operators include Aquaphobia (aquaphobia-ramseyisland.co.uk), Dale Sea Safari (sail-sailing.co.uk), Porthgain Boat Trips (porthgainboats.ndo.co.uk), Ramsey Island Cruises (ramseyislandcruises.co.uk), Shearwater Safaris (boatrides.co.uk) and Venture Jet (venturejet.co.uk).

Broad Haven.

Best seal spotting Take a boat trip to Ramsey, Skomer, Skockholm or Caldey Island. The southwest tip of St Davids Peninsula, Cemaes Head near Cardigan and the Marloes Peninsula are also good spots. The best time to see grey seals is between September and November when they give birth to pups.

Best dolphin spotting Cardigan Bay has a resident population of bottlenose dolphins, while summer witnesses the arrival of common dolphins (sometimes in pods a thousand-strong), as well as humpback, fin, minke and orca whales. Join a boat trip with an operator adhering to the Marine Code (pembrokeshiremarinecode.org.uk). Sea Trust (seatrust.org.uk) operates a lookout from Stumble Head.

Best bird islands Reached by daily boats from Martin's Haven, Skomer is renowned for puffins, guillemots, razorbills and kittiwakes. You can also stay overnight to experience the Manx shearwaters returning to their burrows under cover of darkness. Skokholm's petrels and puffins are best viewed from a boat trip from Dale, while Ramsey can be visited from St Davids. Further offshore, Grassholm is a raucous nesting site for 65,000 gannets during the summer months.

Best cycle trails Cardigan's Cycle Break Centre (cyclebreakswales.co.uk) has set up several easy cycling routes alongside the River Teifi. Other options include St Govans Head (one of the few sections of the Coast

Neyland to Johnston and the 11-km circuit around Llys y Fran reservoir.

Best walks Buggy-friendly paths include the 4-km jaunt from Wisemans Bridge to Saundersfoot Harbour and the 800-m circuit of Pembroke Castle's moat. For a short walk with a convenient café, try the 10-km trail from Nolton Haven to Broad Haven. For something more ambitious, stride out on the 17-km circuit of the Dale Peninsula. The Walkers Coastal Bus Service (pembrokeshire.gov.uk/coastbus) simplifies access to trails, while The Coast Path (pembrokeshirecoast.org/walking) has numerous ideas for circular walks and easy-access paths.

Best attractions Feel the adrenaline rush on the water coaster and 30 other rides at Oakwood Theme Park (oakwoodthemepark.co.uk), cheer on the knights as they battle it out at medieval Pembroke Castle (pembrokecastle.co.uk) and feed the animals at Folly Farm (folly-farm.co.uk).

Best activities A mixture of climbing, swimming, scrambling along rocky shores and flinging yourself off cliff faces, coasteering is the latest wet-and-wild craze to hit Pembrokeshire. Other more orthodox pursuits include scuba diving, sea kayaking, and horse riding. Several dedicated centres, such as the Pembrokeshire Activity Centre (pembrokeshire-activity-centre.co.uk), provide courses in these and other activities.

»» For further information, log on to visitpembrokeshire.com.

Scotland Royal Miles to far-flung Isles

Chances are you won't spot the Loch Ness Monster, but that won't stop your children from staring long and hard at every patch of water they come across in Scotland – and what better way for them to fall under the spell of this beautiful and diverse country. From Edinburgh's historic Royal Mile to the wild and remote Shetlands, kids will find castles to explore, munros to conquer and deserted beaches to lay claim to. And if Nessie proves elusive, they'll be more than satisfied with sightings of whales, eagles and otters during boat trips in the Hebrides.

Kelvingrove, Glasgow.

Edinburgh

Plenty of cities have castles, but not many have a castle perched on an extinct volcano – a double whammy for kid-friendly Edinburgh. A fun way to get an overview of this bonny World-Heritage-listed city is to take a ride through the medieval Old Town and Georgian New Town with Edinburgh Bus Tours (edinburghtour.com).

Next, visit Edinburgh Castle (historic-scotland.gov.uk) to see Scotland's Crown Jewels and the Stone of Destiny. Listen out for the One O'Clock Gun and visit the dungeons to see the Prisoners of War exhibition.

⊙ Inside info

▸▸ The Edinburgh Pass (edinburgh.org/pass) provides free entry to over 30 attractions, plus free city centre bus transport.
▸▸ The Daytripper Ticket (spt.co.uk) is a cost-effective way for families to travel by rail, subway, buses and some ferries throughout Glasgow and Strathclyde.
▸▸ For further information, log on to edinburgh.org and seeglasgow.com

Just below the castle, West Princes Street Gardens is ideal for letting youngsters burn off energy, while teenagers will prefer to exercise their wallets along adjacent Princes Street.

Alternatively, head east from Castle Hill along the Royal Mile – once the main thoroughfare of medieval Edinburgh, linking the castle to the Palace of Holyroodhouse (royal.gov.uk). Flanked by impressive buildings like St Giles Cathedral and Parliament House, it's the toy-crammed Museum of Childhood (cac.org.uk) that will appeal most to kids. On nearby Holyrood Road, Our Dynamic Earth (dynamicearth.co.uk) has an earthquake simulator, a time machine that will whisk you back 15 billion years and a FutureDome where you decide the fate of the planet.

Rearing behind this ultra-modern science centre, you can explore the ancient lava flows of Arthur's Seat, a volcano that blew its top between 350 and 400 million years ago. Rainy-day favourites for younger children include the Brass Rubbing Centre (cac.org.uk) and The Ceramic Experience (theceramicexperience.com), while the excellent Edinburgh Zoo (edinburghzoo.org.uk) is a long-established favourite, whatever the weather.

Edinburgh's most notorious ghost tour, City of the Dead, is hosted nightly by Blackheart Entertainment (blackhart.uk.com) – but be warned: a possible encounter with the MacKenzie Poltergeist is not for the faint-hearted. The Secret City Tour, meanwhile, is suitable for all ages and features stories as diverse as Harry Potter, the invention of Christmas and the origin of Frankenstein's monster.

There are several fine beaches close to Edinburgh, including the popular surf spot of Gullane Bents. Head east towards North Berwick to visit the 12th-century Dirleton Castle, the sandy beach of Yellowcraig and the Scottish Seabird Centre (seabird.org) where you can watch footage beamed live from Bass Rock, 5 km offshore and home to 100,000 gannets between January and October.

Kids' top 10 Highlands & Islands

1 Find out what the real story in Balamory is by taking a ferry from Oban to Mull where the multicoloured houses along Tobermory's waterfront provided the setting for the children's TV programme.

2 Spot the Loch Ness Monster – and if that fails, spy a minke whale on a boat trip from Mull with Sea Life Surveys (sealifesurveys.com) and tick off otters during a safari with Island Encounter (mullwildlife.co.uk).

3 Peer into the spectacular kelp forests around Skye from the Seaprobe Atlantis (seaprobeatlantis.com), Scotland's only semi-submersible.

4 Play king or queen of the castle on the Aberdeenshire Castle Trail (Aberdeen-grampian.com) which links 13 forts – some rugged ruins, others posh palaces.

5 Feed Britain's only herd of reindeer (right) in Cairngorms National Park (cairngormreindeer.co.uk).

6 Discover what it's like to climb on ice at the Glen Coe Visitor Centre (nts.org.uk), then stride outside to explore some of Scotland's most dramatic scenery – and perhaps even 'bag a munro' (a mountain over 914 m in height).

7 Go wild on the treetop trail, adventure playground and water slides of the Landmark Forest Heritage Park (landmark-centre.co.uk) near Aviemore before watching ospreys at the Loch Garten (rspb.org.uk).

8 Practise skiing or snowboarding in the winter wonderland of the Nevis Range (nevisrange.co.uk), Scotland's highest ski area.

9 Pinch yourself to make sure you're not dreaming when you discover the golden sands and turquoise seas of Harris and the Uists in the Outer Hebrides. Other fine beaches include Sandwood Bay on the northwest coast of mainland Scotland and the irresistible tombolo of sand linking Shetland to St Ninian's Isle.

10 Glimpse shipwrecks and marine life through an underwater camera on a Roving Eye Boat Tour (rovingeye.co.uk) and experience life in the 19th century at Corrigal Farm Museum (orkney.gov.uk/heritage) – just two of the highlights on the Orkneys.

» For further information, log on to visithighlands. com and visitthehebrides.com.

Glasgow

Unlike Edinburgh, there are no iconic landmarks in Glasgow, but what this stylish, modern-thinking city lacks in the way of castles and volcanoes it more than compensates for with a buzzing cultural scene and several superb museums. By far the best for kids, the Kelvingrove Art Gallery and Museum (glasgowmuseums.com) has everything from Egyptian mummies to a Second World War Spitfire. Children under five have their own hands-on Mini Museum, while older kids can learn about wildlife, history and art at three discovery centres. Don't miss the webcam link to the Loch Ness Monster,

the 4-m Ceratosaur skeleton and the impressive collection of paintings which includes Salvador Dali's *Christ*.

Highlights at the nearby Museum of Transport include locomotives from the Caledonian and Highland Railways. Nip down to the north bank of the River Clyde and you'll find the 19th-century, three-masted *SS Glenlee*, otherwise known as The Tall Ship at Glasgow Harbour (thetallship.com). On the opposite bank, Pacific Quay is the location of the excellent Glasgow Science Centre (gsc.org.uk), a technological treasure house where kids can tinker with hundreds of interactive exhibits and go

goggle-eyed in the planetarium and IMAX cinema.

East of the city centre, but still on the Clyde, the People's Palace and Winter Gardens (glasgowmuseums.com) reveals Glasgow's social history, while an hour's drive southeast of Glasgow, New Lanark World Heritage Site (newlanark.org) is a beautifully restored 18th-century village where kids can discover what life was like in a Victorian cotton mill.

North of Glasgow, Loch Lomond & The Trossachs National Park (lochlomond-trossachs.org) makes a superb city escape with activities ranging from hiking, cycling and pony trekking to abseiling, windsurfing and lake cruises.

Britain Grown-ups' stuff

When to go
Britain has a mild climate with summer temperatures ranging from 14-30°C. The high season runs from April until October when most attractions are open. School holidays (most of July and August) are very busy, especially at the most popular tourist destinations such as The Lakes, Devon and Cornwall, the Scottish Highlands, Cotswolds and the Pembrokeshire coast.

Getting there
One of the busiest airports in the world, London Heathrow (heathrowairport.com) is served by most major international airports. London has three other main airports (Gatwick, Stansted and Luton), while regional airports include Edinburgh, Glasgow, Cardiff and Manchester. The national carrier is British Airways (britishairways.com), while low-cost airlines include easyJet (easyjet.com), Flybe (flybe. com) and Ryanair (ryanair. com). Ferries operate along 33 routes to England and Wales, arriving at ports on the south, east and west coasts, including Dover, Newhaven, Portsmouth, Harwich, Hull, Liverpool, Fishguard and Holyhead. Prices vary enormously according to season: check ferrycrossings-uk.co.uk or contact operators such as Brittany Ferries

(brittanyferries.com). The only option that doesn't involve travel to Britain by air or sea is to use the Channel Tunnel (eurotunnel.com) from mainland Europe.

Getting around
Its compact size and excellent infrastructure make Britain easy to get around. Self-drive is a flexible option; roads and motorways are well maintained, but bear in mind that major tourist routes can become heavily congested in peak periods and fuel is expensive. All the major car rental companies (Avis, Budget, Hertz etc) can be found at airports. For coach travel try National Express (nationalexpress.com) and Scottish Citylink (citylink. co.uk). For rail travel, Britrail (britrail.com) provides an online booking service for overseas visitors. You can also log on to nationalrail.co.uk for timetables, fares and bookings.

Accommodation
There is no shortage of places to stay in Britain and Ireland: everything from hiring your own private castle to pitching a tent is on offer. Hotels can often be expensive, with family rooms costing upwards of £150/night. Popular family choices include self-catering cottages, farm stays (farmstayuk.co.uk) and family-friendly hotels and guesthouses. Holiday villages have been popular in Britain for decades, ranging from traditional favourites like Butlins (butlins. com) to climate-controlled Center Parcs. Another great British institution, B&Bs can be found everywhere, while the Youth Hostel Association (yha. org.uk) and Scottish Youth Hostel Association (syha.org. uk) provide excellent value accommodation at hundreds of locations throughout Britain. Bridge Street Worldwide (bridgestreet.co.uk) offers apartments in all major UK cities.

Skip the flight

▸▸ **Get on your bike.** Over 16,000 km of the National Cycle Network (sustrans.co.uk) are now open. A third is traffic-free, following disused railway lines and forest tracks, while the rest of the network uses quiet minor roads and traffic-calmed streets in towns and cities.
▸▸ **Island hop** along Scotland's West Coast with an Island Hopscotch ticket from Caledonian MacBrayne (calmac.co.uk).
▸▸ **Take the ferry** to the Isles of Scilly with the Scillonian (ios-travel.co.uk); to the Isle of Man with Steam-Packet Ferries (steam-packet.com); to the Shetland and Orkney Islands with Northlink Ferries (northlinkferries.co.uk); to the Channel Islands with Condor Ferries (condorferries.co.uk); and to the Isle of Wight with WightLink (wightlink.co.uk).

Food & drink

If you're travelling with babies and/or toddlers you may find eating out a frustrating experience, though the days of families being banished to some grubby room at the back, well out of the way of other diners, are, thankfully, a thing of the past. Smoking is banned in all restaurants and pubs. Foreign visitors may find eating times in pubs and hotels limiting (usually 1230-1400 for lunch and 1700-1900 for dinner). In hotels and guesthouses the cooked breakfast (fried egg, bacon, sausages, tomatoes, mushrooms and beans) still reigns supreme. At lunchtime, cafés serve sandwiches and jacket potatoes with various fillings, as well as pasties, paninis and salads. Gastropubs offer more ambitious lunchtime and supper menus, while traditional tearooms are the domain of the cream tea: freshly baked scones with strawberry jam and clotted cream with a pot of tea. For a cheap supper, you can't beat fish 'n' chips, available from takeaways throughout Britain.

Health & safety

No vaccinations are required for entry. Citizens of EU countries are entitled to free medical treatment at National Health Service (NHS) hospitals on production of a European Health Insurance Card (EHIC). For details see nhs.uk. Australia, New Zealand and several other non-European countries have reciprocal health-care arrangements with Britain. Citizens of other countries will have to pay for medical services, except accident and emergency care given at Accident and Emergency (A&E) Units at most (but not all) NHS hospitals. Health insurance is therefore strongly advised for citizens of non-EU countries. The RNLI (rnli.org.uk) produces a guide to beach safety summed up by the FLAGS code: find the red and yellow flags, and swim between them; look at the safety signs; ask a lifeguard for advice about where it's safe to swim; get a friend to swim with you, and stick your hand in the air and shout for help if in difficulty.

Cottages
& holiday parks

Classic Cottages classic.co.uk

Coast & Country Cottages welsh-cottages.co.uk

Coastal Cottages of Pembrokeshire coastalcottages.co.uk

Dales Holiday Cottages dales-holiday-cottages.com

Dorset Coastal Cottages dorsetcoastalcottages.com

Glen Nevis Holidays glen-nevis.co.uk

Lakeland Cottage Holidays lakelandcottages.co.uk

Norfolk Cottages norfolkcottages.co.uk

Northumbria Byways northumbria-byways.com

Rural Retreats ruralretreats.co.uk

Scottish Farmhouse Holidays scotfarmhols.co.uk

Wales Cottage Holidays wales-holidays.co.uk

Butlins butlinsonline.co.uk

Center Parcs centerparcs.co.uk

Haven havenholidays.com

Hoseasons hoseasons.co.uk

John Fowler Holiday Parks johnfowlerholidays.com

Parkdean Holidays parkdeanholidays.co.uk

Park Resorts park-resorts.com

Pontins pontins.com

ⓘ **Fact** file

Country	Time	Language	Currency	Exchange rate approximate	International dialling code	Tourist information
UK	GMT	English, Welsh, Scottish Gaelic	GB pound £	£1 = €1.15	+44	visitbritain.com enjoyengland.com visitscotland.com visitwales.com

Britain Family favourites

Forest Holidays

Where? Cornwall, Forest of Dean, Yorkshire and Scotland.

Why? Forest Holidays' cabins are carefully sited so that you feel an intimate part of the woodland. Double-storey windows flood open-plan living areas with tree-dappled sunlight. Kitchens come with all the mod cons, most cabins have barbecues, flatscreen TVs and DVD players, while a few have an en-suite treehouse attached by an adventurer's bridge. You'll even find a Wii games console in Golden Oak cabins, but don't fret – children get ample opportunity to live in the real world thanks to ranger-led activities that include wildlife watching and forest survival.

How much? Evergreen cabins (sleeping 4-6) £225-913/wk, Silver Birch (sleeping 4) £345-1238, Golden Oak (sleeping 6) £474-1699 or sleeping 8 with attached treehouse £672-2407. Weekend breaks from £127.

Contact Forest Holidays, T+44 (0)845-130 8223, forestholidays.co.uk.

Feather Down Farms

Where? Throughout Britain.

Why? Safari chic with wellies on, Feather Down Farm tents lead the herd when it comes to luxury camping. Lift the flap on these canvas creations and you step into a snug den complete with wood stove, oil lanterns, three bedrooms (including a secret cubbyhole for kids) and everything you need for a relaxing holiday at one of 20-plus working farms across Britain. Each farm has a clay oven for baking potatoes or pizzas, and an honesty shop stocked with local produce. A few even have field spas or the option of renting a private chicken coop. But no matter how you embellish individual sites, the winning formula remains the same: cool camping plus effortless immersion in farm life.

How much? £395-825/wk, £275-575/weekend, £195-525/midweek (Mon-Fri).

Contact Featherdown Farms, T+44 (0)1420-80804, featherdown.co.uk.

Luxury Family Hotels

Where? Woolley Grange, Wiltshire; Ickworth Manor, Suffolk; Fowey Hall, Cornwall; Moonfleet Manor, Dorset; The Elms, Worcestershire.

Why? There's no denying that these hotels are upmarket and unique, offer indulgent spa treatments, a gorgeous array of suites, superb cuisine and quaffable wine lists. What sets them apart from your average Hilton, though, is that adults and children are given equal importance. You might expect facilities like swimming pools, trampolines and playstations, but it's the human touches that add real value – babysitting or baby listening, for example, or OFSTED-registered dens with qualified nannies organizing games and activities.

How much? B&B £140-270/ double room, £185-395/suite, £265-540/interconnecting rooms (children stay free when sharing with parents).

Contact Luxury Family Hotels, T+44 (0)1761-240124, luxuryfamilyhotels.com.

Classic Cottages

Where? Cornwall, Devon, Somerset and Dorset.

Why? Classic Cottages have specialized in the West Country holiday cottage business for over 30 years, so they've had time to build an impressive portfolio of properties (over 530 in Cornwall alone). Take your pick from stone cottages in Mousehole and Coverack, waterside apartments in Falmouth and Newquay, houses overlooking St Ives Bay and the Fowey Estuary, character barns tucked away in the Devon countryside and farms with sweeping views of Dartmoor.

How much? Sleeping six, Penally Cottage (see photo above) overlooks Boscastle Harbour on the north coast of Cornwall and is the perfect retreat for a smuggler's cove-style holiday. One week's rental costs £441-1113.

Contact Classic Cottages, T+44 (0)1326-555555, classic.co.uk.

Center Parcs

Where? Wiltshire, Suffolk, Cumbria and Nottinghamshire.

Why? The transition from the real world to a Center Parcs one requires two things: bicycle and swim gear. Everyone gets around by bike on traffic-free woodland lanes, while the indoor Subtropical Swimming Paradise will become a daily fixture in your itinerary. Activities at Center Parcs are based largely on the three W's – woodland, water and wildlife. You can choose from over a hundred things to do for all ages, from tree trekking and falconry to canoeing and sailing. Each parc has comfortable self-catering accommodation and a range of restaurants for eating out, while the Aqua Sana Spa provides a retreat for saddle-sore grown-ups in need of pampering.

How much? Weekends and short breaks from £239 for a two-bedroom villa, sleeping up to four.

Contact Center Parcs, T+44 (0)8448-267723, centerparcs.co.uk.

Tour operators

In the UK
Blakes Holidays
blakes.co.uk

Camping & Caravanning Club
campingandcaravanning club.co.uk

Center Parcs
centerparcs.co.uk

Feather Down Farms
featherdown.co.uk

Forest Holidays
forestholidays.co.uk

Hoseasons
hoseasons.co.uk

Luxury Family Hotels
luxuryfamilyhotels.co.uk

PGL
pgl.co.uk

Premier Holidays
premierholidays.co.uk

River Deep Mountain High
riverdeepmountainhigh.co.uk

Scotsell Holidays
scotsell.com

The Venture Centre
adventure-centre.co.uk

Youth Hostel Association
yha.org.uk

In the USA
The Backroads
backroads.com

Classic Journeys
classicjourneys.com

Luxury Vacations UK
luxuryvacationsuk.com

The Real Britain Company
realbritaincompany.com

Coast watch – mesmerized by Connemara.

Ireland

Contents

51 **Introduction**

52 **Kids' stuff**

54 **Tots to teens**

56 **Dublin**

58 **East Coast**
58 Co Wicklow

60 **Northern Ireland**
60 Giant's Causeway
60 Mourne Mountains
60 Marble Arch Caves

62 **The Southeast**

64 **The Northwest**

66 **The West**
66 Mayo
66 Roscommon
67 Galway

68 **Shannon**
68 Co Clare
68 River Shannon

70 **The Southwest**
70 Co Cork
70 Co Kerry

72 **Grown-ups' stuff**

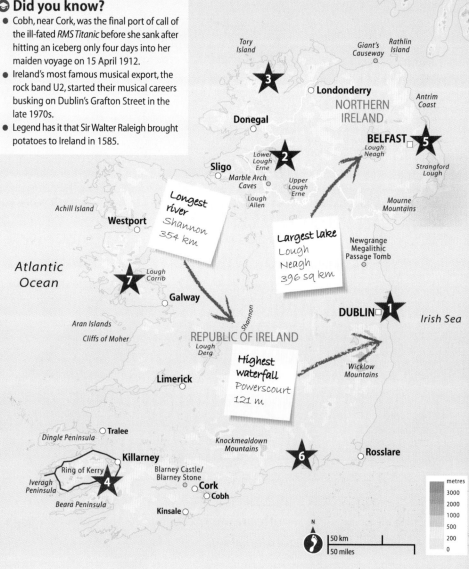

Did you know?

- Cobh, near Cork, was the final port of call of the ill-fated *RMS Titanic* before she sank after hitting an iceberg only four days into her maiden voyage on 15 April 1912.
- Ireland's most famous musical export, the rock band U2, started their musical careers busking on Dublin's Grafton Street in the late 1970s.
- Legend has it that Sir Walter Raleigh brought potatoes to Ireland in 1585.

Tory Island

Giant's Causeway

Rathlin Island

○ Londonderry

NORTHERN IRELAND

Antrim Coast

Donegal ○

BELFAST □

Lough Neagh

Strangford Lough

Sligo ○

Lower Lough Erne

Marble Arch Caves

Upper Lough Erne

Lough Allen

Mourne Mountains

Achill Island

Westport ○

Longest river Shannon 354 km

Largest lake Lough Neagh 396 sq km

Newgrange Megalithic Passage Tomb

Atlantic Ocean

Lough Corrib

Galway ○

Shannon

DUBLIN □

Irish Sea

Aran Islands

Cliffs of Moher

REPUBLIC OF IRELAND

Lough Derg

Highest waterfall Powerscourt 121 m

Wicklow Mountains

Limerick ○

Tralee ○

Dingle Peninsula

Knockmealdown Mountains

Rosslare ○

Killarney ●

Ring of Kerry

Blarney Castle/ Blarney Stone

Iveragh Peninsula

Cork ○

Cobh ○

Beara Peninsula

Kinsale ○

N

50 km
50 miles

metres
3000
2000
1000
500
200
0

Introduction

Hunt for ghosts
➤➤ Malahide Castle in Dublin, page 57

Learn to wakeboard
➤➤ Northern Ireland, page 61

Spot a golden eagle
➤➤ Co Donegal, page 65

Become a chocalatier
➤➤ Co Kerry, page 71

Step back in time
➤➤ Ulster Folk & Transport Museum, page 61

Explore the sand dunes
➤➤ Tramore Strand, page 63

Ride the Connemara Trail.
➤➤ Co Galway, page 67

It's a long way to go to Tipperary, but it's definitely worth the trip… as is the rest of the Emerald Isle – so named for its lush green countryside. Ireland is the third largest island in Europe and lies just off the west coast of Great Britain, separated by the Irish Sea. At just over 300 miles from north to south, it's a great holiday destination for exploring in a relatively short time. In a matter of days kids can totally immerse themselves in the island's myths and legends, guaranteed to fuel the imagination. On the northeast coast they can walk in the footsteps of giants while on the west coast they can go monster spotting in the waters surrounding Achill Island or make the journey over to Tory to meet Ireland's only king. Ireland is a country ripe for adventure with acres of magnificent countryside and hundreds of miles of dramatic coastline providing a fantastic outdoor playground. Visitors are assured of a warm welcome, complementing the mild climate, and making it a very family-friendly destination. The humour, referred to as the 'craic', and hospitality of the Irish people, from north to south, are almost as legendary as the country's Celtic folklore.

Ireland Kids' stuff

O'Sullivan Stew
Puffin Books, 2001
A beautifully illustrated picture book that tells the story of Kate O'Sullivan, a spirited daydreamer who has to try to motivate her fellow villagers to help the local witch in her hour of need. En route there are kidnappings and royal marriage proposals to contend with.
Age 4+

This is Ireland
Universe Publishing, 2008
An updated edition of a classic children's guide from the 1960s, the book is easy to read and filled with charming illustrations. The author takes the younger reader on an enchanting tour of the Emerald Isle, introducing them to the country's history, landmarks and notable people.
Ages 5+

Stories from Ireland – Oxford Children's Myths & Legends
OUP, 2009
Originally told as oral tales from one generation to the next, this book brings together a collection of stories from Irish folklore including *Balor of the Evil Eye and Iubdaan, King of the Leprechauns*. Ages 8+

Tales from Old Ireland
Barefoot Books, 2000
This book and accompanying audio CD contain a collection of seven traditional Irish stories, including the famous Children of Lir. Thought provoking and beautifully illustrated with a helpful resource section, including a guide to pronunciation.
Ages 8+

Leprechaun in Late Winter
Magic Tree House, 2010
An account of how Jack and Annie meet an Irish girl and embark on a magical adventure that changes the little girl's life and sets her on a course to help the Irish people restore their heritage and pride.
Ages 9+

Artemis Fowl
Puffin, 2006
This is the first in a series of books by Eoin Colfer about a 12 year-old criminal mastermind who is intent on kidnapping a fairy. An award-winning tale of intrigue and mystery that sees good and evil battle it out against a fantasy backdrop filled with trolls and elves galore.
Ages 10+

Taste of Ireland
soda bread

What you need
- 170 g self-raising wholemeal flour
- 170 g plain flour
- ½ tsp salt
- ½ tsp bicarbonate of soda
- 290 ml buttermilk

What to do
- Preheat the oven to 200°C.
- Combine the flours, salt and bicarbonate of soda in a large bowl.
- Make a shallow well in the centre and pour in the buttermilk, mixing quickly with a large fork to form a soft dough.
- Turn the mixture onto a lightly floured surface and knead.
- Form into a large round ball, then flatten the dough slightly before placing on a lightly floured baking sheet.
- Cut a cross on the top (traditionally this allows the fairies to escape and helps the bread to cook better) and bake for 30 minutes or until the loaf sounds hollow when tapped. Cool on a wire rack.

Know your leprechauns

① The average leprechaun measures approximately 60 cm tall.

② Leprechauns are the cobblers in the elf community, making shoes for their fellow elves.

③ The money earned from the leprechaun's shoe-making business is stashed in a pot at the end of the rainbow.

④ If you manage to catch a leprechaun (not an easy feat), he is obliged to reveal the whereabouts of the aforementioned pot of gold.

⑤ Never take a leprechaun at his word. They are tricky and mischievous little characters who are not to be trusted!

Ireland Tots to teens

Planning a family holiday to Ireland is straightforward as it's an extremely child-friendly destination. The local tourist board has recently launched a series of brochures and a new website that aim to make visiting Ireland with young children that little bit easier (discoverireland.ie/familyfun). If you are prepared to do a little research in advance, you may also discover some hidden gems that will provide your kids with memories that last a lifetime. To create some excitement before travelling, it's worth buying your kids some reading material to whet their appetite for the country's legends and folklore.

Bundoran Beach, Co Donegal.

Babies

Ireland is an excellent destination for families travelling with babies as it's a fantastic touring country. In recent years the road system has improved dramatically making all four corners of the country accessible within a matter of hours by car. Belfast to Cork (north to south) can be driven in five hours while Dublin to Galway (east to west) takes less than three hours. All the essential baby-related paraphernalia can be bundled into the car, alongside your snoozing little one, leaving you to embark on a road trip that will take you through some of the most breathtaking countryside Europe has to offer.

The main cities are also pram friendly with both Belfast and Dublin having pedestrian shopping areas, alongside open spaces and parks where babies can crawl around.

Toddlers/pre-school

Because Ireland is a relatively compact island, there's no need for long car journeys with fractious toddlers. Take the time in advance to choose the counties you would like to explore further and book one of the many child-friendly hotels, guesthouses or campsites available in each to use as your touring base. This will allow you to bunny hop around the country in short car journeys.

Toddlers love beaches and Ireland's 5000 km of dramatic coastline offers up some spectacular sandy playgrounds for beachcombing and building sandcastles – don't forget to pack a bucket and spade. Travelling with this age group also allows you to visit outside of the school holidays meaning you can usually find stretches of golden sands and dozens of rock pools to enjoy all to yourselves. For safe swimming, look out for beaches awarded a Blue Flag (blueflag.org). Ireland has an impressive 74.

Kids/school age

Imaginations can run wild for school children as spooky castles, ancient ruins and tales of fairy folk and giants are rife in every county. The whole family can also fully embrace the Great Outdoors in Ireland with an increasing number of adventure centres

Get the gift o' the gab

Five miles north of Cork lies the small village of Blarney. On its outskirts is Blarney Castle, dating back to the 13th century and measuring 27 m high. At the top of the castle is the world-famous Blarney Stone, promising the gift of eloquence to all that kiss it. Legend has it that an old woman with magical powers was saved from drowning by the King of Munster. To show her gratitude she cast a spell on the stone in order that the King should kiss it and win favour with all through his speech. Centuries later, over 300,000 people each year make the pilgrimage to Blarney in the hope of attaining the gift o' the gab.

Walk in giants' footsteps

The Antrim Coastline is the setting for one of the world's great drives. It is also home to the legendary Giant's Causeway, often referred to as the 'Eighth Wonder of the World' (giantscausewayofficialguide.com). Over 40,000 basalt columns can be found there, hexagonal in shape and resembling a huge game of stepping stones. While scientists believe they were formed over 60 million years ago by rapidly cooling lava, legend has it that the Irish giant, Finn MacCool, was responsible for their formation when he embarked on a shouting match with the neighbouring Scottish Giant, Benandonner. Finn threw large boulders into the water to form the causeway and challenged the Scottish giant to cross it for a fight. When the mighty Scotsman arrived, he found Finn dressed as a baby and sitting in a hastily made cot on the shore. Assuming this was Finn's son, Benandonner fled in haste, destroying the causeway as he went, fearing what size Finn must be if his baby was already so big!

now operating throughout the country. The range of family activities on offer is vast: from kayaking to windsurfing and climbing walls to zip wires. Check out Killary in Connemara for some great family days (killaryadventure.com). There's nothing funnier than seeing Mum or Dad go for a dip as they attempt an eskimo roll in a kayak!

The Irish coastline also provides some amazing opportunities for spotting marine life. Twenty-four species of the world's whales and dolphins have now been recorded in Irish waters. The minke whales usually arrive off the southwest coast in May with the humpbacks following in late summer and early autumn. Book a marine wildlife tour (whalewatchwestcork.com).

Teenagers

Belfast, Derry, Dublin and Cork are four thriving cities, brimming with fantastic shopping opportunities that should be right up the street of any trendy teenager. The Irish music scene is also alive and kicking with recent exports including Snow Patrol and The Script. Buskers occupy most street corners in Dublin and provide a musical soundtrack as you wander in and out of the shops. The city's famous Grafton Street is a great spot for people watching from one of the local coffee shops and is usually teeming with artists doing their thing.

For a sightseeing experience that might capture the imagination of even the most discerning teenager, the Viking Splash Tour (vikingsplash.ie) in Dublin is worth checking out. Their amphibious vehicles take you around the city, overland and through water, with an amusing commentary about the city's colourful history courtesy of your Viking Chief, dressed in appropriate costume.

Special needs

For further information on specific provision in Ireland, visit discoverireland.ie and search for 'special needs'. There you will find details on accommodation providers, transport options, tourist attractions, etc that all cater for visitors with special needs. For younger family members, Toby World (tobyworld.ie) at Tralee is definitely worth a visit. It has an excellent purpose-built Sensory Room specifically for children with special needs that aims to engage all the senses.

Single parents

Unfortunately the single parent travel market isn't as well developed in Ireland as it is in Britain so finding a tour operator that specializes in this area is very hard. However, Sticky Fingers run an excellent travel website with advice for travelling with children in general as well as a dedicated section for single parent families. Check out their Ireland site on stickyfingerstravel.ie.

Dublin Capital fun

Dublin has to be one of Europe's most vibrant and bustling cities, with a complete A to Z of family attractions starting with the Ark cultural centre for kids and finishing with Dublin Zoo. Over half a million people live in Ireland's capital, famed the world over for its writers, artists and musicians. However, the city is only part of what the Dublin region has to offer visitors. It spreads out along the east coast and is home to some beautiful towns and villages as well as some fantastic sights and attractions. Children of all ages will find plenty here to occupy and amuse. As a nation, the Irish are very family-orientated and nowhere is this more evident than in Dublin itself.

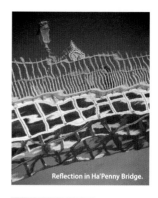
Reflection in Ha'Penny Bridge.

Fun & free

The National Museum in Collins Barracks and the Natural History Museum and National Museum in Kildare Street are all free entry. Dublin is also a great walking city for families. Try a sculpture hunt or download a free podcast of one of Dublin's iWalks (visitdublin/iwalks). Each comes with a full-colour map

◉ Inside info

» Áras an Uachtaráin, the residence of the Irish President, is only open on Saturdays. Free admission tickets are issued at the Phoenix Park Visitor Centre.
» The Dublin Pass (dublinpass. ie) gets you free entry to over 30 of Dublin's tourist attractions as well as discounts on a number of city tours.
» Dublin has a speedy electrical rail service called the DART (Dublin Area Rapid Transport). Taking it from Dun Laoghaire to Howth is a fantastic way to see the coastline in all its glory (irishrail.ie).
» For further information, log on to visitdublin.com.

with points of interest and an entertaining commentary.

Summer months see lots of free events organized by local artists and the city's numerous kids' clubs. Children are invited to experience anything from dance sessions to urban circus skills. The city also has plenty of open spaces for picnicking and enjoying the outdoors. By far the most popular free attraction is Dublin's Phoenix Park (phoenixpark.ie), the world's largest enclosed municipal park. It has an excellent visitor centre and a self-guiding exhibition on the park's wildlife. Every Sunday morning there are free workshops suitable for children aged five years and above.

Travelling further out of the city, Howth Harbour is worth a visit on a sunny day. You can get there via the DART, Dublin's electric train service, and spend a lazy afternoon watching the seals, sampling the cafés and letting the kids loose on the children's playground.

City highlights

For centuries the River Liffey played a major role in the lives of Dubliners and today it's become a visitor attraction in its own right. The Viking Splash Tour (vikingsplash.ie) is a unique way to see more of the city and the Liffey. Boarding an amphibious Second World War vehicle, visitors are met by their Viking Chief before a tour of the city's main points of interest, including the Liffey Quays, begins. En route you'll pass Trinity College, St Stephen's Green and the Government Buildings before plunging into the Grand Canal. It's a truly unique tour, if not the most comfortable.

A must-see for older kids is the Book of Kells Exhibition (bookofkells.ie) at the Old Library in Trinity College, Ireland's oldest university. Step back in time as you wander through the cobbled stones of Trinity and enter the Old Library, constructed in the 18th century.

There you will find portions of the ninth-century manuscript on display. In its entirety it contains the four gospels, beautifully crafted and lavishly decorated. It attracts over half a million visitors every year so be prepared for crowds in the height of summer.

Ireland's most popular visitor attraction is the Guinness Storehouse (guinnessstorehouse.com), located in the heart of the St James's Gate Brewery in Dublin. The Storehouse spans seven floors, with plenty to experience for the whole family, from the state-of-the-art tasting laboratory to an interactive exhibition.

The Irish love their sports and attending a match is often a family event. To soak up the atmosphere at one of the Gaelic games, head for the city 's Croke Park (crokepark.ie) or to hear the roar at a rugby international, make your way to the newly refurbished Lansdowne Road (irishrugby.ie).

Kids' top 10 Dublin

❶ **Ogle** the orangutans or chat with the chimpanzees at one of Ireland's oldest institutions, Dublin Zoo (dublinzoo.ie), located in the heart of Phoenix Park.

❷ **Catch** a wave on the Flow Rider or defy gravity courtesy of the Master Blaster, the Aqua Zone's award winning uphill water coaster at the National Aquatic Centre (nationalaquaticcentre.ie).

❸ **Hunt** for ghosts at 800-year-old Malahide Castle (malahidecastle. com). There's plenty to choose from as spooks are regularly sighted inside the castle and around the grounds.

❹ **Fuel** your imagination and let it run wild at Ireland's only children's museum. Imaginosity (imaginosity.ie) is jam-packed with exciting exhibits and experiences that are guaranteed to wake up all five senses.

❺ **Jump** onboard a Sea Safari (seasafari.ie) and be prepared to have a high-speed adrenaline rush as you take a spin around Dublin Bay, learning about local history and spotting dolphins and puffins enroute.

❻ **Experience** the 70ft Drop Zone at Funtasia (funtasia.ie) in Bettystown, rocketing into the air before plummeting back down to earth.

❼ **Find** out about the history of Ireland's most popular sports and take a behind-the-scenes look at where some of Ireland's biggest sporting fixtures are held each year at the Croke Park Experience (crokepark.ie).

❽ **Watch** a performance at Europe's first custom-designed cultural centre, the Ark (ark.ie), which showcases innovative arts by and for children.

❾ **Ride** in a horse and carriage, feed the ducks or have a picnic at Dublin city centre's favourite park, St Stephen's Green (visitdublin.com).

❿ **Heckle** the puppets at the Lambert Puppet Theatre (lambertpuppettheatre.com). Good old-fashioned fun with regular performances including Cinderella, Snow White and Punch & Judy.

Trinity College.

Croke Park.

East Coast A green & pleasant land

Most families visiting Ireland will venture into Dublin at some point during their stay and from there it's only a hop, skip and a jump into the surrounding counties that make up the east coast. It's an ideal region to explore with kids in tow as, rain or shine, you're never too far away from an activity or attraction that's tailored for families.

Lush pastures in Co Wicklow

Co Wicklow

Co Wicklow is one of Ireland's most beautiful counties with forests, mountains, waterfalls and lakes at every turn. With lots of open spaces and countryside for kids to run amuck in you may not feel the need to take advantage of any of the region's attractions but if you do, there are some gems.

Greenan Farm Museums and Maze (greenanmaze.com) is definitely worth a visit. It's a working hill farm so there are plenty of animals to see year round as well as the museum exhibits, including antique farm machinery and an extensive glass and bottle collection dating back to the early 1800s. However, the main draw for kids is the Dragonfly Nature Trail and the Greenan Maze – a challenging Celtic hedge maze that covers over half an acre and should keep everyone amused for at least a couple of hours.

On a rainy day, head to the National Sea Life Centre (sealife. ie) on Bray's seafront. There you can join in with the Octopus Play Time, eyeball a shark or have a tour of Nemo's Kingdom.

The Clara Lara Fun Park (claralara.com) in Rathdrum is just as much fun to visit as it is to say! It's choc-a-block with outdoor activities and water sports including go karts, rowboats, rafts and a pirate ship. Opening days and times are seasonal so worth checking in advance. For the mums and dads, before you leave Wicklow, if you're familiar with the BBC series *Ballykissangel*, you may fancy visiting the small and very picturesque town of Avoca where all six series were filmed.

Action stations

The region has several outdoor activity centres, so if you're looking for an adrenaline fix you could try Carlingford Adventure Centre (carlingfordadventure. com) in Louth. They run a great Adventure Day course with land-based activities in the morning and water-based in the afternoon.

Alternatively, try the Puddenhill Activity Centre in Meath (puddenhill.com). As well as all the usual centre activities, they have a kids' play zone and petting farm.

The Irish Aquatic Sports

Centre (wakeboarding waterskiing.com) is also in Meath if you fancy trying something even more adventurous. They have wakeboarding and waterskiing lessons for all levels.

If you would rather have a more sedate family experience, Fossey Mountain Springs (fosseymountainsprings.com) in Co Laois offer fabulous trail days, riding western style on horseback through surrounding forestry land. The trails are ideal for the complete novice as well as great fun for the more experienced rider. There is an overnight option that includes a western-style barbecue back at the ranch.

◉ Inside info

▸▸ If possible, try to book your rail fares in Ireland at least seven days in advance in order to take advantage of the cheapest fares available (irishrail.ie).
▸▸ Ireland is walking country so be sure to pack comfortable shoes with a good grip for the whole family.
▸▸ When booking outdoor activities, always use an established company and check their instructor qualifications and health and safety procedures.

Where can I see this?

Powerscourt Waterfall is Ireland's highest at 121 m. It's located two miles south of Enniskerry in Co Wicklow and makes for a great day out and an excellent picnic spot. Its waters flow into the Dargle River and it's completely surrounded by wildlife-rich woodland.

Northern Ireland Natural wonders

In the last decade Northern Ireland has established itself as a must-see destination after years of political unrest. Now back on an even keel, you'll find fantastic facilities and accommodation for families that complement the often breathtaking natural wonders already on offer. Leave the hustle and bustle of Belfast behind and head north to explore the Antrim Coast on one of Europe's most scenic drives, checking out ancient ruins en route. Alternatively, head south to sample the seaside charms of Newcastle where the Mountains of Mourne sweep down to the sea. Travelling over to the west, the Fermanagh Lakelands provide a backdrop to a host of activities from caving to cruising, while further north the rejuvenated city of Londonderry has some of the country's best shopping experiences.

Carrick-a-Rede rope bridge.

Giant's Causeway

Rising spectacularly out of the Irish Sea, and steeped in myth and folklore, the Giant's Causeway has fascinated visitors, young and old, for centuries. Though there are scientific explanations as to how the causeway with its hexagonal basalt columns was originally formed, the story of Finn MacCool is a much more entertaining one (see page 55).

Mourne Mountains

The Mourne Mountains (Co Down) have been the subject of poems and songs and an inspiration to artists for years. It's an area of outstanding beauty with a dozen peaks rising to over 600 m high, including the imposing Slieve Donard. The area is perfect for outdoor activities such as walking, rock climbing, mountain boarding and horse riding. Log on to outdoorni.com for details.

Marble Arch Caves

In Co Fermanagh, the Marble Arch Caves (marblearchcaves. net) have been recognized as a UNESCO Global Geopark and straddle the border between Northern Ireland and the Republic. The show caves are the main attraction in the north and give families the chance to don winter woollies and waterproofs before embarking on an underground adventure together by boat and on foot. It's a fascinating day trip, especially for older kids studying geography.

National Trust

Days out at National Trust (nationaltrust.org.uk) properties are a firm favourite with local families and tourists alike. Old stately homes such as Castle Ward (Co Down) and Castle Coole (Co Fermanagh) are perfect for a rainy day's exploration while their grounds and gardens are ideal for

when the sun reappears. There are scores of family events organized annually, including a summer Mad Hatter's Tea Party at magnificent Mount Stewart (Co Down) and a night of bat hunting at Springhill (Co Londonderry). The ruins at Crom Castle (Co Fermanagh) or the dizzy heights of the swinging Carrick-a-Rede rope bridge (Co Antrim) can both serve to fuel the imagination of most kids.

The great outdoors

All six counties in Northern Ireland are rich with forest parks, lush countryside, spectacular walks and great cycle trails. For families keen on cycling (cycleni. com), try the four-mile circular route at Gosford Forest Park in Co Armagh, or for younger children, the 2½-mile circular route at Castlewellan Forest Park in Co Down. Both are traffic-free and feature castles and woods.

If you prefer to travel on two feet rather than two wheels,

Oxford Island (oxfordisland. com) in Co Armagh has a lovely four-mile walk with interpretive panels en route that provide information on the wildlife and their habitat. You'll also find the Lough Neagh Discovery Centre there. It has interesting exhibitions on display year round and a small café for a well-earned pit stop.

If all of this seems a little sedate, there are lots of alternatives on offer for families with a more adventurous streak. Try mountain biking (summitmountainbiking. com) at Craigavon Lakes, Co Armagh; wakeboarding (ultimatewatersports.co.uk) at Castle Archdale Marina, Co Fermanagh; mountain boarding (qaspactionsports.com) in the Mourne Mountains, or quad biking (fasttrackfarm.com) at Ballywalter, Co Down. There's also a high ropes course at Co

Armagh's Lurgaboy Adventure Centre (lurgaboylodge.com).

Best beaches

In County Antrim you're spoilt for choice with Portstewart Strand, Portrush and Whiterocks Beach. The area is a popular spot for water sports and there's a Kids' Surf Club every morning during the summer holidays, run by Alive Surf School (alivesurfschool. com). Further round the coast is Benone Strand at Limavady. It stretches along the coastline for seven miles and commands views across to Donegal. In Co Down you'll find Tyrella Beach at Downpatrick (the final resting place of Ireland's patron saint, St Patrick) with over 25 ha of sand dunes. Nearby, Newcastle has five miles of golden sands, as well as an outdoor heated swimming pool on the seafront, complete with waterslides.

◉ **Inside** info

▸▸ iLink is a new travel pass that gives unlimited travel across bus and rail service in Northern Ireland. It's valid for different zones and available as a day or week pass for both adults and children (translink. co.uk/ilink).
▸▸ Combine some exercise with a chance to explore Northern Ireland's countryside by walking part of the Ulster Way, a 1000-km circular walking route (walkni. com/ulsterway). And it's free!
▸▸ For further information, log on to discovernorthernireland.com.

Portstewart Strand.

Kids' top 10
Northern Ireland

❶ **Roar** with the lions and parade with the penguins at Belfast Zoo (belfastzoo.co.uk).

❷ **Walk** in the footsteps of giants at Northern Ireland's very own Eighth Wonder of the World, the Giant's Causeway (giantscauseway officialguide.co.uk).

❸ **Step** back in time with Irish settlers as they set sail for America at the Ulster American Folk Park in Omagh or sample life from a bygone era at the Ulster Folk & Transport Museum, Cultra (nmni.com).

❹ **Join** an underground boat trip through the eerie Marble Arch Caves (marblearchcaves.net) and marvel at the stalactites.

❺ **See** a real Egyptian Mummy from the seventh century BC, Takabuti, in her full glory at the Ulster Museum (nmni.com/um).

❻ **Crack** your whip and have a go at being Indiana Jones at the jaw-dropping Carrick-a-Rede rope bridge (nationaltrust.org.uk).

❼ **Discover** what's on offer at Belfast's exciting interactive science and discovery centre, W5-WhoWhatWhereWhenWhy (w5online.co.uk).

❽ **Play** Victorian and dress up at Castle Ward House (nationaltrust. org.uk) before mucking in down on the farm.

❾ **Picnic** in one of the UK's top 20 picnic spots at Tollymore Forest Park at the foot of the Mourne Mountains (discovernorthernireland.com).

❿ **Go** on a wild goose chase at Castle Espie (wwt.org.uk) where almost the entire population of light-bellied Brent geese reside during the winter.

The Southeast Castles & coast

Although Ireland's lush green countryside is often attributed to the rainy weather, it does have plenty of sunny spells and the southeast of the country is known to have Ireland's sunniest climate. The region is made up of four counties – Kilkenny, Carlow, Waterford and Wexford – and every one of them has something to offer families.

Kilkenny Castle.

Region highlights

If you plan to immerse your family in all things medieval when visiting Ireland then your first port of call should be Kilkenny Castle (kilkennycastle.ie). It dominates the skyline, standing tall in the centre of Kilkenny City. Over the centuries it's had many additions and alterations so the current building is a hotchpotch of complicated architectural designs. A tour of the castle and its grounds can make for

◉ Inside info

▸▸ Visit irelandvisitordiscounts.com and download a discount pass for each family member. These are valid at over 90 of Ireland's attractions.
▸▸ Wexford is famous throughout Ireland for its strawberries. The end of June is the best time to visit if you're a strawberry fan as this is when the county has its annual Strawberry Festival (wexfordstrawberryfestival.com).
▸▸ Public holidays in the north and south of Ireland often don't coincide. It's worth checking in advance when planning your trip in order to avoid crowds at attractions and possible bank and shop closures.

an interesting day trip for older children, bringing medieval times back to life.

Dunbrody Abbey (dunbrodyabbey.com) was founded in 1170 and the building was completed 50 years later, c 1220. Although it's an excellent example of a Cistercian Monastery, it's also home to the Dunbrody Maze (formed from over 1500 yew trees) and a nine-hole pitch and putt course. The southeast also offers some fantastic opportunities for experiencing the great outdoors. As well as an array of fabulous beaches, there are plenty of great woodland picnic areas and nature trails to experience.

Kilfane Glen and Waterfall (kilfane.com) is a beautiful garden with streams, tiny bridges, woodland paths and

Freshly caught trout.

18th-century planting that includes wild foxgloves and ferns. The waterfall and thatched summerhouse complete the idyllic setting, making it the perfect location for a lazy afternoon.

Moving up a gear, the Wexford Wildfowl Reserve (wexfordwildfowlreserve.ie) can be explored on foot or on horseback. In the winter over 2000 pale-bellied Brent geese descend on the reserve. They join dozens of other breeds, including Greenland white-fronted geese and Icelandic whooper swans. If you take a closer look, you'll also find European mountain hares, badgers, American mink and red squirrels.

Try casting your nets (and rods) slightly further afield and visit Loch Mahon Lakes (lochmahon.com) in Enniscorthy, Co Wexford for a spot of fishing. Families can hire rods and buy floats, hooks and bait on site. There's even a barbecue area if you fancy cooking one of your rainbow trout for supper.

No description of the southeast would be complete without at least acknowledging

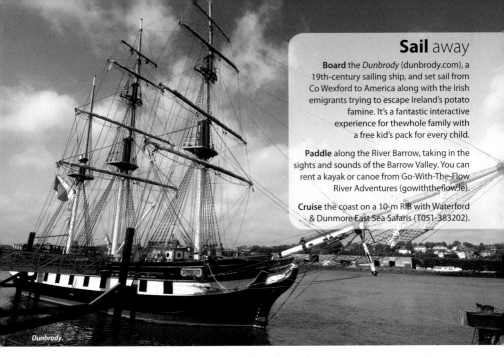

Dunbrody.

the area's most famous export, Waterford Crystal. Sadly, the Ireland factory and visitor centre finally closed its doors in 2009, though Waterford crystal is still produced in several other European locations. Over the past 200 years they have crafted chandeliers for some of the world's most famous buildings.

Best beaches

The Hook Peninsula in Co Wexford is a beautiful area, steeped in heritage as well as being home to some of Ireland's best beaches for families. For swimming and plenty of rock pools to explore at low tide, head to Baginbun Bay. It's a sheltered cove with a lovely sandy beach. Further on you'll find Dollar Bay, famed in local parts for its pirate legend. Apparently pirates buried two tonnes of Spanish milled dollars in the bay in the 1700s. You never know your luck if you're prepared to spend an afternoon beachcombing for buried treasure!

One of the most popular family events in the Wexford calendar is the Duncannon International Sand Sculpting Festival, held every August. Entrants from all over the world compete for the coveted title while beach parties, firework displays, sports competitions and live music take place over the course of the weekend (visitduncannon.com).

Co Waterford has Tramore Strand with its sand dunes and 5 km of gorgeous sandy beach. It's very popular with families with lots of fun to be had exploring the dunes. For some water-based adventuring, you can go on a kayak tour of the area. Qualified instructors will guide you round the islands and into the coves and sea caves dotted along the coast (seapaddling.com).

In Waterford there's also Lawlors and Councillors Strand at Dunmore East. The two beaches merge at low tide and it's an excellent area for families to try snorkelling in the sheltered coves.

The Northwest A breath of fresh air

The northwest can be rugged and wild in parts but always breathtaking and beautiful. When it comes to activities, the emphasis is definitely on the outdoors, making use of the natural resources that can be found on the region's doorstep. The dramatic coastline is a Mecca for surfers, and the countryside and surrounding hills provide a fantastic setting for cyclists and horse riders. The area is an ideal destination for families who want to try something new and adventurous while taking in plenty of fresh air as they go.

Surfing at Sligo.

The coast

Grab a board and embrace the swirling Atlantic waters with the help of one of the local surf schools. Ireland's largest is based in Bundoran where they run a summer kids' camp as well as individual and family group lessons (donegaladventurecentre.net). The surfer's paradise extends along the beaches of Enniscrone and Mullaghmore in Sligo. Donegal's beaches are often lauded as the most beautiful in the world with Bundoran and Dunfanaghy both standing out as family favourites. Strands north and south of Dunfanaghy village provide miles of unspoilt sandy beaches. The local stables also organize beach rides if you would prefer to see more of the coast on horseback (dunfanaghystables.com).

Inland

Killykeen Forest Park is in the heart of the Cavan Lakelands and surrounds the lakes and islands of Lough Oughter. Follow the marked trails and you'll be able to learn about crannogs (ancient lake dwellings) and Iron Age ring forts. Also in Cavan, Dun an Ri Forest Park has riverside walks where you may be lucky enough to see otters playing in the water. Both parks are open 365 days a year and are free to enter.

Cycling is another great way to see more of the northwest. There are bike rental companies in most counties in Ireland but for great service and advice on the best family friendly routes, try Gary's Cycles (garyscycles.com) in Sligo. The staff will be happy to arrange your bike rental and to offer recommendations.

In Leitrim, the Kingfisher Cycle Trail (cycletoursireland.com) is part of the Greenbox Ecotourism project (Ireland's pioneering integrated ecotourism destination). It's the first long-distance cycle trail to be developed in Ireland and offers lots of options, with six different routes and varying levels of difficulty to choose from (over 300 miles of trail in total). The Kingfisher Trail winds its way through the countryside taking in lakes, rivers and forests enroute while also passing through small villages and towns. Dotted along the trail are various types of accommodation and plenty of opportunities to visit local landmarks and to stop and enjoy your surroundings.

◉ Inside info

▸▸ It's always best to visit the attraction website or check with the local tourist offices in advance to confirm opening days and times as many of Ireland's tourist attractions are seasonal.
▸▸ There are direct Aer Arann flights to Donegal from Ireland's capital city, Dublin, and from Prestwick on Scotland's west coast (donegalairport.ie).

Mullaghmore

Kids' top 10 Northwest Ireland

❶ **Spot** a golden eagle at Glenveagh National Park (glenveaghnationalpark.ie), northwest Donegal.

❷ **Twist 'n' Shout** at Bundoran Adventure Park (bundoranadventurepark.com), Co Donegal.

❸ **Whizz** down the fastest waterslide in Ireland at Waterworld (waterworldbundoran.com) in Bundoran.

❹ **Trek** through the Donegal hills or hack over local farmland with Deane's Farm Equestrian Centre (deanesequestrian.ie) in Bruckless, Co Donegal.

❺ **Bounce, race, scramble and climb** at Livewirez (livewirez.ie), a kids' activity centre in Cavan.

❻ **Sail** across Lough Allen in a topper dinghy from the Lough Allen Outdoor Pursuits Centre (allen.ie).

❼ **Drive** a steam train through Barnesmore Gap with the help of a simulator at the Railway Heritage Centre (cdrrl.com) in Donegal Town.

❽ **Dance** with the 'faerie folk' at Gillighan's World (sligotourism.com), Tubbercurry, Sligo.

❾ **See** the Donegal Bay seals from the Waterbus (donegalbaywaterbus.com).

❿ **Step** back in time at the Sligo Folk Park (sligofolkpark.com).

The West A warm Irish welcome

The west of Ireland is by far the most 'Irish' region on the island with the culture colourful and the welcome warm. The emphasis is definitely on the *craic to be had*, and the locals are only too keen to introduce visitors to some, or all, of their favourite pastimes: music, song, dance and horseracing! It's also an area fond of its festivals. There are numerous held throughout the year that should appeal to all members of the family. They range from the Galway Early Music Festival in May through to the International Arts Festival for Children in October, with dozens of others in between. Visiting the west also provides a great opportunity for children to hear the Irish language being spoken first hand. Galway is often referred to as the Bilingual Capital of Ireland because the Galway Gaeltacht (Irish-speaking area) is on its doorstep – *Céad mile fáilte*! (One hundred thousand welcomes!)

Connemara.

Mayo

The heritage town of Westport makes for an ideal base while exploring the wilds of the Mayo countryside. It's a beautiful town with a tree-lined boulevard and stone bridges over the Carrowbeg River. Down at the Quay you'll find a good choice of family-friendly restaurants that cater for all tastes, and plenty of traditional pubs that welcome families. In August the population swells dramatically when the annual Music Festival (westportmusicfestival.com) rolls

Inside info

» Some attractions have early bird discounts so it's worth checking in advance. Pirate Adventure Park at Westport House, for example, offers a 10% discount on a family day ticket if you arrive before 1100.
» If booking a hotel with a kids' club, be sure to check the minimum age, as many of them won't take children under four years.

into town. It's free and it's open air – a perfect way to spend a lazy afternoon, listening to an eclectic mix of traditional and modern music.

Venturing out of town, Ceide Fields (heritageireland. ie) in Ballycastle is an essential stop on any tour of the west. It's the most extensive Stone Age monument in the world with megalithic tombs and dwelling areas stretching out beneath the Mayo boglands for thousands of acres. Even the most techno of teenagers couldn't fail to be impressed by this 6000-year-old ancient wonder.

The town of Cong attracts thousands of visitors every year thanks to the Hollywood movie, *The Quiet Man*. It was filmed on location here almost 60 years ago and put Cong firmly on the tourist map. Even if you aren't familiar with the movie, it's worth a visit as the area is picture-postcard beautiful and has plenty of other attractions, such

as Ireland's School of Falconry (falconry.ie) at Ashford Castle.

Roscommon

Kids will love the Arigna Mining Experience in Roscommon (arignaminingexperience.ie). The underground tour will take you through what was once a working mine and behind the scenes at the coalface. The guides are all ex-miners who can keep the whole family enthralled with tales of their real life experiences.

For younger children, Glendeer Pet Farm (glendeer. com) is a fantastic day out. Although you will find some traditional farm livestock, there are also over 50 species of more unusual birds and animals including llama, ostrich and emus. The farm has an indoor and outdoor picnic area as well as a coffee shop.

One of the most popular attractions in Roscommon is the

scenic Lough Key Forest Park (loughkey.ie). Along with the woodland, lakes and abundant wildlife there are some amazing facilities and activities for kids. A self-guided canopy walk provides a fascinating insight into the park's flora and fauna, while the outdoor Adventure Play Kingdom allows kids to burn off energy on swings, puzzles and climbing frames.

To see a little more of the county, you can abandon the car and go on a family hack, exploring the magnificent Slieve Baun Mountain on horseback with the Mount Cashel Stables (mountcashelstables.com).

Galway

Connemara is dramatic at every turn and makes for a great road trip with plenty of places of interest worth visiting enroute. Connemara's National Park (connemaranationalpark.ie) covers over vast swathes of heath,

bogland and mountainous terrain and in the summer months the park hosts family events including guided walks for kids and special outdoor workshops. You'll also find a herd of the world-famous Connemara ponies roaming free in the park, which should delight most children. To experience some of the more adventurous activities in Galway, try Killary Adventure Company (killaryadventure.com). Based in Leenane, they run lessons in every type of outdoor activity imaginable, including climbing, high ropes, bungee jumping, kayaking, sailing and wake boarding. If the whole family wants to learn some new skills, there's family accommodation available and a range of tailored taster sessions.

Galway City should be part of your itinerary if touring the west of Ireland. It's vibrant and bustling and hosts a fantastic range of festivals throughout the year. One of the most famous is the week-long Galway Races (galwayraces.com) at the end of July. The atmosphere is electric and a visit to the track during the festival's Family Day makes for a great day out.

For a rainy day option, try the Galway Atlantaquaria (nationalaquarium.ie), which is the largest aquarium in Ireland. As well as all of the marine life, it has a Children's Laboratory and a Kids' Science Summer Camp with lots of hands-on activities.

Action stations

❶ **Challenge** yourself in the Boda Borg at Lough Key Forest and Activity Park (loughkey.ie) in Co Roscommon. Suitable for age seven and over, form a team (minimum three members and maximum five) and see if you can beat the Boda Borg, a 47-room building full of tasks and puzzles.

❷ **Ride** on a miniature train, get wet on the Pirate's Plunge flume ride or pedal your boat across the lake at the Pirate Adventure Park at Westport House and Country Park (westporthouse.ie) in Mayo.

❸ **Cycle** through Connemara National Park (connemara nationalpark.com) and experience some of Ireland most beautiful countryside.

❹ **Ride** through Ireland's very own Wild West, along the Connemara Trail in Aille Cross (aille-cross.com).

❺ **Bungee** jump or wake board to get your adrenaline fix at the Killary Adventure Company (killaryadventure.com) in Leenane, Co Galway.

Cycling in Connemara.

Shannon From river to sea

The Shannon region is home to some of Ireland's greatest tourist attractions including its namesake, the River Shannon, and the Cliffs of Moher. It covers counties Clare, Limerick, North Tipperary and South Offaly and is the perfect choice if you are looking for a relaxing family break. The majority of family attractions are located in Co Clare, famous for its scenery and the friendliness of its locals.

Cliffs of Moher.

Co Clare

Co Clare is jam packed with activities and attractions that will appeal to kids of all ages. The Craggaunowen Bronze Age Project (craggaunowen. org) is an award-winning prehistoric park set in over 50 acres of woodland. Visitors get an insight into life in Ireland over 1000 years ago. There are reconstructions of ancient farmsteads, a leather-hulled boat and the chance to see a crannog.

The Co Clare coastline is dominated by the dramatic Cliffs of Moher (cliffsofmoher.ie), standing 214 m high and 8 km wide. The visitor centre is well worth a visit with its exciting interactive exhibits that culminate in a virtual reality

◉ Inside info

▸▸ Book your tickets online to visit the Cliffs of Moher (cliffsofmoher.ie) and save 15%.
▸▸ To fish the River Shannon you'll need a rod licence and a fishing permit (shannon-fishery-board.ie).
▸▸ Currently, you don't need a licence to drive a boat on the River Shannon.

cliff-face experience.

The Burren landscape in Co Clare might look desolate, but it's sparked the imagination of many a young visitor with its almost lunar appearance. It's home to several archaeological sites as well as Ireland's premier showcave, Aillwee (aillweecave. ie) – a relic from the Ice-Age relic with 6-m-high calcite formations and waterfalls. Next door, the Burren Bird of Prey Centre (birdofpreycentre.com) has flying displays of eagles, buzzards and falcons several times a day.

If you prefer fins to feathers, head for Lahinch Seaworld (lahinchseaworld.com) with its aquarium, leisure centre and kids' club. You could also take a Dolphin Tour (discoverdolphins. ie) to Scattery Island – the Shannon Estuary is home to Ireland's only pod of bottlenose dolphins.

Travelling down into Limerick you're at the heart of Irish Rugby. Munster's home ground is Limerick city's Thomond Park (thomondpark.ie). It's a fabulous stadium with an electric atmosphere on match day. Its most famous game was played

in 1978 when Munster became the only Irish side to ever beat the All Blacks. You can tour the grounds and visit the museum in order to find out more about the club's history. Limerick also plays host to Riverfest (festivalslimerick.com) every May. The festival involves water-based competitions, live music, street parties, family events and plenty of craic.

River Shannon

The Shannon flows 344 km through the heart of Ireland, nuzzling into a gentle landscape of floodplains and rolling hills. Travelling all or part of this waterway by river cruiser is not only great fun with children of school age but is also one of the best ways to experience rural Ireland. Carrick Craft (cruise-ireland.com) offers an extensive fleet of two- to eight-berth, fully-fitted cruisers. Rates include full tuition, a detailed captain's handbook and cahrts, plus free mooring at quays and marinas. Banagher makes a good starting base for a week-long cruise. About five hours north, you reach the 6th-century monastic

Go medieval

Bunratty Castle (shannonheritage.com) stands on what was originally a Viking trading camp. Having been fully restored in the 1950s, it is Ireland's most complete and authentic medieval fortress. Inside, it's dressed with 15th- and 16th-century furnishings and has three floors. The castle tour is really interesting but for added fun, it's worth visiting in the evening for the medieval banquet. You'll enter the castle via the drawbridge and receive the 'Bite of Friendship' (bread and salt) in order to protect you within the castle grounds. Inside you'll have a medieval dining experience, complete with mead and traditional (raucous) entertainment.

remains of Clonmacnoise (heritageireland.ie), home of the famous Cross of the Scriptures, a 4-m-tall stone cross etched with Biblical scenes. Backtracking past Banagher, navigational skills are put to the test as you negotiate Meelick Loch. Then it's plain sailing on the vast expanse of Lough derg, stopping at small villages like Castle Harbour and Terryglass. Killaloe, an attractive town with a 13-arch bridge, marks the southern limit of Shannon pleasure cruising.

Clonmacnoise.

The Southwest Emerald in the isle

Ireland's southwest is a very popular holiday destination. Cork City has both an airport and ferry terminal providing a central gateway to the region for tourists. Looking around at the spectacular scenery and visitor attractions on offer, it's easy to see why it has such a draw for families. The blend between heritage and exciting pursuits is just right, so you won't have to look too hard in order to find something that will interest and entertain the whole family.

Youghal

Co Cork

Cork is Ireland's third city, after Dublin and Belfast. Teenagers will enjoy the great choice of shopping opportunities on offer while the rest of the family can enjoy soaking up the city's atmosphere and more traditional charms.

Twenty-five kilometres southeast of Cork you'll find the small town of Cobh (originally called Queenstown). Despite its size, it was Ireland's main emigration port with over 2.5 million Irish leaving from its docks in search of a better life in America between 1844 and 1950. The little town is also famed as the last port of call for the ill-fated *RMS Titanic*. The ship stopped here to collect a further 123 passengers on 11 April 1912 and sunk three days later when it collided with an iceberg in the Atlantic Ocean.

◉ Inside info

▸▸ If driving round the Ring of Kerry, drive in a clockwise direction as tour buses are advised to drive anti-clockwise to make passing easier on the narrow roads in the busy summer months.

The Queenstown Story, covering both the mass emigration and the ship's history, is displayed at the beautifully restored Cobh Railway Station (cobhheritage. com). There's also an interesting walking tour of Cobh called the Titanic Trail (titanic-trail.com).

Continuing on a maritime theme, there are excellent Sea Safari trips that depart from Cork harbour on a daily basis in high season. There are several trips to choose from, including the Grand Harbour Adventure, Dolphin Discovery and Kinsale by Sea Safari (safari.ie). If you do travel to Kinsale you're in for a foodie treat. The town is known as the Gourmet Capital of Ireland thanks to its impressive range of award-winning restaurants and annual Food Festival each October.

On a rainy day you'll find lots to amuse the under 12s at Cork's Monkey Maze (monkeymaze. ie) – the largest indoor activity centre for kids in Europe, with a mulit-tiered giant adventure play maze to keep them occupied until the sun comes out again.

When it does make an appearance, head straight to

Youghal where you'll find miles and miles of Blue Flag beach. As it's the south coast's most popular beach resort, it can get very crowded in the summer months. But this does mean that it caters well for tourists with plenty of entertainment choices along the seafront. For an adrenaline rush, try AquaTrek (aquatrek.ie), where you can learn to powerboat. They also offer a more sedate cruise along the coastline and run a kids' sailing club mid-week.

Co Kerry

There are lots of famous men and women to come out of Ireland over the centuries but few as famous as Dingle's own special son, Fungi the Dolphin! Fungi, then a young bottlenose

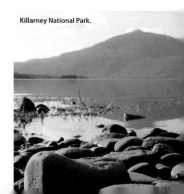
Killarney National Park.

dolphin, arrived into Dingle Harbour in 1984 and has never left. The locals have adopted him as their town mascot and the local tourist trade is thriving as a direct result. People come from miles around to see him and many hire wetsuits and snorkels in order that they might join him for a swim.

There's more to this area than dolphins, however. *National Geographic* once cited the Dingle Peninsula as being 'the most beautiful place on earth'. The Dingle Activities Centre (dingleactivities.com) can offer advice on guided walks, archaeological treasure trails (there are over 2000 sites of interest in this area alone), beachcombing, cycling, horse riding and sailing. There are also trips available to the Blasket Islands (blasketislands.ie) – a 20-minute boat ride that leaves from Dunquin. It's well worth the journey as Great Island is a haven for marine life including whales, dolphins, seals and basking sharks.

When you are ready to move on, the Ring of Kerry and Killarney National Park (killarneynationalpark.ie) should be next on your itinerary. The park is full of great attractions including castles, waterfalls, lakes and islands. It's also home to Muckross House, Gardens and Traditional Farms (muckross-house.ie). The three separate farms with their animals and poultry will be of interest to younger kids while the older ones might enjoy the house and its sunken gardens.

The Ring of Kerry is a tourist trail that starts in Killarney and covers almost 180 km. Many visitors drive the entire route over several days with plenty of stops at the picturesque villages they find along the way. If you'd rather stretch your legs there is a walking track called the Kerry Way and a cycle trail that follows a similar path around the Ring.

If that all sounds too energetic then take advantage of another Co Kerry highlight and jump onboard a steam train for a ride on the Tralee & Dingle Line.

Kids' top 10
Southwest Ireland

❶ **Kiss** the Blarney Stone and receive the gift of eloquence at Blarney Castle (blarneycastle.ie).

❷ **Star gaze** at the Blackrock Castle Observatory (bco.ie).

❸ **Stand** to attention at the Prince August Toy Soldier Factory (princeaugust.ie) in Macroom.

❹ **Visit** over 2500 donkeys at the Donkey Sanctuary (thedonkeysanctuary.ie) in Mallow.

❺ **Learn** to play African drums at Fota Wildlife Park (fotawildlife.ie) at Carrigtwohill in Co Cork. Unity Drums run monthly sessions for kids but if you miss one of these then there's still plenty to do.

❻ **Climb,** abseil and freefall at the Play at Height Adventure Centre (playatheight.com) in Ballinaboola, Co Kerry. For younger visitors there's the Gecko Kids Club with activity pods and playground.

❼ **Learn** how to make chocolate with Lorge the Chocolatier (lorge.ie) in Kenmare. Workshops run bi-monthly and there's plenty of opportunity for tasting!

❽ **Journey** through Killarney National Park and onto 15th-century Ross Castle in an old-fashioned jaunting car (killarneyjauntingcars.com).

❾ **Enter** a wonderland of stalagmites and stalactites at Crag Cave (cragcave.com) in Castleisland, Co Kerry.

❿ **Get** up close with sand tiger sharks at Oceanworld (oceanworld.ie) in Dingle.

Ireland Grown-ups' stuff

When to go

If possible, try to visit Ireland in May, June or September. The weather should be just as good as in July and August but hotels, roads and tourist attractions should all be a little quieter as the local children will be back at school.

The summer months are usually bright and showery, hence the lush green fields that have earned Ireland its nickname of the Emerald Isle. Ireland has an abundance of festivals year round but October is Children's Month when the island celebrates the arts for children and families (childrensfestivals.ie). Though temperatures do fall, they seldom plummet to the extremes that other countries might experience in the winter months. The combined forces of the Atlantic Air and the Gulf Stream ensure that the climate is moderate for most of the year, including the summer when the temperature seldom climbs above the early twenties (centigrade) – a bonus if travelling with young children. In short, there's no such thing as a bad time to visit Ireland, just some months are even better than others!

Getting there

As Ireland is an island, visitors either arrive by air or water. Many families choose the ferry option as it allows them to cram their car full of all the additional travel essentials required when you have children in tow. In the north the main ferry terminals are in Larne and Belfast while in the south you can sail into Rosslare, Dublin, Dun Laoghaire or Cork. There are departure points in Scotland, England, Wales, Isle of Man and France. For specific routes and timetables, visit the following websites – poirishsea.com, stenaline.co.uk, irishferries.co.uk, fastnetline.com, norfolkline.com and steam-packet.com. Special promotions are sometimes available but in general you can expect to pay between £200 and £300 for a return journey with a car and a family of four.

Ireland's main airports are in Belfast and Dublin with a number of smaller ones dotted throughout the country including Derry, Shannon, Cork and Galway. The major airlines serving the island are RyanAir, Aer Lingus, Aer Arann, Flybe, Jet2, BMI and easyJet. If booked far enough in advance, flights with the low-cost airlines can be as low as taxes only for a return flight from Britain.

Getting around

Travelling in Ireland usually poses few problems as the road system in the south has been vastly improved in recent years, as has the rail (irishrail.ie) and bus

Getting afloat on the River Shannon.

network (buseireann.ie) – tourist passes available include the Irish Rover, the Explorer and the Open Road. They all give great savings across the networks and are a popular choice for visitors. The Enterprise rail service is an excellent way to travel between Belfast and Dublin with huge savings to be made if booked online (translink.co.uk). The journey takes two hours and can even make for a fun day trip. In the north, buses and trains can be booked via Translink. All the major car hire operators can be found at airports.

Accommodation

Most families visiting Ireland prefer either the convenience of a hotel or the flexibility of self-catering accommodation. The Sticky Fingers (stickyfingers.ie) website and the Irish Tourist Board's site (discoverireland.ie) can help you to find accommodation that caters for families specifically, listing ones with kids' clubs, crèche facilities and babysitting services. Camping is another popular and less expensive option for families. Getting back to nature can be great fun, as long as the weather holds. Many of Ireland's campsites (camping-ireland.ie) enjoy fantastic coastal or rural locations.

Food & drink
Ireland was the first country in Europe to impose the smoking ban in workplaces in 2004. As a result, all pubs and restaurants are now smoke-free zones, making many of them child-friendly. Traditional Irish food isn't always the healthiest but it is hearty. Some of the most famous dishes are Irish stew (potato, lamb, carrots and onions) and the Ulster Fry (Irish soda and potato breads, black pudding, sausage, bacon, mushrooms and tomato). When it comes to side orders, champ reigns supreme. It consists of thick buttery mashed potato and finely chopped spring onions (scallions), a favourite amongst local children. Seafood is also a speciality throughout the island and if you're looking to enjoy some culinary delights without travelling too far, base yourself in Kinsale in Co Cork, Ireland's foodie capital. The town has its own Gourmet Festival (kinsalerestaurants.com) each October, with most restaurants providing children's options on their regular menu.

Health & safety
Though temperatures seldom rise above the early twenties in the summer months, it's still advisable to pack some high-factor sun cream for the kids. As Ireland offers a fantastic choice of beaches, a UV suit is a good idea for younger children if they'll be exposed to the sun for any length of time while playing on the sand or paddling in the water. Ireland does get its fair share of midges in the summer months, though not as bad as their Celtic cousins in Scotland! The little beasties don't seem to like the wind so

Skip the flight

» Catch a ferry from mainland Britain, Isle of Man or France, arriving into one of Ireland's ports in the north or south (see Getting there, opposite, for relevant website addresses).

» Internally, grab an Irish Rover Bus Ticket and you can hop on and off the buses on both sides of the border. It's also valid for city services in Cork, Limerick, Galway, Waterford and Belfast. Prices start from £56 adult, £32 child for a three-day pass (any three days within an eight-day period).

» Pick up a copy of 'Cycling in Ireland' from one of the local tourist offices and hit one of the 24 cycle routes covering north and south.

tend to swarm inland rather than on the coast. Unfortunately they do get hungry so if you're planning on doing any walking, DEET spray or cream is essential to help ward them off (available at most pharmacists or outdoors shops). The secret weapon used by locals is Avon's own brand of moisturiser, Skin So Soft (avon.com). Emergency services can be contacted by dialling 112 or 999.

ⓘ Fact file

Country	Time	Language	Currency	Exchange rate approximate	International dialling code	Tourist information
Ireland	GMT	Gaelic/ English*	Euro €	£1 = €1.15	+353 (South) +44 (North)	discoverireland.com

* The official language in the south is Gaelic though only 1% of the population speak it on a daily basis. The majority speak English. In the north it's English with a very small number also speaking Ulster Scots.

Ireland Family favourites

Woodlands Park

Where? Tralee, Co Kerry

Why? A four-star family-friendly campsite. Next door is the Aqua Dome (aquadome.ie) with its water slides, lazy river and aqua golf. Special deals available for guests staying at Woodlands.

How much? Two adults and two children with tourer, motorhome or family tent, from €24 per night.

Contact Woodlands Park, T066-712 1235, kingdomcamping.com.

Lusty Beg Island

Where? Lusty Beg Island, Co Fermanagh

Why? A 30-hectare island where imaginations can run wild and children can play to their heart's content. Choose from self-catering or B&B accommodation.

How much? Three-star chalets from £395 per week, or family room B&B from £140 per night.

Contact Lusty Beg Island, T028-686 33300, lustybegisland.com.

Hotel Kilkenny

Where? Kilkenny, Co Kilkenny

Why? Special deals allowing kids to dine free and there's a Kids' Club for four- to 12-year-olds during school holidays. The Club runs 0930 to 1230 and 1700 to 2200 so parents can have a little quiet time for dining.

How much? Family rates from €135 per night B&B.

Contact Hotel Kilkenny, T056-776 2000, hotelkilkenny.ie.

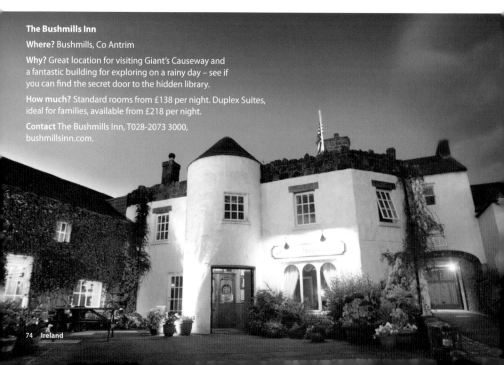

The Bushmills Inn

Where? Bushmills, Co Antrim

Why? Great location for visiting Giant's Causeway and a fantastic building for exploring on a rainy day – see if you can find the secret door to the hidden library.

How much? Standard rooms from £138 per night. Duplex Suites, ideal for families, available from £218 per night.

Contact The Bushmills Inn, T028-2073 3000, bushmillsinn.com.

Kelly's Resort Hotel

Where? Rosslare, Co Wexford

Why? Winner of Best Family Hotel in 2007, Kelly's is legendary for family breaks. It's located on Rosslare's golden beach, stretching over 8 km, and has crèche facilities as well as a great Kids' Club.

How much? Weekend rates from €325 per person. Special discounts available for children.

Contact Kelly's Resort Hotel, T053-913 2114, kellys.ie.

Westgrove Hotel

Where? Naas, Co Kildare

Why? Westgrove runs its own kids' club called Groovies. Activities change daily and range from arts and crafts to team games. It's also only 1 km from Abbeyfield Farm (abbeyfieldfarm.com) where the family can try horse riding and archery.

How much? Deluxe family room from €93 per night.

Contact Westgrove Hotel, T045-989900, westgrovehotel.com.

Dingle Skellig Hotel

Where? Dingle, Co. Kerry

Why? The Dingle Skellig Hotel is on the stunning Dingle Peninsula where kids can try to spot Fungi the dolphin. Facilities include interconnecting family rooms, kids' club and children's tea.

How much? Special B&B offers available from €59 per adult per night and €30 per child per night.

Contact Dingle Skellig Hotel, T066-915 0200, dingleskellig.com.

Tour operators

Responsible Travel
responsibletravel.com

EcoEscape Tours
ecoescape.org

Discover Ireland Tours
discoverirelandprivatetours.com

Five Counties Leisure & Activity Holidays
five-counties-holidays.com

Mayo Horsedrawn Caravan Holidays
horsedrawncaravan.com

Silver Line Shannon Crusies
silverlinecruisers.com

Cycling Safaris
cyclingsafaris.com

McKinlay Kidd
seeirelanddifferently.co.uk

Cycling in the Loire Valley.

France

Contents

79 Introduction

80 Kids' stuff

82 Tots to teens

84 Paris
88 Disneyland Resort
89 Parc Astérix

90 Northern France
90 Normandy and the
northeast
91 Brittany

92 Southwest France
92 Atlantic coast
92 The Dordogne
93 French Pyrenees

94 Loire Valley
94 La Loire a Vélo

96 French Alps
96 Chamonix
97 Tignes-le-Lac
98 Alps ski guide

100 South of France
100 Provence-Alpes-
Cote d'Azur
102 Languedoc-
Rousillon

103 Corsica

**104 Grown-ups'
stuff**

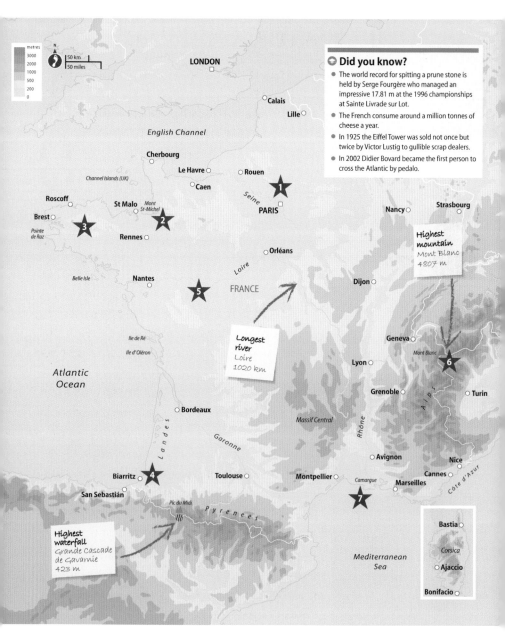

LONDON

Calais

Lille

English Channel

Did you know?

- The world record for spitting a prune stone is held by Serge Fourgère who managed an impressive 17.81 m at the 1996 championships at Sainte Livrade sur Lot.
- The French consume around a million tonnes of cheese a year.
- In 1925 the Eiffel Tower was sold not once but twice by Victor Lustig to gullible scrap dealers.
- In 2002 Didier Bovard became the first person to cross the Atlantic by pedalo.

Cherbourg

Le Havre ○   ○ Rouen

Channel Islands (UK)   ○ Caen

Roscoff   St Malo   Mont   Nancy ○   Strasbourg
Brest ○   St-Michel   PARIS   ○

Pointe   Rennes ○
de Raz

Highest mountain
Mont Blanc
4807 m

Orléans

Belle Isle   Nantes   Dijon ○
FRANCE

Ile de Ré   Geneva ○
Ile d'Oléron   Mont Blanc

Longest river
Loire
1020 km   Lyon ○

Atlantic
Ocean   Grenoble ○   ○ Turin

Bordeaux   Massif Central

Landes   Garonne   Avignon
Rhône   Nice

Biarritz ○   Toulouse ○   Montpellier ○   Cannes ○
San Sebastián   Camargue   Marseilles   Côte d'Azur

Pic du Midi   P y r e n e e s   Bastia ○

Highest waterfall
Grande Cascade
de Gavarnie
423 m   Corsica

Mediterranean   Ajaccio ○
Sea

Bonifacio ○

metres
3000
2000
1000
500
200
0

50 km
50 miles

Seine
Loire
Garonne
Rhône
Alps

Introduction

1 Climb the Eiffel Tower

» Paris, page 84

2 Conquer Mont St Michel

» Normandy, page 91

3 Sail a dinghy or windsurfer

» Brittany, page 91

4 Learn to surf or bodyboard

» Atlantic coast, page 92

5 Cycle to a chateau

» Loire Valley, page 94

6 Ski in the French Alps

» French Alps, page 96

7 Spot a flamingo

» The Camargue, page 101

France is one of the world's most popular holiday destinations. Even the French choose overwhelmingly to stay put *en vacance* and, for that reason, you'll find most places have an intrinsic child-friendliness. The biggest problem you'll face is deciding where to go and what to do. A big city like Paris, for example, might be the last thing on your mind, but even in a world without Disney, you'd still find a city brimming with child-friendly attractions, from scaling the Eiffel Tower to getting down to some serious fun in the interactive science museum at Parc de la Villette. The real boon for families, though, is the ease with which you can combine two or three regions. Sandwiched by a few days on the Normandy coast and an interlude in the Loire, that Paris city break begins to look even more enticing. Likewise, you could make a tasty combo of walking and rafting in the Pyrenees with beach fun on either the Atlantic or Mediterranean coasts. You may decide that some regions deserve your undivided attention: Provence and Brittany spring to mind. Both have idyllic coastlines, loads of activities, medieval castles and Roman ruins. Not forgetting the fine cuisine and cheap wine. France is *tres bon* for parents too.

France Kids' stuff

Books to read

Perraults Fairy Tales

Houghton Mifflin, 1993
This classic collection of fairy
tales from the French founder
of the fairytale genre includes
favourites such as *Cinderella*,
Little Red Riding Hood and
Sleeping Beauty. All ages

Katie Meets the Impressionists

Scholastic, 2007
Find out what happens when
Katie visits an art gallery with
her grandmother and five
famous Impressionist paintings
come to life. A lively and
accessible way of introducing
art to young children. Ages 4-6

The Cows are Going to Paris

Boyds Mills Press, 2002
When the cows get tired of the
fields they decide to visit Paris,
hoofing about in the Louvre and
dining out in posh restaurants. A
hilarious read! Ages 4-8

Eloise in Paris

Simon & Schuster, 1999
Quirky Eloise, *l'enfant terrible*,
takes a trip to Paris. Ages 4-8

Young Chefs French Cookbook

Crabtree Publishing Co, 2001
Have fun with 15 easy-to-
prepare French traditional dishes
with step-by-step instructions.
Bon appetit! Ages 4-8

Degas and the Little Dancer

Frances Lincoln, 2003

The fascinating
story behind
Degas' renowned
clay model of Marie
the ballet dancer is
brought to life in this
beautifully presented book.
Budding ballerinas will be
entranced. Ages 5+

The Three Musketeers

Sterling Juvenile, 2007
Alexandre Dumas' world-
famous tale has been
portrayed in films, television
series and all manner of books.
But have you actually read it
yet? This version is accessible
and well illustrated. Ages 7+

The Mystery of the Mona Lisa

Red Fox, 2006
The Mona Lisa, the most
famous painting in the
world, has been stolen
from the Louvre museum
in Paris. Can Secret Agent
Jack Stalwart find it before
an evil thief takes it out of
the country, never to be
seen again? Ages 7+

Horrible Histories: France

Hippo, 2002
Everything from gruesome
guillotines and foul famines
to a horrible host of kings,
queens and emperors. Find
out lots of revolting facts
about the French Revolution
and how to play hopscotch like
a highwayman. Ages 8+

Taste of France
perfect crêpes

Deliciously light and thin, crêpes are tasty with a little sugar, but douse them in chocolate and ice cream and were talking seriously scrumptious. Here's how to do it at home.

What you need
- 150 g plain flour
- 2 eggs
- 140 ml milk
- 140 ml water
- ¼ tsp salt
- 2 tbsp butter, melted
- oil for cooking

What to do
- Whisk together the flour and eggs; slowly add the milk and water, stirring to combine.
- Add the salt and butter; beat until smooth.
- Heat a lightly oiled griddle or frying pan over medium-high heat; pour on the batter using around a quarter of a cup for each crêpe.
- Tilt the pan with a circular motion so the batter coats the surface evenly.
- Cook for about two minutes until the bottom is light brown; loosen with a spatula, turn and cook the other side.
- Slide on to a plate, add topping and fold into a handy-sized snack.

Play petanque

What you need
- A coin
- 12 metal boules
- 1 cochonnet (small wooden marker ball)
- An area of open ground
- A measure and scoring cards, paper and pens

What to do
- Form two teams of up to three players each. Share out the boules.
- Toss a coin to decide which team goes first.
- Choose a starting point and draw a circle on the ground in which to stand; both feet must remain in the circle until the boule lands.
- The first player throws the cochonnet six to 10 m away and then throws the first boule, trying to get it as near as possible to the cochonnet.
- A player from the other team tries to throw his or her boule closer to the cochonnet (or to knock away the leading boule).
- The team that is farthest from the cochonnet continues to throw.
- When a team has no more boules left the players of the other team take turns to throw theirs and place them as close as possible to the cochonnet.
- The winning team scores a point for each of its boules that has landed nearer to the cochonnet than the closest boule of the other team.
- A member of the winning team throws the cochonnet in the opposite direction from the previous end and play continues until one team reaches 13 points.

Speak French

First Fun with French, Usborne
This DVD/book proves it's never too early to start learning French.

French for Children, McGraw-Hill
Audio CDs for kids, colour activity book and parents CD. Ages 3-9

Essential French for Kids, AA Publishing
A useful guide to take on holiday, this fun book covers making friends, joining in games, ordering food, looking good and hanging out. Ages 9-12

France Tots to teens

To the uninitiated, France might appear rather too sophisticated and aloof for carefree family holidays. But once you see beyond the manicured image of nouvelle cuisine, chic boutiques and immaculate vineyards you'll soon encounter a more down-to-earth, *laissez faire* approach to life. The French understand the needs of families probably better than any other country in Europe. Children's facilities and attractions abound, while the opportunities for camping and self-catering – the two most popular forms of family accommodation in France – are almost endless. For holidaymakers from the UK, it's also straightforward and cheap to nip across the Channel, with or without your car.

Babies

With lots going on around them, buggy-bound babies can be wheeled happily around Paris for hours while their parents soak up the sights, take in a museum or two and indulge in a spot of pavement café culture. As yet unaware of Disneyland, babies will get their kicks from a crawl about in one of the city's parks. Although public transport between Paris and its suburbs is good, you can avoid the hassle of a daily commute by staying in a centrally located self-catering apartment or hotel with babysitting services.

With babies there's a lot to be said for piling everything you need into a car (from bottle sterilizers to bales of nappies) and setting off on your own *tour de France*. Travelling outside school holidays means you can get better deals on accommodation and explore the Mediterranean either side of the fiercely hot months of July and August.

Toddlers/pre-school

Long, meandering car journeys across France don't have quite the same appeal when you've got fractious toddlers strapped in the back who have just discovered the liberating joys of walking.

Fortunately, France has an extensive network of holiday parcs that you can link together in a kind of self-drive dot-to-dot. Many have waterparks and numerous activities for young children, including supervised clubs. You can even find parcs within easy striking range of cities, including Paris.

As for Disneyland, Europe's number one tourist attraction, many parents claim toddlers are too young to get much out of it. Certainly, the big rides, with their height restrictions, will continue to elude them until they are five or six, but that's not to say you won't be able to keep a one- or two-year-old happy for a calmer, more gently paced day with Mickey and his pals.

> **"** We've been to Antibes in the South of France by train which was an exciting experience. It's great to wake up to blue skies and blue seas, and if you're willing to lug your suitcases along endless platforms it's a good way to travel. It's quite expensive, but as long as you think of the journey as being part of the holiday it's OK.
> *Caroline Mewes*

Kids/school age

Adventure beckons for this age range. They'll be up for anything, whether it's a maiden ride on the Goudurix loop-the-loop roller coaster at Parc Astérix, a cycle through the backroads of the Loire Valley or a race to conquer the Eiffel Tower *sans élévateur*.

As with younger children, holiday parcs make an ideal base. However, now that they've reached an age when they can begin to appreciate local culture, you might also want to consider a self-catering *gîte* or villa that's more in touch with rural life.

A visit to the local shops or market is a great way to get kids speaking French. If it's food for thought you're after, then France will stimulate even the most inquiring young minds. In fact, you may decide to sidestep

Sailing boats in Jardin des Tuileries, Paris.

certain aspects of the country's tumultuous history (such as the terrible legacy of the Second World War in Normandy) until your children have studied it at school. Less harrowing historical hotspots include Mont St-Michel, the Loire chateaux, Lascaux's prehistoric cave paintings and, of course, the wonderful museums and landmarks of Paris. For education with a wild twist, you can't beat Brittany with its teeming rock pools or the Alps with their flower- and insect-filled summer meadows.

Teenagers

Paris is cool. So is the French Riviera. Fashion-conscious teenage girls will enjoy browsing the shops, and might even tolerate mum and dad tagging along – as long as they bring their credit cards.

The appeal of camping in

France might be ebbing for this age group (although many parcs hold special activities for teenagers, like discos). A villa is a good alternative – plenty of space for independent-minded, occasionally moody, teenagers. You could even consider renting one that had enough space for them to bring along a friend. All-inclusive resorts should also meet with approval.

For adrenaline-fired adventure, France has numerous possibilities, from surfing on the Atlantic coast to parapenting in the Alps. However, the Côte d'Azure/Provence region scores highest from a teenage perspective – nowhere else combines such an impeccably stylish coastline with a rugged hinterland of gorges and mountains bristling with adventure activities. Explore Worldwide (explore.co.uk) and Exodus (exodus.co.uk) offer teenage-only trips to France.

Special needs

The French ministry of tourism has initiated a campaign to improve access for disabled people travelling in France. Reliable and up-to-date information can be obtained from L'Association des Paralysés de France (www.apf.asso.fr), while *Access in Paris*, available from RADAR (radar.org.uk), provides excellent advice for wheelchair users visiting the city.

Single parents

Acorn Adventure (families. acornadventure.co.uk) provides an infrastructure for supporting single parents on their trips to the Ardeche, the Mediterranean and Normandy. Eurocamp (eurocamp.co.uk) offers discounts for lone-parent families and will even help with unpacking on arrival. Crystal Ski (crystalski.co.uk) offers a discount scheme called One Parent Savers on some of its chalets in locations like Chamonix.

❝❞ Get up early with the children and visit the local boulangerie to buy croissants and baguettes for breakfast. Allow them to ask in French for what you need and let them buy an extra baguette so that on the way back they can nibble both ends (and usually much more) before you reach the breakfast table.

Charlotte Hindle, travel journalist

Paris The Mouse & the Mona Lisa

From Disney to Da Vinci, Paris bridges a cultural chasm that will leave you and your kids reeling. Imagine one day staring at the world's most famous painting and the next coming face to face with a tall mouse dressed in a dinner jacket and bow tie. Whether you're looking to stimulate a spot of art appreciation or simply opting to escape into a land of make-believe, Paris makes a supremely child-friendly city break. In another life (*sans famille*), you may remember Paris as a stylish, romantic place where you wafted between cafés, delved in designer boutiques and lingered in the Louvre. With kids in tow, it's going to be different. Once you accept that fact, you'll begin to see the French capital in a whole new light – and enjoy it no less.

Step to it – climbing the Eiffel Tower.

Tour Eiffel

Champs de Mars, T01-4411 2323, tour-eiffel.fr. Year round, daily from 0930, €4.50-13/adult, €3.50-9.90/youth (12-24), €3-7.50/child (4-11).
➤ Trocadéro Métro, RER Champs de Mars/Tour Eiffel

A riveting romp up this Parisian landmark has to be top of your must-do list. You can take the lift or climb 1665 steps to the second level, from where another elevator is the only way to reach the viewing gallery at 274 m. Just 50 m shy of the tower's flagpole, this often-crowded platform provides superhero views reaching 80 km on a clear day. Apart from giving their parents palpitations (don't worry, its like an iron cage up there), kids will love gazing down on the ant-like columns of traffic and trying to spot other city landmarks. If they start to tire on the climb up (or down), arm yourself with these inspiring and diversionary facts about Gustave Eiffel's engineering

wonder: The Eiffel Tower has over 18,000 metal parts and 2.5 million rivets; it expands up to 15 cm on hot days and took more than two years to build; over 220 million people have visited since it opened in 1889 and it weighs 10,100 tonnes (that's like 2020 elephants standing on top of each other).

Musée du Louvre

99 Rue de Rivoli, louvre.fr. Year round, Wed-Mon 0900-1800, €9/adult, free for under-18s.
➤ Palais Royal Musée du Louvre Métro

You've got to see it, but where do you begin in a gallery displaying over 35,000 works of art? There are several ways families can crack this mighty treasure chest. If you want to remain independent, focus on just four or five major exhibits, such as the *Mona Lisa*, *Venus de Milo*, *Winged Victory* and *Grand Sphinx*. Alternatively, book one of the museum's workshops for children (available for four- to

13-year-olds and lasting up to 2½ hours), or sign up for a guided family tour with Paris Muse Clues – an educational and interactive treasure hunt that takes kids (aged six to 12) from Ancient Egypt to Renaissance Italy, testing their detective skills to lead them ultimately to a prize hidden somewhere beneath the Louvre's glass pyramid.

◉ Inside info

➤ If your kids have Disney on their minds, spend a day there first.
➤ Visit anytime, although it can be hot during August. Christmas lights give the Champs Elysées and Eiffel Tower extra sparkle.
➤ Crêperies make great energy-boosting stops – or, for a real treat, take your pick of 70 ice cream flavours from Berthillon (across the bridge from Notre Dame).
➤ The Métro is a good way to get around, but backpack babies rather than buggy them as there are few lifts. Alternatively, use the River Seine's hop-on, hop-off Batobus boats.

Getting an eye-ful of the Eiffel.

Best of the rest

Catacombe de Paris
Ave de Colonel Henri Rol-Tanguy, T01-4322 4763, catacombes-de-paris.fr. Year round, Tue-Sun 1000-1700, €8/adult, €4/youth (14-26), free for under-13s.
» Denfert Rochereau Métro
A dark side to the City of Light, this macabre museum is piled with the bones of six million Parisians exhumed from the city's overcrowded cemeteries during the late 1700s. Maximum gross factor for teenagers; maximum nightmare potential for littl'uns. Also be warned that there are 130 steps going down into the catacombes and 83 climbing back out again.

Centre Georges Pompidou
Place Georges Pompidou, T01-4478 1233, centrepompidou.fr. Year round, Wed-Mon 1100-2100, museum €12/adult, free for under-18s, family workshops €10 including access to Children's Gallery.
» Rambuteau Métro
Wacky contemporary arts centre with a vibrant spattering of visual and performance art. Don't miss the buskers, 'living statues' and surreal Stravinsky Fountain. Then ride the external escalator and get arty in the Children's Gallery (for six- to 12-year-olds).

Champs Élysées
champselysees.org
» Arc de Triomphe Métro
The city's most famous avenue, dominated by the Arc de Triomphe and Grand Palais. Look out for the Punch and Judy show at Théâtre du Vrai Guignolet. The dialogue is in French, but the gratuitous violence will be all too familiar.

Museum of fun

» Head straight for the gift shop, buy some postcards showing the exhibits and then challenge children to find the actual paintings and sculptures.
» Check at the ticket office whether it's okay for kids to take a sketchbook and pencil into the museum with them.
» Pick a couple of easy themes (such as horses and angels) and challenge kids to spot five each before moving to the next gallery.

Musée National d'Histoire Naturelle (Ménagerie du Jardin des Plantes)

Rue Cuvier, T01-4079 3794, mnhn.fr. Year round, daily 0900-1700, €8/adult, free for under-18s.
» Censier Daubenton Métro
As well as galleries showcasing geology, palaeontology and evolution, this large museum (located next to the Seine) is home to the Ménagerie – one of the world's oldest zoos. The five-hectare park has 240 mammals, 500 birds and 130 reptiles.

Jardin d'Acclimatation

Bois de Boulogne, T01-4067 9082, jardindacclimatation.fr. Apr-Sep, daily 1000-1900, Oct-Mar 1000-1600, €2.90/person, free for under-3s, €2.70/attraction (€32/book of 15 tickets, €48/book of 25 tickets).
» Les Sablons Métro
Quirky amusement park with traditional attractions such as a carousel, hall of mirrors, narrow-gauge train, puppet theatre and pony rides.

Jardin du Luxembourg

» Odéon Métro
Puppet shows, donkey rides, boating pond, children's playground and vintage carousel.

Jardin des Tuileries

» Tuileries or Concorde Métro
Elm-lined avenues lead the eye to famous landmarks such as the Arc de Triomphe and Louvre pyramid. Soak up the atmosphere while the kids sail wooden yachts on the pond.

Montmartre

» Anvers Métro
Hilltop district crowned by the Sacré Cœur basilica. Children will enjoy watching the street artists at work in Place du Tertre.

Musée de la Magie

Rue St Paul, T01-4272 1326, museedelamagie.com (French only). Year round, Wed, Sat, Sun 1400-1900, €9/adult, €7/child (3-12).
» St Paul Métro
Dingy 16th-century cellars provide a creepy setting for magic shows, optical illusions and other tricks of the mind.

Musée d'Orsay

Rue de la Légion d'Honneur, T01-4049 4814, musee-orsay.fr. Year round, Tue-Sun 0930-1800, €9.50/adult, free for under-18s.
» Solférino Métro
One for older children who have perhaps studied the

Impressionists at school and will be entranced by this exquisite collection, which includes Monet's *Blue Waterlilies* and Renoir's *Ball at the Moulin de la Galette*, as well as masterpieces by Cezanne, Degas and Manet.

Cathédrale Notre Dame de Paris

Parvis Notre-Dame, T01-4234 5610, notredamedeparis.fr. Cathedral entrance open year round, Mon-Fri 0800-1845, Sat-Sun 0800-1915, tower entrance Apr-Sep, daily 1000-1830, Oct-Mar, daily 1000-1730, free.
» Cité Métro
Beautiful Gothic cathedral, familiar to many children through Disney's Hunchback of Notre Dame. Climb the South Tower to the Galerie des Chimères to pull faces at gruesome gargoyles lurking between the towers to ward off evil. There are 387 steps and no elevator. The entrance to the tower is located outside the cathedral on Rue de Cloître Notre-Dame.

Parc de la Villete (Cité des Sciences et de l'industrie)

Ave Corentin-Cariou, T01-4005 7000, cite-sciences.fr. Year round, Tue-Sat 1000-1800, Sun 1000-1900, €6/person for La Cité des Enfants, €8/person for Expositions d'Explora (under-7s free), €3/person for Argonaut submarine (under-7s free), €10.50/person for La Geode. Discounts on combination tickets.

▸ Porte de la Villette Métro

Enormous park containing the Cité des Sciences et de l'Industrie, a high-tech, hands-on science museum where kids can tinker with physics and biology. Head straight for the captivating Cité des Enfants. A section for children aged two to seven is divided into themed areas designed to challenge, inspire and inform. Another area for five- to 12-year-olds is crammed with hundreds of interactive challenges for enquiring young minds. Once your children have finished splitting the atom, operating robots, running the European space programme or playing at being Archimedes, spend some time exploring the Argonaut submarine (once the pride of the French navy) or Expositions d'Explora (showcasing the latest developments in the world of science), then take in a movie at La Géode (a giant hemispherical IMAX cinema) or go starry-eyed at the new 3D planetarium.

Left: Little devil – a gargoyle on Notre Dame.

🏛 Visit Versailles

Château de Versailles
Place d'Armes, Versailles, T01-3083 7800, chateauversailles.fr. Palace open Apr-Oct, Tue-Sun 0900-1830, Nov-Mar, Tue-Sun 0900-1730, garden open Apr-Oct, daily 0800-2030, Nov-Mar, Tue-Sun 0800-1800, passport ticket to estate €16/adult, free for under-18s.

▸ RER C from Paris to Versailles Rive Gauche station

Built in the mid-17th century, the enormous Château de Versailles provides a glimpse into the opulent tastes of the French monarchy during the reign of Louis XIV. Located 21 km southwest of Paris, the chateau has no fewer than 700 rooms and 6300 paintings. Pace yourself and be selective. Highlights include the Queen's Apartment and Hall of Mirrors – 73 m long and shimmering with 357 mirrors. Outside you'll find the largest palace grounds in Europe – 100 ha of elaborate flower beds, symmetrical paths, the 1.6-km-long Grand Canal and Versailles' famous fountains.

Paris How to do Disney

Disneyland Resort Paris
Marne-la-Vallée, T01-6030 6030,
disneylandparis.com. Year round,
daily from 1000 (check website
for 'extra magic hours'), 1-day
ticket (valid for either Disneyland
Park or Walt Disney Studios)
€45/adult, €38/child (3-11), 2-day
hopper ticket (valid for both parks)
€96/adult, €81/child, 3-day hopper
ticket €119/adult, €101/child.
Check online for special offers
and packages.
➤➤ RER to Marne-la-Vallée/Chessy

If you're thinking of taking the kids
to Paris and not spending at least
one day at Europe's most popular
family attraction, forget it. At best,
they'll never speak to you again;
at worst they'll do something
spiteful in the Louvre when you
drag them there instead. In any
case, Disneyland, for all its zigzag
queues and rictus smiles, is great fun
whether you're a Cinderella-doting
five-year-old, an adrenaline-hungry
teenager or the 40-something
paying for it all.

When to go
Well, it sure isn't Florida, so be
prepared for an invigorating range
of unpredictable European weather.
The upside of visiting in winter, of
course, is that queues are shorter
and you can get special deals.

How to get there
The train is the easiest and most
relaxed option. If you're staying in
Paris take the RER (40 minutes from
the city centre) or, if you're travelling
from further afield, hop on Eurostar.
Either way you'll arrive at Marne-la-
Vallée/Chessy station right outside
the park entrance.

Where to stay
It depends on whether you want

to spend a day at Disney or make
a long weekend (or more) out of
it. If it's the latter, pick one of the
hotels near Disneyland – several are
run by Disney so you'll be able to
live the magic (breakfast with Chip
'n' Dale, etc) even after the parks
have closed. For a Paris holiday that
simply includes a day trip to Disney
you'll get better value by staying in
a mid-range city hotel or a suburban
holiday park, such as Camping
International in Maison-Laffitte.

What to do
There are two parks: Disneyland and
Walt Disney Studios. If it's your first
time, focus on Disneyland where you
will find five distinct zones.

The entrance leads straight
to **Main Street USA**, a nostalgic
evocation of small-town America
in the early 1900s, complete with
horse-drawn streetcars and ice-
cream parlours. Autograph hunters
will find Mickey, Minnie and the
Disney Princesses here.

Walk through Sleeping Beauty
Castle to **Fantasyland** where Peter
Pan's Flight, It's a Small World,
Mad Hatter's Tea Cups, Lancelot's
Carousel and the Flying Dumbos are
always a hit with children.

Discoveryland features several
big rides, including the revamped
Space Mountain: Mission 2 roller
coaster (minimum height: 132 cm),
Buzz Lightyear Laser Blast (where
you score points by zapping Zurg
and other nasties) and Star Tours
(a simulator flight to the Moon
of Endor). Children can test their
driving skills on the Autopia
track (minimum height: 132 cm),
descend 20,000 leagues under the
sea in Captain Nemo's Submarine
and discover what it's like to be
miniaturized in the old favourite
Honey, I Shrunk the Audience.

Frontierland has the runaway

Cinderella's Castle,
Buzz Lightyear and
Crush's Coaster. © Disney

rollercoaster, Big Thunder Mountain
(minimum height: 102 cm), the
spooky Phantom Manor, Pocahontas
Indian Village, paddle steamer rides
and live shows at the Chaparral
Theatre, while **Adventureland** has
Pirates of the Caribbean, Adventure
Isle, Captain Cook's Pirate Ship and
another wayward rollercoaster,
Indiana Jones and the Temple of
Peril (minimum height: 140 cm).

Remember to intersperse the
big rides with some of the smaller,
queue-free attractions, such as Le
Passage Enchanté d'Aladdin with its
exquisite scenes of Agrabah – and
be sure to stake out a good spot on
Main Street to view the daily parade.

Right next door to Disneyland
Park, **Walt Disney Studios** puts you
centre-stage in a world of a special

effects, animation and big-screen drama. The Studio Tram Tour takes you behind the scenes, while big rides include The Twilight Zone Tower of Terror (an elevator ride from hell, with random drops of up to 13 floors; minimum height: 103 cm), Stitch Live! (an interactive encounter with the animated alien) and Moteurs... Action! (a stunt show spectacular with high-speed car chases). Based on *Finding Nemo*, Crush's Coaster (minimum height: 107 cm) is an indoor/outdoor spinning rollercoaster ride, in which you explore real-life underwater scenes, meet Bruce the veggie great white shark and battle against the East Australian Current. Cars Race Rally takes you for a spin along Route 66, while Rock n Roller Coaster (minimum height: 120 cm) inflicts Aerosmith music and high-speed loops and turns.

At park closing time, nearby **Disney Village** continues to buzz with its plethora of shops, restaurants, cinemas and live shows.

How to save time

⏵ Use FastPass – a polite way of queue jumping. Just insert your entrance ticket into a FastPass machine and you'll receive a designated time when you can board the ride by a special, often queue-free, entrance. The catch, of course, is that you can only FastPass one ride at a time.

⏵ Parent Switch allows parents with young children to take turns on adult rides, without queuing twice.

⏵ Take a picnic into the park with plenty of drinks.

⏵ Leave the park well before closing time if you want to eat in Disney Village – otherwise the queues are huge. Alternatively book a table at one of the Disney hotels as you arrive in the morning.

Parc Astérix Let's hear it for the Gauls

Never mind the Romans. Astérix and Obélix are fighting their greatest battle against Mickey and his pals. It's no surprise that Disneyland reigns supreme when it comes to Europe's top theme park attraction, but don't write off Parc Astérix. To get the most out of this eclectic park it helps if you are familiar with the comic strip. Follow these five steps to get well and truly addicted to the antics of those indomitable Gauls.

① Read the books
"The year is 50 BC. Gaul is entirely occupied by Romans. Well, not entirely... one small village of indomitable Gauls still holds out against the invaders." So sets the scene for the adventures of Astérix, created by René Goscinny and Albert Uderzo in 1959 and now translated into 107 languages with over 320 million copies sold worldwide. Orion (orianbooks.co.uk) has relaunched 24 re-inked, re-coloured and re-designed titles in the series, including *Astérix and the Falling Sky*, *Astérix and the Soothsayer*, *Astérix in Corsica*, *Astérix and the Normans*, *Astérix the Legionary*, *Astérix the Gaul*, *Astérix and Cleopatra* and *Astérix the Gladiator*.

② Know the characters
A cunning little warrior who never passes up the chance of a perilous mission, **Astérix** gets his superhuman strength from the magic potion brewed by village druid **Getafix**. Astérix's inseparable companion **Obélix** fell into the potion when he was a baby. Addicted to wild boar, the menhir delivery man is followed everywhere by **Dogmatix**, who howls whenever a tree is cut down. Meanwhile, **Vitalstatistix**, the village chief, is constantly afraid that, one day, the sky will fall on his head.

③ Watch the film
Astérix and the Vikings (2007).

④ Visit the official website
gb.asterix.com.

⑤ Visit the theme park
Parc Asterix
Plailly, T03-4462 3434, parcasterix.fr (French only). Apr-Oct, times and days vary, €39/adult, €29/child (3-11).
⏵RER B3 from Paris to Roissy Charles de Gaulle, then Parc Asterix bus
By Toutatis, let the fun begin! Tucked into forest 30 km north of Paris, Parc Astérix is divided into five lands – Gaul, Roman, Greek, Viking and Through the Ages. There's an authentic Gaulish Village where you can meet characters from the comic strip, a Roman Arena and numerous adrenaline-charged rides. For top thrills, don't miss Tonnerre de Zeus (minimum height: 120 cm) – Europe's biggest wooden roller coaster reaching speeds of 80 kph along its 1.2 km length. Goudurix (minimum height: 140 cm) is a 950-m loop-the-loop roller coaster which sends you upside down no less than seven times; La Trace du Hourra (minimum height: 120 cm) is a 60-kph Gaulish bobsled; while the Menhir Express water ride has a 13-m splash drop.

Northern France En vacance sur la mer

A seaside holiday. That's what lures most families to Northern France. And who can blame them. From the vast sandy beaches of Normandy to the Atlantic-gnawed cliffs and sheltered coves of Brittany, this varied stretch of coastline is paradise for anyone armed with a bucket, a spade and a shrimping net. History, too, comes alive along this shore – from megalithic standing stones at Carnac to the D-Day beaches of the Second World War. And to crown it all you've got Mont St-Michel, an excuse for a Famous Five-style adventure if ever there was one.

Normandy beach.

Normandy & the northeast

For many families arriving from the UK by cross-Channel ferry, Normandy and Pas de Calais are simply gateways to a wider-reaching *tour de France*. However, don't overlook the regions' mixture of family-friendly beaches and evocative historical sites.

Best beaches
The coastal strip between Calais and the Somme estuary is basically one long beach. Look out for resorts with Kid Station status, indicating children's facilities and high standards of safety and cleanliness. They include Wissant (vast expanse of sand, good spot for land-yachting), Wimereux (gently shelving beach and shallow sea, ideal for children learning to windsurf) and Hardelot (sheltered beach backed by dunes). Le Touquet-Paris-Plage is another popular resort with everything from waterparks to carousels. Further west, near Le Havre, Trouville is one of Normandy's favourite family

beaches (quieter and more relaxed than its chic neighbour, Deauville). Meanwhile, the Péninsule de Cotentin has some excellent beaches south of Granville, with a long promenade for walking or cycling. And if all that sand starts to drive you crazy, retreat to the Somme Estuary and spend a day birdwatching at La Parc Ornithologique du Marquenterre, a prime site for spotting seabirds and migrants.

Battleground tour
The D-Day landings endowed Normandy with one of the most poignant legacies of the Second World War. Starting at Caen drive north to Ouistreham and Pegasus Bridge where troop-laden gliders landed just after midnight on 6 June 1944, spearheading the huge allied invasion codenamed Operation Overlord. At Arromanches a museum and 360-degree cinema describes how an artificial port (known as the Mulberry Harbour) was built here in just 12 days to secure allied supply routes.

Further along the D514, you reach Omaha Beach where American troops met fierce German resistance. On the clifftop at Colleville-sur-Mer the 9387 graves at the American Cemetery provide a stark reminder of the heroism and sacrifices of D-Day.

Bayeux
If your kids are studying William the Conqueror at school, then seeing the 11th-century Bayeux Tapestry will bring 1066 and the Battle of Hastings into vivid relief (and just think how impressed their history teacher will be). The embroidered linen measures 70 m in length and took nuns 10 years to stitch.

◉ **Inside** info

▸▸ Self-drive touring is the easiest and most popular way to go.
▸▸ The Channel can be chilly, so consider wetsuits for the kids.
▸▸ For coastal diversions, try the famous lily pond at Giverny (home of Impressionist artist Claude Monet) or go canoeing in Parc Naturel Régional Normandie-Maine to the south of Caen.

Kids' top 10 Brittany & Normandy

① **Conquer** Mont St-Michel (pictured), a 1000-year-old fortified abbey perched on a rock in the middle of a bay and guarded by lethal tides and whiffy mudflats. Climb through a steep warren of streets, hemmed in by wonky half-timbered houses to reach the Gothic abbey – a major pilgrimage site in the Middle Ages and still hugely popular.

② **Taste** delicious local delicacies, from chocolate-smeared crêpes to smoked sausages (or just stick with the crêpes), at one of Brittany's numerous markets.

③ **Walk** to Pointe du Raz, the Lands End of France, and strike an epic pose as you gaze across the Atlantic towards America.

④ **Count** (or rather lose count) of the 3000-odd menhirs and other megalithic shenanigans at Carnac, a prehistoric conundrum dating from 4500 to 1800 BC. Resist the temptation to 'do an Obélix'.

⑤ **Cruise** to the Sept-Iles, home to 20,000 pairs of seabirds (don't even attempt to count these), including a raucous gannet colony. Departures from Perros-Guirec.

⑥ **Learn** to sail a windsurfer, catamaran or sand yacht at the St-Malo Surf School (surfschool.org).

⑦ **Discover** the secret life of a rock pool, from lightning-fast blennies to bumbling hermit crabs. Beware of tide times and those razor-sharp oyster-encrusted rocks.

⑧ **Cycle** 35 km of biking trails on La Belle Île.

⑨ **Vote** for your favourite beach, but sample lots first, including the sand sensations at Audierne, La Baule, Carnac, St Cast, Dinard, Douarnenez, Perros-Guirec, Trégastel-Plage and La Trinité-sur-Mer.

⑩ **Explore** Océanopolis (see right), Brest's mega-aquarium where you'll see everything from pipefish to penguins.

Wet wonders

Nausicaa
Bologne-sur-Mer, T03-2130 9898, nausicaa.fr. Year round, daily from 0930, €17.40/adult, €11.20/child (3-12).
Teeming with reef fish, the Tropical Lagoon aquarium at Nausicaa is mesmerising and there are also sharks, sea lions and penguins to be found at this cutting-edge aquarium with its enormous tanks, discovery areas and thought-provoking environmental themes. Don't miss the new Steer South! attraction – a virtual voyage with Jean-Michel Cousteau and his children.

Océanopolis
Brest, T02-9834 4040, oceanopolis. com. Year round, daily from 0900 (opening times vary), €16.20/adult, €11/child (4-17), €60.40/family.
Divided into polar, tropical and temperate seas, Océanopolis has Europe's largest penguin colony, seven species of shark, a 13-m coral reef and a boardwalk through tropical rainforest. A touchpool and seal rescue centre adds a splash of local sea life.

Southwest France Surf & turf

There's plenty to keep families occupied in this corner of France, from surfing on the Atlantic coast and hiking in the Pyrenees to canoeing, cycling and horse riding in the Dordogne. Combine all three regions and you will probably need another holiday to recover. But you will also have experienced something of the extraordinary diversity of landscapes that France is renowned for – from serpentine rivers snug in gorges to wide sandy beaches ravaged by Atlantic breakers.

A river runs through it – The Dordogne.

Atlantic coast

The southwest coast of France is one long, wild, wave-swept beach – give or take a sheltered bay or two. For a surfing holiday you won't find anywhere better in Europe. There are surf schools scattered along the length of the coast with a concentration around Biarritz in the south. You'll find no shortage of waves to suit all ages and abilities, but choose beaches that are supervised by lifeguards. Families with younger children will appreciate more tranquil spots, like Basin d'Arachon – a huge bay protected from the Biscay bruisers and a popular spot for gentler watersports like sailing and kayaking. You can also visit the nearby Dune du Pyla (or Pilat), Europe's largest sand dune

at 110 m high, from where there are great views and a brilliant excuse for a roly-poly. Boat trips in the bay, meanwhile, are often rewarded with sightings of dolphins and seabirds. Take your pick of numerous campsites and holiday parks, as well as family-friendly resorts like Biscarosse, Mimizan and Moliets.

The Dordogne

Caves, castles, clifftop villages – it's small wonder the Dordogne is such a magnet for holidaymakers – and that's before you've cajoled canoeing, horse riding and cycling into your itinerary. No visit is complete without a stroll around Domme – a fortified town (or *bastide*) with narrow streets, a market square and stomach-lurching views from a terrace perched atop a precipitous cliff. Below the village you can explore a large stalactite-filled cave. West of Domme, medieval masonry at Château de Castelnaud is brought to life through a wonderful range of workshops where kids can learn how to

fire a crossbow and devise the perfect strategy for laying siege to a castle – not necessarily the kinds of skills you might want your little darlings to acquire, but great fun nonetheless. Hugging the base of a steep cliff looming above the river, La Roque-Gageac is a fascinating place that's been inhabited since prehistoric times. You can climb to cave forts bored in the cliffs and visit a garden of subtropical plants that thrive in the warm microclimate. The honey-stone town of Sarlat is also worth visiting, particularly during the Saturday market where you can see, and try, local delicacies such as foie gras, chestnuts, walnuts, mushrooms and truffles.

◉ **Inside** info

▸▸ Horse-riding centres can be found throughout the region.
▸▸ As well as quiet backroads, cycling is possible on the car-free Piste Cyclable running southeast from Sarlat to the River Dordogne.
▸▸ For the perfect canoe trip, plot a course that takes in the main sights of La Roque-Gageac, Domme and Castlenaud, stopping at the latter for lunch.

They may not be as high or as grand as the Alps, and you might struggle to name any actual peaks, but what the Pyrenees lack in size and notoriety they more than compensate for with spectacular scenery, abundant wildlife and a wide range of activities. For families, the Pyrenees also score highly for their accessibility to both the Atlantic and Mediterranean coasts, making it a cinch to combine some huff and puff in the mountains with a week relaxing on the beach.

Mountain trains

These are ideal if you are lugging around a baby in a papoose or have small children. Just south of Biarritz, Le Petit Train de la Rhune rattles its way to 905 m above Basque Country, while Le Petit Train d'Artouste, accessible by cable car from Lac de Fabrèges, climbs high into the central Pyrenees. Admire views of Lurien (2826 m) and Palas (2974 m) before walking the short distance to Lac d'Artouste.

Cable car rides

Another easy way up and down the mountains is to take the cable car to the top of Pic du Midi. In just 15 minutes you'll be whisked from La Mongie to the summit (2877 m), where there's an interesting observatory and museum.

Walks

This is what it's all about! Pack a picnic and some warm, waterproof clothes and hit the trails. If you only have the time (or energy) for one hike, make sure it's in the Cirque de Gavarnie – about 50 km south of Lourdes. If the children seem reluctant to walk, plonk them on a donkey (you can hire one at the village of Gavarnie), then follow the path into the vast natural amphitheatre of the cirque. You can't miss the 400-m Grande Cascade, but also keep an eye out for alpine flowers, such as edelweiss, and mountain birds like the chough and wallcreeper. Bonus points if you spot a golden eagle or lammergeier. Bonus points with bells on if you spot a brown bear (there's only a handful of them left around these parts).

Caves

Going underground may seem like an odd thing to do with all the gorgeous scenery available topside. But the Pyrenees is a great spot for caves, and chances are you're going to get at least one rainy day anyway. When you do, make a dash for either Grottes de Bétharram (near Lourdes) or Grotte de Lombrives (near Tarascon-sur Ariège). Both are positively dripping with stalactites and bristling with stalacmites; there are guided tours and even underground train rides.

Other activities

For children around 11 and up, the Pyrenees offers plenty of activities guaranteed to get the pulse racing, including whitewater rafting, river boarding, potholing, rock climbing, abseiling, canyoning and *via ferrata*. Some you might not have heard of – others you may wish you'd never heard of when you see your loved ones grappling with ropes and ladders on a precipitous mountain route that is part-hike, part-scramble (that's *via ferrata*) or disappearing over the lip of a waterfall wearing a wetsuit, a crash helmet and a devilish grin (one of the thrills of canyoning).

◉ **Inside** info

▸▸ Barèges and La Mongie share one of the largest ski areas, while other winter resorts include Font Romeu and Les Angles.

▸▸ Summer activities like walking can be adapted to suit any age, while rafting, body-boarding, rock climbing and canyoning (available at several outdoor centres) are better suited to older children.

▸▸ Nearby towns worth visiting include Foix, where you can row a boat along an underground river, and the pilgrimage site of Lourdes.

▸▸ See page 125 for the Spanish Pyrenees and Andorra.

Loire Valley Exploring chateau country

Forget your traditional touring holiday: it might be time to ditch the car. The Loire Valley presents too good an opportunity for a family-friendly, eco-friendly alternative. It's called La Loire à Vélo, a signposted itinerary made up of minor roads and cycling tracks that allows you to pedal through the gently undulating, chateaux-speckled countryside of one of Europe's most beautiful river valleys. Easy to plan and easy to pedal, La Loire à Vélo forms part of a grand plan to link Nantes with Budapest via a 2400-km cycle route. But first things first – hand over the car keys and reach for your helmets…

Views from the riverbank.

La Loire à Vélo

Relax. No one is expecting you to cycle the entire Loire à Vélo route (800 km from Cuffy in the Cher region to St-Brévin-les-Pins in Loire-Atlantique). And, if your thighs cramp at the mere thought of two-wheel, leg-powered transport, all of the Loire highlights on the following cycle trails can easily be visited in the comfort of your car.

◉ Inside info

▸▸ Take the TGV high-speed train from Paris to Orléans, Blois, Tours or Angers.
▸▸ Most people bring their own bikes, but there are also several hire centres along the route.
▸▸ A baggage-forwarding service is provided by hotels, guesthouses and campsites.
▸▸ Agencies offer cycling packages, including accommodation, bike hire and itineraries.
▸▸ Cycling distances between centres can be as little as 6 km, there are literally hundreds of rest stops and even a number of sites specially labelled as being fun and educational for kids.

Chateaux Trail

Lestiou – Candé-sur-Beuvron, 51 km
Following riverbanks as far as St-Dyé, this route visits the ancient port of Chambord with its long stone quayside, as well as the majestic 400-room Château de Chambord – the largest in the Loire with a famous double-turn spiral staircase and great views from the roof terrace. Small roads then lead you to the Château Royal de Blois before continuing on tree-lined routes to the peaceful town of Candésur-Beuvron.

Unfaithful Trail

Tours – Langeais, 32 km
Must-see sights in Tours include the cathedral and the timber-framed buildings of the medieval quarter. Then it's off along the banks of the River Cher, cycling to Château de Villandry, one of the most family-friendly in the Loire with spectacular gardens to explore and even a maze and children's playground.

Riverbank Trail

Langeais – Chinon, 40 km
Château d'Ussé on the willow-swept River Indre is another favourite with kids. Charles Perrault is said to have been inspired to write the tale of *Sleeping Beauty* after visiting this fairytale castle of turrets and spires. Cycling through vineyards, the route continues to Chinon, overlooked by a medieval fortress.

Confluence and Caves Trail

Chinon – Saumur, 41 km
More vineyards line this route as it meanders towards the beautiful village of Candes-St-Martin and the Royal Abbey of Fontevraud, Europe's largest monastic complex. To get to Saumur and its castle, the trail follows a hillside riddled with ancient troglodyte dwellings that are now used as wine cellars or mushroom-growing beds.

Château d'Ussé.

Float away

You can rent kayaks (with or without a guide) by the hour, half-day or full-day at towns such as Amboise, Angers and Saumur. **Loire Aventure** (Ile d'Or, Amboise, T02-4723 2652, loire-aventure. fr) can kit you out with two- or three-seater Canadian canoes and drive you upriver for a gentle 10-km paddle downstream. Rates are usually around €15/person for a half-day trip.

Show time

Futuroscope
Near Poitiers, T02-7499 8049,
futuroscope.com. Feb-Oct, daily,
plus weekends and holidays Nov-
Jan, €35/adult, €24/child (5-16).

Maximum wow factor is guaranteed at Futuroscope (pictured above) with its giant-screen 3D IMAX shows and interactive adventure rides.

Puy du Foy
Les Epesses, T02-5157 3547,
puydufou.com. Apr-Sep, times vary,
€30/adult, €17/child (5-13).

A theme park for wannabe time travellers, Puy du Fou allows you to witness rampaging Vikings, gladiator battles, knights in shining armour and the exploits of the Three Musketeers in breathtaking live shows with special effects and stunts. There are also reconstructions of historical villages to explore and, during summer, the Cinéscénie evening show spectacular.

Other châteaux

Château d'Angers
Château d'Angers is renowned for its Apocalypse Tapestries, but kids are more likely to enjoy running riot on the ramparts that link its 17 impressive towers.

Château de Brézé
Perfect for a rainy day, Château de Brézé has an incredible system of underground tunnels to explore.

Château de Chenonceau
Château de Chenonceau has a 16th-century farm and a waxwork museum. Children will

Château de Brézé.

love paddling a boat under the chateau's arches.

French Alps Peak perfection

The snow has melted, the ski lifts are closed and the pistes are smothered in alpine flowers. Summer is coming and it's time to head to the mountains. Several alpine resorts alternate effortlessly between winter ski Mecca and action-packed summer destination, making them a perfect alternative to the traditional family seaside holiday. Just think of all that invigorating alpine air, comfortable temperatures, healthy outdoor activities and beautiful scenery. Your kids may never want to see a bucket and spade again.

La Mer de Glace.

Chamonix

If you can't do it in Chamonix, it probably doesn't exist. From river rafting and rock climbing to parapenting and summer tobogganing, Chamonix has got to be your top choice for non-stop activities. Just don't expect a cutesy alpine village. This bustling Savoy town has 10,000 hotel and guesthouse beds, dozens of restaurants, a casino and sports centre. But what Chamonix lacks in intimacy it more than compensates for with breathtaking views of Mount Blanc, 330 km of footpaths and an extensive network of cable cars and mountain railways.

Kids activities

Don't miss the summer luge (planards.com) – a 1820-m concrete bobsleigh run that's suitable for all ages (although young children must be accompanied by a parent). Bikes can also be hired and then, of course, there's good old-fashioned walking. Take your pick from gentle forest ambles to high-altitude hikes. Two favourite starting points are the Aiguille du Midi cable-car station at 3842 m and Le Brévent, with its famous views across the valley towards the seven summits of the Mount Blanc massif – each one rising to over 4000 m. At Vallorcine, a gentle trail weaves through summer meadows of bistort, studding the ground like a massed array of pink ice-lollies. The track culminates at the Bérard waterfall, where you can scramble through a cleft to stand behind the cascade – quite an adventure for littl'uns.

Rock climbing (minimum age six) and ice-climbing (minimum age 12) are also available. Then there's whitewater rafting (for children aged 10 and up), horse riding and, if it rains, swimming and bowling in the large indoor sports complex.

66 99 Reaching over 11 km in length, the largest glacier in France snakes beneath an imposing range of saw-tooth peaks, a frozen tongue in a maw of rocky fangs. If you asked a young child to draw some mountains this is what they would look like: all pointy and improbable. Inevitably, though, it was not the scenery or hiking potential of La Mer de Glace, near Chamonix, that captivated our children so much as the little red mountain train we had taken to reach it. At Montenvers Station, a cable car whisked us down to the glacier itself where you could walk inside a man-made ice grotto, complete with frozen sculptures.

Will

◉ **Inside** info

» Allow 90 minutes to drive from Geneva or nine hours from Calais.
» Nip through the Mount Blanc tunnel into Italy or take the scenic route via Aiguille du Midi and Pointe Heilbronner, using three different cable cars.

Left: On a wing and prayer – parapenting near Mt Blanc. Above: On a slippery slope – hiking at Chamonix and riding the luge.

Best family day out
Board the rack-and-pinion railway for a spectacular alpine journey to Le Mer de Glace. Expect to pay around €55 for a family ticket (compagniedumontblanc.com), which includes return train fares, cablecar rides and entrance to the Grotte de Glace.

One for the grown-ups
Take a leap of faith on a tandem parapente flight. Strapped to a pilot, you'll get airborne from either Brévent or the Aiguille du Midi and spend 30 minutes or so riding thermals and swooping over forested slopes.

Tignes-Le-Lac

Built around a natural lake and surrounded by snow-capped peaks, Tignes is around three hours' drive from Geneva or 1½ hours from Chamonix.

Kids activities
For maximum thrills try whitewater rafting near Centron and Gothard, or a 4WD safari on the high alpine trails in Vanoise National Park. Then there's horse riding, mountain biking, canyoning, quad biking, *via ferrata* and the adventure assault course in Tignes-les-Brevières. Pony riding is available

for children as young as three, while slightly older kids can learn to sail on the lake.

Best family day out
From Tignes-val-Claret take the funicular and connecting cable car to reach the glacier beneath 3656 m Grand Motte. Here you will find the best summer skiing in France (with access to about 20 km of runs), not to mention stupendous views.

One for the grown-ups
Europe's highest golf course can be found at Tignes-le-Lac. Be sure to book a tee-off time during high season.

🎿 Alps ski guide

How to choose the perfect family resort

1 Does it meet everyone's needs? Do you have a baby that will need crèche facilities, or teenagers who will be bored senseless without a snowboarding half-pipe to practice their eggflips and corkscrew 540s?

2 Does it have other activities available? A resort that offers extras like husky sledding, ice skating, bowling or an indoor swimming pool can be a godsend in bad weather or if – shock, horror – you discover that your child just doesn't like skiing.

3 Does it have easy access to ski lifts and a diverse range of runs to suit everyone in the family, from infant novices to adult powder-carvers? Short legs quickly get tired when walking in ski boots, so compact resorts with well-linked slopes are a bonus.

4 Does it have ski classes for children of different ages and abilities? Do the instructors speak English?

5 Does it offer chalet or hotel accommodation that's suitable for children? Exclusive occupancy of a chalet means you don't have to worry about your kids disturbing other guests – or being kept awake after bedtime.

6 Does it involve a long journey from home? What are the options for self-drive, flying or taking the train?

7 Does it have a good reputation for being family-friendly? Saas Fee in Switzerland, for example, is a car-free resort, which instantly gives it family appeal. Other resorts, however, are exclusive and expensive.

Resort	Country	Altitude (m)	Distance to airport (km)	Nursery areas	Pistes			Snow-boarding		Lifts					Activities
					Beginners	Intermediate	Advanced	Parks	Pipes	Funiculars	Cable cars	Gondolas	Chairlifts	Drag lifts	
Arinsal	AND	1500	172	2	19	18	5	1	2	0	1	1	11	13	S·T·SM
Obergurgl	AUS	1930	97	2	12	15	8	1	1	0	0	4	12	7	IS·SS
St Anton	AUS	1300	100	3	48	71	31	2	2	1	6	3	36	36	S·T·IS·SR
Kaprun	AUS	800	80	2	55	50	25	1	0	0	4	7	15	28	S·IS·B·T·HR
Neustift	AUS	1000	220	2	21	23	10	1	2	0	0	5	8	19	S·IS·T·SR·SS·IC
Les Arcs	FRA	2000	135	6	144	66	29	5	1	1	3	12	66	58	IS·SM·B·IC·SR
Avoriaz	FRA	1800	88	3	150	110	28	10	3	0	3	11	82	110	SR·B·IS·SS
Courcheval *	FRA	1850	128	12	183	119	33	5	3	3	3	34	69	71	IS·S·HS·SM·T
Chamonix	FRA	1035	100	4	41	25	13	0	0	0	6	6	17	12	S·IS·SR·SS·HS·T
La Plagne	FRA	2100	149	6	144	66	29	5	1	1	3	12	66	58	IS·B·S·SR·HS
La Rosière	FRA	1850	170	3	32	29	12	1	0	0	1	0	17	19	SS
Tignes **	FRA	2100	165	3	80	35	16	2	1	2	4	4	45	36	HR·HS·B·SM·SS
Cervinia	ITA	2050	140	8	18	33	16	7	0	0	0	7	13	13	B·IC·IS·S·SS
La Thuile	ITA	1441	150	3	32	29	12	1	0	0	1	0	17	19	S·SS
Grindelwald	SUI	1050	195	3	15	28	8	1	1	2	1	2	11	7	S·IS·B·SS·T
Saas Fee	SUI	1800	230	2	13	14	7	2	2	1	4	3	1	13	S·T·IS·HS·IC·SS

Snow business like family skiing – specialist operator Esprit Ski (espritski.com) provides nursery care, children's ski classes and clubs.

Checklist: keeping kids safe and happy

» **Two-piece ski suit** – for easy access when the need arises.
» **Thermals** – a cold child is a grumpy child.
» **Ski mittens** – easier for children to manage than gloves.
» **Sunblock** – psychedelic colours available for trendy teenagers (and tots).
» **UV goggles** – don't fall off like sunglasses, and offer better protection.
» **Energy-boosting snacks** – stick a bag of raisins in their pocket.
» **ID tag** – write your mobile phone number on it; clip inside child's pocket.
» **Crash helmet** – an essential, whether you buy one or hire one.

Key to table

* Figures cover the Three Valleys area (can also be skied from Méribel)
** Figures cover the Espace Killy area (can also be skied from Val d'Isère)

B	Bowling
HR	Horse riding
HS	Husky sledding
IC	Ice-climbing
IS	Ice skating
S	Swimming
SM	Snowmobiling
SR	Sleigh rides
SS	Snowshoe walks
T	Tobogganing

South of France Coast with the most

The Cannes Film Festival, Monte Carlo Grand Prix, Châteauneuf-du-Pape… the South of France is where legends are created and stars are born. It's where the world's mega-rich park their palatial launches and strut their stuff along the promenades of glitzy resorts. So not much on offer for families then? Don't you believe it! This venerated strip of Mediterranean coastline may be *trés* posh in places, but it's also irresistibly kid-friendly. Not only is the Côte d'Azure and Languedoc-Rousillon coastline star-studded with coves and beaches, but you won't have to go far inland to find action-packed gorges, wonderful wildlife and a good spattering of Roman ruins and medieval hilltop villages.

Côte d'Azur.

Provence-Alpes-Côte d'Azur

The region of Provence-Côte d'Azur is one of France's most popular destinations and it's easy to see why. Family holiday staples like sandy beaches, warm sea and sunshine, come in bucket-loads along the French Riviera, but with its head in the Alps and its toes dabbling in the Camargue, adventure is never far away.

Arles.

Le Pont du Gard.

Best beaches
You're spoilt for choice. The stretch of coast between St Tropez and St Raphael has

◉ Inside info

» Fly to Nice or take the TGV train from Paris to Avignon.
» July-August can be stifling, beaches and roads are crammed and prices take a hike; try to visit in cooler, less crowded months.
» Accommodation ranges from hotels and apartments to campsites and gîtes; consider travelling with another family and renting out a large villa with pool.

wonderful coves and beaches – just don't expect to have one all to yourself. Not only does beach towel space become a precious commodity during peak season, but parking can be a challenge too. Your best bet is to arrive early. Family favourites include Plage d'Agay, Cannes Plage, Cassis Plage and Fréjus Plage. All but Plage d'Agay have good sand for building castles. There are also several Aqualand waterparks along the Côte d'Azur, each one with a spaghetti tangle of daredevil waterslides.

Aix-en-Provence
There are more than 100 fountains in this elegant town

where you can visit Cézanne's studio, explore the market (Tuesday, Thursday and Saturday) and enjoy a drink in one of the cafés along tree-shaded Cours Mirabeau. The perfect place to introduce kids to a spot of Provençal culture.

Arles
A Roman treasure hunt awaits children visiting this market town on the banks of the Rhône. Corinthian columns and fragments of ancient temples seem to sprout from every street corner. You can't miss the well-preserved amphitheatre (Les Arénes) or the Théâtre Antique, but will you find the remains

🌀 **Adventure** Provence

The Camargue
Saddle up and ride a pony or bicycle into the watery wilderness where the Rhône meets the sea. Famous for its white horses, black bulls and pink flamingos, the Camargue is a like a breath of salt-laden fresh air after the flashy resorts along the Côte d'Azur. You can hire your trusty mount at Ste-Maries-de-la-Mer. Pony treks are suitable even for beginners, while the Digue à la Mer is designed for walkers and cyclists. Allow at least half a day to pedal to the lighthouse and the flamingo-nesting site at Etang du Fangassier. Remember to take a pair of binoculars – the Camargue is also home to some 400 other bird species, including ducks, egrets, herons and kingfishers.

Gorges du Verdon
Don wetsuits and helmets for a splash through mainland Europe's deepest river gorge. Canyoning (minimum age eight) in France's so-called Grand Canyon provides an epic perspective of sheer cliffs towering 700 m overhead as you negotiate a tortuous river by swimming, abseiling, jumping off waterfalls and sliding down natural water chutes. Other excellent spots for watersports are Gorges de l'Ardèche near Vallon Pont d'Arc and Gorges du Tarn near Parc National des Cévennes.

Parc National du Mercantour
An idyllic spot in the Alpes-Maritimes, Mercantour is a refuge for a unique blend of alpine and Mediterranean flora and fauna. It's also prime walking country with opportunities for both short ambles and adventurous hikes.

Gorges du Verdon.

of the Roman circus where 12 chariots once raced side by side?

Avignon
The fortress-like façade of the Palais des Papes dominates this walled city. Explore the maze of medieval streets, take a spin on an antique carousel in Place de l'Horloge, then visit Le Pont d'Avignon for a good old nursery rhyme singalong.

Monaco
The tiny principality that thinks big. Teenagers will love ogling the launches gleaming in the harbour, while younger children will enjoy the aquarium at the Musée Océanographique and the glass-bottom boat trips that depart from Quai des Etats-Unis.

Le Pont du Gard
Part of an ambitious Roman scheme to convey water to the city of Nîmes via a 50-km-long aqueduct, Le Pont du Gard is now a World Heritage Site (kids may prefer to think of it as an early attempt to create the ultimate waterslide). The visitor centre has an interactive programme for children aged five to 12 where they can experience life as Gallo-Roman pupils, devise ways of controlling water and become archaeologists and naturalists. during high season.

Smell the flowers
A walk or cycle ride on the Plateau de Valensole packs a perfumed punch between June and early September when the famous lavender fields of Provence reach their purple prime. Grasse, meanwhile, is the capital of the world's perfume industry. Join a tour around one of its many perfume houses or visit during mid-May for the Fête de la Rose.

Languedoc-Rousillon

Best known for the bucket-and-spade appeal of its fine Mediterranean coastline, the Languedoc-Roussillon region has a fascinating hinterland dotted with hilltop castles and impressive abbeys.

Pick of the beaches goes to Argèles-sur-Mer and Cap d'Agde, both with long sandy stretches and the added attractions of waterparks, aquaria, mini-golf and the like.

Inland, you'll find the Cathar castles of Queribus, Peyrepertuse and Puilaurens – each one perched atop a seemingly unassailable cliff. Young children may find it hard to conquer these largely ruined forts (and parents will want to keep them on a short reign when they see some of the unguarded drops). Adventurous kids, however, will love the challenge (and counting the steps).

For something less crumbly, visit the restored fortress city of Carcassonne (carcassonne-tourisme.com). Guarded by 52 towers and 3 km of battlements, it's an exciting place to roam, despite the crowds and inevitable rash of souvenir shops. Beyond the main entrance (Port Narbonnaise) lies a medieval mishmash of narrow streets. The 12th-century Château Comtal is worth exploring, as is the Gothic St-Nazaire basilica. In the lower town, an interactive museum called Im@ginarium brings the Middle Ages to life. A short distance outside Carcassonne, Lac de la Cavayere provides light relief in the form of swimming and pedal boats.

Towering achievement – lay seige to the walled city of Carcassonne.

Corsica Isle of adventure (& beaches)

Corsica seems a world away from the rampant resorts and crowded beaches that stereotype much of the Mediterranean. Although it receives its fair share of summer holidaymakers, this enigmatic island remains one of the truly wild and unspoiled gems of the region. An island of contrasts, Corsica has a kaleidoscope of busy ports and impenetrable pine forests, ancient citadels and plummeting sea cliffs, jagged mountains and sandy beaches. If you're after a family holiday that combines adventure and fun by the sea, then look no further.

Cliff-hanger – Bonifacio.

Highlights

Beaches
In the northwest, the gently shelving bay at Calvi has sunbeds, restaurants and watersports. Nearby Algajola, Ile Rousse and Lozari are also popular with families. St Florent has some of the best beaches in the northeast, while Campomoro, Propriano and the coves at Cappiciola are worth checking out in the southwest. With fine white sand and brilliant turquoise water, Palombaggia in the far south is stunning, but can get very busy during the height of summer.

Bonifacio
A medieval town perched on 60-m-high limestone cliffs near the southernmost tip of Corsica, Bonifacio rears above a marina packed with gleaming yachts and launches and lined with outdoor restaurants – a far cry from the ninth and 10th centuries when the town thrived on fishing and piracy. Explore the old town, have lunch by the marina, then take a boat trip to gaze up at the lofty citadel.

Les Calanques de Piana
Children will enjoy spotting faces and shapes in these weird granite formations on the west coast between Ajaccio and Calvi.

Col de Bavella
The long-distance GR20 path traverses Col de Bavella, but for those with less stamina several short walks are also available, including a two-hour jaunt to the Trou de la Bombe, a peculiar 9-m-wide hole that has been eroded through a rock face.

Inside info
» You can fly direct from the UK to Bastia or take a ferry (corsica-ferries.fr) from the French or Italian mainland. Crossings take between two and 5½ hours.
» Daytime temperatures during the hottest months of July and August can exceed 35°C.
» A homage to the wind, Festival du Vent (lefestivalduvent.com) takes place in Calvi during October with everything from kite flying to parades.
» Further information: visit-corsica.com

Island safari
Corsica can be a real treat for the senses – and a thrill for any young nature detective. You only have to stroll through its wonderful *maquis* (the ubiquitous scrubland of the Mediterranean) to smell the heady pot-pourri of herbs crushed underfoot. Can you identify white and pink rock rose, yellow broom, wild rosemary and lavender? You'll probably hear the staccato beat of woodpeckers hammering holes in ancient cork oaks and the electro-whirring of cicadas filling the warm sultry air. See if you can track down one of these acoustic insects – the trunks of olive trees are a good place to start. Then try your luck at catching the grasshoppers that flicker around your feet like green sparks or spotting the redstarts and green-speckled Tyrrhenian lizards that chase flies along the ancient dry-stone walls. If you're really lucky you may find a Hermanns tortoise, now extinct on the European mainland. There are no vipers on Corsica, but you might stumble upon a harmless Aesculapian snake basking in the sunshine. Remember to cast the odd glance skyward – Corsica has several birds of prey, including red kites and Bonelli's eagles.

France Grown-ups' stuff

When to go

Spring is an ideal time to visit **Paris** – the days are getting longer and temperatures haven't reached the muggy extremes of high summer. In fact, many Parisians flee the city during August to escape the heat. The capital has plenty of festive sparkle during December, which is also a good time to visit **Strasbourg**'s Christmas market. Skiing in the **Alps** is best from January to March, although summer is also a wonderful time to visit the mountains, with alpine meadows in full bloom, plenty of warmth and sunshine and no shortage of lakes to swim in. The **south of France** has hot, dry Mediterranean summers – too hot for some families who might prefer the milder **Atlantic coast** (albeit with its less predictable sunshine). The best time to visit **Corsica** is from May to early July and September to October. Weather forecasts for various French regions can be found at meteo.fr/meteonet.

Getting there

Through its SkyTeam Alliance network, Air France (airfrance.com) connects 199 destinations in 85 countries via its hub at Paris Charles de Gaulle (CDG) airport. Expect to pay from around £90 for a return flight between London and Paris and US$640-1100 for a return fare from New York.

British Airways (britishairways. com) has flights to Ajaccio, Basel, Bordeaux, Geneva, Grenoble, Lyon, Marseille, Montpellier, Nantes, Nice, Paris CDG and Toulouse. Low-cost airlines operating between the UK and France include easyJet (easyjet. com), Ryanair (ryanair.com), Flybe (flybe.com) and BmiBaby (bmibaby.com).

Getting around

Driving in France is a pleasure thanks to its comprehensive road network, although venturing by car into Paris is not recommended. The autoroute system has service stations at approximately 40-km intervals and *aires* (rest areas with toilets and recreation areas but no food or fuel services) every 10 km. Plan your self-drive in France by using the route planner facility provided by Michelin (michelin.com). Car rental companies include Avis (avis.fr), Europcar (europcar.fr)

and Hertz (hertz.fr).

France has a modern and fast **rail** system. Take Eurostar to Paris, connect with TGV (tgv. com), France's high-speed train service, and you could be in Marseille or Bordeaux just three hours later. Regional express trains, known as TER, connect smaller towns. You can book an InterRail pass, allowing three, four, six or eight days' travel in one month from Rail Europe (raileurope.co.uk).

Getting around in cities is usually very straightforward and economical thanks to efficient Métro, bus and tram systems.

Accommodation

The most popular family options are either to rent a **gîte** (a self-catering cottage or house) or to stay at a **holiday park** in a mobile home or pre-pitched tent. A directory of accredited gîtes is administered by Gîtes de France (gites-de-france.

Skip the flight

➤➤ **Sail across the Channel** with P&O Ferries (poferries.com) from Dover to Calais (70-90 minutes) or with Brittany Ferries (brittanyferries.com) from Portsmouth to Caen (six hours), Portsmouth to St-Malo (8½ hours), Poole to Cherbourg (four hours; Fastcraft 2¼ hours) or Plymouth to Roscoff (five hours). Speed Ferries (speedferries.com) has a 50-minute Dover-Boulogne service from just £20 one-way, while Transmanche Ferries (transmancheferries.com) operates to Boulogne, Dieppe and Le Havre.
➤➤ **Take your car** through the Eurotunnel (eurotunnel.com) from Folkestone to Calais in just 35 minutes. Shuttle trains depart up to four times an hour.
➤➤ **Hop on Eurostar** (eurostar.com) from St Pancras International for high-speed trains direct to Paris, Lille, Avignon, Disneyland and the French Alps.
➤➤ **Catch a bus** with Eurolines (eurolines.co.uk) from London's Victoria Coach Station to Paris, via Eurotunnel or ferry.

fr). Average prices per week vary from €440 in the high season to €265 in the low season. Available during the school holidays, a carefully selected range of children's *gîtes* organizes special activities for kids aged four to 15. Companies specializing in cottage and villa rental in France include Allez France (allezfrance. com), Dominiques Villas (dominiquesvillas.co.uk), Rentals France (rentalsfrance.com) and VFB Holidays (vfbholidays.co.uk).

Camping France (camping france.com) has an online reservation system for over 10,000 campsites. As well as searching by region, you can select various criteria, such as sites with kids' clubs or beach access or waterparks. Many of the most popular holiday parks have superb facilities, including well-equipped mobile homes, swimming pools and waterslides, entertainment programmes and sports. Try Canvas Holidays (canvasholidays. com), Eurocamp (eurocamp. com), Keycamp (keycamp.ie) and Siblu (siblu.com).

Center Parcs (centerparcs. com) has two villages in France, one in Normandy and the other in Loire-et-Cher, while organized adventure holidays are available with Acorn Venture Holidays (acorn-venture.com) and PGL (pgl.co.uk). Esprit (esprit-holidays.co.uk) and Mark Warner (markwarner.co.uk) are the leading family specialists in winter and summer holidays in the French Alps, while Club Med (clubmed.com) has an all-inclusive resort with children's facilities in Provence.

Food & drink
The French love their food and you'll find everything from informal brasseries and family-run bistros cooking local dishes to Michelin-starred restaurants serving nouvelle cuisine. To save money, have your main meal at lunchtime when many restaurants serve a *menu du jour* for around half what it might cost in the evening. Be brave and introduce your kids to a few regional specialities. Along the **Brittany** and **Normandy** coasts, *assiette de fruits de mer* is a seafood platter of crayfish, oysters, prawns, mussels, crab and whelks which kids will enjoy dissecting even if they don't eat much. A sure hit from this region, though, are crêpes and galettes – pancakes with either sweet or savoury fillings. *Tarte tatin*, upside-down apple tart, should also go down a treat. **Mediterranean** dishes are some of the tastiest of all. Anything 'á la provençale' promises a delicious concoction of olive oil, garlic, tomatoes, onions and herbs. Duck and geese dishes feature prominently in **southwest France** and the **Pyrenees** – too rich for many kids, but as with anywhere in France, you'll always find standard fare like steak-frites. In the **Alps**, cheese fondues and *gratin dauphinois* (sliced potatoes baked in milk) are always popular with children, while traditional lamb stew and *fiadone* (lemon cheesecake) should tempt them in **Corsica**.

Health & safety
The sun can be strong in France during midsummer, so pack plenty of high-factor suncream and make sure children get some shade during the middle of the day.

Mosquitoes can be irritating in some areas, so it's also a good idea to take insect repellent.

(i) **Fact** file

Country	Time	Language	Currency	Exchange rate approximate	International dialling code	Tourist information
France	GMT+1	French	euro €	£1 = €1.15	+33	france.guide.com

France Family favourites

Chateau des Ormes

Where? Dol-de-Bretagne, Brittany.

Why? Lively holiday park set in 100 ha of chateau parkland with 18-hole golf course, waterpark with four-lane waterslide, indoor pool complex and all-weather football pitch. Children's clubs are available for toddlers through to teenagers and there is an extensive activity programme.

How much? Basic prices for 12-night holidays range from £287 to £1403 for two adults and all children under 18, staying in a Classic Midi mobile home (sleeping six), including mid-week Dover-Calais crossings with P&O Ferries. You can pay a supplement to upgrade your mobile home. A Villagrand Deluxe, for example, costs an additional £24 to £51 per night.

Contact Keycamp Holidays, T+44 (0)844-844 1000, keycamp.co.uk.

Also try... other Keycamp sites in Brittany, such as Les Menhirs at Carnac Plage or De la Baie at Trinity-sur-Mer.

La Baume

Where? Fréjus, French Riviera.

Why? Well-equipped parc with every amenity imaginable, from Fun Stations for kids aged four and above to a soundproof disco for over-16s. On-site activities include tennis, football, basketball, skateboarding, archery and cycling and there are lovely beaches nearby if you can tear yourself away from the parc's two outstanding pool complexes.

How much? Basic prices for 12 nights in a two-bedroom Comfort mobile home range from £437 to £1887, including P&O ferry crossing from Dover to Calais. Upgrade to a three-bedroom Comfort home for an extra £9 to £25 per night. Ready-pitched 'supertents' are also available for £341 to £1247 for a 12-night holiday.

Contact Eurocamp, T+44 (0)844-406 0402, eurocamp.co.uk.

Also try... Eurocamp's Esterel site at St Raphal or Les Pecheurs at Roquebrune-sur-Argens.

Domaine de Dugny

Where? Blois, Loire Valley.

Why? Four-star parc in the heart of the Loire Valley, close to the region's chateaux and other attractions. As well as an indoor and outdoor pool with waterslides, Domaine de Dugny offers children's play areas, archery, bike hire, boules, crazy golf, fishing, pedalos, table tennis, volleyball and free football tournaments for all age groups. Handy holiday extras include linen and towel packs, baby packs, food baskets for late arrivals and three free children's clubs for kids aged one to 14.

How much? From £267 for seven nights in May, including return Dover-Calais ferry and staying in a two-bedroom Esprit mobile home with terrace (sleeps up to six).

Contact Siblu, T+44 (0)871-911 2288, siblu.com.

Also try... Siblu's Domaine de Litteau site in Normandy or La Croix du Vieux Pont for a good-value location close to Paris, Disneyland and Parc Astérix.

Disneyland Hotel

Where? Disneyland Paris.

Why? Ultimate Disneyland hotel overlooking Disneyland Park and just a three-minute walk to Walt Disney Studios Park and Disney Village. As well as enjoying facilities like an indoor swimming pool, spa and Club Minnie playroom, guests receive a FastPass and have plenty of opportunities for meet 'n' greet sessions with Disney characters. The hotel also boasts family rooms.

How much? From £281 per adult (based on two sharing) for two days/one night, including accommodation, breakfast and Disney Parks entrance. Check website for kids' discounts, free places and special packages.

Contact Disneyland Hotel, hotels.disneylandparis.co.uk.

Also try... Disney's Hotel New York, Newport Bay Club, Sequoia Lodge, Hotel Cheyenne, Hotel Santa Fe and Davy Crockett Ranch.

Villa Chavaz

Where? Cappiciolo, Corsica.

Why? This spectacular beachside villa (sleeping up to six) overlooks Valinco Gulf and has a path leading through its garden to a secluded sandy beach.

How much? From £548 per person, based on six sharing and including return flights from London, car hire, taxes and a welcome hamper.

Contact Corsican Places, T+44 (0)845-330 2059, corsica.co.uk.

France Family favourites

Country Kids & Country Tots

Where? Herault, near Montpelier.

Why? With its complimentary crèche, splash-pool, play area, petting farm and two free nights' babysitting, this stylish self-catering accommodation appeals particularly to parents with babies and toddlers. There's also a huge range of nursery and play equipment on hand, so you can even revert to the days of packing lightly. The grounds include a tennis court, heated swimming pool and a farm shop fully stocked with homemade ready-meals.

How much? From around €3000 to €5000 per week for a family of four.

Contact Baby Friendly Boltholes, T+44 (0)845-489 0140, babyfriendlyboltholes.co.uk.

Also try... Baby Friendly Boltholes' equally decadent Maison Cypres at Le Sarraíl near Carcassone, or the aptly-named Wide Open Space Villa on the edge of the historic town of Montauroux in Provence.

Villa du Lac

Where? Cazaux, Atlantic coast.

Why? Located close to surfing beaches and the famous Dune du Pyla, this modern house makes a comfortable family base, with four bedrooms, fitted kitchen, living/dining room and 10-m swimming pool. Shops and restaurants are within easy walking distance, as is a lake offering swimming, fishing, waterskiing and cycling.

How much? One week rental from €706 to €1883 per week, including a return Channel crossing for one car and up to five passengers.

Contact French Affair, T+44 (0)20-7381 8519, frenchaffair.com.

Also try... French Affair's Villa Larros, a magnificent house located near Gujan-Mestras and the picturesque harbour of Larros. Ideal for two or three families to share, the villa boasts six bedrooms, three bathrooms, plus extensive grounds and an outdoor pool.

Les Hauts de Bruyères

Where? Loir et Cher.

Why? Special features of this well-equipped Center Parcs include the Experience Factory (with miniature golf, play areas, crêperie and electric cars), subtropical waterpark with lagoons, waves, slides and waterfalls, Aqua Sana spa and a forest assault course using a network of suspended bridges, beams and lianas.

How much? From €1255 for a week in August (or from €904 in May) staying in a two-bedroom Comfort Villa with terrace (ideal for a family of four).

Contact Center Parcs, T+31 (0)10-498 9754, centerparcs.com.

Also try... Center Parcs' showpiece French property Le Lac d'Ailette, close to Paris and Disneyland and with Canadian-style villas, a beautiful lakeside setting and stunning winter garden. Other Center Parcs villages in France include Les Bois in Normandy and, new for 2010, Domaine des Trois Forêts in de Moselle region.

Opio en Provence

Where? Near Nice, Provence.

Why? Tucked into olive groves and pine forests, this spectacular all-inclusive resort boasts stylish accommodation and a wide range of facilities, including four swimming pools, Turkish bath and sauna, nine-hole golf course, Mini Club Med for four- to 11-year-olds, Circus School, and teen-only spaces.

How much? Expect to pay around £6200 per week for a family of four during August (or £3200 in May), including flights, meet-and-greet transfers, accommodation in interconnecting rooms, all meals, snacks and drinks, Mini Club Med childcare, activities and entertainment.

Contact Club Med, T+44 (0)871-424 4044, clubmed.co.uk.

Also try... other Club Med resorts, such as La Palmyre Atlantique on the Arvi Peninsula or Cargèse on the island of Corsica.

Chalet Hotel Sapinière

Where? Chamonix, French Alps.

Why? Ideal for a summer or winter holiday, the Sapinière has superb views of Mount Blanc and is just a few minutes' walk from the children's ski area. A childcare programme caters for children aged from four months to 12 years. During winter there are kids' snow clubs and ski classes, while in summer, Alpies and Teen Rangers clubs offer activities such as husky walking and rock-climbing.

How much? Winter rates from £579 to £1169 per week per adult, including flights, transfers, breakfast and dinner; see website for child discounts, free children's places and lots of other goodies like free children's lift passes. Summer packages cost £399 to £499 per week per adult, accommodation and meals only.

Contact Esprit Holidays, T+44 (0)1252-618300, esprit-holidays.co.uk.

Also try... Esprit's new Chalet Hotel Mariande in Alpe d'Huez.

Tour operators

The Adventure Company
adventurecompany.co.uk

Canvas Holidays
canvasholidays.co.uk

Center Parcs
centerparcs.com

Club Med
clubmed.com

Crystal Holidays
crystalholidays.co.uk

Esprit Holidays
esprit-holidays.co.uk

Eurocamp
eurocamp.co.uk

Exodus
exodus.co.uk

Explore Worldwide
explore.co.uk

Families Worldwide
familiesworldwide.co.uk

Headwater
headwater.com

Inntravel
inntravel.co.uk

Keycamp
keycamp.co.uk

Mark Warner
markwarner.co.uk

Neilson Active Holidays
neilson.co.uk

PGL
pgl.co.uk

Powder Byrne
powderbyrne.co.uk

Siblu
siblu.com

Praia de Odeceixe on the
Algarve's Atlantic coast.

Contents

113 **Introduction**

114 **Kids' stuff**

116 **Tots to teens**

118 **Central Spain**
118 Madrid
119 Extremadura

120 **Northern Spain**
120 Vizcayan Coast
120 Cantabria
121 Galicia

122 **Catalonia**
122 Barcelona
124 Costa Brava
124 Costa Daurada
125 Costa del Azahar,
     Costa Blanca &
     Costa Cálida
125 Spanish Pyrenees

126 **Andalucía**
126 Seville

126 Ronda
126 Granada
127 Sierra Nevada
127 Costa del Sol
127 Coto Doñana

128 **Balearic Islands**
128 Mallorca
128 Menorca
128 Ibiza &
     Formentera

130 **Canary Islands**
130 Gran Canaria
131 Lanzarote
131 Fuerteventura
132 Tenerife

134 **Portugal**
134 Lisbon
135 The Algarve
136 Madeira
136 The Azores

138 **Grown-ups'
     stuff**

Spain & Portugal

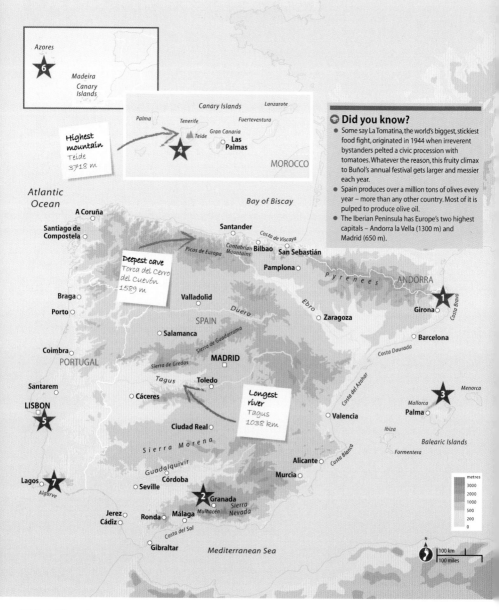

Azores

Madeira
Canary
Islands

6

Canary Islands   Lanzarote

Palma   Tenerife   Fuerteventura
              Gran Canaria
Highest   Teide   Las
mountain   Palmas
Teide
3718 m   MOROCCO

4

Atlantic
Ocean   Bay of Biscay
        A Coruña
                         Santander
Santiago de   Costa de Viscaya
Compostela   Cantabrian Bilbao
                 Picas de Europa Mountains San Sebastián
Deepest cave   Pamplona
Torca del Cerro
del Cuevón   Pyrenees   ANDORRA
1589 m
Braga   Valladolid   Girona
                         Duero   Ebro   Costa Brava
Porto   SPAIN   Zaragoza
                 Salamanca   Barcelona
Coimbra   Sierra de Guadarrama   Costa Daurada
PORTUGAL   MADRID
         Sierra de Gredos
         Tagus   Toledo
Santarem   Cáceres   Menorca
LISBON   Longest   Mallorca
                         river   Palma
5   Tagus
         Ciudad Real   1038 km   Valencia
                                             Ibiza
         Sierra Morena   Balearic Islands
              Guadalquivir   Alicante   Costa Blanca   Formentera
Lagos   Córdoba   Murcia
7   Seville
Algarve
         Jerez   Ronda Málaga Mulhacén Sierra
         Cádiz   Costa del Sol Nevada
                 2 Granada
              Gibraltar   Mediterranean Sea

Did you know?

- Some say La Tomatina, the world's biggest, stickiest food fight, originated in 1944 when irreverent bystanders pelted a civic procession with tomatoes. Whatever the reason, this fruity climax to Buñol's annual festival gets larger and messier each year.
- Spain produces over a million tons of olives every year – more than any other country. Most of it is pulped to produce olive oil.
- The Iberian Peninsula has Europe's two highest capitals – Andorra la Vella (1300 m) and Madrid (650 m).

metres
3000
2000
1000
500
200
0

N
100 km
100 miles

Introduction

Explore the 'Wild Coast'
▸▸ Catalonia, page 122

Admire the Alhambra
▸▸ Andalucía, page 126

Find the perfect beach
▸▸ Balearic Islands, page 128

Conquer a volcano
▸▸ Canary Islands page 130

See the seven seas
▸▸ Lisbon, page 134

Island hop in the Atlantic
▸▸ Madeira & the Azores, page 136

Discover a secret cove
▸▸ The Algarve, page 135

With its stunning beaches, almost-guaranteed sunshine and excellent value for money, it's not hard to see why Spain is such a popular family holiday destination. And while Portugal has less in the way of beach resorts and nightlife than its Iberian neighbour, it's still a friendly, fun place to take kids. Don't be put off by the reputation of certain Costas and islands for crowded beaches and rowdy nightlife. You can always find smaller, quieter resorts or travel in the low season – particularly to year-round destinations like the Canary Islands. There are also plenty of opportunities for getting off the beaten track, from roaming the Spanish steppes of Extremadura to island-hopping through the mid-Atlantic archipelago of the Azores. And if that sounds too taxing (or too far from the beach) there is always scope for adding an adventurous twist to a traditional seaside holiday – whether you combine northern Spain's coast with some action-packed days in the mountains of the Picos de Europa or head inland from the Costa del Sol on a cultural quest to Granada and Seville.

Spain & Portugal Kids' stuff

Books to read

Prince of the Birds
Frances Lincoln, 2005
In a story adapted from Washington Irving's *Tales of the Alhambra*, Ahmed, the Prince of Granada, lives in a high tower, with only birds for friends. Through his ability to communicate with them he finds true love in the form of a princess locked in a faraway tower. To win her hand he must conquer his fears before they can finally escape together on a flying carpet. Ages 5+

The Life and Work of Salvador Dali
Heinemann, 2005
Part of a series on the lives and works of great artists, this 32-page book delves into the surreal world of Spanish painter, Salvador Dali – well known for his weird and wonderful paintings, such as *The Persistence of Memory*. Ages 5+

The Story of Ferdinand
Penguin, 1997
An endearing classic with exquisite illustrations, *The Story of Ferdinand* tells the tale of a bull who would much rather sit under a cork tree smelling the flowers than enter the bullfighting ring. Ages 5+

Toro! Toro!
Collins, 2002
Set in Andalucía, against the backdrop of the Spanish Civil War, this is the moving tale of Antonito and the young bull that he has hand-reared and wishes to spare from the fate of the bull ring. A delightful story, full of drama. Ages 6+

Ferdinand Magellan and the First Voyage around the World
Chelsea House, 2000
A biography of the daring Portuguese sea captain who commanded the first expedition that sailed around the world. Ages 7+

With Love from Spain, Melanie Martin
Yearling, 2005
In this diary of her family holiday in Spain, 11-year-old Melanie dances flamenco, tries Spanish food, visits museums and falls in love. Ages 8+

Asterix in Spain
Orion, 2004
When Pepe, the kidnapped son of a Spanish chief, escapes from his Roman captors, who should find him but those indomitable Gauls, Astérix and Obélix. Faced with the task of returning Pepe to his father, the gallant heroes must brave mountains, bullfights, Roman legions and the annoying habits of young Pepe. Ages 8+

Snorkel wise

Get gear that fits
▸▸ Hold the mask up to your face and breath in through your nose. If it sticks to your face, it fits.

Spit and polish
▸▸ To stop the inside of your mask misting over, rub a little spit over the glass, then rinse thoroughly.

Practise in a swimming pool
▸▸ Get used to breathing through a snorkel. If water seeps into your mask, tread water and pull the lower edge of the mask away from your face to allow it to drain out. A burst of air should shoot any water out of your snorkel.

Ready for the sea
▸▸ Start in a calm, shallow area. For buoyancy wear a life jacket or wetsuit. Use a relaxed, fluttering kick with your flippers. If you're doing it right, there should not be too much splashing. Every few minutes lift your head above the surface to check that currents haven't taken you too far from the shore. Always be aware of boats and stay clear of breaking waves. Wear a rash vest, smother the back of your neck and legs with waterproof sunblock and avoid snorkelling during the middle of the day.

Taste of Spain gazpacho

This Spanish cold tomato soup makes a great starter or a simple lunch. It's also really easy to make. Here is the Andalucían variety.

What you need
▸▸ 1 kg plum tomatoes
▸▸ 1 small onion
▸▸ 1 small green pepper
▸▸ 1 small chubby cucumber
▸▸ 1 small cup olive oil
▸▸ 4 tsp vinegar
▸▸ 200 g white bread soaked in water
▸▸ salt and pepper
▸▸ glass of water (optional)
▸▸ garlic cloves, peeled and crushed
▸▸ bowl of diced tomatoes, red and green peppers, cucumber, onion and croutons to garnish

What to do
▸▸ Blend the tomatoes, onion, pepper, cucumber, vinegar, bread and oil.
▸▸ Add the water and garlic to suit your own taste; the water will make it less strong, while the garlic will make it stronger.
▸▸ Add salt and pepper to taste and put the mixture in a bowl. Chill for at least an hour, the colder the better (you can add ice cubes if you like).
▸▸ Serve in bowls with side dishes of the diced vegetables and croutons for people to add themselves.

Craft like Picasso

▸▸ Take a look at some of Picasso's famous paintings. Notice the way that he sometimes painted pictures of faces, with lots of different views.
▸▸ Take a piece of modelling clay (that doesn't need to be kiln-dried) about the size of a tennis ball. Flatten it to make a circle, around 4 cm thick.
▸▸ Use clay tools to draw a line from the top to the bottom of the circle that shows a side view (or profile) of a face.
▸▸ On the other side of the line, draw one eye facing forward.
▸▸ Add raised features such as lips, eyebrows and a nose also facing forward on that side.
▸▸ Score, or make little marks, with your clay tool and then use a wet finger to help seal the features in place.
▸▸ At the top of the face make 10 holes for adding hair later.
▸▸ Allow the clay to dry completely before painting; then insert pipe cleaners into the holes to create wacky hair.

Spain & Portugal Tots to teens

Planning a family holiday to Spain, Portugal or any of their islands is not only straightforward, but can also offer excellent value for money. Accommodation ranges from self-catering apartments and resort hotels to holiday villages with tents and mobile homes, while food covers everything from burgers and pizzas to tapas bars where children can try lots of small traditional dishes. Although you will usually find a friendly welcome wherever you go, the Portuguese have a special weakness for children – particularly babies and toddlers. Children in both Spain and Portugal are treated like mini-adults and it's not unusual to see them in restaurants with their parents late at night.

Babies

Avoid the hot and crowded summer season – it will still be warm enough in spring and autumn to enjoy Spain's Mediterranean resorts. The main resort beaches have play areas, while babysitting is usually available in the larger hotels. High chairs are not always common, so consider bringing a collapsible travel seat that attaches to a chair.

Toddlers/pre-school

The quietest resorts include Llafranc on the Costa Brava, San Pedro de Alcántara on the Costa del Sol and Dénia on the Costa Blanca. In the Balearics, Menorca is the most laid-back island for young families. There are some excellent beaches on the Algarve, although some are strafed by strong Atlantic currents and winds – fine for beachcombing and playing chicken with the waves, but dangerous for swimming. If you

are unfazed by the longer flight, the Canary Islands are an ideal choice for toddlers. With warm, sunny weather year-round, you can travel outside the busy school-holiday season and still enjoy good beach weather. For ultimate flexibility, opt for a self-catering apartment and hire car; for onsite facilities choose a family resort.

Kids/school age

Although you are restricted to busier school-holiday periods with this age group, crowded beaches at least provide guaranteed playmates for your children. They will also be able to enjoy a wide range of beach-based activities, from snorkelling to trips in glass-bottom boats. Popular tourist spots always have a waterpark (Siam Park in Tenerife being the latest and most spectacular) and there are also several excellent theme parks, such as PortAventura on the Costa Daurada. Rather than restricting yourselves entirely to

❝❞ I love Spain because it's always hot. I love walking along the sandy beaches collecting seashells. And I also love eating swordfish.

Lottie Gale (age 9)

the beach, however, consider a trip that combines the coast with the mountains. In northern Spain, for example, a week or so relaxing on Cantabria's lovely sandy bays can easily be followed by a multi-activity adventure in the Picos de Europa, while southern Spain's Costa del Sol combines well with walking or horse riding in the Sierra Nevada. If you just want a taster of the high ground, try Tenerife where a day or two clambering about on the volcanic slopes in Teide National

Special needs

Most tourist offices can provide information on accessible accommodation. Disabled holiday specialists Can be Done (canbedone.co.uk) lists several properties in Spain and Portugal that offer facilities such as wheel-in showers and pool hoists. Also try Accessible Travel & Leisure (accessibletravel.co.uk).

Single parents

The Adventure Company (adventurecompany.co.uk) has single-parent departures on its eight-day Active Pyrenees adventure break in Andorra. One-parent family holiday specialists Single Parents on Holiday (singleparentsonholiday. co.uk) and Mango (mangokids. co.uk) both offer group trips to rural Andalucia. Try Eurocamp (eurocamp.co.uk) for single-parent discounts on holidays to the Costa Brava, Costa del Sol, northern Spain and the Algarve.

Park will give kids a real sense of achievement. Educationally, Spain's premier museums and galleries are in Madrid – quite a sophisticated destination for kids until you factor the Warner Bros theme park into the equation. For an insight into the country's history and culture you could also combine the Spanish capital with Extremadura, but you'll need an itinerary that's short and sweet to keep kids interested. Valencia's super-modern City of Arts and Sciences is a guaranteed hit with children, as is Lisbon's Parque das Nações with its superb oceanarium.

Teenagers

If it's lively beach resorts you're after, Spain has them in bucket loads – although you should steer clear of the rowdiest fleshpots on Ibiza or along the Costa Blanca. As well as buzzing nightlife and a similarly aged, like-minded crowd to hang out with, most teenagers are up for a sporty challenge whether it's learning how to sail, windsurf or waterski. And when the beaches begin to pall, there are always the waterparks, theme parks and shops – particularly in cities like Barcelona which teenagers will love for its trendy vibe and wacky art scene.

For multi-activity breaks, The Adventure Company (adventurecompany.co.uk) has teenage trips to Andorra, while Explore Worldwide (explore. co.uk) has dedicated teenage departures to Spain, Mallorca and the Azores.

Top: Pedal to the peaks – family cycling in northern Spain's Picos de Europa.

❝❞ Praia do Barril near Tavira in Portugal's Algarve is a long stretch of vanilla sand, with umbrellas for hire, clean showers and toilets, and a shady outdoor restaurant where you can always get a table. But its trump card for kids is simple and overwhelming: you reach it by taking a five-minute miniature train ride across the lagoon.

Dan Linstead, Editor, Wanderlust magazine

Central Spain What? No Costas?

Central Spain may be a long way from the beach, but there is still enough in this region to keep children happy on holiday. At first glance, Madrid's reputation for fine art doesn't exactly make it an easy sell to kids. If you're desperate to see the capital's famous Prado, Thyssen or Reina Sofía galleries, you'll need to dangle a pretty tempting carrot under your children's noses – preferably in the form of the Warner Bros Park south of the city. Once you've seen some of Madrid's traditional (and not so traditional) highlights head west to Extremadura, an unspoilt region with fascinating birdlife and history (but alas, still no Costas).

Museo del Prado.

Madrid

City highlights

If you have time to visit just one of Madrid's three world-class art museums, the Museo del Prado (museoprado.mcu.es) should be top of your list. Inside you'll find a wealth of paintings by Spanish masters Goya and Velázquez, as well as an impressive collection of Italian and Flemish works. Highlights for children include

◉ Inside info

⟫ The Tourist Travel Pass from Madrid Card (madridcard.com) provides unlimited travel on bus, metro and suburban train routes for between one and seven days.
⟫ If you plan to visit all of Madrid's art highlights, buy a ticket for the Art Walk (El Paseo del Arte), available at the Prado, Thyssen and Reina Sofía galleries.
⟫ Look for beautifully illustrated tiled street plaques in the old quarter of Madrid.
⟫ For an energy-boosting snack, try *chocolate con churros*.
⟫ For further information, visit esmadrid.com and turismo-en.sigimo.com.

Las Meninas by Velázquez where the infant Margarita is fussed over by her ladies-in-waiting. Goya's so-called Black Paintings may be too harrowing for young children – although teenagers will probably delight in the gross-factor of *Saturn Devouring his Son*. Also worth tracking down is Caravaggio's *David Victorious over Goliath*, an exquisite study in light and shadow.

For more art appreciation, head to the Museo Nacional Centro de Arte Reina Sofia (museoreinasofia.es) to see Picasso's anti-war masterpiece *Guernica*, or to the Museo Thyssen-Bornemisza (museothyssen.org) to study paintings by Rembrandt, Raphael and others.

A short walk from the galleries, the Parque del Retiro has plenty of space to run around, as well as boats to hire on the lake and a Sunday afternoon puppet show. On the opposite side of central Madrid, you'll find Palacio Real (patrimonionacional.es),

Madrid's extravagant Royal Palace with its lavishly decorated dining hall and throne room

From central Madrid, take the metro west to Batán to reach Casa de Campo, a former royal hunting ground that's home to Parque de Atracciones (parquedeatracciones.es), an amusement park with hanging roller coasters, free-fall rides and water chutes. The Tranquillity Zone offers more relaxing activities such as a jungle boat cruise, while younger children have their own special area with roller coasters, water rides, puppet theatres and an adventure playground.

Also in Casa de Campo, Parque Zoológico (zoomadrid.com) has everything from koalas and tigers to dolphins and sharks, while Faunia Madrid (reached by taking the metro east to Valdebernardo) recreates various ecosystems, from polar to tropical.

For waterparks, try Aquópolis de Villanueva de la Canada or Aquópolis de San Fernando de Henares (aquopolis.es).

Warner Bros Park

San Martín de la Vega, T902-024100, parquewarner.com. Mar-Nov, from 1100 (days and times vary), €37/adult, €28/child, free for children less than 90 cm in height.

» A short bus or train ride south of Madrid city centre

Warner Bros Park is divided into five themed areas. Peruse the shops, cafés and cinemas along Hollywood Boulevard before witnessing a spectacular stunt show (based on Batman, Lethal Weapon or Police Academy) at Movie World Studios.

Some of the biggest rides can be found in Superheroes World, including The Vengeance of the Enigma – a 100-m vertical tower drop (minimum height: 130 cm) and the 90-kph Superman roller coaster (minimum height: 132 cm).

Old West Territory keeps the adrenaline pumping with a giant wooden roller coaster and various water rides.

Cartoon Village, meanwhile, is where you can meet Tweety, Bugs Bunny and other Looney Tunes characters, and ride the new Correcaminous Bip Bip – a roller coaster based on the Roadrunner (minimum height: 130 cm or 100 cm if accompanied by an adult).

Gentle rides for little ones include Scooby-Doo spinning cups, while the park's loudest screams are usually generated by the 106-kph Stunt Fall coaster (minimum height: 137 cm).

⑪ **Where** can I see these?

White storks nest on chimneypots, church towers and rooftops throughout Extremadura – a remote and little-visited region of central Spain. In Parque Natural de Monfragüe, the Peña Falcón provides a suitably precipitous nesting site for griffon, Egyptian and rare black vultures which you can observe from viewpoints along the road opposite. Elsewhere in the park, easy walking trails probe the oak woods and herb-rich grasslands of the *dehesa* – the perfect habitat in which to spot hoopoes and rollers. Extremadura's cultural highlights include the Monasterio de Guadalupe, the Roman monuments of Mérida, the medieval hilltop town of Trujillo and the maze of streets in the old town of Cáceres.

Northern Spain The green side of Spain

Stretching from the Pyrenean foothills to the crinkle-cut shoreline of Galicia, the Atlantic coast of northern Spain has everything from rugged cliffs to sandy bays, fishing villages and holiday resorts. What it doesn't have, though, is the almost guaranteed heat and sunshine of the Mediterranean Costas: a small price to pay, perhaps, for less crowded beaches and quieter resorts. But northern Spain appeals to families in search of more than sun, sand and sea. Lush broadleaf forests sweep up the flanks of the Cantabrian Mountains, with adventure-rich national parks like Picos de Europa just a short distance inland. There are also caves to be explored – many with prehistoric paintings – while a wonderful procession of cathedrals, churches and monuments mark the pilgrimage route to Santiago de Compostela.

Vizcayan Coast

Stretching east from the busy commercial port of Bilbao, the rugged Basque coastline has a long history of fishing, and at the Museo del Pescador in Bermeo you can catch the whole story, from whales to anchovies. Just beyond Bermeo

◉ Inside info

» Sail from Portsmouth to Bilbao with P&O Ferries (poferries.com) or from Plymouth to Santander with Brittany Ferries (brittany-ferries.com) and you stand a good chance of spotting whales, dolphins and basking sharks in the Bay of Biscay.
» Inland from Bilbao, Pamplona is renowned for its annual fiesta, Los Sanfermines (6-14 July), in which bulls stampede through the frenzied, crowded streets of the city.
» For further information, visit euskadi.net, infoasturias.com, turismodecantabria.com and turgalicia.es.

the coastal road diverts inland following a scenic route along the west bank of the Oka River estuary to Gernika. It was here in 1937 that German and Italian planes unleashed a devastating bombing raid, killing over 1600 people – an outrage vividly portrayed in Picasso's powerful *Guernica* painting on display in Madrid (see page 118).

A few kilometres north, the Cuevas de Santimamiñe are worth a visit, although the chamber with the prehistoric cave drawings of bison is closed to the public. Cantabria's caves (see below) might be more satisfying. Following the west bank of the estuary back to the coast, you reach Mundaka, an attractive old harbour town renowned for its long surf break. Continuing east, Lekeitio has a couple of good beaches, but for the ultimate Basque holiday resort look no further than San Sebastián (sansebastianturismo.com).

Surrounded by hills and overlooking the beautiful horseshoe bay of La Concha, San Sebastián has loads for kids to do – from swimming and sailing to ogling sharks in the aquarium near the town's old quarter.

Cantabria

A region blessed with a heady mixture of golden-sand beaches (particularly at Laredo and Santander) and a spectacular mountainous hinterland, Cantabria not only has the best of northern Spain's scenery, but it also has the added attraction of some fascinating prehistoric caves. The most famous of these are the Cuevas de Altamira (museodealtamira. mcu.es) where charcoal and ochre images of bison, deer and horses festoon a rock face. In order to protect the original drawings (created by

Langre beach in Cantabria. Right: Picos de Europa.

Cro-Magnon communities up to 14,000 years ago) a replica of the cave is open to visitors. For a glimpse of the real thing head to Cuevas del Castillo, a des-res for cave dwellers from as early as 130,000 years ago. Here you can see animal drawings as well as some 50 hand prints. Kids will also enjoy the nearby Cabárceno Wildlife Park where African elephants, rhinos and other exotic beasts roam a 750-ha swathe of the Peña Cabarga Nature Reserve.

For a proper taste of northern Spain's great outdoors, though, you need to set your sights on the Parque Nacional de los Picos de Europa. Easily accessed from either Santander or the Asturian town of Oviedo, this dramatic chunk of the Cordillera Cantábrica is home to vultures, eagles, chamois, wolves and bears, as well as a dazzling array of butterflies and orchids. The riverside village of Potes makes a good base. You will

find several adventure operators here (offering activities ranging from mountain biking, whitewater rafting and horse riding to paragliding and 4WD tours), while nearby Fuente Dé is the setting for a dramatic cable-car ride.

Galicia

The coast to the north of this westernmost province of Spain, especially the Costa da Morte, is wild and windswept – fine for a scenic drive and an invigorating picnic on a headland, but not exactly what you'd call child-friendly. Instead, head for the Rías Baixas on Galicia's southwest coast. This series of deep inlets has a milder climate and safer beaches, especially at the resort of Panxón. There are good watersports facilities at Vilagarcia de Arousa, while the

tiny island of A Toxa is worth a visit to see its church, which is covered in scallop shells.

🔊 **Puppy** power

A living sculpture sustained by an internal irrigation system, the Puppy sits obediently outside Bilbao's extraordinary Guggenheim Museum (guggenheim-bilbao.es) where it contrasts with the museum's titanium-clad façade.

Catalonia Beautiful Barcelona

A superb family holiday destination, Catalonia caters for all ages, whether you have 10-year-olds in search of mountain adventure, teenagers in search of city chic or toddlers in search of sand and sea. Rivalling Madrid for cultural importance, child-friendly Barcelona is the vibrant capital of this diverse region which stretches from the 3000-m peaks of the Pyrenees to the sandy bays of the Costa Daurada. One of Europe's original package-holiday destinations, Catalonia's rugged Costa Brava continues to draw the crowds, while inland attractions include the mesmerizing Monastery of Montserrat.

Three-day action plan

➤ **Day 1** Start at Plaça de Catalunya, a large square at the heart of the city, and walk down La Rambla, a 1-km-long pedestrian thoroughfare adorned with colourful pavement mosaics and thronging with cafés, bird and flower stalls, buskers, street artists and spray-painted human statues. About halfway down you can detour to the left to see Barcelona's magnificent Gothic Cathedral. At the end of La Rambla, take the lift up the Monument a Colom where Christopher Columbus stands

atop an 80-m column. The views are spectacular. You'll be able to see the dramatic and otherworldly spires of Gaudí's Sagrada Família (although you should schedule time for a close-up visit to this extraordinary church). From the Monument a Colom, stroll a little way along Avinguda de les Drassanes to Museu Marítim (museumaritimbarcelona.com) where Barcelona's seafaring tradition is brought to life with imaginative exhibits and special effects. Nearby at Port Vell, admire the beautiful schooner, *Santa Eulàlia*, before walking across the pontoon of Rambla de Mar to visit L'Aquarium (aquariumbcn.com) – one of Europe's largest, with a walk-through shark tank. Other attractions in Port Vell include an IMAX cinema, the submarine *Ictíneo II* and the Museu d'Història de Catalunya (en.mhcat.net), a child-friendly museum that allows children to experience Catalan history through dressing up and role-play. Boat trips are available with

Las Golondrines (lasgolondrinas.com) and on the catamaran Orsom (barcelona-orsom.com), while sandy beaches with play areas and cafés can be found at both Port Vell and Port Olímpic. For something more peaceful, make for the green oasis of Parc de la Ciutadella just to the east of Port Vell. Here you'll find a boating lake, a fountain and shady paths to explore, as well as the Parc Zoològic with its dolphin shows, pony rides, adventure playground and children's farm.

➤ **Day 2** Take the metro to Paral.lel from where a funicular connects with the cable-car station on Avinguda de Miramar. A thrilling ride up Montjuïc Hill leads to Castell de Montjuïc with its far-reaching views of the city. There's a military museum inside the castle,

◉ **Inside** info

➤➤ Barcelona divides nicely into three family-friendly sections: La Rambla and Port Vell, Parc de Montjuïc and Tibidabo.
➤➤ The Barcelona Card (available from the tourist office – see below) allows free travel on public transport as well as discounts at various museums and attractions.
➤➤ For further information, visit barcelonaturisme.com.

although most kids will be happy enough exploring the gardens, which are littered with ancient cannon. On the opposite side of Parc de Montjuïc, the majestic Palau Nacional houses the Museu Nacional d'Art de Catalunya (mnac.es), renowned for its Romanesque church frescos. Admittedly, children will be more captivated by the cascades and fountains outside, but if you're determined to instil some cultural appreciation there's always the nearby Poble Espanyol (poble-espanyol. com), an open-air museum with streets, squares, buildings and monuments from around Spain.

It's a bit touristy, but kids will enjoy the handicraft workshops, street entertainers and puppet shows.

▸ **Day 3** From Plaça de Catalunya take the open-topped Bus Turístic to Parc Güell, a colourful and wacky mishmash of pavilions, benches, archways and other architectural shenanigans hatched from the playful mind of Gaudí. Continue north to Avinguda del Tibidabo and take the funicular up 517-m-high Tibidabo hill where colour-coded paths and nature trails probe the woodlands of Parc de Collserola. Round off the day at the 100-year-old Parc d'Atraccions del Tibidabo (tibidabo.es) which has traditional funfair rides as well as some more modern, white-knuckle embellishments.

Opposite and right: Mosaic tiles at Gaudí's Parc Guell.
Left: Sagrada Família.

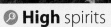

🔍 **High** spirits

Built into a mountainside 40 km northwest of Barcelona, the **Monestir de Monserrat** is the spiritual heart of Catalonia and was built on the spot where La Moreneta – a statue of the Virgin Mary – was hidden from the Moors. Reach the monastery by car or train, then take the cable car or rack railway up the mountain. The Montserrat Visita Card (montserratvisita. com) includes tickets for the rack railway or cable car, Montserrat Museum, and lunch in the café.

Catalonia Coast & mountains

Costa Brava

The 200-km 'Wild Coast' of Catalonia is an enticing mixture of golden beaches, rocky cliffs and bustling resorts. At its northern end, Roses has sheltered beaches and makes a good base for visiting the fishing village of Cadaqués and the Dalí museum in Figueres. Further south, the small resorts of L'Escala and L'Estartit have a thriving sardine fishery and are close to the Greco-Roman ruins of Empúries. Don't miss a snorkelling or kayaking trip to the offshore Medes Isles, available through Medaqua (medaqua.com). Palafrugell has three of the Costa Brava's finest beaches (Calella de Palafrugell, Llafranc and Tamariu), while the popular resort of Platja d'Aro has a 2-km stretch of lifeguard-patrolled beach and lively nightlife. A beautiful old fortified town above the sheltered sweep of Platja Gran beach, Tossa de Mar has a watersports centre at Cala Llevadó. The busiest and liveliest stretch of the coast, Lloret de Mar suits families with teenagers in search of watersports and a buzzing nightlife. The catamaran *Sensation* (catamaransensation.

com) operates sailing trips between Blanes and Lloret de Mar, while the Jardí Botànic Mar I Murta gardens makes a pleasant retreat from the coast. Waterparks along the Costa Brava include Aquabrava (aquabrava.com) in Roses, WaterWorld (waterworld.es) in Lloret de Mar and Marineland (marineland.es) south of Blanes.

Costa Daurada

Stretching south of Barcelona the 'Golden Coast' is renowned for its long sandy beaches. Sitges is a long-established and trendy resort, but not as popular as Salou – one of Spain's prime Mediterranean hot spots. Here you will find the gently shelving beaches of Platja de Ponent and Platja de Llevant, with smaller, less crowded coves towards Cap Salou. Beyond this lies Le Pineda with more beaches and the waterpark Aquopolis (aquopolis.com). Just inland, kids will be desperate to visit Costa Daurada's legendary theme park, PortAventura (portaventura.com). There are five lands to explore – China, the Far West, Polynesia, Mexico and the

Above: Peñon d'Ifach, La Ciudad de las Artes y de las Ciencias. Opposite: Costa Brava.

Spanish Pyrenees

The Parc Nacional d'Aigüestortes is a beautiful tapestry of peaks, forests, lakes and streams offering wonderful walking trails, particularly around Lake Sant Maurici. Further west lies Baquera-Beret (baqueira.es), a popular ski resort with over 40 pistes. During summer, children aged six and above can take part in an excellent activity programme including team games, horse riding, archery, craft workshops and picnics in the mountains. For older children and teens there's canyoning, whitewater rafting, climbing and hiking. Nearby Vall d'Aran is the perfect place to spot some of the Pyrenees' rare butterflies and perhaps even glimpse a golden eagle or bearded vulture. Further west still, in the province of Aragón, the Pyrenees reach their most dramatic in Parque Nacional de Ordesa – a rugged melange of peaks, canyons and densely wooded valleys.

Mediterranean. With no less than eight loop-the-loops, the Dragon Khan roller coaster used to be the ultimate thrill ride at PortAventura, but then along came Furius Baco, which accelerates its passengers from 0 to 135 kph in three seconds. More stomach-clutching moments are available on Hurakan Condor, a 42-storey free-fall tower. Families with younger children will find plenty of softer options, including the Sea Odyssey submarine ride and spinning Armadillos. In addition to three on-site hotels, PortAventura also boasts the Caribe Aquatic waterpark, so it looks like you'll be spending at least two days here.

Costa del Azahar, Costa Blanca & Costa Cálida

The sun-drenched beaches of the Costa del Azahar, Costa Blanca and Costa Cálida attract millions of holidaymakers each year. In the north of Valencia, the main resorts of Costa del Azahar include Benicassim, Oropesa and Peñíscola, which has a fortified old town enclosing a maze of narrow streets. There's an Aquarama (aquarama.net) waterpark in Benicassim, while inland

attractions include the ruined medieval castle of Morella. Further south, boats carry visitors through the flooded subterranean passages of the Coves de Sant Joseph, while Sagunt has the remains of an ancient fortress dating back to Roman times. Aside from being a departure point for ferries to the Balearic Islands (see page 128), the regional capital of Valencia is home to the futuristic Ciudad de las Artes y de las Ciencias (cac.es) which contains a hands-on science museum, IMAX cinema, planetarium and aquarium. Following the coastal road south, you reach L'Albufera, a freshwater lake that supports over 250 bird species. The Cap de la Nau marks the transition to the Costa Blanca with the resort of Dénia offering a mixture of sandy and rocky beaches. The Costa Blanca's most dramatic landmark, the 332-m-high limestone bluff of Peñon d'Ifach, rises above the harbour town of Calp from where you can take a boat trip to admire the impressive coastline. A short distance inland, the mountain village of Castell de Guadalest is a popular day trip from resorts along this stretch of coast.

Andalucía Sunny southern Spain

For sheer variety, Andalucía is hard to beat. Even if you opt for a beach holiday on the Costa del Sol, that still puts you within range of excursions to the lofty wilderness of the Sierra Nevada and the cultural gems of Ronda and the Alhambra. Further west, Seville and the Parque Nacional del Coto Doñana make a great city break/safari combo, while the Costa del Sol itself has several options for beach-free days, from the caves at Nerja to the Rock of Gibraltar.

Alhambra palace.

Seville

Andalucía's beautiful capital is rich in heritage and most of its historical highlights are within easy walking distance of each other. Just how much you see in the way of Moorish and Renaissance architecture, however, will depend on your children. You can always use Isla Mágica (islamagica.es) as a bargaining tool – an outing to this theme park with its roller coasters, waterslides and free-fall towers on Isla de la Cartuja is easily worth a day of sightseeing in return. Start with Seville

66 99 **Up in the foothills of the Sierra Nevada, the tracks linking the villages and pastures provided ideal avenues of exploration for our children. We passed men leading donkeys and working threshing machines, while just 40 minutes away were the busy resorts of the Costa del Sol.**

Mike Wynne, Walks Worldwide

Cathedral (catedraldesevilla.es), a vast Gothic creation built on the site of a great mosque. Originally built as a minaret in 1198, La Giralda now serves as the cathedral's belltower. Designed to accommodate a man on horseback, 35 ramps help smooth the climb to the top. Back at street level, explore the maze of narrow streets in Seville's historic centre (on foot or by horse-drawn carriage). Pause to admire the exotic royal palace, Real Alcázar (patronato-alcazarsevilla.es), before finding a tapas bar to sample some traditional Andalucían fare. Next, head west to Torre del Oro in the adjacent district of El Arenal. This Moorish tower contains a small maritime museum and is also the starting point for cruises on the Guadalquivir. If your kids need to burn off some energy, make instead for Parque de María Luisa.

Ronda

Just half an hour's drive from the Costa del Sol (see opposite), Ronda is the most visited of Andalucía's *pueblos blancos* (white towns). However, it's

worth contending with the crowds of day trippers simply to see Ronda's spectacular clifftop setting – the Puente Nuevo bridge spanning a 100-m-deep cleft to link the old town with the new.

Granada

Although young children won't necessarily appreciate the Romanticism or subtle beauty of the Alhambra, this incredible medieval Arab palace – the best preserved in the world – is something you simply have to show your kids. A large complex of palaces, pools and patios with gardens at one end and a ruined fortress at the other, the Alhambra demands at least a full morning or afternoon. Your tickets will show an allocated time when you are allowed to enter the most famous section known as the Palacios Nazaríes. Highlights here include the Salón de Embajadores, a sumptuously decorated throne room, and the Patio de Arrayanes, a peaceful courtyard with a long rectangular pool reflecting the graceful arches of surrounding arcades. At the western end of the Alhambra, children will relish the chance to explore the more rugged 13th-century Alcazaba fortress where they can climb the Torre de la Vela for stunning views of the Sierra Nevada.

Sierra Nevada

Home to mainland Spain's highest mountain, Mulhacén (3482 m), and a haven for various endemic plants and rare butterflies, the Sierra Nevada has been protected as a national park since 1999. It also boasts Europe's southernmost ski resort – Solynieve (Pradollano), at 2100 m – which has a good range of pistes and a half-pipe. Las Alpujarras, a region of fertile valleys dotted with almond orchards, vineyards and olive groves on the range's southern flanks, is an ideal place to introduce children to a rural and non-commercialized part of Spain. Based in one of the region's Moorish-style villages you can explore the mountains on foot, horseback or bike.

◉ **Inside** info

▸▸ Stretching from Málaga to Gibraltar, the Costa del Sol receives on average around 300 days sunshine a year.
▸▸ Avoid queues at the Alhambra by booking tickets in advance at alhambratickets.com.
▸▸ For further information, log on to andalucia.org.

Kids' top 10 Costa del Sol

❶ **Find** the best beaches, whether you want lots of action at Torremolinos or something more low-key at Torre del Mare.

❷ **Escape** into the mountains of the Sierra Nevada for cool air, cool views and cool mountain biking or horse riding.

❸ **Spot** film stars and celebrities in Marbella (marbella.com). Ogle their luxury yachts in the marina, browse stylish shops in the old town and then hit the beach at Playa de Don Carlos.

❹ **Conquer** the 450-m-tall Rock of Gibraltar (gibraltar.gi) and meet the famous Barbary macaques, Europe's only wild primates (pictured below). Then take to the sea on a Dolphin Safari (dolphinsafari.gi) in search of whales, dolphins and porpoises in the Straits of Gibraltar.

❺ **Delve** underground into the Cuevas de Nerja (cuevadenerja.es), a spectacular cave system where a 32-m-tall limestone column in the Hall of the Cataclysm is recognized as the world's largest.

❻ **Learn** about sea turtle conservation at the SeaLife Centre (sealifeeurope.com) in Benalmádena.

❼ **Discover** the unspoilt beaches of Cabo de Gata, a nature reserve in Almería province that can be visited from the resort of San José.

❽ **Reach** new speeds on the waterslides at Aqualand (aqualand.es) in Torremolinos where highlights include the 22-m free-fall Kamikaze, an artificial surf beach and the rubber ring Boomerang ride.

❾ **Enjoy** the fun of the fair at Benalmádena's Tivoli World (tivoli.es).

❿ **Go** east to find the Wild West at Almería's Mini Hollywood, a spaghetti western movie set where you can watch staged shoot-outs.

ⓗ **Wetland** wonder

A 50,000-ha wilderness of marshland, sand dunes and scrub woodland, Parque Nacional del Coto Doñana is located south of Seville. Rarities include the imperial eagle, purple gallinule and Spanish lynx. An important stopover for migratory birds, including the greater flamingo, the wetlands of the Coto Doñana recede during summer making it easier to spot mammals like deer, boar and wild cattle. Access is by guided tour only, although several visitor centres on the park's outskirts provide birdwatching opportunities and nature trails. At the Centro de Visitantes El Acebuche there's an exhibition, café and shop.

Balearic Islands Holiday heaven in the Med

Renowned for inexpensive package holidays, fine beaches and lively nightlife, the Balearic Islands are well-established family favourites. However, there's more to this Mediterranean archipelago than crowded sands and wild nightclubs. The islands of Mallorca, Menorca, Ibiza and Formentera have a diversity to suit all tastes – from the cultural sights of Mallorca's capital to the quiet, unspoilt beaches of Menorca and Formentera. Accommodation ranges from boisterous resorts to rustic farmhouses, while children will find no shortage of activities both on and off the beach.

Mallorca

Best beaches Mallorca's coastline is dimpled with countless coves including those at Cala d'Or, Illetes and along the rugged west coast. The island also has several longer stretches of beach, the most desirable being on the dramatic northern peninsula where Platja de Formentor is lapped by calm turquoise water.

Best activities Snorkelling is excellent from any of the island's rocky coves, while birdwatching is rewarding during spring and autumn when migrant species use the S'Albufera wetlands as a stopover. Illa Dragonera, a tiny island off the west coast, is a lovely spot for a picnic and a walk; for more challenging hikes look to the mountains of the Serra de Tramuntana.

Best parks For wild and wacky water rides choose from Western Park (westernpark.com) in Magaluf, Aqualand (aqualand.es) in both Magaluf and El Arenal, and Hidropark (hidropark.com) at Puerto de Alcudia. Just west of Palma, Marineland (marineland.es) has dolphin and sea lion shows, while the Auto-Safari Park near Portocristo provides close encounters with giraffes, rhinos and monkeys.

Best days out Mallorca's capital, Palma, has a new aquarium (palmaaquarium.com), which combines well with a visit to the cathedral and the 14th-century Castell de Bellver. A series of spectacular caverns on the east coast, the Coves del Drac, can be explored by boat and on foot, while further north the Cuevas de Artà exit dramatically on to the open sea.

Menorca

Best beaches Many of the north coast beaches, like Cala Pregonda, are deserted gems, accessible only by boat or on foot. One of the most popular resorts, Cala Santa Galdana, overlooks a beautiful crescent-shaped cove on the south coast, while just to the west, Cala en Turqeta has aquamarine water, sea caves and shady pines.

Best activities Don't expect as much in the way of watersports and beach facilities as you find on Mallorca and Ibiza. Boat trips are an ideal way of exploring Menorca's beautiful and unspoilt coastline, while pony trekking along the island's rural tracks is available from horse-riding centres at Maó, Ferreries and Ciutadella.

Best parks The Los Delfines Aquapark (aquacenter-menorca.com) is located at Ciutadella.

Best days out Bronze Age ruins are scattered throughout the interior of Menorca. Some of the larger, more impressive ones, like Trepucó and Torre den Gaumes, are worth visiting with children, but not in the heat of midday. Combine them with a beach visit or a trip to Ciutadella or Maó – both of which have interesting harbours and café-lined squares.

Ibiza & Formentera

Best beaches A busy resort, with a sandy beach, safe swimming and plenty of watersports, Es Canar is a family favourite on Ibiza. With fine sand and sparklingly clear water, the sheltered bay of Cala Vadella promises excellent swimming and snorkelling, as well as boat trips. On Formentera, the large, sandy sweep of Platja de Migjorn boasts excellent facilities.

Best activities Glass-bottom boat trips operate from several beaches on Ibiza, including lively Sant Antoni where Club Náutico de Sant Antoni also offers sea kayaking and sailing tuition. For birdwatching, head to Estiny Pudent, a saltwater lagoon on Formentera where flamingos mingle with herons, stints and other waterbirds during late summer and autumn.

Best parks Waterparks on Ibiza include Aqualandia at Cap Martinet and Aguamar at Platja den Bossa.

Best days out Cycling is possible on both islands (route leaflets are available from tourist offices), while horse riding is offered by Ibiza's numerous stables. Formentera is just an hour's boat ride from Ibiza's south coast.

Cape Formentor, Mallorca.

Canary Islands All-action archipelago

The Canaries have a split personality. At one extreme you could bake yourself on a beach for two weeks, eat English food and restrict your sightseeing to discos and waterparks, while at the other you could go truly wild, whale watching, climbing volcanoes, learning to scuba-dive and hiking through ancient forests. There's a huge range of things to see and do in the archipelago, but the three characteristics that all four major islands share in abundance are sun, sand and sea. Quite simply, there is nowhere better in Europe to plan a winter beach escape with the kids.

Dunas de Maspalomas.

Gran Canaria

Third largest of the Canary Islands (after Tenerife and Fuerteventura), Gran Canaria receives over three million holidaymakers each year. Most zip down the motorway on the island's east coast to resorts like Playa del Inglés, Maspalomas and Puerto Rico where apartment blocks and high-rise hotels crowd golden-sand beaches. Activities in the sunny south range from windsurfing (steady breezes at Playa del Inglés and Pozo Izquierdo) to camel riding. Just north of Maspalomas, Aqua Sur

◉ **Inside** info

›› Regular flight and ferry services operate between the three islands in the Eastern Province, while rental cars are available at airports and ferry terminals.
›› Sea temperatures range from 18°C during winter months to 25°C in summer.
›› For further information, log on to grancanaria.com and turismolanzarote.com.

(aqualand.es/grancanaria) is one of the biggest waterparks in the Canary Islands with no fewer than 33 waterslides. You'll find a roller coaster and other jollities at nearby Holiday World, while go-karting (for children as young as five) is available at San Agustíns Gran Karting Club. For a triple whammy of themed days out you can witness a Wild West shoot-out at Sioux City, performing parrots at Palmitos Parque and crocodile shows at Agüimes' Crocodilo Park.

After that lot you'll either need a week recovering on the beach or else you will be yearning to see a more natural side to the island. If it's the latter, Spirit of the Sea (dolphin-whale.com) offers two-hour cetacean-spotting cruises from the harbour in Puerto Rico. Alternatively, you could make tracks across the Dunas de Maspalomas, a spectacular swathe of sand dunes sandwiched between Playa del Inglés and Maspalomas.

However, the two areas where Gran Canaria really

shakes off its package-holiday image are along the cliff-strewn west coast and in the central highlands. Allow at least a full day to explore the rugged volcanic interior of the island. Not only are there several traditional mountain villages to visit, but there are also numerous possibilities for walks, including a moderate 6.5-km hike to the base of Roque Nublo – a dramatic basalt spire. In the north of the island, you'll find plantations of orange, mango and papaya trees in the valleys around Agaete and exotic plants at the botanical garden in Tarifa.

Las Palmas, Gran Canaria's capital, is also worth a visit. In addition to Museo Elder (an interactive science museum and IMAX theatre), kids will be intrigued by the Guanches mummies on display in Museo Canario and the exploits of Christopher Columbus depicted in Casa de Colón. That's assuming, of course, you can drag them away from the city's beach – a 3-km curve of enticing sand.

Roque Nublo in the mountainous heart of Gran Canaria.

Timanfaya, Lanzarote.

Lanzarote

Arid, barren and windswept, Lanzarote's volcanic interior has a stark and haunting beauty. Children probably won't notice the lack of trees on the island – they'll be too mesmerized by the volcanic carnage wrought by the Montañas del Fuego in Parque Nacional de Timanfaya. Can you imagine their faces when your guide demonstrates how the volcano is dormant, not extinct, by shoving sticks into a crevice where they instantly ignite? And that's after you've ridden camels up the cinder-strewn slopes for spectacular views across the park's ochre-red volcanic cones. Timanfaya is an essential day trip on Lanzarote, but you will spend most of your

time on the coast. The majority of visitors stay in Puerto del Carmen, a sprawling resort with hotels, bars, restaurants and discos, but none of the high-rise brashness that has blighted parts of Tenerife and Gran Canaria. Another good family option is Playa Blanca at the southern tip of Lanzarote, where you'll find hidden coves and gorgeous stretches of golden sand. The north of the island is also worth exploring. Visit the old capital of Teguise on Sundays to buy handicrafts at the weekly market, before continuing on to Cueva de los Verdes, a 6-km-long lava tube that you can explore on guided tours. The nearby Jameos del Agua lava caves have been cleverly landscaped to incorporate a restaurant and swimming pool.

Fuerteventura

Compared with the other main islands in the Canaries, tourism is still in its infancy on Fuerteventura. The two most

popular resorts are in the south at Península de Jandía and in the north at Corralejo. Both have spectacular beaches, although Corralejo has the added attraction of a massive belt of sand dunes. The former fishing village also boasts the Baku Water Park (bakufuerteventura. com), glass-bottom boat trips to the tiny offshore Isla de los Lobos and a 40-minute ferry service to Lanzarote. A popular day trip in the south, Oasis Park (lajitaoasispark.com) in La Lajita combines an animal park, garden and camel farm.

Corralejo, Fuerteventura.

Kids' top 10 Tenerife

1 Burrow through tunnels of *laurisilva* (ancient forests of laurel and myrtle) that festoon the slopes of the Anaga Massif in the east of Tenerife.

2 Spot pilot whales and dolphins on a boat trip out of Las Américas (choose an operator that follows guidelines for minimizing disturbance to the whales).

3 Experience the thrill of scuba-diving at Los Gigantes Diving Centre (divingtenerife.co.uk), which offers two-hour Discover Scuba adventures (minimum age 14 if accompanied by a parent or guardian).

4 Talk to the animals at Loro Parque (loroparque.com) in Puerto de la Cruz, where you'll find the world's largest collection of parrots, as well as a breeding colony of penguins.

5 Track down a dragon tree at Parque del Drago in Icod de los Vinos.

6 Splash out at the waterpark Aqualand Costa Adeje (aqualand.es/tenerife) or take a dip in the natural saltwater pools along the coastline of Puerto de la Cruz.

7 Ride a camel at El Tanques Camello Centre or a pony at the Oasis del Valle in the Oratava Valley.

8 Climb Mount Teide, the highest point in the Canary Islands at 3718 m – or at least have a good scramble on its volcanic slopes. Keep an eye out for Teide Eggs – magma boulders created by the same principles that make snowballs grow when rolled downhill. Families with young children can opt for the eight-minute cable-car ride to within 160 m of Teide's summit.

9 Sample as many beaches as possible. Some of the island's most family-friendly include Playa de las Teresitas (1.5 km of imported Sahara sand, close to Santa Cruz de Tenerife and sheltered by a breakwater), El Médano (2-km stretch of golden sand fringed by calm, shallow waters, perfect for windsurfing) and Playa Fanabé (Blue Flag beach with lots of watersports).

10 Visit Siam Park, one of Europe's largest waterparks, Thrill rides include the Dragon, Volcano, Tower of Power (a 28-m vertical drop slide), a six-lane racing slide and rapids galore. Wave Palace boasts the world's largest artificial waves reaching a height of 3 m), while more placid waters can be found on the Mai Thai lazy river ride. Siam Park also has a superb Thai-themed cocktail of aquariums, restaurants, a sea lion cove and even a floating market.

» Siam Park, T+34 (0)902-060000, siampark.net. Apr-Oct, daily 1000-1800, Nov-Mar, daily 1000-1700, €28/adult, €18/child (3-11).

Main pic and top: Mount Teide. Above: pilot whale. Above right: Laurel forest.

66 99 The path burrowed into a mossy tunnel of overhanging trees. It was shadowy and quiet, the air tinged with the loamy odour of decay. Occasionally sunlight penetrated the canopy, splashing colour across the forest floor, or a gap in the trees would be filled with a bright filigree of waves breaking on the coast far below.

Will

Portugal Lisbon & beyond

Few families look further than the Algarve when it comes to holidaying in Portugal, and who can blame them? Not only is it largely sheltered from cool Atlantic winds and ocean currents, but its coastline is notched with a glorious succession of sandy coves and beaches, some of which have smugglers' den written all over them. There's also an endless variety of boat trips to choose from, as well as a good range of family-friendly accommodation. So why even consider going to Lisbon instead? Well, for starters, the Portuguese capital has plenty to appeal to youngsters, particularly at the Parque das Nações. However, it's only when you start contemplating a few days in Lisbon as the prelude to an island odyssey in Madeira or the Azores that the Algarve begins to seem less of a foregone conclusion.

Pradrão dos Descobrimentos, Lisbon.

Lisbon

There are three main areas in Lisbon worth visiting with children. The most central is the city's hilltop citadel, Castelo de São Jorge. This huge walled compound contains the tiny neighbourhood of Santa Cruz do Castelo as well as the Inner Battlements – a kind of castle-within-a-castle where children can scamper between watchtowers and gaze across

 Inside info

» The Lisboa Card (askmelisboa. com) includes free public transport and admission to museums and monuments.
» Save money at the Parque das Nações by purchasing a Cartão do Parque, which provides free entry to the Oceanarium and Knowledge Pavilion, a return ride on the cable car and a discount on bike rental.
» For further information, log on to visitlisboa.com.

the rooftops of the city below. Originally a Moorish fort (but captured by Afonso Henriques in 1147), the castle is believed to be the site of Lisbon's earliest settlement, dating as far back as the 6th century BC. However, the period of Portuguese history that is most likely to capture the imagination of kids is the Age of Discovery. Belém, Lisbon's westernmost suburb, reached by tram 15 from the city-centre square of Praça da Figueira, is home to the 52-m-tall Pradrão dos Descobrimentos monument depicting famous Portuguese mariners, such as Vasco da Gama and Magellan. Standing at the prow of the sculpture, with a caravel in hand, is Henry the Navigator, while on the pavement nearby a huge world map is etched with the routes taken by the explorers during the 15th and 16th centuries. A monument to the wealth of the Age of Discovery, the beautiful Mosteiro dos Jerónimos, set

a little way back from the waterfront at Belém, contains the tombs of Vasco da Gama and Henry the Navigator. Two museums in the monastery's west wing cover archaeology, shipbuilding and navigation but be sure to leave time to visit the nearby Torre de Belém, a wonderful 16th-century defensive tower on the River Tagus with battlements, watchtowers and a dungeon.

Oceanário
Parque das Nações, T+351 (0)21-891 7002, oceanario.pt. Year round, daily from 1000, €11/adult, €5.50/child (4-12), €26.50/family.
» Vermelha Metro to Oriente station. Lisbon's leisure hot spot, Parque das Nações (parquedasnacoes. pt) is a guaranteed hit with children. Built on the site of the city's Expo 98 world fair, the parque boasts gardens, restaurants, shops, the impressive canopied Portugal Pavilion and even a cable car

Algarve coast.

running along its length to the 145-m-tall Torre Vasco da Gama. The highlight, however, is Oceanário, one of the world's largest aquariums, and one of the most imaginatively designed. Based on a Global Ocean theme, its central exhibit comprises a giant 7-m-deep aquarium from which four distinct zones radiate. These cover the North Atlantic, Antarctica, temperate Pacific and tropical Indian Ocean – from both above and below the surface. One moment you are watching sea otters frolicking on a rocky shore; the next you're peering through the swaying fronds of a kelp forest. Look out for star appearances from penguins, sea dragons, wolf eels, cuttlefish, manta rays and blacktip sharks. The Pavilion of Knowledge or Ciência Viva (pavconhecimento.pt) will also captivate kids. Permanent exhibitions at this science centre include Exploratorium where you can touch a tornado and make a gigantic bubble, and the Unfinished House where three- to six-year-olds can grapple with construction tools and scamper over scaffolding.

Kids' top 10 The Algarve

1 **Discover** beach heaven at Lagos, exploring the small, sheltered bay of Praia de Dona Ana, hemmed in by cinnamon-coloured sandstone cliffs, or revel in the space of 4-km-long Meia Praia, the Algarve's longest beach. A short distance to the east of Lagos, the combination of golden beach and lively nightlife at Portimão's Praia da Rocha will appeal to teenagers.

2 **Cruise** through the myriad waterways of the Parque Natural da Ria Formosa (ilha-deserta.com), spotting birds and collecting shells on a deserted island. Alternatively, explore the reserve on foot by walking the 3.2-km São Lourenço nature trail across saltwater marshes and lagoons.

3 **Snorkel** in the shallows off Albufeira's Praia da São Rafael, a beautiful sandy bay surrounded by cliffs and rock formations riddled with caves. Located in front of the old quarter of Albufeira, Praia dos Barcos is renowned for its fleet of colourful fishing boats.

4 **Surf** on the Atlantic coast at Praia do Armado, Carrapateira, or seek out calmer waters in the rock pools at low tide.

5 **Paddle** a canoe on the Alvor Estuary (outdoor-tours.net), hauling out on a tidal sandbank for a game of beach volleyball and a swim.

6 **Ride** a high-speed RIB (rigid inflatable boat) out of the marina at either Lagos or Portimão in search of dolphins, orcas and sharks. Dolphin Seafaris (dolphinseafaris.com) offers daily 90-minute trips.

7 **Stalk** the battlements of Silves Castle, a Moorish stronghold built on the site of a Roman fort, and then visit the excellent Museu Arqueológico in the town below.

8 **Sail** in search of smugglers' caves aboard the *Santa Bernada* (santa-bernarda.com), a replica of a 500-year-old Portuguese *caravela*.

9 **Plan** a day at the park, taking your pick from theme parks like Zoomarine (zoomarine.com), A Cova dos Mouros (minacovamouros.sitepac.pt) and Krazy World (krazyworld.com) or waterparks such as Aqualand Algarve (aqualand.pt) near Alcantarilha.

10 **Escape** the crowds by heading north to Praia de Odeceixe, a stunning Atlantic beach that's perfect for sandcastle-building, body boarding or a walk at low tide. Curling behind the beach, the estuary of the River Seixe is ideal for canoeing and there are cafés and a beach shop nearby.

Ragged-tooth shark at Oceanário.

Cable-car ride in Funchal.

Terra Nostra Gardens.

São Miguel coastline.

Madeira

A dot in the Atlantic, 608 km from Morocco and almost 1000 km from Lisbon, Madeira is a subtropical gem with year-round appeal. In Funchal, the island's capital, children will enjoy setting sail on a replica of Columbus' *Santa Maria*. Whale watching off the coast is also rewarding with almost guaranteed sightings of fin, sei, sperm and pilot whales during summer months. Don't miss the cable-car ride to Monte or the famous street toboggan ride back down again. Swimming is possible along Funchal's Lido Promenade or you could head east to Santa Cruz where the Praia das Palmeiras has a children's play area and pedal boats for hire. Highlights on Madeira's north coast include the natural rock pools at Porto Moniz and the São Vicente Caves where you can explore 700 m of lava tunnels. At Santana there's a theme park devoted to the history, science and traditions of Madeira, while hardy walkers will find plenty of challenging trails in the island's rugged interior. For a 30-minute taster, try the straightforward trail between Rabaçal and the Risco Waterfall. If even that sounds too much like hard work, nip over to Porto Santo, a small island lying 37 km to the northeast of Madeira and boasting a superb 9-km beach.

The Azores

Scattered some 1300 km west of Lisbon, this isolated archipelago will appeal to adventurous families who enjoy walking and island hopping. Each island has its own character and special appeal. Starting in the west, Flores is one of the most beautiful, with hydrangea hedgerows lacing the island in bright cerulean each July. Graciosa is renowned for the Furnas do Enxofre, a sulphur lake located in a cave beneath the island's Caldeira. On Faial, the historic port of Horta is worth a day of exploration, as is Capelhinos, where an eruption in 1957 added 2 sq km to the island. With its dramatic sea cliffs and deep valleys covered in lush vegetation, São Jorge is a magnet to walkers, as is Pico with its challenging ascent of Ponta do Pico. Whale watching (particularly for sperm whales) is also excellent from Pico, with three-hour boat trips from Lajes available from Espaco Talassa (espacotalassa.com). On Terceira, highlights include the World Heritage Site of Angra do Heroísmo, a town that once formed the hub of Atlantic trading routes. The twin volcanic lakes of Sete Cidades – one blue, one green – can be found on São Miguel, the largest and most diverse of the islands. However, be sure to also visit Gorreana, the site of Europe's only tea estate, and the spa town of Furnas where you can see bubbling mud pools and hissing vents. Nearby Terra Nostra Gardens is a haven of exotic flora, while a drive out to Nordeste on the east coast provides wonderful clifftop views. Dramatic scenery is also a drawcard for Santa Maria. This peaceful island has terraced vineyards at Maia and, unusually for the Azores, a white sandy beach at Praia Formosa.

◉ **Inside** info

▸▸ The nine islands of the Azores range in size from 17-sq-km Corvo to 746-sq-km São Miguel; the five Madeiran islands cover an area of roughly 795 sq km.
▸▸ For further information, log on to madeiratourism.org or visitazores.org.

❝❞ As soon as I got in the water and put my head under, there were dolphins everywhere, making clicking noises and moving around a lot. I saw six in front of me playing. It was really good. The sea was very deep!

Henry (age 10)

🌊 **Swim** with wild dolphins

The Dolphin Connection (dolphinconnectionexperience.com) offers holidays swimming with wild dolphins in the Azores, where it is not uncommon to meet pods of up to 200 individuals. Each 10-day trip includes six three-hour boat trips. The recommended minimum age is seven years old and all children (and adults) are given snorkel training in a pool prior to venturing into the open ocean. Professionally trained guides (with RLSS Aquatic Rescue certification) are always on hand to help children develop snorkelling confidence, while local experts provide talks on the biology and conservation of the archipelago's renowned whales and dolphins.

Spain & Portugal Grown-ups' stuff

When to go
If possible, try to visit Spain and Portugal during May, June or September to avoid the blistering heat and tourist crush of midsummer. In the south, you can often rely on decent weather as early as April or as late as October – although the sea will be warmer, especially around the **Balearic Islands**, during the latter period. If you have no choice but to visit southern Spain in the peak summer season, remember that you can retreat to the mountains to escape excessive heat. The Atlantic-facing Costa de la Luz in **Andalucía** receives cooling breezes, as do parts of the **Algarve**. Despite the **Canary Island's** celebrated year-round sunshine, the island's geography does create local variations. For example, between late autumn and early spring you can experience frost in Tenerife's El Teide National Park during the morning and be sunbathing on Playa de las Américas by the afternoon. The south of the island is sunnier than the north where trade winds bring more cloud and rain. Generally speaking, though, the archipelago has enviable weather with ample sunshine, little rain and an average annual temperature of 23°C. In the **Azores**, locals will tell you to expect all four seasons in one day. In general, expect warm temperatures (up to 27°C in summer, dropping to around 13°C in winter) and a chance of rain in any month. Visit between May and September if you are keen to go whale-watching, sailing or fishing. Walking is good year-round, but to witness the island's famous azaleas and hydrangeas in flower, June and July are best.

Getting there
One of the most inexpensive ways of reaching Spain or Portugal is by charter flight, although departure and arrival times are not always ideal. For **scheduled flights**, Iberia (iberia.com) has the most extensive network in the region. Starting prices (including taxes) for return flights from Heathrow include Madrid (£112), Barcelona (£102), Seville (£104), Tenerife (£169) and Mallorca (£162). Iberia also flies from several regional airports in the UK, as well as Dublin and the United States. British Airways (britishairways.com) serves several destinations on the Iberian peninsula. SATA Air Açores (sata.pt) operates a direct service from London Gatwick and Dublin to São Miguel in the Azores, as well as flights from Lisbon, Madeira, Toronto, Boston and Montreal. For **budget flights** to Spain and Portugal you're spoilt for choice, with a wide range of UK regional airports covering the region. easyJet (easyjet.com)

serves Madrid (from Bristol, Edinburgh, Gatwick, Liverpool and Luton), Bilbao (Stansted), Barcelona (Bristol, Gatwick, Luton, Liverpool, Newcastle and Stansted), Lisbon (Bristol, Gatwick, Liverpool and Luton), Faro (Bristol, East Midlands, Gatwick, Liverpool, Luton and Newcastle) and Funchal (Bristol and Stansted) in addition to various routes to Alicante, Almeria, Ibiza, Mahon, Malaga, Murcia and Palma. Ryanair (ryanair.com) has an equally comprehensive network with flights to Alicante, Almeria, Barcelona, Faro, Feurteventura, Jerez, Madrid, Malaga, Murcia, Palma, Santander, Tenerife and Valencia. Air Berlin (airberlin.com) serves Barcelona, Malaga and Ibiza, while Thomsonfly (thomsonfly.com) has many flights to the Balearic and Canaries, as well as to Alicante, Barcelona, Faro, Lisbon, Malaga and Valencia.

Getting around
Trains operated by RENFE (renfe.es) provide a high-speed service between Madrid and other cities such as Seville and Barcelona. **Buses** also provide a relatively efficient service between major towns in both Spain and Portugal, but you will need to hire a **car** to explore off the main routes. Major car-hire companies are represented in most cities and airports, including Avis

Sunny smiles – beach life in Spain and Portugal.

Skip the flight

›› **Sail across the Bay of Biscay** from the UK to northern Spain. Services operate between Portsmouth and Bilbao with P&O Ferries (poferries.com) and between Plymouth and Santander with Brittany Ferries (brittany-ferries.co.uk).

›› **Take the train** from London to Madrid or Barcelona, using Eurostar (eurostar.com) to Paris and then changing to a sleeper service to Spain. Bookings can be made online at Rail Europe (raileurope.co.uk).

›› **Catch a ferry** from Spain to the Balearics with Iscomar (iscomar.com) with departures from Barcelona, Valencia and Dénia. Trasmediterránea (trasmediterranea.es) operates ferries to both the Balearic and Canary Islands. High-speed catamarans are used for the shorter routes, while on longer journeys the ferries have many of the facilities you'd expect on a cruise liner, such as a swimming pool, restaurants and cinema. Book online with Direct Ferries (directferries.co.uk).

(avis.com), Europcar (europcar. com) and Hertz (hertz.com). Unless you take organized coach trips, car hire is also essential for getting around the Balearics, Canaries and Azores. In the Balearics, inter-island **ferry** services are operated by

Trasmediterrínea (see right). Island hopping in the Canaries is possible with connections by plane, ferry and jetfoil. All of the islands in the Azores are linked by the domestic airline SATA (see left) and Transmaçor ferries (transmacor.pt).

ⓘ **Fact** file

Country	Time	Language	Currency	Exchange rate approximate	International dialling code	Tourist information
Spain	GMT+1*	Spanish	Euro €	£1 = €1.15	+34	spain.info
Portugal	GMT**	Portuguese	Euro €	£1 = €1.15	+351	visitportugal.com

*Canary Islands GMT, **Azores GMT-1

Spain & Portugal Grown-ups' stuff

Accommodation
You can choose from a vast range of accommodation in Spain and Portugal, from family hotels, luxury resorts and villas to apartments, farmstays and holiday villages. One of the most economical options for families is to rent a **rural house** (*casa rurale*) where you can expect to pay around €400 per week for a simple village property to €1000-plus for something more luxurious with a pool and garden. Try Colours of Spain (coloursofspain. com) for an online directory, or book through regional associations such as RAAR (raar.es) in Andalucía; Ruralia (ruralia.com) in Asturias; and Ruralverd (ruralverd.com) in Catalonia. Casas Cantabricas (casa.co.uk) offers self-catering properties and small, family-run hotels in northern Spain, Pyrenees Accommodation (pyreneesaccommodation. com) has a selection of family hotels in the Spanish Pyrenees and Inns of the Canary Islands (innsofcanaryislands.com) has a portfolio of character accommodation on Tenerife and other islands in the Canaries.

For **city breaks**, try Madrid B&B (madridbandb. com) for two- and three-bedroom apartments in Spain's capital, Loving Barcelona (lovingbarcelona.com) for apartments in Catalonia's trendy

urban hot spot and Hotel Real Palacio (realpalaciohotel.com) for a central location and good children's facilities in Lisbon.

For **seaside villas** with pools, try James Villa Holidays (jamesvillas.co.uk), which offers properties in Mallorca and the Algarve from as little as €440 per villa. Meon Villas (meonvillas. co.uk) and Simply Travel (simplytravel.co.uk) also have a good selection. To make your money go even further, book a package with an operator like First Choice (firstchoice.co.uk) or Thomson (thomson.co.uk).

Camping is another excellent option for the budget-conscious. Canvas Holidays (canvasholidays.co.uk), Camping Life (campinglife. co.uk), Eurocamp (eurocamp. com), Keycamp (keycamp.com) and Siblu (siblu.com) represent all the region's best sites.

Food & drink
Eating out is a family affair in Spain and Portugal and it's not unusual to see children in restaurants late at night. Some highly salted dishes are not advisable for babies and toddlers, but that still leaves plenty of choice particularly if you pick and mix from a tapas menu with its breads, dips and other goodies. Some regional specialities to tempt adventurous children include *botifarra amb mongetes* (Catalan sausages and white beans),

Life revolves around the pool at a family villa on the Algarve.

66 99 In the Azores, try *pudim naõ sei*, which translates as 'pudding with no name'– it resembles something that one of Pico's earthquakes might do to a load of chocolate mousse, sponge cake, peaches and cream.
Will

gazpacho (chilled tomato soup), *tortilla Española* (a thick potato and onion omelette), *frango assado com piri-piri* (a spicy chicken dish from the Algarve), *leitão à bairrada* (roasted suckling pig, popular

Kids' top 10
tapas nibbles

1 *Almendras* Fried and salted almonds.

2 *Calamares fritos* Squid rings and tentacles dusted with flour and fried in olive oil.

3 *Chorizo* Sausage flavoured with paprika and garlic.

4 *Costillas* Spare ribs.

5 *Croquetas* Deep fried croquettes made with chopped ham, chicken or fish.

6 *Diabolitos picantes* Spicy mini hamburgers.

7 *Gambas a la plancha* Prawns.

8 *Soldaditos de Pavia* Cod fingers fried in batter.

9 *Patatas bravas* Fried potatoes with a spicy red sauce.

10 *Tortilla Española* Potato and onion omelette.

in Portugal) and *empanadas* (pastry parcels stuffed with tuna or ham). Don't forget to try *paella*, Spain's famous rice dish with beans, tomato, paprika and either meat or seafood.

Health & safety
Spain and Portugal are generally safe countries to visit. The European Health Insurance Card (EHIC) entitles you to emergency medical treatment. Drinking water is safe and standards of food hygiene are generally good. Be wary, however, of tapas dishes that may have been left out for a while or reheated.

Seafood snack – *gambas a la plancha*.

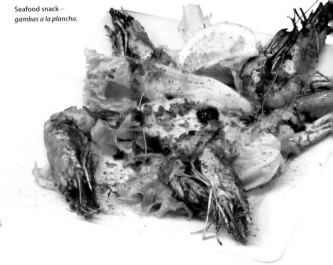

Spain & Portugal Family favourites

Cambrils Park.

Cambrils Park

Where? Salou, Costa Daurada.

Why? This beautifully landscaped holiday park has a fantastic pool complex with waterslides and squirting elephants! On-site facilities include tennis, football, minigolf and a Tiger Club for five- to 12-year-olds, while the beach (800 m away) has a range of watersports. Self-catering is a piece of cake thanks to the park's bakery and supermarket, and there's also a restaurant and takeaway for eating out.

How much? From around €450, based on two adults and up to three children sharing a two-bedroom Esprit+ holiday home for seven nights.

Contact Siblu Holidays, T+44(0) 871-911 2288, siblu.com.

Camping Cabopino

Where? Costa del Sol.

Why? Eurocamp not only offers discounts to single-parent families, but its easy-going camping holidays are the ideal place for both children and adults to meet new people, whether popping to the shop for baguettes in the morning or lazing around the pool. Children, meanwhile, will also enjoy making friends at the free kids' clubs.

How much? From around £435 for two adults and up to four children under 18 years for seven nights in a mobile home, including return Dover to Calais ferry crossings.

Contact Eurocamp, T+44(0) 844-406 0402, eurocamp.co.uk.

Casa Olea

Where? Priego de Córdoba, Andalucía.

Why? Tucked into the heart of Andalucía, halfway between Córdoba and Granada, this luxurious six-room guesthouse is surrounded by ancient olive groves and provides an authentic experience of rural Spain. The nearby riverside woodland is teeming with wildlife, including wild boar. Casa Olea is perfect for a walking or mountain-biking holiday exploring local villages, while home comforts include stylish bedrooms, a swimming pool and sun terrace and delicious locally-sourced food.

How much? From around €80 per room, including breakfast, plus €10 for an extra child's bed.

Contact Casa Olea, T+34 696-748209, casaolea.com.

Spain & Portugal Family favourites

Cal Rei Petit

Where? Puerto Pollenca, Mallorca.

Why? Just five minutes' drive to sandy beaches, this three-bedroom villa has mountain views and is surrounded by beautiful gardens with olive and fig trees. As well as a swimming pool, family-friendly touches include a modern well-equipped kitchen, stair gates and air-conditioning.

How much? From €616 per week, including car rental.

Contact Mallorca Farmhouses, T+44 (0)118-947 3001, mfh.co.uk.

Hotel Presidente

Where? Portinatx, Ibiza.

Why? Located in a quiet, family-friendly part of Ibiza, away from the nightclubs, Hotel Presidente is surrounded by pine trees and overlooks a beach. Some of the hotel's 270 rooms sleep four and there's also a free kids' club for three- to 12-year-olds.

How much? B&B from around €1200 for one week in August, based on two adults and two children sharing a room.

Contact Hotel Presidente, T+34 971-320576, hotelpresidenteibiza.com.

Finca el Almendrillo

Where? Granada, Andalucía.

Why? Set in lovely countryside, Finca el Almendrillo sleeps up to 20 is well placed for visiting either Granada or the coast. Superbly equipped for parents, you'll find everything from high chairs to bottle sterilizers. There's also a fenced-off pool, a courtyard for riding bikes, a local goat farm and horse riding.

How much? From around €2450 per week.

Contact Finca el Almendrillo, T+34 620-525739, granada-farmhouse.com.

The Balearics beckon – you're never far from a stunning beach in Mallorca.

Tennis academy at La Manga Club.

La Manga Club

Where? Costa Calida.

Why? One of the world's best holiday destinations for active families, La Manga runs junior sports academies in golf, tennis, football, dance, rugby, karate and cricket. Other activities include scuba-diving, waterskiing, horse riding, sailing, quad-biking and kayaking.

How much? A two-bedroom View Apartment in the family-friendly Hyatt Las Lomas Village costs from around €150 per apartment per night.

Contact La Manga Club, T+34 (0)968-331234, lamangaclub.com.

Pine Cliffs Resort

Where? Albufeira, Algarve.

Why? Pine Cliffs offers a range of family-friendly accommodation, from two-bedroom apartments to four-bedroom villas with private pools. The resort's Porto Pirata for children has wooden ships, a swimming pool, remote-control boats, a playground, bouncy castle, bicycle track, volleyball pitch and an 18-hole minigolf course.

How much? Expect to pay around €3300 during peak season for a week's B&B for two adults and one child.

Contact Pine Cliffs Resort, T+351 (0)289-500300, pinecliffs.com.

Tour operators

In the UK
The Adventure Company
adventurecompany.co.uk

Club Med
clubmed.com

Eurocamp
eurocamp.com

Families Worldwide
familiesworldwide.co.uk

First Choice Holidays
firstchoice.co.uk

Freewheel Holidays
freewheelholidays.com

Headwater
headwater.com

Individual Travellers
individualtravellers.com

Keycamp
keycamp.com

Mark Warner
markwarner.co.uk

Portuguese Affair
portugueseaffair.com

Powder Byrne
powderbyrne.com

Siblu
siblu.com

Spanish Affair
spanishaffair.com

Sunvil
sunvil.co.uk

Thomson Holidays
thomson.co.uk

In the USA
Abercrombie and Kent
abercrombiekent.com

Adventures by Disney
abd.disney.go.com

Tauck Bridges
family-travel.tauck.com

Thomson Family Adventures
familyadventures.com

Pigeons in the Piazza – flights of fancy in
St Mark's Square, Venice. Right: The giant
hand of Constantine, Rome.

Italy

Contents

149 Introduction

150 Kids' stuff

152 Tots to teens

154 **Rome**
156 City escapes

158 **Tuscany**
158 Siena
158 Leaning Tower
of Pisa
158 Lucca
160 Florence

162 **Venice**

166 **The Lakes**
166 Lake Garda
167 Milan

168 **Umbria
& Le Marche**
168 Assisi
168 Perugia

170 **Puglia**
170 Bari & Trani
170 Alberobello
170 Lecce
170 Otranto

172 **Bay of Naples**
172 Naples
172 Pompeii
173 Sorrento & the
Amalfi Coast

174 **Sicily**

175 **Sardinia**

176 **Grown-ups'
stuff**

Largest Lake
Garda
370 sq km

Mont Blanc

Lake Maggiore

Lake Como

4

Turin

○ **Milan**

Lake Garda

3

Verona
Po
Padua

○ **Venice**

○ **Parma**

Highest mountain
Mont Blanc
4807 m

○ **Genoa**

Bologna

Longest river
Po 650km

Ligurian Sea

2

○ **Lucca**

Florence

SAN MARINO

○ **Pisa**

Conero Peninsula

○ **Siena**

Lake Trasimeno

Perugia
○ **Assisi**

Adriatic Sea

Elba

ITALY

5

Corsica (France)

Tiber

Tremiti Islands

ROME □ **1**

Gargano Peninsula

6

○ **Bari**

Naples Vesuvius

Sardinia

○ **Lecce**

metres
3000
2000
1000
500
200
0

Tyrrhenian Sea

N

100 km
100 miles

○ **Cagliari**

Stromboli

Aeolian Islands

Ionian Sea

○ **Palermo**

Taormina
Mt Etna

Sicily ○ **Catania**

7

○ **Syracuse**

Mediterranean Sea

◎ Did you know?

- At least 5000 animals and gladiators were killed during the Colosseum's 123-day inaugural games in AD 90.
- Venice has 116 islands and 409 bridges.
- You can walk around the Vatican, the world's smallest country, in less than an hour.
- The world record holder of the fastest time to eat a 12-inch pizza is not Italian, but a Belgian called Tom Waes who took 2 minutes 19.91 seconds.

Introduction

1 Find out how ancient Romans lived

▶▶ Rome, page 154

2 See the Leaning Tower of Pisa

▶▶ Tuscany, page 158

3 Explore the canals of Venice

▶▶ Venice, page 162

4 Swim and sail on Lake Garda

▶▶ The Lakes, page 166

5 Go medieval in a hill town

▶▶ Umbria & Le Marche, page 168

6 Relive the days of Pompeii

▶▶ Naples, page 172

7 Stand on an active volcano

▶▶ Sicily, page 174

It's one of those places you have to visit at least once in a lifetime – but should you leave Italy until the kids are older and more likely to appreciate its cultural and historical treasures? Of course not! Kids love Italy, and Italians love kids. Not only are the locals barmy about *bambinos*, but they also know a trick or two when it comes to feeding them. With a staple diet of pizza, pasta and pastries (supplemented, of course, with copious *gelato*), your children should have more than enough energy for at least a taster of Rome, Florence or Venice (Italy's triumphant trio of World Heritage cities). Don't be bamboozled into thinking you've got to see all the museums and ancient sites, and pay homage to every Michelangelo masterpiece – experiencing Italy has just as much to do with spending an afternoon in a piazza, lingering over lunch, playing around the fountain and, you guessed it, pillaging the local *gelato* parlour. Beyond the cities, Italy's beautiful countryside encompasses rolling hills, mountains and lakes – perfect for a relaxed break in a villa with a pool. There's no shortage of beaches for more traditional family holidays, while locations like Naples and Sicily add a bit of spark to sightseeing days, courtesy of Vesuvius and Mount Etna.

Italy Kids' stuff

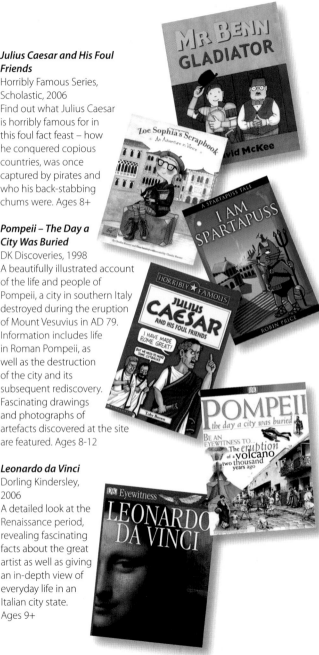

Mr Benn – Gladiator
Andersen Press, 2005
Mr Benn's adventures always see
him visiting a costume shop,
choosing an outfit and then
travelling to that era via a special
door. This time Mr Benn turns
gladiator. But can the gentle
character steel himself to join
in with such violent games?
Ages 4+

Zoe Sophia's Scrapbook:
An Adventure in Venice
Chronicle Books, 2006
Zoe Sophia and her dog, Mickey,
embark on the adventure
of a lifetime when they visit
great aunt Dorothy in Venice.
Zoe's scrapbook brings the
enchantment of Venice to
life, with its gondolas and
glassblowers. But when Mickey
gets lost in the maze of canals,
the excitement really begins.
Ages 6+

I Am Spartapuss
Mogzilla, 2005
This humorous series is set
in Rome in AD 36, when the
mighty Feline Empire ruled the
world! Spartapuss, a ginger cat,
becomes imprisoned by the
evil emperor Catligula and is
finally released into a school
for gladiators. Spartapuss must
fight and win his freedom in
the Arena before his opponents
make dog food out of him!
Ages 8+

Julius Caesar and His Foul
Friends
Horribly Famous Series,
Scholastic, 2006
Find out what Julius Caesar
is horribly famous for in
this foul fact feast – how
he conquered copious
countries, was once
captured by pirates and
who his back-stabbing
chums were. Ages 8+

Pompeii – The Day a
City Was Buried
DK Discoveries, 1998
A beautifully illustrated account
of the life and people of
Pompeii, a city in southern Italy
destroyed during the eruption
of Mount Vesuvius in AD 79.
Information includes life
in Roman Pompeii, as
well as the destruction
of the city and its
subsequent rediscovery.
Fascinating drawings
and photographs of
artefacts discovered at the site
are featured. Ages 8-12

Leonardo da Vinci
Dorling Kindersley,
2006
A detailed look at the
Renaissance period,
revealing fascinating
facts about the great
artist as well as giving
an in-depth view of
everyday life in an
Italian city state.
Ages 9+

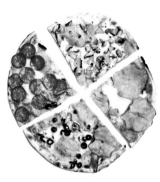

Taste of Italy
perfect pizza

Pizzas are plentiful throughout Italy, and making them from scratch at home – base and all – is a lot simpler than you might think.

What you need
» 1 tsp dried yeast
» 1 tsp sugar
» 150 ml warm water
» 225 g plain flour
» Tomato sauce such as passata or tomato paste
» Grated cheese
» Favourite toppings such as tuna, ham, mushrooms, sweetcorn, olives and pineapple

What to do
» Mix the yeast, sugar and water. Leave to rest in a warm place for about 10 minutes (until the yeast and sugar has dissolved).
» Add flour and mix to make a firm dough, adding extra flour if required.
» Roll out to make your pizza base.
» Bake for about 10 minutes at 180°C.
» Spread the tomato sauce over the base and then add the grated cheese and other toppings.
» Bake for 10-15 minutes at 180°C depending on the thickness of the pizza base.

Make a mosaic
» Study examples of Roman mosaics in books and on websites.
» Decide on the picture or pattern you want to create. Roman mosaics often featured animals or geometric designs.
» Draw your design on to card.
» Cut up small pieces of coloured paper, magazines or comics. Sort them into colour groups.
» Stick them on to your design, thinking carefully about where you place the colours to highlight the details of your design.

Play camicia
You can play this Italian card game with a normal set of 52 cards, or use an Italian pack (often 40 cards). This is a game of pure luck for two players. The aces, twos and threes are the attack cards (suits are ignored).

» Deal out the cards evenly.
» Players take turns to place their top card face-up in a pile on the table. If the card is normal, no action is taken and play passes to the other player.
» When an attack card is played by one of the players, the other player has to add to the exposed pile the number of cards corresponding to the face value of the attack card – that is one card for an ace, two cards for a two, and three cards for a three.
» If all the cards played in response to an attack are normal, the attacking player takes the pile of played cards and adds them to his or her hand. If one of the cards played in response to an attack is an attack card itself, the former attack is finished, and the new attack takes place.
» The player who runs out of cards is the loser.

Italy Tots to teens

Kids are welcome everywhere in Italy. You will have no problem getting them to adapt to the local cuisine (assuming, of course, they like pizza, pasta and ice cream), while accommodation ranges across the entire family-friendly spectrum, from campsites and holiday villages to beach resorts and self-catering villas. If there's one potential fly in the *gelato* it's that major tourist attractions can become very crowded and unbearably hot during the summer – so try not to overdo the sightseeing.

Tuscan toddler.

Babies

Italy promises a well-earned rest for new parents. Most hotels offer babysitting if you arrange it in advance, but a far more relaxing alternative is to rent a villa. Self-catering might not sound like much of a rest, but it suits a lot of new parents desperate to maintain feeding and sleeping routines. If renting a car, check that the safety standards of any children's seats provided are up to scratch or, better still, consider bringing your own. Don't forget sunshades for car windows. With

66 99 Italian piazzas are great places to go with kids. They're lined with restaurants, and a lot are car-free so the kids can run around in safety – and in view – while parents enjoy a drink or a meal. We always found waiters happy to make space for high chairs, which most restaurants had.

Jason Hobbins

a baby in tow you're unlikely to want to embark on an ambitious sightseeing tour of Rome (in fact, you'd be wise to avoid all Italian cities during the fierce heat of midsummer). However, even a modest medieval town in Tuscany can reduce you to a gibbering wreck trying to cajole a pushchair along its cobbled streets and pavements. To preserve sanity, take an all-terrain three-wheeler buggy or a backpack-style baby carrier.

Toddlers/pre-school

That villa with a pool still sounds very tempting with children of this age. However, you do need to be extra-vigilant about pool safety: holiday villages may well have fenced-off pools and lifeguards on duty; private villas may well not. For a seaside holiday, Italy has no end of lovely beaches to choose from, especially in Sicily, while the northern Lakes offer a freshwater alternative (just remember to pack jelly shoes for the kids so they can negotiate the pebbly beaches). Historical and cultural sights are always a

challenge with children of this age. The concepts of queuing, keeping quiet in cathedrals and art galleries, staying behind security barriers and not mauling priceless works of art are all completely alien to them. This doesn't necessarily mean that your Italian sojourn need be culturally bereft. Car-free city piazzas can provide toddlers with (supervised) freedom while you admire the façades of the *duomo* (cathedral) or the *palazzo*. And you can always take it in turns to sightsee – one parent entertains the kids while the other snatches an hour or two of Bernini browsing.

Kids/school age

In Italy, vast swathes of the school curriculum come to life. Few places are more synonymous with famous artists, brilliant minds and ancient cultures. The food is an education in itself; the language is fun to learn; and to top it all, Italy scores top marks on the geography front, with everything from volcanoes to vast limestone caverns. There

Gondolas on the
Grand Canal, Venice.

Special needs

An increasing number of hotels, restaurants, monuments and galleries are installing facilities, such as ramps and lifts, to assist wheelchair users. CO IN Sociale (coinsociale.it) provides information and assistance for disabled travellers in Rome. For excellent advice on accessible travel around Venice, try Informahandicap Venezi (comune.venezia.it) which provides several ideas for 'itineraries without barriers'.

Single parents

Eurocamp (eurocamp.co.uk), Keycamp (keycamp.ie) and Siblu (siblu.com) offer special deals for single parents at their holiday camps in Italy. Most also have babysitting services or activity clubs (for toddlers to teens) where you can sit back and relax while the kids are entertained.

is a downside though. Few museums and galleries have the special children's facilities or activities that you find in northern Europe. Nor is there much in the way of hands-on science centres. At this age they at least have the potential to enjoy a full day's sightseeing; and if not then you can always resort to bribery (a double scoop of *gelato* for the *duomo* and we'll throw in a waterpark for the Renaissance exhibition). Don't forget, though, that there is far more to Italy's heritage than shuffling around daunting museums and galleries. Most kids will leap at the challenge

of climbing the steps to the top of a medieval bell tower, while sites like Pompeii and the Colosseum instantly ignite a child's imagination. And then, of course, there's all the purely fun stuff, from theme-park rides at Gardaland in northern Italy to snorkelling in the crystal-clear coves of Sicily.

Teenagers

Although sometimes a little too far off the beaten track for their liking, villas (with chill-out pools) are still a good option for teens – particularly if they bring along a friend or two.

Holiday parks and resorts, with their clubs and activities, are also a good bet. Pick a location that provides a couple of teen mainstays, such as a city for shopping and nightlife and a beach or lake for watersports and hanging out with mates. As for sightseeing, you might find that teenagers are more in tune with their iPods than the Italian Renaissance. If it's wow factor they need, concentrate on the big sights in Venice and Rome. The Adventure Company (adventurecompany.co.uk) and Explore Worldwide (explore. co.uk) offer teenage departures on their trips to Italy.

Rome Those about to sightsee, we salute you!

Touring Rome with kids requires a gladiatorial effort. It's a hot, sprawling, chaotic city packed with ancient monuments, museums, churches and galleries. Throw in the Vatican and it will feel like two city breaks rolled into one. But before you sidestep Italy's vibrant capital, just think what you will be missing: Michelangelo's Sistine Chapel ceiling, the Pantheon, the Roman Forum, the Colosseum... kids will feel like time travellers as they explore these historical icons. Just make sure you don't enslave them in a non-stop history lesson – Rome's lighter side (*gelato*, fountains, parks, shopping, etc) will help to ensure your conquest of the city is enjoyable as well as informative.

Trevi Fountain.

Three-day action plan

» Day 1 Start with the Colosseum. It opens at 0900 and can be reached by Metro Line B to Colosseo station, as well as by bus or tram. It's not only big and impressive, but it's the one sight in Rome that children are most likely to relate to – especially teenagers

who have watched Russell Crowe strut his stuff in *Gladiator*. You can join an organized tour or explore the ruins on your own. Be sure to stand centre stage where warriors, slaves and wild beasts engaged in deadly combat nearly 2000 years ago. Try to imagine the roar of the 70,000-strong crowd, and don't miss the maze of tunnels and pens

where lions, tigers and other animals were held prior to the slaughter. About 200 cats still prowl the Colosseum – challenge your kids to see how many they can spot.

Now that your children are fired up about ancient Rome, take them to see the adjacent Roman Forum (Foro Romano), a patchwork of ruined triumphal arches, basilicas and temples that once formed the city's civic and ceremonial heart. You can access it from Via Dei Fori Imperiali, but kids will grasp the layout better if you walk up the small hill behind the Colosseum and enter the Forum by the Arch of Titus on Via Sacra – the street along which victorious commanders paraded their spoils of war. Don't even attempt to see everything in the Forum. By now it will be approaching midday and you'll be getting hot and hungry. Make a beeline for the House of the Vestal

Virgins and the vaulted Basilica of Constantine and Maxentius, then hop in a taxi or bus (or walk if you have the energy) to Piazza Navona. Built around three flamboyant Baroque fountains, this beautiful square is lined with palaces and pavement cafés, and is usually bustling with street performers and artists. It's a great place to boost your children's energy levels aided, no doubt, by *tartufo*, a chocolate ice cream, fudge and cherry concoction served at Tre Scalini. From Piazza Navona, it's a short walk to the Pantheon, the best-preserved ancient building in Rome, where kids will be intrigued to discover an 8.3-m-wide hole (or *oculus*) in the dome. From the Pantheon, take bus route 116 to Villa Borghese, a large park where kids can rent bikes and boats or ride ponies – just rewards for all that sightseeing earlier in the day.

▸▸ **Day 2** By now, the Vatican City will seem irresistible, but you're risking cultural overload (and rebellion) by taking kids to the city state straight after a day hotfooting it around ancient Rome. Save the Vatican for your third day and keep day two relatively laid-back. Teenagers may want to check out

the big names in *haute couture* along Via Conditti or scour Via del Corso for anything from CDs to shoes.

Nearby is the famous Trevi Fountain which is particularly beautiful when floodlit at night. Don't forget to toss a coin into the fountain, throwing it over your shoulder to ensure a safe return visit to the Eternal City. A little further north, the rococo monument of the Spanish Steps (ablaze with azaleas in May) is another popular spot from which to soak up the city's atmosphere. The best *gelato* in the Trevi neighbourhood is at San Crispino on Via della Panettaria, while pick of the pizzas can be found at Pizzeria da Ricci on Via Genova.

Afterwards, assuming you can stomach it, wander over to the Capuchin Crypt on Via Veneto where the bones of dead monks adorn the walls. Alternatively, for something equally macabre, head south along Via Appia Antica to visit the Catacombs (catacombe.roma. it) – a labyrinth of cemeteries where roughly hewn and dimly lit corridors are lined with tomb niches. Some, like the Catacombs of San Domitilla, still contain human bones.

Best of the rest

Galleria Borghese
This small museum in the Villa Borghese gardens contains an exceptional collection of Bernini sculptures, as well as paintings by Raphael and Caravaggio. Reserve tickets online at galleriaborghese.it.

Musei Capitolini
Located on Capitoline Hill, these two magnificent museums contain some of Rome's greatest treasures. In Palazzo Nuovo, look out for the famous sculpture of the *Dying Galatian* and the original second-century, bronze statue of Emperor Marcus Aurelius astride his horse (a replica is in the star-shaped *piazza* between the two museums). In the Palazzo dei Conservatori kids will be wowed by the outsize body parts from the Colossus of Constantine and intrigued by the bronze, Lo Spinario, which depicts a boy trying to remove a thorn from his foot.

Museo Nazionale Romano
Split into two sites, the National Museum of Rome houses outstanding Classical art, including the inspiring mosaic of the *Four Charioteers*.

◉ **Inside** info

▸▸ The three-day Roma Pass (romapass.it) offers free admission to the first two museums and/or archaeological sites visited and full access to public transport.
▸▸ Bring binoculars so kids can see the details on the ceiling of the Sistine Chapel.
▸▸ For further information, visit romaturismo.it, and vatican.va.

Rome Vatican City

» Day 3 The Vatican might only cover an area of 43 ha, but what the world's smallest state lacks in size it more than makes up for with historical, cultural and religious esteem. The quickest way to get there is by Metro Line A to Ottaviano San Pietro, from where it's a short walk to St Peter's Square. This vast papal-audience ground is flanked by the 284 columns of Bernini's Colonnade (great for hide and seek) and punctuated at its centre by an obelisk brought from Egypt in AD 37. But inevitably you will be drawn towards the massive façade of St Peter's Basilica, the world's largest church. Doors open daily at 0700, but you won't be allowed inside wearing sleeveless tops, shorts or above-knee-length skirts. Suitably

attired, steer your children towards the first nave on the right where Michelangelo's exquisite marble carving, Pietà, depicts a grief-stricken Mary cradling the crucified body of Jesus. For children, one of the highlights of a visit to the Vatican is to climb St Peter's 136.5-m-high dome from where there are superb views across the rooftops of Rome. You can take a lift part of the way, but that still leaves you with some 330 steps.

By now your kids will be developing a healthy respect for Michelangelo (St Peter's dome was his design), but if there's one Michelangelo masterstroke that you've simply got to show them, it has to be the ceiling art of the Sistine Chapel. To reach it you need to navigate the immense art treasury of the Vatican Museums. It's a 20-minute walk from the entrance of the museum

complex to the Sistine Chapel without even pausing to admire the wealth of Roman antiquities and Renaissance paintings. What, if anything, you decide to linger over will depend on how your children are bearing up and how much queuing you've had to endure. Ultimately, though, those nine colourful scenes from *Genesis* (which took Michelangelo four painstaking years to complete, mostly while lying on his back at the top of a scaffold) are usually enough to lift the eyes and the spirits of even the most jaded child.

Below: Michelangelo's Pietà.
Opposite: St Peter's Church; interior of the dome; St Peter's Square.

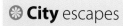

☸ City escapes

Tivoli
Located 28 km east of the city, this country escape for ancient Romans has temples and gardens, but is best known for nearby Hadrian's Villa, a lovely place to picnic or explore.

Acquapiper
Cool relief from city sightseeing, Acquapiper waterpark (aquapiper. it) is located on the road to Tivoli.

Lake Bracciano
This large crater lake set in beautiful countryside to the northwest of Rome is ideal for a refreshing swim during summer.

Tuscany Leaning towards Pisa?

A beautiful Tuscan villa set amongst cypress trees and vineyards, a day or two marvelling at the art treasures of Florence and a lazy tour between historic hilltop towns like San Gimignano. No wonder Tuscany is one of Italy's best-loved destinations. But won't kids find it too sophisticated? Or just plain boring? Not if the villa has a pool and you transform your cultural forays into an adventure trail of medieval streets to be explored, bell towers to be conquered and *gelato* to be sampled.

Siena.

Siena

At 102 m in height, the Torre del Mangia is one of the tallest medieval towers in Italy. Challenge your kids to climb the 505 steps to the top from where there are superb views across Siena's medieval maze of lanes and *piazzas*. Afterwards, relax with a picnic on the Piazza del Campo – you can get supplies from the grocery store down Via di Salicotto. One of Europe's greatest public squares, the fan-shaped Campo has been used for everything from bullfights to executions, but it is now famed for its Palio, a fiercely contested bareback horse race that takes place twice a year. Nearby, the Piazza del Duomo is dominated by Siena's magnificent Gothic cathedral, which contains sculptures by Michelangelo.

Leaning Tower of Pisa

Piazza Duomo, opapisa.it. Apr-Sep, daily 0830-2000, Oct-Mar (times vary), cathedral and *piazza* €2/person (free for under-10s), tower €15/person.

Italy's most recognizable landmark, the Leaning Tower of Pisa has immense appeal to children. The ultimate stack of building blocks teetering on the brink of collapse, there's something intrinsically childlike about the eight-storey belfry. Recent engineering work stabilized the 12th-century wonky wonder, reducing its lean to around 5 m from the vertical. It's now safe to climb the 294 steps to the top, but only as part of a 30-minute guided tour (minimum age eight). Most people contemplate the tower (and the splendid *duomo* and baptistry) from the lawns of the Campo dei Miracoli – a lovely spot for a picnic. If your kids are crestfallen because they're too young to climb the tower, try to placate them with the medieval alternative in the northwest corner of the Campo – it's free and there's no age limit.

Lucca

Founded by the Romans in 180 BC, Lucca's crowning glory is the 11th-century cathedral of San Martino – unless, of course, you're an opera fan in which case you will want to call in at Puccini's birthplace on Via di Poggio. Children, on the other hand, will be drawn to Lucca's massive 16th-century ramparts which encircle the town and are wide enough for you to walk or cycle on – a popular elevated circuit shaded by overhanging trees. To the northeast of Lucca, Collodi has a Pinocchio theme park (pinocchio.it) in recognition of the fact that Carlo Lorenzini penned the story of the wooden puppet here in 1881.

◉ Inside info

≫ Trains are quick and efficient, but a hire car is the best way to explore Tuscany's backroads and hill towns.
≫ The compact city centre of Florence is easily explored on foot.
≫ Siena's Palio horse race takes place on 2 July and 16 August.
≫ For further information, log on to firenzeturismo.it, terresiena.it, pisaturismo.it, and luccaturismo.it.

Best hill towns

Children will feel like they've walked into a fairy tale (or a scene from *Lord of the Rings*) in San Gimignano (sangimignano.com). No fewer than 14 weather-beaten stone towers (originally there were 72) rear above a skyline that has remained largely unchanged since the Middle Ages. For the best views, scramble up the ramparts of the Rocca, a ruined 14th-century fortress tucked into the eastern side of the town. Torre della Diavola (She-Devil's Tower) houses the Museo della Tortura, containing enough gruesome torture instruments to make children squirm with delight.

In the far east of the region, Cortona (cortona.net) has all the sweeping views, medieval alleyways and Renaissance art that you'd expect from a Tuscan hill town. What sets it apart from the others, though, is its rich Etruscan heritage, evident in the many ancient tombs dotting the surrounding countryside. You can see artefacts from this early civilization, including an oil lamp dating back to the 5th century BC, in the Museo dell'Accademia Etrusca. Follow Via S Margherita to the Fortezza Medicae – the views towards Lake Trasimeno make it worth the steep climb. Other hill towns worth visiting include Montepulciano and Montalcino.

Best beaches

Not far from Pisa or Lucca, the sandy beach resort of Viareggio has a promenade lined with cafés and shops. There's more sand to the north at Forte dei Marmi, while the best beaches on the island of Elba – reached by ferry from Piombino – are on the west coast.

Defying gravity – the Leaning Tower of Pisa.

Kids' top 10 Florence

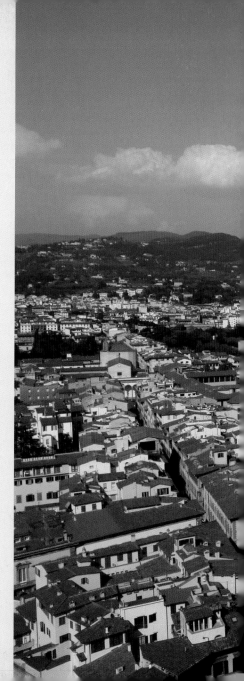

1 Rise above it all by climbing the orange-tiled dome of the *duomo* (or adjacent *campanile*) for stupendous views and then, back at ground level, marvel at the famous bronze doors of the baptistry and the colourful Byzantine mosaics that decorate the ceiling above the cathedral's font.

2 Plan a treasure hunt in the Uffizi (uffizi.firenze.it), ticking off at least one painting by each of the following masters: Leonardo da Vinci, Michelangelo, Botticelli, Bellini, Raphael, Rembrandt, Rubens, Van Dyck and Caravaggio. An extra scoop of *gelato* afterwards if you correctly identify *The Birth of Venus* by Botticelli.

3 Grapple with science at the Museo di Storia della Scienza (imss.fi.it), which not only features two of Galileo's telescopes, but also has demonstrations of his experiments on motion. Look out, too, for early maps and globes, and a gruesome collection of 19th-century surgical instruments. An interesting excursion from Florence, the Museo Leonardiano di Vinci (leonet.it) displays wooden models of some of da Vinci's famous inventions, from a flying machine to a tank.

4 Meet Michelangelo's *David*, a 5.2-m statue of the biblical hero who slayed Goliath. The original sculpture is in the Galleria dell'Accademia (where you'll have to pay and queue), so settle instead for the copy in Piazza della Signoria.

5 Reward yourself with *gelato* for every museum, art gallery, cathedral and church that mum or dad drag you into. One of the best *gelato* parlours in the city is Vivolis on Via Isole delle Stinche, where only a triple scoop will do.

6 Indulge in a spot of window-shopping along Ponte Vecchi, the oldest surviving bridge in Florence (built in 1345) and famous for its antiques and jewellery shops.

7 Escape to Boboli Gardens for a game of hide-and-seek amongst the statues, box hedges and cypress trees – or find a shady spot for a picnic.

8 Browse the colourful stalls at Mercato Centrale for fruit, vegetables and flowers, as well as local Tuscan fare, like wild mushrooms, truffles and *porchetta* (roast suckling pig).

9 March over to the Museo Stibbert (museostibbert. it) where a spectacular column of armour-clad knights rides on horseback through a grand hall.

10 Don't stop at *gelato* when there are all kinds of other Florentine sweets and pastries to sample, such as *ricciarelli* (honey and almond cakes dusted with sugar).

Falling for Florence
– taking in the view from
the top of the *duomo*.

Venice Piazzas, palazzos & pigeons

It's going to be busy and expensive – and oppressively hot if you go in summer. And there might be the occasional fraught moment, cajoling your buggy up and down countless bridge steps, restraining your toddler from nose-diving into yet another canal or preventing teenagers from playing havoc with your holiday budget in all the fancy boutiques. But will any of this stop you from going? Of course not. Venice is irresistible – an exciting watery maze, a fantasy city of palaces and churches slowly sinking beneath the waves. Go there soon while it manages to keep its head above water.

Canal art.

One-day action plan

The moment you stroll into Piazza San Marco (St Mark's Square) your children are likely to say one of three things:

» Can we feed the pigeons? No problem. Vendors sell bags of sweetcorn for €1.

» Can we climb up there? Yes. The views from the top of the 98.5-m Campanile are exhilarating, but be prepared to queue. Help kids pass the time

◉ Inside info

» Valid for 12 hours, two days or a week, the Venice Card (venicecard. com) offers unlimited use of public transport, toilets and nurseries, as well as free admission to various museums and cultural sites.
» Venice is joined to the mainland by a causeway, but the best way to arrive is by *vaporetto* (actv.it), a waterbus network linking the city to Marco Polo Airport, Punta Sabbioni (Cavallino), Santa Maria Elisabetta (Lido) and other islands in the lagoon.
» For further information, visit turismovenezia.it.

by challenging them to count the arches in the Palazzo Ducale (Doge's Palace).

» Can we go on a gondola? Maybe. There's a gondola mooring at the edge of Piazza San Marco, but you'll pay a premium rate. For a quicker, cheaper, but less romantic option, *traghetto* gondolas shuttle back and forth across the Grand Canal.

Once you've fed the pigeons and conquered the Campanile, explore the warren of alleyways and canals between Piazza San Marco and Ponte di Rialto (Rialto Bridge), delving into shops along the way. There's a Disney Store near Ponte di Rialto, but if it's fantasy you're after, nothing beats the views of the Grand Canal from the most graceful and famous bridge in Venice. Nearby, you can board a *vaporetto* waterbus for a cruise along the Grand Canal, passing elegant old *palazzos* and famous landmarks like the Accademia (a treasure trove of Venetian paintings) and the

fine Baroque church of Santa Maria della Salute. Vaporetto routes 1 and 82 will take you back to Piazza San Marco. Spend some time admiring the exquisite façade of the Basilica San Marco. Five mosaics adorn each of the doorways to this Byzantine beauty, while the four Horses of St Mark (replicas of the bronze originals kept inside) prance above the main entrance. You may well feel compelled to enter this great building – kids will be entranced by the mosaic floor and the dazzling Ascension Dome – but leave time for the Palazzo Ducale where highlights include a torture chamber.

Other highlights

Museo Storico Navale
(Campo S Biagio) A shrine to ships of every kind, from Chinese junks to a replica of the Doge's ceremonial barge.

Base camp

You could splash out on a converted palace, luxury hotel or even rent a canal-side apartment in Venice, but most budget-conscious families opt to stay outside the city.

Curling out from the mainland towards the east of Venice, the Cavallino Peninsula (turismocavallino.it) – also known as the Litorale del Cavallino – makes an ideal family base. Not only is it packed with holiday resorts, but it also boasts a 15-km stretch of sandy beach and one of Italy's top water parks, known as Aqualandia (aqualandia.it).

While water slides and crazy golf might seem a million miles from your dreamy-eyed vision of Venice, don't underestimate their usefulness as a negotiating tool. The kids get a day at Aqualandia, but only after you've perused the art collections in the Doge's Palace or Accademia.

As for reaching Venice, Cavallino is perfectly placed, with regular boats departing from Punta Sabbioni and taking around 30 minutes to cruise to Ca' di Dio – a 10-minute walk from St Mark's Square.

Museo di Storia Naturale

(Salizzada del Fondaco dei Turchi) Contains an aquarium and a 4-m-tall dinosaur skeleton of *Ouranosauris nigeriensis* discovered in the Sahara.

Glassblowing

Take a ferry to the island of Murano where skilled craftsmen have been forging fine Venetian glass for over 700 years.

Gliding along in a gondola.

Venice Exploring a sinking city

" It's mid-August and we're on a ferry that's more crowded than a Ganges Delta riverboat during rush hour. We're making slow progress to the world's most adult, romantic, couply city. And it's hot – the kind of heat that usually makes kids whingy and clingy. But the voices around me are hushed because the Campanile is coming into view, rising like a giant exclamation mark above a sun-spangled sea.

"Is it really floating on the water?" chime Joe and Ellie, adding a touch of innocent wonder to this most magnificent of city approaches. The six-year-old twins look shocked when I tell them it's actually sinking. As soon as we disembark, Joe stamps on the pavement and Ellie seems reassured.

The queues for the Campanile and Palazzo Ducale are Disneyesque. Not that it matters – all Joe and Ellie want to do is feed the pigeons, which allows their parents ample time to gawp at the head-spinning façades of Piazza San Marco. It's only when an overgenerous handful of birdfood leads to Ellie being mobbed that we tear ourselves away and search for something cooling and calming.

Unfortunately, the gondoliers are charging €150 for a 40-minute punt – €200 if you want to include Rialto Bridge. So instead we delve into the wonderful maze of narrow streets beyond St Mark's Square and feign interest in Gucci handbag shops for quick doses of air-con before the staff get wise and evict us.

The shops selling masks and little glass ornaments captivate the twins – as does the spectacle of Rialto Bridge where day trippers are scrumming down on the parapet, five or six deep, for a glimpse of the Grand Canal. There is something surreal about being wedged in this mêlée of pixel-popping humanity while below you people glide serenely past in gondolas, trailing their fingers in the water... but Joe and Ellie seem genuinely entranced by the graceful curve of *palazzos* and the non-stop bustle of boats.

We extract ourselves from the crowds, buy ice creams and catch a waterbus back to St Mark's Square. There's just time to feed the pigeons again (which are now so bloated they have almost lost the ability of flight) before catching our ferry back to Cavallino.

So is it worth taking young kids to Venice? Of course! Just don't expect a romantic meal at a pavement café or a lingering look inside St Mark's Basilica. Instead, you'll experience the innocent fun of exploring a labyrinthine city floating on water. You'll also introduce your children to one of the world's cultural icons. And you'll spend a lot of money on pigeon food.

Will

Bird grains – feeding the ravenous
hordes in St Mark's Square.

The Lakes Italy's water wonderland

Lake Como is peaceful and relaxed, Lake Maggiore is romantic and sophisticated and Lake Garda is a bustling summer playground. That may be oversimplifying the allure of northern Italy's three major lakes (all share stunning scenery, elegant lakeside towns, a rich historic and artistic heritage and plenty of beaches and watersports), but there's no denying the obvious family appeal of Lake Garda. Largest of the trio, it has over 120 beaches and a wide range of places to stay, from villas to campsites. The medieval fortress town of Sirmione makes a great day out, but the real clincher as far as kids are concerned is Gardaland, Italy's answer to Disney World.

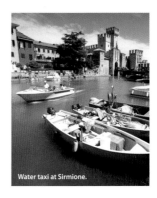
Water taxi at Sirmione.

Lake Garda

Located at the tip of a narrow peninsula protruding from the southern shore of Lake Garda, Sirmione is dominated by the 13th-century castle, Rocca Scaligera. Children will enjoy marching across the drawbridge and storming the towers and battlements, which are almost totally surrounded by water. When they've finished raining imaginary arrows on the tour boats below, lead them down the narrow lane along one side of the ramparts to a string of small beaches – all with good stone-skimming potential. Looping back into the heart of Sirmione you'll find streets and squares lined with galleries, craft shops, pizzerias and *gelato* parlours. Buy an ice cream and sit on the jetty wall, feeding the ducks and watching the ferries come and go. At the tip of the peninsula (which you can reach by following the Passeggiata Panoramica along the eastern shore) are the remains of a vast, sprawling Roman villa known as Grotte di Catullo – a lovely spot to contemplate the lake views.

Another child-friendly highlight in the south of Lake Garda is Gardaland (see right), but it's also worth spending a day or two exploring further north – either by ferry or by driving along the lakeside road. Heading up the west coast, you pass several towns and villages well endowed with medieval churches and castles, neoclassical mansions

and idyllic waterfronts bristling with yachts and launches. Stop at Gardone Riviera to see the fine collection of alpine, Mediterranean and subtropical plants in the Giardino Botanico Hruska before pushing on up to the lake's northern tip where the approach to Riva del Garda is hemmed in by towering cliffs. With its lifeguard-patrolled swimming area and shady lakeside park, Riva is popular with families, while nearby Tobole gets the thumbs up from windsurfing and sailing aficionados. Pretty much everywhere you go, however, you'll find watersports galore from luxury speedboat cruises to banana-boat rides. If it floats, you'll find it on Lake Garda.

If you base yourself on the southeast shore of Lake Garda you are around 40 km from Verona with its spectacular Roman Arena. Love-struck teenagers will no doubt want to swoon over Casa di Giulietta where Romeo is said to have climbed to Juliet's balcony.

⊙ Inside info

» There are good motorway connections between Milan and all three major lakes.
» Lakeside roads can become extremely busy during peak summer months, so use the network of ferries instead (gardanotizie.it/navigarda).
» Beaches are mostly pebbly, so take jelly shoes or wetsuit boots for kids.
» For further information, log on to milanoinfotourist.com, lagodigarda.it, lakecomo.org, and distrettolaghi.it.

◉ Tour Milan

Start by taking the elevator up the dome of the *duomo*. The Roof Terraces are bristling with spires adorned with some 3500 statues depicting saints, animals and monsters. Descend to Piazza Duomo, bearing right towards the vast iron and glass-domed arcade of the Galleria Vittorio Emanuele II. Inside you'll pass shops and cafés before emerging at the other side facing Milan's famous opera house, Teatro alla Scala (teatroallascala. org). A short walk from the

northwest of Milan's historic centre, Castello Sforzesco houses a large art collection, while the adjacent Sempione Park is an appealing green space with a lake.

Nearby Santa Maria delle Grazie is famous for Leonardo da Vinci's masterpiece, *The Last Supper*. Measuring 8.5 m wide and 4.6 m tall, the famous scene can be found above the doorway in what was once the convent's refectory. Reservations are required and a maximum of 25 people are admitted at a time – and only then for 15 minutes viewing. Is it worth it? The painting is in a fragile condition, so see it while you can is one argument. But far more interesting to kids is the Museo Nazionale della Scienza e della Tecnologia (museoscienza. org) on Via San Vittore, where a gallery is devoted to wooden models

of inventions based on Leonardo sketches. The museum also has a wide range of interactive science exhibits covering topics as diverse as acoustics and astronomy. There's not much in the way of English interpretation, but kids will easily figure out what to do.

Other child-friendly museums include the Museo di Storia Naturale and the Planetarium. Both are on Giardini Pubblici – a large city park. If the city gets too much, take the Metro Line 1 to Primaticcio, followed by bus route 64 which passes Aquatica (parcoaquatica.com), a waterpark in Milan operated by Gardaland. Teenage girls, however, will more likely want to stay central in Milan's fiendishly fashionable quadrilatero, where all the top Italian and international designer labels can be found, from Gucci to Prada.

Gardaland

Near Peschiera, T045-644 9777, gardaland.it. Apr-Sep, daily from 1000, Oct, weekends, plus Christmas, from €22/person, €19 for under 10s, free for children under 1 m tall.

Italy's largest theme park, Gardaland is like Disney, SeaWorld and Universal Studios rolled into one. The park has five themes – fantasy, adventure, energy, live shows and the Palablu dolphinarium – but anything goes at Gardaland. One moment you could be floating through the African jungle on the Tunga river cruise and the next you're witnessing a shoot-out at the Rio Bravo Wild West village. From exploring a

pirate ship to delving into the myth of Atlantis, Gardaland will leave your head spinning. As well as the floorless roller coaster, Blue Tornado (right), big rides include Space Vertigo (a 40-m tower drop), Magic Mountain (a loop-the-loop roller coaster) and Sequoia Adventure (a bizarre ride where you spin round and upside down as if you were the chain on a chainsaw). For hot summer visits, there are plenty of water rides with potential for cooling splashes, like Jungle Rapids and Colorado Boat. And there is also plenty to keep little ones happy in Fantasy Kingdom with its train ride, tree house and animal farm. Don't miss 4D Adventure

or the live theatre shows, which include everything from Broadway spectaculars to Gardaland on Ice. More themed fun can be found just up the road towards Lazise, where Caneva World (canevaworld.it) pushes the boundaries of reality even further with its triple whammy of an Aqua Paradise waterpark, a Movieland Studios full of stunt rides and simulators and a Medieval Times arena complete with tournament.

Umbria & Le Marche Escape the crowds

Unlike many of Italy's more visited regions, Umbria and Le Marche have little in the way of gold-star family attractions. There are no must-see Roman arenas, leaning towers or volcanoes – but what you will find is a gentle, rural and unspoilt part of Italy with rolling countryside dotted with medieval castles and hilltop towns, fine stretches of sandy beaches along the Adriatic coast and spectacular national parks in the Apennine mountains. It's the perfect place to relax and experience a less hectic side to Italian life with plenty of the cultural and scenic highlights you'd expect from somewhere like Tuscany, but without the crowds.

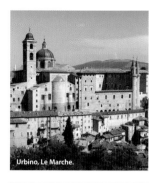
Urbino, Le Marche.

Assisi

If there's one must-see in Umbria, it's this medieval hill town. The magnificent Basilica di San Francesco is renowned for its frescos depicting the life of St Francis, who is buried here. See if your kids can spot the beautiful *Sermon to the Birds*, one of the remarkable Giotto frescos that, like many works of art in the basilica, was carefully restored after the 1997 earthquake. From the basilica, walk to Assisi's main square, Piazza del Comune, for *gelati* on the steps of the fountain. From Assisi, a scenic route climbs the slopes of Monte Subiaso before

descending to Spello where the church of Santa Maria Maggiore has frescos depicting scenes from the New Testament.

Perugia

Umbria's old capital is riddled with narrow medieval streets and there's also a museum containing prehistoric, Etruscan and Roman artefacts. It won't take long, however, before your kids latch on to the fact that Perugia is home to Italy's most famous confectionary. Italian for 'kisses', *baci* are creamy dark chocolates with rich hazelnut centres, wrapped in poetic love notes. Shops along pedestrianized Corso Vannucci are laden with the stuff, but for the ultimate sweet treat you can tour the Baci factory in Perugia's San Sisto suburb. Make arrangements at the tourist information office near the *duomo*. Just 2 km to the west, Città della Domenica (cittadelladomenica.com) is an animal park with various rides and attractions.

Other Umbrian highlights

In the north, Gubbio is a medieval hill town with terracotta-tiled houses and pink-stone palaces set against the thickly wooded slopes of the Apennines. Lake Trasimeno in the west has small sandy beaches and clear warm water, perfect for swimming and watersports, while lakeside towns like Castiglione del Lago offer trips to Isola Maggiore, an island known for its lace-making. Highlights in southern Umbria include the 80-m-high 14th-century aqueduct, Ponte delle Torri, in Spoleto, and the elaborate façade of the *duomo* in Orvieto. To escape into the wilds of the Apennine mountains, head for Monti Sibillini (sibillini.net), a national park with great potential for hiking and horse riding.

Le Marche

To the east of Umbria, Le Marche has the added attraction of almost continuous sandy

⦿ Inside info

>> The A1 motorway between Florence and Rome skirts the western side of Umbria, and there are also good rail and bus links.
>> The A14-E55 and a good rail service link the coastal resorts of Le Marche.
>> For further information, log on to umbria2000.it, and turismo.marche.it.

beaches running the length of its Adriatic coastline. The most picturesque section is the Conero Peninsula, a dramatic seascape of limestone cliffs, sandy coves and turquoise waters. The three resorts in the area, Portonovo, Sirolo and Numana, can get busy in summer, so consider taking a boat trip to one of the quieter coves along the coast. Head inland from Ancona (Le Marche's main town) and you enter the foothills of the Apennines, dotted with medieval towns like Urbino and Ascoli Piceno. Visit the spectacular cave system of Grotte di Frasassi (frasassi.com), the mighty fortress at San Leo and the tiny republic of San Marino (visitsanmarino.com). In the south of Le Marche there are wonderful scenic drives through the Monti Sibillini.

66 99 The countryside is miraculously unspoilt – even in August it was quiet. We managed to balance our need to soak up the atmosphere in some medieval towns (aided by the customary bribe of *gelati*) with swimming and tennis for the children. Eating out is a joy – there's always something on the menu that children will love.

Alison Rippon

Castelluccio di Norcia, Umbria.

Puglia Land of the trulli

Tucked into the heel of Italy, this little-visited province may not have the cultural clout of Rome, Florence or Venice, but what it lacks in notoriety it more than compensates for with a quirky range of monuments – from Neolithic tombs and Gothic cathedrals to the curious *trulli* houses. And even if you are not a culture vulture, Puglia has plenty of rich pickings. Natural highlights include the lovely beaches and forests of the Gargano Peninsula, the spur on Italy's heel, while 20 km offshore lie the Tremiti Islands, an unspoilt cluster of limestone islands.

Alberobello – *trulli*, madly, steeply.

Bari & Trani

Most tourists arrive at this busy Adriatic port to catch a ferry to Greece or Croatia. If you find yourself with a few hours to spare in Bari, head to the old district of Città Vecchia to explore the castle. Also worth a look, Bari's Basilica di San Nicola is one of Puglia's earliest churches (begun in 1087), while further north along the coast, Trani's Norman *duomo* (San Nicola Pellegrino) rises above a harbour filled with blue-hulled fishing boats. One of the most striking of Puglia's monuments can be found inland from Trani on the central limestone plateau

known as Le Murge. Built around 1240, Frederick II's Castel del Monte is a perfect octagon in shape, with a hefty tower at each corner.

Alberobello

A large swathe of this town is pimpled with over 1000 *trulli* – tiny, conical-roofed houses sprouting from narrow streets like stone toadstools. Constructed entirely of local limestone, each circular dwelling is no larger than a garden gazebo; most are whitewashed while a few are daubed with strange pagan symbols. Kids will love exploring this World Heritage Site, particularly since many *trulli* are now used as craft or souvenir shops.

Lecce

Dubbed the Florence of the Baroque, Lecce is renowned for its elaborate architecture. The imposing façade of the 16th-century Santa Croce church is dominated by a large rose window surrounded by

66 99 With its immaculate stone-flagged lanes and elegant houses, Locorotondo commands sweeping views across the Valle d'Itria – dotted with *trulli* and scrawled with the rich terracotta of freshly ploughed soil.

Will

intricately sculpted columns and friezes where saints, dragons and gargoyles crouch in niches like seabirds on a crowded cliff. Lecce is also famed for its papier-mâché figures, often depicting nativity characters.

Otranto

Pleasure boats and fishing trawlers form orderly rows across the turquoise shallows of Otranto's harbour where, 3500 years ago, Mycenaean traders beached their ships. These Bronze Age forays were a precursor to the first Greek colonies in Italy. A scenic route hugs the coast south of Otranto, weaving past medieval

◉ Inside info

▸▸ The historic centres of most towns are compact and easily explored on foot.
▸▸ Buses and trains serve many destinations, but for ultimate flexibility rent a car at one of the region's airports.
▸▸ From Naples, allow three hours to drive to Bari.
▸▸ For further information, log on to pugliaturismo.com.

A fisherman tends to his nets in Trani.

Lecce.

watchtowers, limestone caves and small seaside villages.

Best beaches

Dotted with sandy coves and beaches, the rugged Gargano Peninsula (parcogargano.it) is popular with holidaymakers, as are the Tremiti Islands, accessible by boat from Termoli.

★ **Local** buys

Finely-sculptured papier-mâché figures (often depicting nativity characters) can be found in Lecce. Alberobello is renowned for its rugs and fabrics, and the *trulli* district is also a good place to purchase local pasta and olive oil.

Gargano Peninsula.

Bay of Naples In the shadow of Vesuvius

Italy's third largest city, Naples is hot, crowded and chaotic. Not only are its pavements as congested as its roads, but scooters often fail to distinguish between the two. So why bring kids here? First and foremost, Naples is the jumping-off point for excursions to Pompeii – the most enigmatic ruins you'll find anywhere. And then there's the Amalfi Coast – a bit on the posh side, but nevertheless a fine excuse for beach hopping and a breathtaking coastal drive. But even Naples itself is worth a day or two of sightseeing. If the castles and archaeology museum don't do it for your kids, at least you can introduce them to some of Italy's most authentic pizza and ice cream.

Castel Nuovo, Naples.

Naples

An ideal place to start is Castel Nuovo. Not only does this striking fortress lie at the city's heart, but its ramparts afford views towards Mount Vesuvius brooding across the Bay of Naples. Nearby, in striking contrast, is the Galleria Umberto I with its glass-domed roof built in the late 1800s. Continue walking around Piazza Trieste e Trento to Caffè Gambrinus – the city's prime spot for pastries and ice cream. Kids can then run off their sugar high in the paved expanse of Piazza del

Plebiscito while parents admire the magnificent façade of the Palazzo Reale – once one of the Mediterranean's most important royal courts. A short walk along the seafront leads to Castel dell'Ovo, the oldest castle in Naples, parts of which date from the ninth century. It now shelters a small marina and several popular restaurants.

Located in the heart of central Naples, Spaccanapoli threads a tourist lifeline between numerous churches, statues and historic buildings. A narrow canyon-like street, it is one of the most vibrant parts of the city. Street vendors crowd the cobbles, while shops are crammed with everything from pasta and pastries to Neapolitan masks and clay nativity scenes. Cafés overflow with locals sipping coffee, while open-air restaurants serve delicious pizza Margherita. One church definitely worth visiting on Spaccanapoli is Santa Chiara – if only to relax in its garden-framed cloister, which

is beautifully decorated with hand-painted tiles. At the end of Spaccanapoli, turn right on Via Toledo (Naples' main shopping street) and continue walking up the hill until you reach the Museo Archeologico Nazionale. Must-sees include *Hercules* and other famous statues from the Farnese Collection. Many relics from Pompeii and Herculaneum have also found sanctuary here, including some wonderfully intricate mosaics. There is also a fascinating scale model of the Pompeii excavations – the perfect primer before visiting the actual ruins.

Pompeii

T081-857 5331, pompeiisites.org. Nov-Mar, daily 0830-1700, Apr-Oct, daily 0830-1930, €11/adult, €5.50/youth (18-24), free for under-18s.
» Train Circumvesuviana, stopping at Pompei Scari or Pompeii Santuario. Set the scene for your kids: It's August in the year AD 79. For several days, small earthquakes have shaken Pompeii, but

Inside info

» Calm sanctuaries for frayed nerves include the cavernous nave of the *duomo* and the cloisters of Santa Chiara; for somewhere to let kids run around in traffic-free safety, try Piazza del Plebiscito.
» The Circumvesuviana train service connects Naples with Pompeii and Sorrento.
» For further information, log on to inaples.it, amalficoastweb.com, and guidevesuvio.it.

Positano, Amalfi Coast.

otherwise life in the thriving Roman city continues as normal. Then, on the afternoon of the 24th, Vesuvius suddenly erupts, shooting a column of ash over 30 km into the atmosphere. Fearful of Vulcan, the Roman God of Fire, the people of Pompeii cower at the sight. Then terror and blind panic seizes them as a cloud of superheated, poisonous fumes and volcanic debris sweeps down the volcano killing everything in its path. The eruption lasts 19 hours, by which time Pompeii lies buried beneath 6 m of pumice and ash, while nearby Herculaneum has vanished beneath a deep layer of mud and lava.

Such was the ferocity of the eruption that both settlements were petrified in time. At the excavated ruins of Pompeii, look for cart tracks along Via dell'Abbondanza and visit Modesto's bakery where several loaves of carbonized bread were found. Perhaps too haunting for youngsters, the Garden of the Fugitives contains over a dozen plaster casts of human victims – adults and children – frozen in anguished postures as they succumbed to the onslaught of ash and lethal fumes. There are other areas of Pompeii that you might wish to steer kids away from – particularly the brothels where frescos depict the wares of prostitutes in graphic detail. Otherwise, must-sees include the well-preserved temples, baths and theatres, as well as the House of the Vettii with its colourful friezes.

Frozen in time – a Pompeii victim.

Sorrento & the Amalfi Coast

A dramatic coastline of white limestone cliffs along the southern boundary of the Bay of Naples, the Sorrento Peninsula is not your typical family seaside destination. Villages cling to its precipitous slopes, beaches are few and far between, and much of the accommodation tends to be quite up-market. Nevertheless, Sorrento makes a good base for exploring the surrounding area (including Pompeii and Herculaneum). The town has a range of shops and restaurants, and you can take a boat trip to the island of Capri (35 minutes). Continue around the peninsula and state road 163 begins to twist and turn along the spectacular Amalfi Coast. The fishing village of Praiano and the pastel-tinted houses of Positano, stacked like Lego blocks against the cliffside, are just some of the highlights.

Sicily Melting pot of cultures

Just 3 km from the toe of Italy, Sicily is an island of contrasts where rolling wheatfields, olive groves, vineyards and citrus plantations hold sway beneath the brooding hulk of Europe's largest volcano. While Mount Etna puffs away in the east, holidaymakers seek out Sicily's sandy beaches or explore its wealth of archaeological sites – a rich legacy of the many civilizations that have left their mark on this fiery and fascinating island.

Thar she blows – Etna erupts (again).

Volcanoes

Constantly simmering and regularly boiling over in spectacular pyrotechnic displays of bright red sparks and molten lava, 3370-m Mount Etna is one of Italy's most impressive (and unexpected) sights. Not only is it Europe's largest volcano, but it is also one of its most active. Parents might be a little alarmed to discover that it's possible to step foot on the slopes of Etna. Few volcanoes, however, are more closely monitored and, as long as you arrange a guided tour, you should be safe. Take the Circumetnea Train (circumetnea.it) from Catania to Nicolosi and Zafferana for walks on old lava flows. Remember to bring warm clothing, sturdy shoes and sunglasses to protect your eyes from windblown grit. Jeep tours start from the Rifugio Sapienza Etna Sud and follow the line of the cable car that was destroyed in the 2001 eruption. For a less intimidating volcanic escapade, take a boat trip from Milazzo on Sicily's north coast to the Aeolian Islands, a volcanic archipelago where you can swim and snorkel from black-sand beaches, collect fragments of pumice floating in the sea and delve back in time at the archaeological museum in Lipari. To the north of the main group of islands lies Stromboli – a feisty little volcano that has been active for more than two millennia.

⊙ Inside info

» A city with diverse architecture, from Arabic to art nouveau, Palermo (palermo tourism.com) is Sicily's regional capital.
» You will find most types of accommodation on Sicily, from resorts hotels and self-catering villas to farmstays and campsites.
» For further information, log on to regione.sicilia.it/turismo, and parcoetna.ct.it.

Temples & castles

Sicily's top historical sites include the ancient Greek theatre at Taormina (Sicily's first resort), the Roman hunting lodge of Villa Romana del Casa, the lavish mosaics inside the Norman cathedral at Monreale and the magnificent Greek temple ruins at Agrigento (pictured right) and Selinunte. Among Sicily's numerous castles ripe for rampart-romping and dungeon-delving, try Castello di Eurialo, Castello di Lombardia and Castello di Venere.

Best beaches

Just to the north of Palermo, Mondello has the island's most lively beaches with lots of facilities. A little further to the west, Lo Zingaro, Sicily's first nature reserve,

protects 7 km of rocky coastline on the Gulfo di Castellammare. You can reach this idyllic spot (keeping an eye open for Bonelli's eagle and peregrine falcons) either by walking along the coastal path or by taking a boat trip. Don't forget masks and snorkels – there are several gorgeous coves with crystal-clear waters. At Selinunte in the southwest there's a large sandy beach just below the temples and a nearby Acquasplash waterpark. Other sandy stretches along the south coast include Eraclea Minoa, Scoglitti and Donnalucata. In the southeast corner of the island, Vendicari has beautiful sandy beaches set in a nature reserve.

66 99 The Sicilians just seem to adore babies. We had a young couple run halfway across the airport to say *ciao* to Amelia and even teenage boys were happy to play peek-a-boo with her on buses. Once, on the bus to Taormina, it was so packed there was nowhere for us to sit. Amelia was gently but firmly taken from us and passed to a grinning grandmother who entertained her until we reached our destination.

Su Taylor

Sardinia

A beautiful island with a rugged interior smothered in herb-scented *macchia* (scrubland) and a shoreline alternating between isolated coves and long sandy beaches, Sardinia makes a superb family-holiday destination – whether you like to hike and bike or flop on a beach.

There's plenty of family accommodation available, from country villas to coastal hotels like Forte Village, where kids can be kept happily occupied without you ever needing to leave the resort. It would be a shame, however, not to track down at least one of Sardinia's quirky *nuraghe* (ancient stone structures dating from 1800 to 300 BC) that you will find dotted around the island. The Museo Archeologico Nazionale in Sardinia's capital, Cagliari, provides an insight into the people who created them.

As for the best beaches, they are not just confined to the exclusive Costa Smeralda in the northeast. Look to the northwest and to the east near Cala Gonone for equally enticing coves and aquamarine waters. At the latter don't forget to take a boat trip to the famous sea caves, Grotta del Bue Marino.

Italy Grown-ups' stuff

When to go

Italy has a varied climate, based on its distinct geographical regions. In the north, expect cold Alpine winters and warm, wet summers; in the **Po Valley** the summers are hot and dry and the winters are cold and damp; the rest of Italy has a wonderful climate of long hot summers (with temperatures consistently over 25°C) and mild winters, with cooler weather and a chance of winter snow in the **Appenines**.

Italy's historic sites and cities are busy and crowded from spring to October and the heat can be oppressive during the midsummer months of July and August. Remember, though, that you can always escape into the cooler hill towns when the heat gets too much. Be aware that **Rome** and the Vatican City will be packed with pilgrims at Christmas and Easter, and that **Venice** triples its population during Carnevale in February. Consider visiting Venice in the low season (October to March) – everything stays open and gondola rides will be cheaper!

Getting there

Milan, Verona and Bologna are the key transport hubs in northern Italy; Rome and Naples in the south. The national carrier, Alitalia (alitalia.com), flies from Europe and the United States to all major cities in Italy. Check their website for special promotions, but expect to pay from around £90 for a return fare between Heathrow and Rome, or £120 for a return to Naples (via Rome). Alitalia's return fares between New York and Rome start from around $675. British Airways (britishairways.com) flies to 11 Italian destinations, including Rome, Naples, Milan, Pisa, and Bologna. Rates start at around £75 for a return flight between London Gatwick and Rome.

For **budget flights** to Italy, BMI British Midland (flybmi.com) serves Naples, Rome and Venice; easyJet (easyjet.com) flies to Milan, Turin, Venice, Pisa, Rimini, Rome, Naples and Sicily; and Ryanair (ryanair.com) covers over 20 Italian destinations including cities in Puglia, Sicily and Sardinia as well as all the major hubs.

Getting around

Travelling within Italy usually poses few problems, particularly in the north of the country, where the road, bus and rail networks are modern and efficient. Alitalia (alitalia.com) operates an extensive network of **internal flights** as do low-cost operators such as Alpieagles (alpieagles.com) and Club Air (clubair.it).

Fly-drive deals are often the cheapest way to arrange **car hire**. Most rental agencies are located at major Italian airports. Motorways, although generally good, can become heavily congested at weekends and during peak periods. One way to avoid the busy routes is to take the **train**, which provides good value and is especially useful if you want to link two or more cities (where you'd be crazy to attempt to drive yourself). Trenitalia (trenitalia.com) has an online reservation system.

Italy also has a large and well-developed network of **ferries** that ply routes between offshore islands, as well as making international crossings. SNAV Collegamenti Marittimi (snav.it) operates ferries between Civitavecchia and Olbia (Sardinia) and Palermo, and from Naples to Palermo, Capri and Ischia. Also try Grand Navi Veloci (gnv.it).

The best way to get around Italian cities varies from place to place. For example in Venice, waterbuses or *vaporetti* are abundant; in Rome, buses are most useful; and in Milan there is an efficient metro. You will often find that walking is quicker than taking a taxi or bus through congested streets.

Accommodation

Families are spoilt for choice when it comes to places to stay in Italy – you will find everything from beachside campsites and rural farmstays to resorts, hotels and converted *palazzos*.

Skip the flight

» **Get a coach pass** with Eurolines (eurolines-pass.com) linking classic cities such as Venice, Florence, Milan, Rome and Naples.

» **Take your car** by train to Italy. Dutch company Auto Slaaptrein (autoslaaptrein.nl) operates a weekly motorail service from June to September between s'Hertogenbosch (a short drive from the Channel ports of Hoek van Holland or Rotterdam) to Bologna. The train runs overnight with couchettes and sleepers southbound on Friday nights, northbound on Saturday nights.

» **Travel by train** from London to Rome. Book a ticket with Eurostar (eurostar.com) to Paris. Cross Paris by Métro to the Gare de Bercy and connect with the Palatino sleeper train to Rome. Bookings can be made online at raileurope.co.uk.

Lake Garda ferry.

Most **hotels** welcome children, even if they have no special facilities. Some of the cheaper hotels may not be able to supply cots, but most hotels will provide an extra child's bed if required. Many of the big international hotel chains have a presence in Italy, including Best Western (bestwestern. com) and Starwood Westin (starwoodhotels.com).

Most of Itay's **self-catering** accommodation is generally of a high standard, and is often in wonderful locations. The Associazione Nazionale per l'Agriturismo (agriturist. it) represents more than 2000 farms, villas and mountain chalets and offers reasonably priced accommodation. For something unusual, contact Apulia Bella (apuliabella.com) to arrange a stay in a converted *trullo* in the Puglia region.

For an online directory of Italian **campsites** and resorts, log on to camping.it.

For **holiday villages** offering accommodation in well-equipped chalets and tents, try Eurocamp (eurocamp.co.uk), Keycamp (keycamp.com), Siblu (siblu.com) and Vacansoleil (vacansoleil.co.uk).

ⓘ Fact file

Country	Time	Language	Currency	Exchange rate approximate	International dialling code	Tourist information
Italy	GMT+1	Italian	Euro €	£1 = €1.15	+39	enit.it

Italy Grown-ups' stuff

Food & drink

Food is an obsession in Italy and a quintessential part of Italian lifestyle. If your children enjoy pizza, pasta and ice cream they won't go hungry. However, encourage them to try some of the regional specialities in the table below, if only to supplement their diet of pizza margherita, spaghetti bolognese and *gelato*.

Health & safety

It is strongly recommended that you have good medical and travel insurance prior to visiting Italy. EU citizens should ensure they have a European Health Insurance Card (EHIC), which entitles the holder to emergency medical treatment. It does not cover you for medical repatriation, on-going medical treatment or treatment of a non-urgent nature.

Italy is generally a safe place to visit, with few health and safety risks. There is a small risk of contracting Leishmaniasis from an infected sand fly bite or Lyme disease from a tick bite.

Crime levels in Italy are generally low. The biggest risk to tourists is petty crime such as bag snatching – particularly in major tourist spots. Try to keep valuables hidden from view.

Top 30 gelato flavours

Know your ananas from your bananas with this guide to popular *gelato* flavours.

- ★ **Albiocca** *apricot*
- ★ **Ananas** *pineapple*
- ★ **Bacio** *chocolate with hazelnut*
- ★ **Banana** *banana*
- ★ **Caffe** *coffee*
- ★ **Ciliega** *cherry*
- ★ **Cioccolato** *chocolate*
- ★ **Cocco** *coconut*
- ★ **Cocomero** *watermelon*
- ★ **Crema** *egg-yolk custard*
- ★ **Fragola** *strawberry*
- ★ **Frutti di bosco** *wild berries*
- ★ **Lampone** *raspberry*
- ★ **Limone** *lemon*
- ★ **Macedonia** *fruit salad*
- ★ **Malaga** *raisin*
- ★ **Mandarino** *tangerine*
- ★ **Mela** *apple*
- ★ **Menta** *mint*
- ★ **Mirtillo** *blueberry*
- ★ **Nocciola** *hazelnut*
- ★ **Panna** *whipped cream*
- ★ **Pera** *pear*
- ★ **Pesca** *peach*
- ★ **Pistacchio** *pistachio*
- ★ **Pompelmo** *grapefruit*
- ★ **Stracciatella** *chocolate chip*
- ★ **Tarocchio** *blood orange*
- ★ **Tiramisu** *tiramisu*
- ★ **Vaniglia** *vanilla*

Regional specialities

Rome	*Spaghetti alla carbonara*	Spaghetti cooked with raw egg, Parmesan cheese, cracked black pepper and *pancetta* (bacon).
Tuscany	*Panforte*	Fruit cake made with chewy nougat, fruits and spices.
	Donzelle	Fried dough balls.
	Crostini	Rounds of bread toasted and brushed with olive oil, plus various toppings such as chunks of tomato.
	Tiramisu	Dessert with a creamy sauce of mascarpone and eggs between layers of sponge drenched in coffee or liqueur.
Venice	*Pasta e fagioli*	Bean soup with home-made pasta.
Umbria	*Schicciata*	Similar to pizza crust, bread baked with olive oil and sometimes with onions.
Sicily	*Cassata*	Sponge cake, ricotta cream, marzipan and candied fruits.
	Granita	Fruity iced drink.

Italy Family favourites

Villa Pia

Where? Lippiano, Tuscany.

Why? Stylish, yet relaxed and homely, Villa Pia is an 18th-century manor house within easy reach of Florence and Siena for sightseeing and eating out. In addition to four family suites, with interconnecting bedrooms and private bathroom, there is a living room and kitchen with help-yourself fridge. Boasting wonderful views, the villa has two swimming pools, a sandpit, trampoline, adventure play areas and an all-weather tennis court.

How much? Adults from €500 per week, children from €200 per week, full board.

Contact Villa Pia, T+39 (0)75-850 2027, villapia.com.

Club Med Kamarina

Where? Ragusa, on the southwest coast of Sicily.

Why? This 96-ha beachside holiday village has something for all ages, from catamaran sailing, rollerblading and tennis to swimming in one of three pools. Kids' clubs include a Mini Club Med for children aged four to 10 and Club Med Passworld for youngsters up to 17. For grown-ups there's a Club Med Spa, Turkish bath and aqua fitness classes.

How much? All-inclusive weekly rates from around €1000 per adult. Check online for special offers

Contact Club Med, T+44 (0)871-424 4044, clubmed.co.uk.

Tuscan View Apartments

Where? Montaione, Tuscany.

Why? A perfect base from which to explore the hill town of San Gimignano, this working estate has lots to keep families happy, from tennis to horse riding. There is even a bar, restaurant and mini-market selling the estate's honey and olive oil. Equipped with living rooms and kitchenettes, the apartments are located in attractively restored farmhouses.

How much? One week's rental of a two-bedroom apartment (sleeping four) costs from £415 per person, including Dover-Calais ferry crossings.

Contact Inntravel, T+44 (0)1653-617004, inntravel.co.uk.

Tour operators

The Adventure Company
adventurecompany.co.uk

Crystal Active
crystal-active.co.uk

First Choice Holidays
firstchoice.co.uk

Inntravel
inntravel.co.uk

Keycamp Holidays
keycamp.com

Lakes and Mountains Holidays
lakes-mountains.co.uk

Powder Byrne
powderbyrne.com

Sunvil Discovery Italy
sunvil.co.uk

Villas 4 You
villas4you.co.uk

Italy Family favourites

CaSavio Campsite

Where? Cavallino, near Venice.

Why? Venice is just a bus and boat ride away from this large holiday camp, which not only has a vast swimming pool complex, but is also located next to a sandy beach. Accommodation ranges from five-person tents to well-equipped mobile homes sleeping up to seven. Onsite facilities include a supermarket, restaurant and pizzeria, while activities range from minigolf and table tennis to cycling, canoeing and archery. Fun Station kids' clubs operate during high season.

How much? Seven nights in a two-bedroom Villanova mobile home start from around €300 per party.

Contact Keycamp Holidays, T+44 (0)844-844 1000, keycamp.co.uk.

Also try... Foresteria Valdese di Venezia (foresteriavenezia.it) in central Venice where rates start at around €120 for a four-bed room with bathroom.

Hermitage Hotel

Where? La Bidola Bay, Elba.

Why? With a variety of interconnecting rooms, the Hermitage makes a great bolt hole for families. There's plenty to keep kids occupied, with windsurfing, waterskiing, jet-skiing, banana boating and boat hire available from the private beach. In addition to three saltwater swimming pools (including a children's pool), the hotel also offers tennis, golf, mountain biking, volleyball, five-a-side football and pétanque. For adults there's a wellness centre.

How much? From around £1100 per adult and £580 per child for seven nights half-board accommodation, UK return flights and transfers.

Contact Powder Byrne, T44 (0)208-246 5300, powderbyrne.com.

Also try... Chia Laguna (scottdunn.com), a stunning family resort on Sardinia with excellent kids' clubs and a wide range of watersports.

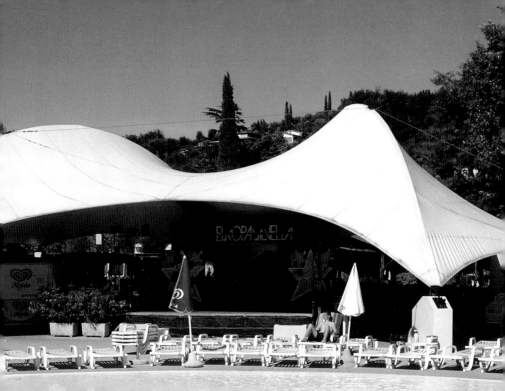

Europa Silvella

Where? Lake Garda.

Why? With its own lakeside beach, this well-equipped holiday park is ideal for watersports. It also has its own swimming pool, along with a range of other facilities, including shop, takeaway and restaurant. Accommodation is available in six-berth tents or mobile homes – all with shade. The Gardaland theme park is just 33 km away.

How much? Seven nights in a Venezia mobile home cost from around €440 for two adults and up to four children under 18 years old, including return midweek P&O ferry crossings between Dover and Calais.

Contact Eurocamp, T+44 (0)844-406 0402, eurocamp.co.uk.

Contents

185 **Introduction**

186 **Kids' stuff**

188 **Tots to teens**

190 **Low Countries**
190 Brussels
190 Wallonia
190 Flanders
192 Amsterdam
193 Luxembourg

194 **Germany**
194 Berlin
195 Coast & islands
195 Black Forest
195 Touring routes

198 **Switzerland**
198 Bernese Oberland
198 Graubunden
199 Valais
199 Lucerne

200 **Austria**
200 Vienna
200 Salzburg
201 Carinthia
201 Styria
201 Tyrol

202 **Grown-ups' stuff**

Central Europe

Swishing down a Swiss ski slope. Right: Edelweiss.

metres
3000
2000
1000
500
200
0

N

50 km
50 miles

Baltic Sea

Rügen

North Sea

Frisian Islands

○ **Hamburg**

NETHERLANDS

○ **Bremen**

Elbe

☐ **BERLIN**

2

☐ **AMSTERDAM**

Hanover ○

Hook of Holland

○ **Rotterdam**

GERMANY

Rhine

Harz Mountains

○ **Bruges**
○ **Ghent**

Flanders

☐ **BRUSSELS**

1

○ **Cologne**
○ **Bonn**

BELGIUM

Ardennes

Frankfurt ○

LUXEMBOURG

☐ **PRAGUE**

○ **Nürnberg**

Danube

4

Black Forest

Wasserfaelle Gutach

Munich ○

VIENNA ☐

Salzburg ○

Bodensee

Zürich ○

LIECHTENSTEIN

Lake Lucerne

SWITZERLAND

AUSTRIA

Tyrol

Grossglockner

Styria

BERN ☐

5

Graubünden

Carinthia

6

A   l   p   S

Lake Geneva

Bernese Oberland

Geneva ○

Valais

Matterhorn

Dufourspitze

Lyon ○

Milan

Longest river
Danube
2850 km

Largest city
Berlin, population 3.39 million

Highest mountain
Dufourspitze
4634 m

◉ Did you know?

● Amsterdam has 1281 bridges, 2000 houseboats and 600,000 bicycles.

● Belgium produces 172,000 tons of chocolate each year, which is equivalent to 1000 solid chocolate blue whales.

● The Manneken Pis in Brussels has over 700 costumes in the City Museum, including an Elvis jumpsuit.

● Liechtenstein is the world's largest exporter of false teeth.

● Mountains cover more than 70% of Switzerland.

Introduction

★1 Find out where Tintin was created
›› Belgium, page 190

★2 Explore the canals of Amsterdam
›› Netherlands, page 192

★3 Tour the Castle Road
›› Germany, page 196

★4 Experience all of Europe in one park
›› Germany, page 195

★5 Stand on top of the world
›› Switzerland, page 198

★6 Get active in the Alps
›› Switzerland and Austria, pages 201

At first glance, the problem with Central Europe is that everywhere surrounding it looks more exciting. Head north to Scandinavia, south to the Mediterranean, east to Poland and the Baltics and west to France. But keep focused, keep staring straight ahead, because Central Europe not only offers an excellent range of family-holiday options, but it's also less crowded (and sometimes better value) than its higher-profile neighbours. Belgium, the Netherlands and Germany all have sandy beaches along the North Sea coast, while Austria and Switzerland have countless lakes that are perfect for swimming and watersports. The region has plenty of family-friendly hotels, guesthouses and holiday villages; public transport is super-efficient, and the cuisine features chocolate, chips, cheese and waffles. As for adventure, you will find every kind of action sport available in the Austrian and Swiss Alps, from rock climbing to whitewater rafting, while the Low Countries promise more in the way of gentle touring and cycle routes. In Germany you can follow in the fairy-tale footsteps of the Brothers Grimm, in Austria you can take your cue from *The Sound of Music* and in Switzerland you can ride on some of the world's most spectacular mountain railways.

Central Europe Kids' stuff

Books to read

Play, Mozart, Play!

Greenwillow, 2006
Artist Peter Sís introduces the child genius, Wolfgang Amadeus Mozart. Ages 3-8

The Complete Brothers Grimm Fairy Tales

Random House, 2006
With over 700 pages, this illustrated volume contains every published story by the Brothers Grimm, including well-known classics like *Cinderella*, *The Frog Prince*, *Hansel and Gretel*, *Little Red Riding Hood*, *Rapunzel*, *Rumpelstiltskin* and *Snow White*. Ages 4+

The Adventures of Tintin

Egmont, 2007
Read three classic Tintin adventures – *The Castafiore Emerald*, *Flight 714 to Sydney* and *Tintin and the Picaros* – by Belgian cartoon-strip supremo, Hergé, in volume 8 of this latest series of compilations. Ages 6+

Heidi

Puffin, 2009
Johanna Spyri's classic tale of a little Swiss girl who is sent to live with her grandfather in a mountain hut high in the Alps – an idyllic life that's shattered one day when Heidi is brought back to Frankfurt by her aunt Dete. Ages 8-11

Diary of Anne Frank

Longman 1989
The tragic, deeply moving and inspiring story of a Jewish girl living in Amsterdam who is forced into hiding during the Holocaust. Ages 12+

Grow a tulip

Did you know that over nine billion flower bulbs are produced in the Netherlands every year? Tulips are some of the easiest to grow. Just follow these simple steps:

▸ Decide on a colour scheme or pattern.

▸ Purchase your bulbs; generally the bigger the bulb, the bigger the bloom.

▸ Prepare the soil by removing rocks and adding some compost and bone meal.

▸ Plant the bulbs any time during autumn, placing them around 15-20 cm apart, and at a depth that's roughly twice the width of the bulb.

▸ After flowering, let the plant continue to grow until it dies back naturally.

Kick a backside 360-degree spin

This is one of the easiest and safest advanced tricks to learn.
» Make sure you start the spin on the kicker before you take off.
» Drive your front shoulder towards your back foot and wind your arms in front of you, before unwinding them towards your back just as you approach the jump.
» After leaving the kicker you'll be flying backwards; keep turning your upper body, and you should still be travelling upwards, spinning blind until you're at your highest point in the jump.
» Keep turning those shoulders in the direction of the spin as you get ready to land. Don't forget, the board needs to travel 360 degrees, so keep that board turning.
» Using your arms for balance, prepare for the oncoming landing. Bring the board to the ground and meet the floor with a fully extended body, your board pointing perfectly forwards and your weight centred over the board.

Yodel like a local

» Find a remote mountain pasture with plenty of echo potential.
» Take a deep breath, open your mouth wide and sing, 'Hodl oh-ooh-dee'.
» Try it again, going high-pitched on the 'ooh'.
» Now practise 'Hodl-ay-ee-dee', going up a note on the 'ee'.
» Put the two lines together, and you're yodelling.
» Optional: finish with a 'heh-ee-dee-ho-ooh-dee-yo'.

Toblerone
bite-size facts

» The famous Swiss chocolate is named after creator, Theodor Tobler, and *torrone*, a type of Italian nougat.
» The first Toblerone was sold way back in 1908.
» Toblerone's unique shape is based on Switzerland's Matterhorn.

Taste of Germany perfect pretzels

Hailing from southern Germany in the 12th century, the humble pretzel is now a popular snack worldwide. This recipe shows you how to make soft pretzels, traditionally served in Bavaria for breakfast and accompanied by *weisswurst* (white sausage) and sweet mustard.

What you need
» 775 g flour
» 4 tbsp brown sugar
» 2 tsp salt
» 1 tbsp yeast dissolved in water
» 2 tbsp baking soda
» 1 egg

What to do
» Mix 300 ml of warm water with the yeast, brown sugar and salt.
» Gradually add the flour and mix to form a smooth dough.
» Chill the dough for an hour and then divide it into six pieces.
» Roll out each piece until it is slightly thicker than a pencil.
» Arrange each dough string into an upside-down U-shape.
» Hold the ends of each string and twist them together.
» Flatten the ends with your fingers, then bring them to the top of the pretzel pressing them into the dough.
» Place the pretzels on a greased baking tray and leave them to rise for about 30 minutes.
» Boil 600 ml of water, add the baking soda, then dip each pretzel in the solution for about 10 seconds before placing them back on the baking tray.
» Beat the egg with one teaspoon of water, then brush it over the pretzels.
» Sprinkle the pretzels with salt, sesame seeds, cheese or cinnamon.
» Bake for around 15 minutes until golden brown.

Central Europe Tots to teens

Travelling with kids in Central Europe is a breeze. The Dutch in particular are relaxed and friendly, but you'll find families are generally welcome wherever you go. Children receive discounts on admission to most major sights, and often travel free on the slick public transport systems that operate across the region. You'll also have no problem finding family-oriented accommodation and places to eat.

Babies

Take the low ground or the high ground. Buggy-friendly Amsterdam is ideal for a relaxed city break, just as Austria or Switzerland are perfect for an alpine jaunt or two while your baby is still light enough to be lugged around in a carrier or papoose.

Flying from the UK to anywhere in Central Europe is quick and simple, but with a baby in tow you might feel happier piling everything you need into your car and taking a ferry to Belgium or the Netherlands.

Don't forget that several hotel brands in the region, such as Kinderhotels and KidsHotels, offer all-inclusive packages with outstanding childcare for the tiniest of tots – not to mention some pampering incentives for their parents.

Toddlers/pre-school

Amsterdam's reputation for being family-friendly might not strike a chord with parents of hyperactive toddlers. One glance at a city map and all those canals is enough to give any parent instant palpitations. The same could be said for the Alps with its mountain paths and precipitous drops. In both cases, toddler reins are essential.

The big boon with this age group, of course, is that you can sidestep the busy school-holiday periods and take advantage of cheaper travel deals and less crowded cities, beaches or ski slopes. Just watch the weather though. Central Europe's climate can be unpredictable at the best of times – stray too far either side of mid-summer and that balmy beach holiday on the North Sea coast could be decidedly damp and chilly. Still, there's always Center Parcs where it's permanently subtropical thanks to their dome-covered water worlds. You'll find them in Belgium, the Netherlands and Germany.

Kids/school age

Holiday villages, such as Center Parcs and Eurocamp, are a great option for children of this age who often have limitless energy and require constant stimulation. Active holidays in Central Europe can include anything from cycling in the Low Countries to learning how to rock climb in the Alps. You can also satisfy many a childhood passion by touring one of Germany's themed routes, such as the Castle Road or Fairy Tale Route, and spending time at world-class theme parks like Europa-Park and Legoland.

From an educational point of view, Central Europe has plenty of lessons in store for children, from Van Gogh's strokes of genius to Salzburg's intriguing brush with salt.

Teenagers

When children begin learning about the world wars at school, Central Europe will inevitably loom large in their minds. The tragic, thought-provoking story of Anne Frank, the Jewish teenager who hid from the Germans for over two years in a tiny annexe that is now a

On a mountain high in Switzerland.

" We are not a skiing family, but we decided to give it a go this year. Our children are six and three. To our complete astonishment, our week's skiing holiday was one of the most successful ever. Why? Firstly, we skied at Easter which meant the weather was warm (warm kids equals happy kids). Secondly, both Daisy and Poppy had gone ice-skating a couple of times in the UK and developed a taste for balance and ice, which I am sure helped them stay upright on skis. Thirdly, we punctuated the skiing day with breaks for delicious, hot chocolate which both children looked forward to when they were getting tired.

Simon Calder, Senior Travel Editor, The Independent

museum in Amsterdam, will grip many teenagers. So too will the rise and fall of the Berlin Wall – again, meaty stuff, but something that teenagers can at least begin to grasp the magnitude and meaning of.

Of course, you probably won't get teenagers within a hundred miles of either Amsterdam or Berlin unless you tempt them with something

slightly less bitter. Fortunately, both cities carry the sweet promise of retail heaven, as well as a suitably trendy café and arts scene. For teenagers who prefer the sound of thrills over tills, head for the mountains for year-round action sports. The Adventure Company (adventurecompany.co.uk) offers teenage departures on its trips to Switzerland.

Special needs

In Belgium, Toegankelijk Reizen (toegankelijkreizen.be) has information on accommodation and transportation for people with disabilities. The Netherlands Board of Tourism (holland. com) issues a *Holland for the Handicapped* brochure, while in Germany, NatKo (natko. de) promotes tourism for all people. In Austria, IBFT (ibft.at) has information on barrier-free tourism. Mobility International Switzerland (mis-ch.ch) has information on wheelchair-accessible travel, accommodation and attractions in Switzerland.

Single parents

Single Parents on Holiday (singleparentsonholiday.co.uk) offers both winter and summer holidays in Austria, while Crystal (crystalski.co.uk) offers discounts for one-parent families on its Austrian skiing holidays. Special lone-parent deals are also available with Eurocamp (eurocamp.co.uk) and other camping operators.

Low countries Big fun in Little Europe

Belgium, Netherlands and Luxembourg might not cause the biggest blips on family-holiday-planning radars, but there's more to this diminutive trio than chocolate, windmills and a dismal reputation in the Eurovision Song Contest. They tend to be the kinds of places you drive through on the way to your family holiday, but linger in Luxembourg, for example, and you will discover some beautiful countryside and one of Europe's most spectacularly situated capitals. Belgium and the Netherlands, on the other hand, not only share a long stretch of sandy coastline but possess a liberal scattering of theme parks, cycling routes and other family attractions. Amsterdam emerges as the region's most child-friendly city with its 'green light' district of museums and parks.

Walibi theme park.

Brussels

Belgium's capital is nothing if not diverse. At one extreme you have the bureaucratic edifice of the European Union headquarters, at the other a statue of a little boy peeing into a fountain. An obligatory first stop on any family sightseeing tour of the city, Le Manneken Pis (manneken-pis.com) has been eliciting sniggers from children since it was unveiled in 1619 on the corner of Rue de l'Etuve and Stoofstraat. The city's most

 Inside info
⟩⟩ Sandy beaches, up to 500 m wide at low tide, run between Knokke-Heist and De Panne.
⟩⟩ Brussels has several green oases, including Parc du Cinquantenaire, Brussels Park, Egmont Park and Duden Park.
⟩⟩ Grand Place and Place Sainte Catherine in Brussels host a Christmas market and nightly sound and light show during December.

significant historical landmark, however, is the Grand Place, a beautiful square surrounded by ornate buildings dating from the 13th century. It's in complete contrast to Atomium (atomium. be) – a massive molecule of nine escalator-linked spheres rearing above Bruparck in northern Brussels. Not far from the mighty atoms you'll find Mini-Europe (minieurope. com), a quirky collection of 300 pint-sized monuments, plus an IMAX cinema and waterpark. Other child-friendly attractions include the Musée des Enfants (museedesenfants.be), Musée des Sciences Naturelles de Belgique (sciencesnaturelles. be) and the interactive exhibits at Scientastic (scientastic.be). The Centre Belge de la Bande Dessinée (comicscenter.net) showcases Belgium's comic-strip heroes, including Hergé of Tintin fame. Several cartoon-adorned buildings around the city form part of an outdoor exhibition known as the Comic Strip Route.

Wallonia

Occupying the southern half of Belgium, Wallonia's big crowd-puller is Walibi Belgium (walibi.be), a theme/water park combo boasting over 50 rides, including seven roller coasters and a 140-m river run through rapids and waterfalls. For more natural thrills, go underground at the Grottoes of Han (grotte-de-han.be) or kayak along the River Lesse (lessekayaks. be). To give your brain a buzz, head for the Eurospace Centre (eurospacecenter.be) or Pass (pass.be), an interactive science adventure park.

Flanders

Deeply moving lessons in the mindless brutality of two world wars can be found in cemeteries and museums throughout northern Belgium, including the Memorial Museum Passchendaele 1917 (passchendaele.be) near Ypres,

where, in 1917, casualties exceeded 500,000 in 100 days for a gain in territory of just 8 km. On a lighter note, the North Sea coast has sandy beaches, while Ghent and Bruges have canals to explore and chocolate shops to peruse.

Battle plan

Located 20 minutes' drive south of Brussels, the site of the Battle of Waterloo (waterloo1815.be) has an excellent visitor centre, battlefield tours and a puzzle book to help children aged seven to 12 decipher the strategies that led to Napoleon's defeat. Don't miss the re-enactments of cavalry and artillery manoeuvres at Lion Mound Hamlet every weekend in July and August.

Little squirt - the Mannekin Pis in Brussels.

The Dutch capital may have something of a steamy image, but it gets an emphatic green light when it comes to travelling with kids (see right). This is largely due to its spider's web of 13th-century canals – a great excuse to transform boring old city sightseeing into something far more exciting. You can get afloat on a pedal boat, but you'll see more on a canal tour boat (canal.nl). Keep an eye out for De Pozenboot, a houseboat moored on the Singel that has become a refuge for stray cats. You can also hire bikes at several locations in the city (Vondelpark has safe paths, as well as a café, paddling pool and puppet theatre). Alternatively, hop on a tram (museumtram-amsterdam.nl)

Kinderdijk.

◉ Inside info

➥ For value and flexibility, consider staying outside Amsterdam. Molengroet campsite (molengroet.nl) is close to beaches, but just 40 km from the city centre.
➥ For an insight into how the Dutch lived in times gone by, visit the Open Air Museum (openluchtmuseum.nl) on the outskirts of Arnhem.
➥ For theme parks, try De Efteling (efteling.com) or Linnaeushof (linnaeushof.nl).
➥ The island of Texel has the Maritime and Beachcombers Museum (texelsmaritiem.nl).

at Centraal Station for the 20-minute ride to Amsterdamse Bos, a woodland park with space to run around.

Best cycle routes

Flower bulb route
Petal power meets pedal power. This 30-km route between Haarlem and Sassenheim (near Leiden) passes through the dazzling bulb fields of southern Holland – at least, they will be when the daffodils and tulips are in bloom during April and May. Purchase a route guide at the tourist office in Lisse.

North Sea route
Stretching from Den Helder to Boulogne-sur-Mer, the

Dutch part of this coastal epic is still 300 km long – so be sure to do it in a northerly direction to make the most of tailwinds. Apart from beaches, dunes and seaside resorts like Scheveningen, highlights on the ride include the Oosterschelde storm-surge barrier in Zeeland.

Windmill route
A 43-km spin through the Alblasserwaard area in southern Holland. Start near Kinderdijk (which has a row of 19 beautifully preserved windmills), then it's plain sailing as you follow the signposts through a typical Dutch polder landscape of rivers, reedbeds and lush meadows.

Bike to the beach.

Kids' top 10 Amsterdam

1. **Pedal** a four-seater canal bike around the waterways.

2. **Ogle** a Van Gogh (or revere a Rembrandt) at either the Van Gogh Museum (vangoghmuseum.nl) or Rijksmuseum (rijksmuseum.nl).

3. **Climb** the 85-m-tall tower of Westerkerk church for a pigeon's-eye view of the city.

4. **Find** out what makes your brain tick, discover how to purify water and uncover the science behind adolescence at the hands-on technology museum, NEMO (see box, bottom right).

5. **Travel** back in time as you board the replica Dutch East Indiaman *Amsterdam*, moored at NEMO while the Scheepvaart Museum (scheepvaartmuseum.nl) undergoes renovation.

6. **Cycle** out of town to Amstelpark to see the well-preserved De Rieker windmill, built in 1636 and a favourite subject for Rembrandt.

7. **Marvel** at the tragic, yet inspiring, story of Anne Frank at Anne Frankhuis (annefrank.nl), the secret annexe in which the Jewish teenager and her family hid from the Nazis for 25 months during the early 1940s.

8. **Discover** what it was like to live on a houseboat in the old days at the Houseboat Museum (houseboatmuseum.nl).

9. **Cook** up a feast at KinderkookKafé (above left), where kids get to prepare, cook and serve meals.

10. **Run** wild at TunFun (tunfun.nl), a subway-turned-adventure playground for one- to 12-year-olds.

Luxembourg

The Grand Duchy may be little more than a dot on the map, but it crams in everything from a World Heritage-listed capital to the forested hills of the Ardennes and the wine region of the Moselle Valley. Perched on a rocky promontory, Luxembourg city offers fine views over the Pétrusse Valley, particularly from the Place de la Constitution. Walk along the Chemin de la Corniche up to the Bock – a cliff where Count Sigefroi laid the foundations for a fortress more than 1000 years ago. All that remains is a honeycomb of underground passages known as the Bock Casemates. These, and other highlights, can be visited on a City Safari Tour for families that leaves from the tourist office at Place Guillaume. Heading north towards the Ardennes, Bourschied Castle is worth a detour, as is the National Military Museum in Diekirch with its displays of the 1944 Battle of the Bulge. The Ardennes is ideal for exploration by bike. Well-signed routes vary in length from 10 km to 40 km and there are some specifically for kids.

Finding NEMO

NEMO
T+31 (0)20-531 3232, e-nemo.nl.
Year round, Tue-Sun 1000-1700, plus Mon (Jun-Aug), €12/person, under-3s free.
Designed in the shape of a ship's prow, Amsterdam's largest science museum contains five floors of interactive exhibits, with themes ranging from 'The search for life' and 'Codename DNA' to 'Amazing constructions', 'Teen facts' and 'Future Fuel'.

Germany Fast rides & fairy tales

Nice cars, good beer, fine composers – but surely not that great for family holidays? Well, actually, yes. Germany might lack the charisma of the Spanish Costas or the magnetism of Disneyland Paris, but what it lacks in big names and notoriety it more than compensates for with a veritable cheer-fest of family attractions, ranging from island retreats in the Baltic Sea to roller-coaster mayhem at Europa-Park. What's more, Germany is easy to reach and a piece of (Black Forest) cake to get around, whether you're cruising the autobahn towards Berlin or dawdling along the Fairy Tale Route on the lookout for the seven dwarves.

Rugen.

Berlin

Germany's happening capital doesn't exactly buzz with family appeal, but don't overlook it as drab or uninviting. There's plenty to keep families interested for a day or two – although older children will definitely get more from the city. In addition to iconic landmarks like the Brandenburg Gate, Berlin's defining moments of post-war history are best revealed at Haus am Checkpoint Charlie (mauermuseum.de), a small museum documenting the rise and fall of the Berlin Wall and the numerous, often fatal, attempts made to flee East Germany. If you visit just one other museum in Berlin, make sure it's the Pergamon Museum (smb.spk-berlin. de) – one of the collection of museums on Museum Island where pride of place goes

to the Hellenistic masterpiece, the *Pergamon Altar*, a frieze of sparring gods and giants that dates from the second century BC. Continue into the adjoining Ancient Near East collection and you will find other amazing artefacts, including a truly monumental reconstruction of the Babylonian Ishtar Gate and Processional Way.

Berlin may be heavy on history, but light relief for kids is available in the form of the excellent Berlin Zoo (zoo-berlin. de) with its famous sculptured Elephant Gate and extensive animal collection. Don't miss the Hippopotamus House where you can view the lumbering 'river horses' from both above and below water. The aquarium is also worth a visit, particularly for its walk-in Crocodile Hall, black-tip reef sharks and breeding jellyfish.

Take the U5 underground or M17 tram to the city's outskirts and you'll discover Tierpark (tierpark-berlin.de), a 160-ha landscape zoo with spacious open-air enclosures for everything from pachyderms to primates.

Coast & islands

Germany's North Sea coast has no shortage of sandy beaches, including the 12-km-long St Peter-Ording. Avid naturalists should head to the Elbe estuary off Cuxhaven where the islands of the Hamburg Wattenmeer National Park are popular with terns and seals. Just to the north, Schleswig-Holstein Wattenmeer National Park provides a memorable, if messy, opportunity to venture into the world's largest contiguous area of mudflats – a rich wildlife habitat that, for safety reasons, should only be explored on a guided tour. On Germany's Baltic coast, the island of Rugen (ruegen.de) makes a superb family-holiday base, with everything from sea promenades and sandy beaches to boat trips.

Black Forest

Home of the cuckoo clock, the Black Forest in southwest Germany can easily be toured by road, but you'll feel much better walking – especially after indulging in a slice or two of ubiquitous cherry-filled chocolate cake. A guided trail lasting from one to 10 days starts at Triberg (triberg.de) where you can also take a day hike to the 160-m Wasserfaelle Gutach, the highest cascade in Germany. St Märgen also makes a good base for walks, while Furtwangen's cuckoo clock museum is worth a quick visit.

Europa-Park

Rust, T01805-776 688, europapark.de. Apr-Oct, daily 0900-1800, Nov-Dec 1100-1900, €27-35/adult, €24-31/child (4-11).

Reaching speeds of 130 kph and centrifugal forces of 4 G, Silver Star (the biggest rollercoaster in Europe, minimum height 140 cm) is just one of the 100-plus rides and attractions at this outstanding theme park. Other highlights include Fjord Rafting through Scandinavia and an interactive Atlantis Adventure where you explore a sunken citadel armed with laser harpoons. But it's the themed streetscapes of 12 European countries, from Greece to Russia, which may well leave the most lasting impression.

Left: Brandenberg Gate, Berlin.
Right: Silver Star coaster at Europa-Park.

◉ **Inside** info

›› Several cities, including Berlin and Hamburg, have super-saver cards, offering free travel on public transport and free or discounted admission to major attractions.
›› Satisfy sweet-tooth cravings at the Chocolate Museum in Cologne (Köln) and the Haribo factory in Bonn.
›› Germany has an extensive cycle route network (adfc.de) and over 5000 'bike-friendly' places to stay (bettundbike.de).

Germany touring routes

Heidelberg.

Castle Road

burgenstrasse.de
Mannheim to Prague: 1000 km

Tales of witches, knights and dragons add zest to this long-established scenic tour of castles and palaces in Germany and the Czech Republic. In Heidelberg Castle, for example, children can discover the 'witch's bite' – a crack in an iron door ring where a witch tried to force entry to the castle using her teeth. Several castles organize costumed festivals, ghost tours and medieval banquets. You'll also encounter medieval games in towns like Bad Wimpfen, while others, such as Ansbach and Schwetzingen, run special guided tours for children. Other highlights include the impressive fortifications of Auerbach, the medieval imperial city of Nürnberg and the ancient towns of Bamberg, Coburg, Kronach, Kulmbach and Bayreuth. The Castle Road is a designated cycle route and there are also coach tours and train stations along its length. Other child-friendly highlights include Sea Life Speyer (sealifeeurope.com) near Heidelberg – a series of aquariums evoking the various habitats of the Rhine from alpine source to Rotterdam harbour – and Zirndorf's Playmobil Fun Park (playmobil.de) where the knight's castle stands alongside a pirate ship, gold mine and jungle ruins.

The Toy Road

spielzeugstrasse.de
Nurnberg to Waltershausen: 300 km

Site of an international toy fair (toyfair.de), Nürnberg is an appropriate place to start this trail through a land of dolls, teddies and model railways – although don't forget that Legoland (legoland.de) lies well to the south of the route near Gunzberg. A short distance from Nürnberg is the Playmobil Fun Park (see left), while the town of Fürth is home to several major toy manufacturers and a puppet festival in May. Coburg dotes on dolls, Weidhausen tends towards teddies, while Neustadt not only has copious amounts of both (in the Museum of the German Toy Industry), but also has a doll and teddy bear doctor. Educational toys are on display at Friedrich Froebel's memorial museum in Oberweissbach; Lauscha is the birthplace of christmas tree baubles, while Ohrdruf's claim to fame is the rocking horse and porcelain doll. Don't miss the massed display of gnomes at Trusetal Gnome Park (note that sledgehammers and golf clubs must be left at the entrance).

Fairy Tale Route

deutsche-maerchenstrasse.com
Bremen to Hanau:
600 km

Kassel.

The road to enchantment starts in Bremen, birthplace of the Brothers Grimm, whose timeless fairy tales come to life as you travel north. There's a chance you might meet Snow White and the Seven Dwarves in the Weserbergland hills. Schwalmstadt, meanwhile, is Little Red Riding Hood country, while Mother Goose waddled about in the Werra Valley. Sleeping Beauty nodded off in Sababurg Castle, Cinderella had a ball at Polle Castle, Rapunzel let her hair down in Trendelburg and, of course, Hamlyn is where the Pied Piper (pictured right) led his rats on a merry dance. In just about every town you will find fairy-tale tours, theatre shows, museums, and picture-perfect half-timbered buildings. At the heart of the Fairy Tale Route, Kassel is home to the Brothers Grimm Museum and also hosts a summer folklore festival and fairy-tale Christmas market. Don't miss the Bremen Town Musicians, on stage every Sunday between May and September.

German Alpine Road

germany-tourism.de
Lindau to Berchtesgaden: 450 km

Königssee.

Stretching between Lakes Constance and Königssee, the German Alpine Road links a healthy succession of forests, meadows, lakes and farming villages – all set against the backdrop of the Bavarian Alps. No less than 20 lakes and some 25 castles, abbeys and palaces can be found along the historic route. Don't miss the island town of Lindau on Lake Constance, the Linderhof Palace at Ettal or the fairy-tale castles of Füssen. Many lakes offer watersports and, if you're feeling really energetic, you can cycle the German Alpine Road using a special track that runs along part of its length. Cable cars and chairlifts, meanwhile, whisk you into the mountains where there's no shortage of walking trails and skiing areas.

Switzerland Clockwork holidays

The great Swiss outdoors has more family-friendly attractions than you can shake a ski stick at. From nature trails and mountain railways to gold panning and whitewater rafting, boredom is easily banished in the squeaky-clean, rosy-cheeked land of Heidi and Peter the Goatherd. Public transport runs with typical Swiss precision and there are even 30-odd resorts and nearly 50 hotels that have been cited as particularly family friendly. Any downsides? Well, Switzerland can be pricey, but you'll find family travel passes (plus some Toblerone therapy) will help to sweeten the pill. See page 98 for a round-up of winter ski resorts.

Lake Lucerne paddlesteamer.
Below: Marmot.

Bernese Oberland

Eiger, Mönch and Jungfrau reign supreme above the Bernese Oberland (berneroberland. ch), Switzerland's ultimate outdoor playground and the setting for such classic alpine destinations as Interlaken and Gstaad. For peak perfection, set your sights on Jungfraujoch (jungfraubahnen.ch), a breathtaking visitor centre

◉ **Inside** info

▸▸ The Swiss Pass (swisstravel system.ch) permits unlimited free travel by train, bus and boat (including scenic routes like the Glacier Express), plus free entry to 400 museums.
▸▸ Swiss holiday resorts that have a range of services geared specifically to the needs of children and parents are awarded a Families Welcome label (swisstourfed.ch).
▸▸ Zurich Airport (zurich-airport. com) has a children's playground with a trampoline and Alouette helicopter, as well as 75-minute tours of the apron, runways and nature reserve.

perched on a mountaintop with giddy views of summits and glaciers. You reach the top of Europe using three rack-and-pinion trains and, once there, you can visit the Ice Palace and go hiking, dog sledging and summer skiing.

Another summit that's easily bagged is 2190-m Stockhorn (stockhorn.ch), reached by cable car from Erlenbach in just 20 minutes. The views from the top take in everything from distant Mont Blanc to the lakes of Thun and Brienz.

More down-to-earth adventures include Aldeboden Flower Trail (adelboden.ch), a gentle 3-km amble from the Hahnenmoos Pass to Sillerenbühl with drawings and information to help you identify alpine flora. If you prefer something more fluffy, try the Marmot Trail on Betelberg Mountain. Kids aged four to 10 will also enjoy the Dwarf Trail (alpenregion.ch).

Upping adrenaline levels slightly, the Bernese Oberland is riddled with hiking and biking

opportunities, and there's also whitewater rafting on the Saane (swissraft.ch).

Graubunden

Family highlights in this eastern canton include luggage-free hiking holidays in the Engadine, Val Bregalia, Val Poschiavo and Swiss National Park (engadinferien.ch), where your bags are transported from hotel to hotel leaving you to carry little more than a pack lunch and a stash of cable-car tickets. For hiking with a literary twist, skip along the Heidi Adventure Path above Maienfeld.

Gold panning (gold-rush. ch) is available on the Rhine at Disentis, while those who splash about on the Inn River at Scuol will be rewarded with some gold-star whitewater rafting (engadin-adventure.ch).

Valais

With the Matterhorn and numerous other 4000-m giants straddling the French and Italian borders, it's little wonder that Valais is a magnet to rock climbers. Children can get to grips with ropes and carabiners on the Aletsch Fixed-Rope Trail (alpincenterbelalp.ch), a four-hour scramble around Gibidum Reservoir. Also on offer are two-day adventures, combining *via ferrata* and a glacier hike or rafting on the Rhône and canyoning through the Massa Gorge. Slightly more contrived, but no less fun, is Aquaparc (aquaparc.ch) at Le Bouveret on the shores of Lake Geneva.

Lucerne

Highlights in Lucerne include the 14th-century Chapel Bridge and Weinmarkt – an old city square surrounded by buildings adorned with elaborate frescoes, while the *Dying Lion of Lucerne* is a rock sculpture described by Mark Twain as 'the most mournful and moving piece of stone in the world'. The Lake Lucerne Navigation Company (lakelucerne.ch) operates five vintage paddle steamers and 15 modern cruisers. The most interesting section of the lake is the Urnersee where you can intersperse ferry travel with walks along the 35-km lakeside Swiss Path.

Kids' top 10 Switzerland

1 **Race** down the Churwalden toboggan run (pradaschier.ch) at speeds of up to 40 kph.

2 **Hoof** up the Binn Valley on a mule trek (bergland.ch).

3 **Sleep** in a fairy-tale castle at Mariastein-Rotberg (youthhostel.ch).

4 **Spot** ibex and marmots in Swiss National Park (nationalpark.ch).

5 **Strike** it lucky at Grabenmühle (grabenmuehle.ch), trout fishing or panning for gold.

6 **Swing** like Tarzan at Pilatus Seilpark (pilatus.ch), a suspension rope park in central Switzerland suitable for kids aged eight and above.

7 **Ride** Switzerland's oldest steam cog railway up 1678-m Rothorn Kulm (brienz-rothorn-bahn.ch).

8 **Discover** sweet sensations on the Chocolate Train from Montreux to the Nestlé factory in Broc, or visit Schoggi Land in Flawil (schoggi-land.ch).

9 **Ride** a cool scooter-bike from Belalp to Blatten along 7 km of mountain paths and surfaced roads (brig-belalp.ch).

10 **Meet** Peter the Goatherd in Savognin (savognin.ch) or live like a shepherd for the day at Alpine Museum Riederalp (riederalp.ch).

Pick of the resorts Saas Fee

Kids activities For those with energy, try horse riding, mountain biking and hiking some of the 350 km of marked footpaths; for those who want an easier way up and down the mountains take the cable car to the start of the Feeblitz summer toboggan run. Husky buggies (think mushing on wheels) are also available.

Best family day out A 40-minute drive away, Zermatt and the Matterhorn are well worth a visit. Closer at hand, however, is the 3500-m Mittelallalin, reached by cable car and underground railway. Here, you can find out about glaciers in the Ice Pavilion and have lunch in the world's highest revolving restaurant. Summer skiing is also available.

Austria Music to your ears

Altogether now: "Doe, a deer, a female deer; ray, a drop of golden sun..." Welcome to the land of the family singalong. Resistance is utterly futile. If you're not singing it, you'll be humming it. And if it's not a ditty from *The Sound of Music* it will be Falco's *Rock Me Amadeus* or, worse still, an impromptu yodelling session. Depending on their age, your children will either join in with gusto or shrink away in disgust. Salzburg, Austria's musical maestro-piece, is great fun for kids, while Vienna, with its Lipizzaner stallions, is somewhat more refined. But it's only out on the mountain paths, the bike trails and the sparkling lakes that you'll tune in to the some of the best sounds in Austria – the rarefied silence of alpine wilderness.

Lipizzaner stallion.

Vienna

Horse-lovers will be enchanted by Vienna's Spanish Riding School (srs.at) where the famous Lipizzaner stallions strut their stuff. You can book tickets online for the limited performances that take place, usually on Sundays, throughout the year. However, there's a stampede to get them, so you may have to settle for the Morning Exercises (daily, except Mondays) when the white beauties are put through their paces. Rarer, but

more accessible, creatures can be viewed at Schönbrunn Zoo (zoovienna.at), which not only has giant pandas, a Borneo rainforest habitat and a polarium, but also does its bit for the less fortunate equines of this world – namely the endangered Turkmenian donkey and Mongolia's Przewalski horse. To escape horses altogether, take a spin on the 65-m-tall Riesenrad (wienerriesenrad.com), Vienna's iconic Ferris wheel which first cranked into life in 1897. For a more hands-on view of the past, the Schönbrunn Palace (schoenbrunn.at) has a kids' museum where you can learn how to lay a royal table and dress up as a prince or princess.

Salzburg

There's something you should know before visiting Salzburg: most of the locals have never seen *The Sound of Music*. They don't wander around singing *Edelweiss* and they haven't

erected a statue of Julie Andrews in the city centre. They do, however, appreciate its tourism potential, so if you want to see movie locations, like the Mirabell Gardens where Maria and the Von Trapps sang *Do-Re-Mi*, simply sign up to one of the many Sound of Music Tours (panoramatours. com). Try to spare some time, though, for Mozart. You can see his memorial in Mozartplatz Square in the heart of the old town. Of the two Mozart museums in Salzburg, the house at Getreidegasse 9 (containing his concert violin, clavichord and other memorabilia) is probably of more interest to children.

Salzburg's baroque splendour was financed largely through sales of salt mined from the Durrnberg. At Salzwelten Hallstatt (salzwelten. at) you can explore the ancient mines, descending into their depths on thrilling wooden slides (reaching over 60 m in length) to an underground lake

● Inside info

>> The Vienna Card allows unlimited free travel by underground, bus and tram for 72 hours, plus discounts at over 200 attractions, shops and restaurants.
>> Allow a week to pedal along the easy, level Danube Cycle Path from Passau to Vienna.
>> A drive of about one hour from Vienna, the Sonnentherme Lutzmannsburg (sonnentherme. com) has a spa and adventure waterpark.

⚠ **Take** the high road

Drive along the Grossglockner High Alpine Road (grossglockner.com) into the heart of the Hohe Tauern National Park for views of Austria's highest mountain, the 3798-m Grossglockner, soaring above the Pasterze glacier. There are four themed children's playgrounds along the way, as well as an Alpine Nature Show Museum.

where salt was dissolved from the surrounding rock. To add a pinch of creepiness to the experience, you'll also learn of the remarkable discovery in 1734 of a miner who, having died during a tunnel collapse centuries earlier, became naturally embalmed in the salt.

Salzburg's white gold brought immense wealth to its prince archbishops and one of them, Markus Sittikus, indulged in a summer palace, known as Hellbrunn (hellbrunn.at). Sittikus, who evidently loved a good laugh, designed all sorts of push-button pranks, from trick fountains and spurting grottoes to a stone dining table where all but one of the seats is rigged with a water jet. Bring a sense of humour and change of clothes.

Carinthia

Austria's southernmost province has some 1270 lakes, 200 of which are suitable for swimming. Other summer

activities include hiking and cycling, while winter snows create over 800 km of pistes. One of the region's most popular family attractions is Minimundus (minimundus.at) where you can see the world in miniature.

Styria

Located in southeast Austria, Styria's forest-draped hills are perfect for biking (there are over 5000 km of cycle trails), while lakes and rivers offer boating, fishing and whitewater rafting.

Tyrol

This magnificent alpine region in western Austria is the country's adventure playground, with everything from horse riding, mountain biking and marmot-spotting (in Hohe Tauern National Park, hohetauern.at) to climbing and year-round skiing. Prepare to be dazzled at the Swarovski Crystal World (kristallwelten. swarovski.com) in Wattens, and to be spooked at Hexenwasser Hochsöll (hexenwasser.at), a land of witchcraft in Hohe Salve.

Pick of the resorts Kaprun

Kids' activities The highlight of any visit to Kaprun is a trip to the Kitzsteinhorn glacier where, year-round, you can ski, snowboard, toboggan or try your hand at snow-scooting. Down in the valley, there's easy cycling to nearby Zell am See where you can hire rowing boats on the lake. Alternatively, you can go horse riding, rock climbing, tandem paragliding or whitewater rafting on the Salzach River.

Best family day out An hour's drive from Kaprun, the 11th-century Werfen Castle (filming location for *Where Eagles Dare*) perches dramatically on a 150-m-high rock and has an excellent falconry show. Equally impressive are the nearby ice caves a subterranean Narnia world of blue-ice stalactites and frozen waterfalls.

Central Europe Grown-ups' stuff

When to go

The most popular time is summer unless, of course, you're going for the winter sports. Snow cover lasts from December to March in the alpine valleys of **Austria** and **Switzerland**, although in higher regions you can often eke out a skiing holiday as late as April or May (some resorts, like Kaprun, offer summer skiing). In the **Netherlands**, April is the best month for seeing daffodils in bloom; May for tulips. In **Germany**, the forests are golden-hued in autumn, a time when resorts are less crowded and the weather less settled.

Getting there

Several airports in the region are major international hubs, particularly Schipol (Amsterdam) and Frankfurt. National carriers include Austrian Airlines (aua.com), KLM (klm.com), Lufthansa (lufthansa.com) and Swiss Air (swiss.com). Expect to pay from around €130 for a return **flight** between London and Amsterdam with KLM. The Dutch carrier operates an extensive European and global network, linking up with Northwest Airlines to serve numerous cities in the United States. Low-cost airlines serving Central Europe from the UK and Ireland include easyJet (easyjet. com), with flights to Amsterdam, Berlin and Zurich, and Ryanair (ryanair.com), which flies to Brussels, Frankfurt, Karlsruhe-Baden and Salzburg. Air Berlin (airberlin.com) also has an extensive network with return fares between London and various German cities from as little as €70.

Getting around

Public transport is excellent throughout the region. If you arrive in **Brussels** by Eurostar your ticket includes travel to any other Belgian station within 24 hours (b-rail.be). Bus services are operated throughout Belgium by TEC (infotec.be).

In the **Netherlands**, a slick rail network (ns.nl) can whisk you from Schiphol Airport to Amsterdam in just 16 minutes. Once in the capital you can rent a bicycle from around €6 per day, or explore the city by Canal Bus (canal.nl).

In **Luxembourg**, the Luxembourg Card (ont.lu/card-en) provides free travel on trains and buses, plus free admission to over 50 attractions in the Grand Duchy – a one-day family card costs €20.

Germany's rail network is operated by Deutsche Bahn (bahn.de), with InterCityExpress (ICE) trains capable of reaching speeds of 320 kph. Some ICE trains have a Kleinkindabteil (or toddler compartment) reserved for families with small children. Most major German cities boast

🎫 **Ticket** to ride

Trading hiking boots, map and compass for a public transport pass and a pair of sensible shoes places a whole new perspective on travel in Switzerland. It takes the puff out of the views, makes more sense if you have very young children and puts you in touch with more of the country's cultural highlights. Switzerland's rack railways have been shuttling tourists up and down the mountains since the late 1800s.

an underground, bus and tram system, and in many you'll find Welcome Cards offering discounted admission to various tourist attractions, as well as unlimited travel on local public transport.

As you might expect, super-efficient, integrated public transport systems reach their peak in **Switzerland**. The Swiss Travel System (swisstravelsystem.com) offers a variety of travel passes for making use of the country's network of over 20,000 km of rail, bus and boat routes. The Swiss Pass allows unlimited free travel on the entire network, including scenic routes like the famous Glacier Express (glacierexpress.ch), city trams and buses, a 50% discount on several mountain railways and cableways and free entry

to 400 museums. A four-day pass costs from around €230 per adult, while children aged between six and 15 travel free if accompanied by a parent. Coaches in Switzerland are operated by PostBus (postauto.ch) and trains are run by Swiss Federal Railways (sbb.ch). RailAway (railaway.ch) offers winter and summer excursions combining discounted fares and admission to various attractions.

Austrian Federal Railways (oebb.at) connect major towns and cities in **Austria**, while various cruise operators offer excursions on the Danube (ddsg-blue-danube.at).

Accommodation
There are Center Parcs (centerparcs.com) in Belgium, Netherlands and Germany, each one with

Skip the flight
» **Take Eurostar** (eurostar.com) from London St Pancras to Brussels, a 111-minute journey with fares from around £70 return. Onward connections are possible to Amsterdam by high-speed Thalys (thalys.com) or Germany by Deutsche Bahn (bahn.de). Switzerland is also served by fast, reliable inter-European rail services.
» **Catch a bus** Eurolines (eurolines.com) has an extensive service across Central Europe.
» **Take the ferry** from the UK to France (see page 104), Belgium or the Netherlands. P&O Ferries (poferries.com) has 14-hour services from Hull to Zeebrugge and Rotterdam; Stena Line (stenaline.com) sails from Harwich to Hook of Holland with one-way fares starting from around £50 for a car plus driver.
» **Use Eurotunnel** (eurotunnel.com) to reach mainland Europe, then access the superb motorway network.

ⓘ **Fact** file

Country	Time	Language	Currency	Exchange rate approximate	International dialling code	Tourist information
Belgium	GMT+1	French Dutch	Euro €	£1 = €1.15	+32	visitbelgium.com
Netherlands	GMT+1	Dutch	Euro €	£1 = €1.15	+31	holland.com
Luxembourg	GMT+1	French German	Euro €	£1 = €1.15	+352	visitluxembourg.com
Germany	GMT+2	German	Euro €	£1 = €1.15	+49	germany-tourism.de
Switzerland	GMT+1	German French Italian	Swiss Franc	£1 = CHF1.75	+41	myswitzerland.com
Austria	GMT+1	German	Euro €	£1 = €1.15	+43	austria.info

Central Europe Grown-ups' stuff

its own special attractions (see opposite). Camping holidays are available throughout Central Europe with Canvas Holidays (canvasholidays.com), Eurocamp (eurocamp.com) and Keycamp (keycamp.ie). Also try Select Sites (select-site.com). Ski specialists offering all-inclusive family packages to Austria, Switzerland or both countries, include Esprit (esprit-holidays.co.uk), Mark Warner (markwarner.co.uk) and Powder Byrne (powderbyrne.com).

In **Belgium**, Belsud (belsud. be) offers a comprehensive range of accommodation in Brussels, Wallonia and the Ardennes, including farmstays, rural *gîtes*, horse-riding *gîtes*, apartments and holiday villages. Also try Gîtes de Wallonie (gitesdewallonie.net) and Logis de Belgique (logis.be).

Germany has more than 2500 campsites, most of which are open from April to October. There are also 600 youth hostels (djh.de) and a huge choice of self-catering properties and B&Bs (bed-and-breakfast.de). For farm holidays, browse the selecton at landtourismus.de. Hotels that cater specifically for families include Dorfhotels (dorfhotel.eu), Familotel (familotel.de) and Kinderland (kinderland.by). Europa-Park also has some great themed hotels.

Switzerland offers a range of family-friendly accommodation, from igloos

(iglu-dorf.ch) and mountain huts (sas.cas.ch) to sleeping in giant barrels at Trasadingen (feste-feiern.ch). Over 40 KidsHotels (kidshotel.ch) offer quality family accommodation, with well-equipped play areas, children's menus and baby essentials if you need them. Some even provide free childcare during the high season, as well as a weekly programme of activities. Another long-established family favourite, Reka (reka. ch), operates several holiday villages around Switzerland, each one with a relaxed mixture of self-catering cottages, playgrounds, swimming pools and occasionally a wellbeing centre for the grown-ups. Farm holidays from around €250 per week are available from Swiss Holiday Farms (agrotourismus. ch). Swiss Youth Hostels (youthhostel.ch) have good-value family rooms and self-catering kitchen facilities, while Bed and Breakfast Switzerland (bnb.ch) has an online directory with rates from €20.

Austria's all-inclusive, full-board Kinderhotels (kinderhotels.com) are well known for their outstanding childcare. English-speaking childminders are provided free of charge (even for babies as young as seven days old) for up to 60 hours a week. Baby and toddler equipment is provided free of charge, and all food is organic.

Food & drink

Although you will find a cosmopolitan range of restaurants, cafés and fast-food outlets everywhere you go, be sure to try one or two regional specialities. In **Belgium**, kids will love getting to grips with *gauffres* – thick waffles dripping with chocolate, strawberry or raspberry sauce and doused with whipped cream. The **Netherlands** has *poffertjes*, small pancakes dusted in sugar; **Germany** has the formidable Black Forest cake; **Austria** has strudels and **Switzerland** and B∍lgium, of course, are magnets to chocoholics.

On the savoury front, **Germany** is renowned for its sausages – but be warned: they are not always your typical barbecue bangers. In **Switzerland**, fondues, raclettes and rosti should all go down a treat with children – as long as they haven't overdosed on Toblerone beforehand.

Health & safety

Apart from a small risk, during spring, of contracting illnesses from tick bites in forested parts of Germany, no special health precautions are necessary for travel in Central Europe. Remember that strong currents can affect the North Sea coast, so always check whether it's safe to go swimming.

Central Europe Family favourites

Out on the lake at Center Parcs.

Center Parcs at a glance

Belgium	**Erperheide**	⟩⟩ Aqua Mundo in an Asian fishing village setting, indoor play world.
	De Vossemeren	⟩⟩ Aqua Sana wellbeing centre, Discovery Bay in jungle setting, indoor skate arena.
Netherlands	**De Kempervennen**	⟩⟩ Montana Snowcentre, outdoor high adventure experience, waterskiing and dive college.
	Het Meerdal	⟩⟩ Aqua Mundo with 101-m water slide, Mini Baluba indoor playworld.
	Het Heijderbos	⟩⟩ Aqua Mundo with wild-water rapids, horse-riding school, tropical dome with jungle expedition.
	De Eemhof	⟩⟩ Aqua Mundo with body-boarding Flow Rider, magnetic climbing in Action factory, watersports centre.
	Port Zélande	⟩⟩ Sail and dive college, Adventure Factory, close to Zeeland coast.
Germany	**Bispinger Heide**	⟩⟩ Aqua Mundo with Dragon Rock water spout, Aqua Sana spa.
	Park Hochsauerland	⟩⟩ Aqua Mundo, crazy river.
	Park Heibachsee	⟩⟩ Indoor play world, watersports.
	Butjadinger Kuste	⟩⟩ Aqua Mundo with crazy river.

Tour operators

In the UK
The Adventure Company
adventurecompany.co.uk

Bents Tours
bentstours.com

Canvas Holidays
canvasholidays.com

Crystal Holidays
crystalholidays.co.uk

Esprit
esprit-holidays.co.uk

Eurocamp
eurocamp.co.uk

Families Worldwide
familiesworldwide.co.uk

Inntravel
inntravel.co.uk

Keycamp Holidays
keycamp.ie

Lakes & Mountains Holidays
lakes-mountains.co.uk

Mark Warner
markwarner.co.uk

Powder Byrne
powderbyrne.com

VFB Holidays
vfbholidays.co.uk

In the USA
The Backroads
backroads.com

Classic Journeys
classicjourneys.com

Ski Europe
ski-europe.com

Contents

209 Introduction

210 Kids' stuff

212 Tots to teens

214 Athens

218 The Peloponnese
218 Ancient Mycenae
218 Epídaurus
218 Ancient Olympia
219 Nafplio

219 Halkidikí

222 Greek islands
222 Corfu
222 Kefalloniá
223 Kos
223 Lésvos
224 Límnos
224 Rhodes
224 Santoríni
224 Skiathos
225 Zákynthos

226 Crete
226 Irákleio
226 Palace of Knosós
226 Samariá Gorge

228 Cyprus
228 South Cyprus
228 North Cyprus

230 Istanbul

232 Turkish coast
232 Northern Aegean
232 Southern Aegean
233 Turquoise Coast
234 Mediterranean
    Coast

**236 Grown-ups'
    stuff**

Greece & Turkey

Scuba-diving in the Aegean.
Right: Tower of the Winds, Athens.

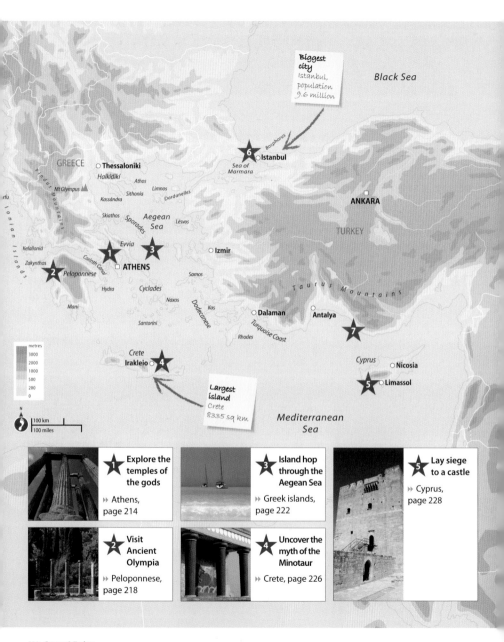

Biggest city
Istanbul,
population
9.6 million

Black Sea

6 Istanbul
Bosphorus
Sea of
Marmara

ANKARA

GREECE
Thessaloniki
Halkidikí
Athos
Limnos
Sithonia
Dardanelles
Mt Olympus
Kassándra

Skiathos
Sporades
Lésvos
Aegean
Sea

TURKEY
Izmir

Kefaloniá
Evvia
3
1
Corinth Canal
ATHENS
Peloponnese
2
Zakynthos
Samos

Hydra
Cyclades
Naxos
Kos
Dodecanese
Dalaman
Antalya
7
Taurus Mountains

Mani
Santorini
Rhodes
Turquoise Coast

metres
3000
2000
1000
500
200
0

Crete
Irakleio
4

Cyprus
Nicosia

5 Limassol

Largest
island
Crete
8335 sq km

Mediterranean
Sea

N
100 km
100 miles

1 Explore the
temples of
the gods
▸▸ Athens,
page 214

3 Island hop
through the
Aegean Sea
▸▸ Greek islands,
page 222

5 Lay siege
to a castle
▸▸ Cyprus,
page 228

2 Visit
Ancient
Olympia
▸▸ Peloponnese,
page 218

4 Uncover the
myth of the
Minotaur
▸▸ Crete, page 226

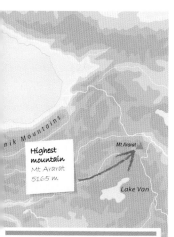

Highest
mountain
Mt Ararat
5165 m

nik Mountains

Mt Ararat

Lake Van

◎ Did you know?

- When a child loses a tooth in Greece it is thrown on the roof for good luck (the tooth not the child).
- Two of the Seven Wonders of the Ancient World stood in Turkey – the Temple of Artemis at Ephesus and the Mausoleum of Halicarnassus in Bodrum.
- The word 'astronaut' is derived from the Greek words *ástron* (star) and *nautes* (sailor).
- Glass beads are a popular talisman which Turks believe ward off the 'evil eye'.
- Pausanias, a Greek geographer who lived in the second century BC, is credited with writing the first ever travel guide, *Description of Greece*.
- The Turks introduced tulips to the Netherlands in the 1500s.

★ 6 Delve into a Turkish bazaar

» Istanbul, page 230

★ 7 Cruise on a sailing *gület*

» Turkey, page 232

Introduction

The people are friendly, the sea is warm, the sunshine is guaranteed and the accommodation and food won't upset the contents of your wallet or your children's stomachs. No wonder Greece and Turkey are such popular family holiday destinations. You probably went there as a kid yourself and know just the place with that perfect beach or laid-back taverna. The Greek islands are the undisputed stars of the region, spattering the azure Aegean with over 2000 irresistible reasons to pack your bags and go Greek. Only a few dozen islands are holiday hotspots, but such is their diversity that you could easily spend a lifetime sampling them. Well-established favourites include Corfu, Rhodes and Crete. Then there's Cyprus and the coasts of Turkey and the Peloponnese – all with enough sandy beaches, ice-cream kiosks and banana-boat rides to satisfy most kids. There's also a lot to be said for combining beach bliss with a little culture. The Greeks practically invented the stuff, so it would seem rude not to spend a day or two exploring the historical wonders of Athens or strutting your stuff in Ancient Olympia. Istanbul, meanwhile, carries more shock with its culture, but its hectic bazaars and flamboyant architecture will leave most children wide-eyed with wonder.

Greece & Turkey Kids' stuff

Books to read

Aesop's Fables
Usborne, 2007
Book/CD pack of famous tales, such as *The Hare and the Tortoise* and *The Thirsty Crow* from the most moral-minded of Greek storytellers. Easy-reading text. Ages 5-8

Greek Myths for Young Children
Usborne, 1999
Pandoras Box, *Theseus and the Minotaur* and *Jason and the Golden Fleece* are just three of the classic tales in this beautifully illustrated collection. Ages 5+

The Wooden Horse of Troy
Book House, 2004
Trojan prince, Paris, abducts Helen, the beautiful wife of King Menelaus, in a crime that unites Greek armies against Troy. Featuring cartoon-style illustrations, this book also has a who's who section and pronunciation guide. Ages 7+

The Groovy Greeks
Scholastic, 2007
Gods that ate their own children, doctors that tasted their patients' earwax… it's all here in Terry Deary's Horrible History, along with other revolting facts about food, war and sport in Ancient Greece. Ages 8+

How Would You Survive as an Ancient Greek?
Franklin Watts, 1999
What would you wear? How would you make a living? And what would happen to you if you cheated at the Olympic Games? Ages 8+

My Family and Other Animals
Puffin, 2006
Gerald Durrell's classic account of how his family moved to Corfu in the 1930s is humorous and insightful. Share Durrell's passion for creatures great and small and gain an insight into Greek culture and family life. Ages 12+

Troy
Scholastic Point, 2006
Adele Geras brings the most famous war in history to life through the eyes of two sisters. Marpessa is gifted with God-sight, while Xanthe has the healing touch. But Aphrodite, Goddess of Love, decides to play with their hearts… and contrives for them to fall in love with the same young warrior. Ages 12+

Taste of Greece & Turkey baklava

A sticky and irresistible pastry that's impressive to look at and easy to make.

What you need
- 400 g ground almonds
- 250 g butter
- 2 tsp cinnamon
- 1 pinch cloves
- 500 g filo pastry
- lemon juice
- 250 ml thyme honey
- 2 tsp vanilla extract
- 450 ml water

What to do
- Mix together the almonds, cinnamon and cloves.
- Butter four sheets of pastry and place in a deep pan or dish.
- Spread a thin layer of nuts and spices on top of the pastry sheets, then add two more sheets of pastry.
- Repeat the process, using the last four sheets for the top layer.
- Cut the baklava into squares; make sure you cut all the way through.
- Top with the remaining butter and bake in a medium-hot oven for 45 minutes.
- Mix the sugar, honey, vanilla, lemon and water and boil in a saucepan for five minutes.
- Pour over the baklava (removing any froth) and serve cold.

Go like Hercules

The year is 708 BC and you've been training hard for 10 months, living life as a soldier. Your challenge is to win the first ever pentathlon event (discus and javelin throwing, wrestling, 180-m sprint and leaping – a kind of long jump). Try these tricks and tips to claim glory, fame and that all-important olive wreath.

- **Javelin** Take a long run up, put all your weight on your stronger foot before you throw. Use your whole body's strength and, remember, don't cross the line.

- **Discus** Hold a heavy object in your stronger hand, bend your knees and hold out both arms in front of you. Spin slowly at first, gradually increasing speed before letting fly.

- **Sprint** Ask two friends to hold a rope (the finish line) at chest height. Run as fast as you can to the line; when you are a couple of paces from the finish, lean forwards, flinging both your arms back and looking down at the floor in a winning chest dip.

- **Wrestling** Stand on one leg and ask a friend to do the same. Practise keeping your balance while gently pushing each other.

- **Leaping** The run up is the key – get your strongest foot planted just before the line to give yourself the best chance. Spring forward and try not to lean back.

Guide to Gods Roman names in brackets

★ **Aphrodite** (Venus) Goddess of love and mother of Eros (Cupid).
★ **Apollo** (Apollo) God of music, poetry and healing.
★ **Ares** (Mars) God of war.
★ **Artemis** (Diana) Goddess of hunting and Apollo's twin.
★ **Athena** (Minerva) Goddess of wisdom and guardian of Athens
★ **Demeter** (Ceres) Goddess of earth and fertility.
★ **Dionysos** (Bacchus) God of wine and merriment.
★ **Hades** (Pluto) God of the Underworld and brother of Zeus.
★ **Hephaestus** (Vulcan) God of the forge.
★ **Heracles** (Hercules) God-hero famed for completing the seemingly impossible Twelve Labours set by Eurystheus, King of Mycenae.
★ **Hermes** (Mercury) Messenger of the gods.
★ **Poseidon** (Neptune) God of the seas and brother of Zeus.
★ **Zeus** (Jupiter) Father of the gods and supreme deity.

High and mighty – the goddess Athena.

Greece & Turkey Tots to teens

Turks and Greeks love children. They dote on them and are usually very forgiving of their moods. Don't be surprised, for example, if your irritable, scowling, post-tantrum toddler receives a squidge on the cheeks and some affectionate hair ruffling rather than a disapproving glance from the locals. While shopping you might find storekeepers spontaneously lavishing balloons, sweets and other freebies on your little darlings, while waiters will often go out of their way to cater for children at restaurants and cafés. Accommodation, meanwhile, covers the entire family-friendly spectrum, from activity-packed all-inclusive resorts to self-catering rural villas.

Greek island sailing.

Babies

Should you really even consider Athens with a baby? What would possess you to drag him, her or, heaven forbid, them around one of the hottest, busiest cities in Europe? After all, most things you will want to see, like the Acropolis and Ancient Agora, are about as buggy-friendly as an SAS assault course. City pavements are either narrow, wonky or non-existent and can you imagine the havoc you'd create pushing your Mamas and Papas three-wheeler into a Pláka curio shop crammed with imitation Greek vases? Still determined to go?

66 99 We love Turkey: the people, food, culture, history, climate, scenery… In fact, there isn't much we don't like, except perhaps the driving and the odd earthquake.

Maxine Browning

Well, the good news is that, during the run-up to the Athens 2004 Paralympics, access for wheelchair users in the city was greatly improved (see opposite). This doesn't mean families with prams or pushchairs can use the wheelchair lift on the north side of the Acropolis, but it does mean that they can take advantage of the fully accessible metro and other improved access facilities around the city.

Of course, you could ditch the wheels altogether and carry your baby around in a papoose or sling. Just be extremely wary of doing this during summer when it becomes insanely hot. If you're determined to feast your eyes on propylaea, stoas and the like, it will be far more relaxing to base yourself at a comfortable beachside hotel or apartment in the Peloponnese and make brief forays to Corinth, Epídaurus or ancient Mycenae.

Plenty of Greek islands also have ancient ruins, so you can combine the odd day's sightseeing with a

predominantly beach-based holiday. The same applies to the Turkish coast. As for Istanbul, it could well be as hot and challenging as Athens. Hygiene may be more of a concern, but one thing is certain: locals will fall over themselves to help you, your baby and your buggy.

Toddlers/pre-school

This could possibly be an even worse age to take children to Athens or Istanbul than when they were babies. Not only are they still largely buggy-dependent (for naps or when they get tired of toddling), but they are heavier to push and more prone to accidents when you set them free. Having said that, this is a great time for taking them to the Peloponnese, Halkidikí, Greek islands or Turkish coast. You might need to ask yourself whether these destinations are worth flying the extra distance (with a fractious, fidgety toddler) when you could have a similar Mediterranean beach holiday in Italy, France or Spain. Ultimately, of course, it all comes down to personal preference. But for sheer variety and value, Greece and Turkey are hard to beat.

Kids/school age

Ancient Greece storms on to the school curriculum around the age of seven – a time when your mini Greek warrior (or goddess) will be thrilled at the prospect of a family odyssey. They are better able to cope with bewildering cities like Athens at this age, although it's still crucial to take precautions against heat and sun exposure. Don't forget to help fire their imagination when visiting ancient ruins (see page 229 for some tips). As with all ages, there are plenty of kids' clubs at excellent resorts throughout Greece, but don't assume this type of accommodation is the only one that will meet with approval. A villa tucked into a forested mountainside on Corfu, for example, might be just the kind of thing to unleash the budding Gerald Durrell in your child.

Teenagers

Mass tourism in parts of Greece and Turkey have spawned the kind of nightlife that might well appeal to your teenager, but most parents of this age group will be happier in a more controlled resort environment where there are special activities and social areas provided for teens. The Lakitira Summer Beach Resort on Kos, for example, caters superbly for teenagers. Available from Mark Warner (markwarner.co.uk) it has an Indy Activ Club where 14- to 17-year-olds can hang out at their own beachfront centre. Organized activities include water polo and pool gladiators, while evening entertainment could be anything from floodlit volleyball to quizzes and discos. This style of resort is also an excellent opportunity for teenagers to learn a new sport, such as kitesurfing, sailing or scuba-diving. The Adventure Company (adventurecompany. co.uk) and Explore Worldwide (explore.co.uk) offer teenage departures on their trips to Greece and Turkey.

66 99 A short stroll from Myrina on Límnos brings you to a sheltered cove of fine sand and shallow water. There's an excellent taverna behind the beach serving delicious, fresh grilled sardines. Be warned: when a big ferry crosses the bay some unexpectedly large waves wash on to the beach a few minutes later.

Celia and Alan Littlefield

Special needs

Greece is slowly addressing access issues, helped in no small part by the 2004 Paralympics which spearheaded the need to improve facilities for the disabled. There is now a wheelchair elevator on the Acropolis, although once at the top the ground is irregular and littered with fragments of marble. Athens airport and the metro both have good access, while the larger catamarans are usually the best option for getting to islands. Athens's National Archaeological Museum is accessible, as is the main floor of Irákleio's museum on Crete. Many parts of Knosós are also wheelchair-friendly, but watch out for sudden unprotected drops. In Rhodes, many lanes of the old city are cobbled but generally negotiable. Visit greecetravel.com/handicapped for further information on accessible sites, hotels and tours including Greek sailing tours for the disabled.

Located in relatively flat areas, Turkish resorts like Dalyan are better suited to wheelchair users – check what facilities are available before booking.

Single parents

Single Parent Holidays (singleparentsonholiday.co.uk) offers affordable quality holidays to many popular destinations including Crete, where you stay in a four-star hotel on a private sandy beach, close to the villages of Stalis and Malia with superb facilities for children and adults. Mango (mangokids.co.uk) offers group holidays for single parent families to Paphos, Cyprus.

Athens Ancient gods & heavenly isles

You don't need to be Athena (the goddess of wisdom) to fathom why Greece is such a popular holiday destination for families. Boasting fantastic beaches, warm, sheltered seas and an easy-going atmosphere, the Greek islands are legendary. With holiday bliss scattered so liberally throughout the Aegean Sea, the Greek capital is always going to have a hard time vying for attention. But spare a thought, and a day or two in your itinerary, for Athens. It's a hot and chaotic city, but the ancient sites truly are amazing. And then there's the Peloponnese, that large, spiky peninsula clinging to the mainland like a stubborn maple leaf. There are more crumbly old wonders here (so that'll impress your history teacher), but the Peloponnese, like Halkidikí in the north, is also blessed with an enticing coastline of beaches and laid-back tavernas.

Marble maidens – the Caryatids.

City highlights

To sightsee in Athens is to romp through the ages. With a little bit of planning, a modest itinerary, sun hats and a healthy dose of imagination you'll be able to fill your children's minds with riveting tales of gods, heroes, villains and geniuses.

◉ Inside info

▸▸ The Acropolis and Ancient Agora are within easy walking distance of each other.
▸▸ Modern, cheap and efficient, the metro (ametro.gr) links major archaeological sites, as well as the port of Piraeus, from where ferries depart for the islands.
▸▸ The modern tram service (tramsa.org) links central Athens with the city's southern suburbs and the coast.
▸▸ Many sites and state museums (culture.gr) close early afternoon.
▸▸ Cool off by getting a day pass to the Athens Hilton pool or seeking shade in the pine forests at Moní Kaisarianí on Mount Ymittós.

The Acropolis

T210-321 4172, acropolisofathens.gr.
Year round, daily from 0800,
€12/adult, free for under-19s.
Acropolis Museum: Dionysiou
Areopagitou St, T210-900 0900,
thecropolismuseum.gr. Year round,
Tue-Sun 0800-2000, €1/adult.
▸▸Red line metro to Acropoli.
Still rising supreme above Athens, this 90-m-high global icon is the crowning glory of ancient Greece. But as with any ruin you will need to bring it to life for kids. So, picture the scene as you walk through the grand temple gateway of the Propylaea: you are following in the footsteps of the Panathenaic Procession when, 2500 years ago, the people of Athens marched through the city to the Acropolis bearing a special robe to honour their patron goddess, Athena. Beyond the Propylaea, towering bronze statues would have reared either side of you – one of Athena Promachos (so dazzling she could be seen by

ships sailing towards Athens) and the other of a Trojan horse. But it was the Parthenon that drew the crowds on. Inside this magnificent temple, with its 46 columns and 13,400 blocks of marble, stood another statue of Athena – a 12-m beauty, clad in gold and ivory and bearing a huge shield.

The exterior of the temple was lavishly adorned with sculptures and brightly coloured friezes – most of these have succumbed to erosion, wars or theft, but you can still imagine something of the fine detail of the Acropolis temples by seeking out the Porch of the Caryatids. You'll find it on a building called the Erechtheion (a sacred site where Poseidon and Athena are said to have fought for control of the city) where, instead of columns, exquisitely carved priestesses support the roof.

Spend some time admiring the views of the surrounding

Crowning glory – the Acropolis.

city, then visit the Theatre of Herodes Atticus, added to the Acropolis by the Romans in the second century AD and still used for performances during the summer Festival of Athens (greekfestival.gr). By now you'll probably need some shade and a rest, so head for the pine-clad hills to the west of the Acropolis for a picnic. Philopáppou Hill is the classic vantage point from which to admire the Parthenon. Imagine the scene in 1687 when Turks ruled Athens and used the temple as a gunpowder store. You're in the Venetian

army trying to wrestle control of the city; you aim your cannon towards the Parthenon, light the fuse and… kaboom! It's a wonder archaeologists were able to piece any of it together again. You'll find more mind-blowing stuff at the sensational new Acropolis Museum with its state-of-the-art displays.

Ancient Agora
odysseus.culture.gr. Year round, daily from 0800, €4/adult, free for under-19s.

▸▸Green line metro to Monastiráki. If anything, kids will be able to

relate more to the Agora than the Acropolis. This was where the nitty-gritty of daily mortal life was carried out in ancient Athens. You'll be able to find the remains of everything from law courts and markets to schools and a prison. The most obvious building is the replica of the Stoa of Attalos – a two-storey shopping arcade. The original version, opened in 138 BC, would have housed 42 shops, but the modern one contains the Agora Museum. Inside, see if you can find the children's toys and an ancient potty.

Pláka and Monastiráki

Lying to the north of the Acropolis, these historic districts are chock-a-block with ancient ruins, as well as some more modern goodies. Among the contemporary highlights are the curio shops along the pedestrianized streets of Pandrósou and Adrianoú and the flea market at Platéia Avissynías. There are also dozens of cafés, tavernas and restaurants. If your kids are game for more old stuff, however, start with the Roman Agora where you can challenge them to spot all eight winds depicted on the 12-m-tall Tower of the Winds – a multi-purpose sundial, water clock, weather vane and compass devised by Andronikos around 150 BC. Nearby Anafiótika is a tangle of narrow streets hemmed in by whitewashed houses nuzzled up against the Acropolis.

Syntagma

Ermoú street links Monastiráki with this city-hub district centred on Plateía Syntágmatos. However, it's more fun to ride the metro – the underground station at Syntagma is a veritable museum of Athenian history with displays of relics uncovered during its excavation. Above ground, take a minute to watch the traditionally attired soldiers high-stepping in slow motion by the Monument to the Unknown Soldier, then seek refuge in the National Gardens. There are children's play areas here, as well as shady benches,

Chariot relief carving, Ancient Agora.

a duck pond and a café. Walk through the gardens and you'll emerge opposite the Temple of Olympian Zeus. It's a whopper, although only 15 of the original 104 17-m-tall columns remain.

Lykavitós Hill

Departing every 10 minutes from Ploutárchou Street a funicular railway scales 277-m Lykavitós Hill. At the top you'll find cafés and an observation deck with Olympian views of the Acropolis and other landmarks.

Best museums

National Archaeological Museum
Patissíon, T210-821 7724, namuseum.gr. Year round, Mon 1330-2000, Tue-Sun 0830-2000, €7/adult, free for under-19s.
School-age children studying the Ancient Greeks will find more than enough inspiration at this extraordinary and recently renovated museum. Star exhibits include the Mask of Agamemnon (a gold death mask discovered at Ancient Mycenae – see page 218) and a collection of bronze statues (*Poseidon, Horse with the Little Jockey*, and *Youth of Antikythira*) salvaged from ancient shipwrecks. It's a huge collection, so prioritise or devise a treasure hunt for your children to find their favourite characters from Greek mythology.

Benáki Museum
Koumbari, T210-367 1000, benaki.gr. Year round, Mon, Wed, Fri, Sat 0900-1700, Thu 0900-2400, Sun 0900-1500, €6/adult, free for under-18s.

The Benáki Museum houses an exceptional collection of Greek treasures, including simple but striking Cycladic figurines (2600-2500 BC), El Fayum portraits (dating from the third century AD) and a magnificent 17th-century map of Greece. Of particular interest to kids, however, is the wonderful display of toys dating from antiquity to 1970 and ranging from costumed dolls to intriguing board games.

Other museums worth an hour or two include the **Acropolis Museum** (see page 214), **Museum of Greek Popular Musical Instruments** (bouzoukis and lutes galore), the **Hellenic Children's Museum** (interactive displays and activities), the **Museum of Greek Children's Art** (paintings inspired by an annual children's competition), the **Museum of Greek Folk Art** (costumes and shadow puppet theatre) and the **War Museum** (weapons and strategies from Mycenean battles to the Second World War).

City escapes

➤➤ Catch a ferry from Piraeus to one of the islands in the Saronic Gulf. Aegina has beaches at Perdika and Agia Marina, Hydra has a beautiful harbour lined with tavernas and shops and Spétses has beaches at Agioi Anárgyri and Agia Paraskeví.

➤➤ Hop on a bus for the two-hour drive south to Cape Soúnion and watch the sun set behind the Temple of Poseidon.

➤➤ Join an organized tour or rent a car and drive three hours' north to Delphi – a spectacular ruin on the flank of Mount Parnassós where ancient Greeks communed with gods through the mysterious oracle.

Cape Sounion.

The Peloponnese Myth meets history

Cross over the Corinth Canal to the Peloponnese and watch your children's faces light up as you explain that this was the birthplace of winged wonder-horse Pegasus and the evil snake-headed Hydra. Tell them about Greek hero, Heracles (or Hercules to the Romans) who battled here to complete the daunting Twelve Labours. It's all myth, of course, but that won't stop your kids' imaginations running riot when you explore the ancient sites of this enigmatic peninsula.

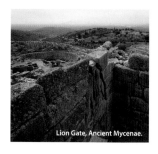
Lion Gate, Ancient Mycenae.

Ancient Mycenae

Rearing from a rugged mêlée of mountains and ravines, this 3300-year-old Bronze Age citadel leapt to fame in 1867 when archaeologist Heinrich Schliemann discovered what he thought was the grave of a legendary king. "I have gazed upon the face of Agamemnon!" he proclaimed – moments before it crumbled to dust as he lifted the gold death mask (now on display in the National Archaeological Museum, page 216). You can still see the grave circles where Schliemann toiled, but far more exciting are Ancient Mycenae's Cyclopean

walls, so-called because later generations, who had lost the ability to move such massive rocks (weighing an average of six tons), believed that the giant, Cyclops, must have had a hand in it. In places they still tower 15 m above you. Even more mind-blowing is the Lion Gate at the citadel's main entrance, where a 12-ton lintel has been raised 3 m off the ground. An unsurpassable feat? Don't you believe it. The nearby Treasury of Atreus has a 9-m-long lintel weighing 120 tons – twice the weight of the heaviest rock at Stonehenge.

Epídaurus

Snug in a cluster of hills clad in pines and oleanders, Epídaurus boasts the best-preserved theatre in Greece. Try to visit before the tour buses arrive so that you can demonstrate its near-flawless acoustics. Get the kids to sit 55 rows up in the spectacular scoop of tiered seats while you stand on the stage and whisper something. They should be able to hear every word.

Ancient Olympia

For sporting fans these incredible ruins are a must-see. Inhabited as early as 4000 BC, Ancient Olympia only achieved esteem as a religious and athletics centre in 776 BC when the first Olympic Games were held there. Many of its treasures are displayed in the Olympia Archaeological Museum, including fine statues, temple reliefs and various sporting artefacts. Check out the Stone of Bybon, a 144-kg rock with the inscription, 'Bybon, son of Phorys, threw me above his head with one hand'. An Olympian feat if ever there was one. Exploring the ruins themselves, you can almost imagine the roar of the crowd as you walk beneath the archway leading to the stadium where running races were held. You can still see the starting line, marked in stone with grooves for athletes' toes. Challenge your kids to a race and then have them in fits of giggles (or disbelief) when you explain that ancient Greek athletes competed

◉ **Inside** info

›› You can visit the Peloponnese sites of Corinth, Epídaurus or Ancient Mycenae on whistle-stop tours from Athens.
›› A rental car will provide freedom and flexibility to visit the sites at your own pace.
›› The Epídaurus Festival, when Greek dramas are held at the ancient theatre, takes place in July and August.
›› For details of ancient sites, log on to odysseus.culture.gr.

Epidaurus.

naked. Other essentials at Olympia include the remains of the Temple of Zeus and the reconstructed colonnade of pillars surrounding the Palaestra (a training centre for boxers, wrestlers and jumpers).

Nafplio

An elegant city with airy squares and narrow streets choked with bougainvillaea and geraniums spilling from wrought-iron balconies, Nafplio is perfect for a spot of curio browsing and a relaxed meal at a pavement café.

Best beaches

Head to the south and west coasts. You'll find sandy bays and clean, warm seas near Methoni, Pylos and at Porto Kayio on the Mani Peninsula. Stamped like a disc of turquoise in the rocky shoreline, Voidokiliá near Pylos is a sheltered, shallow-water gem. Further north, top beaches include Kalogria, a 6-km stretch of sand bordered by pine trees. On the east coast, Tolon is a popular resort offering watersports and boat trips.

Halkidikí holiday heaven

Dangling into the northern Aegean Sea like a cow's udder, Halkidikí has three peninsulas. Two of them – Kassándra and Sithonía – have some of the best sandy beaches in Greece and a good choice of holiday resorts to go with them, while the third – Athos – is an autonomous republic ruled by monks. You have to be male and obtain special permission to visit this hallowed ground, although boat trips from Ouranoúpoli offer views of holy Mount Athos and the monasteries that lie beneath it. Be sure to tear yourself away from the beach for at least a day in order to explore the northern part of Halkidikí. Here you'll find the prehistoric troglodyte dwelling of Petrálona Caves and the birdwatching haven of Lake Korónia. Further afield, there are Macedonian treasures to peruse in the Thessaloníki Archaeological Museum and walking trails to pound on the slopes of Mount Olympus.

›› Greece's second city, Thessaloníki, is the international gateway to the region.
›› Although the best family holiday resorts are located in Halkidikí, there are other options further east at Alexandroúpoli.
›› Halkidikí has more Blue Flag beaches than any other region in Greece.
›› Take a ferry from Kavála to visit the northern Aegean islands or from Thessaloníki to reach the Sporades.

Kids' top 10 Greece

❶ Cruise on a *caique* – a traditional Greek sailing boat – island hopping through the Cyclades, dropping anchor in deserted bays to swim and snorkel.

❷ Hunt for brilliantly tacky souvenirs, like painted wooden donkeys and miniature Greek statues, among the streets and flea markets of Pláka and Monastiráki in Athens.

❸ Challenge mum or dad to a sprint in the 2700-year-old stadium at Ancient Olympia – and win.

❹ Search for chameleons in the dunes near Giálova Lagoon (near Pylos in the Peloponnese) – one of the only places in Europe where you can find African chameleons.

❺ See a Mediterranean monk seal before they become extinct. They're one of Europe's most endangered mammals (only around 500 are left), but you might be lucky enough to glimpse one in the seas around Alónissos – there are boat trips to Sporades Marine Park.

❻ Ogle the gold treasures discovered at Ancient Mycenae and now on display in the National Archaeological Museum in Athens.

❼ Explore the ruins of the Palace of Knosós on Crete, pretending it's the legendary labyrinth of the Minotaur – a fearsome beast, half-bull and half-man, that devoured young victims lost in the maze.

❽ Learn to sail a yacht around the Greek Islands (see page 235).

❾ Make lots of new friends on the beach, in the resort or at the kids' club.

❿ Imagine what happened to the legendary city of Atlantis when the Santorini volcano erupted some 3500 years ago.

“” Youngsters love playing hide-and-seek at ancient ruins, collecting stones or chasing grasshoppers, while older children will enjoy the detective challenge of working out what's what.

Will

Voidokiliá, near Pylos on the Peloponnese, with the lagoons of Giálova in the background.

Greek islands Plan your odyssey

Look at a map of Greece and it's almost as if someone has shaken a pepper pot over the Aegean Sea, such is the abundance of islands and islets scattered between Turkey and mainland Greece. Some, like Corfu, attract hundreds of thousands of tourists each summer, while others remain quieter and less developed. Somewhere in this archipelagic constellation you're bound to find a particularly bright star – an island that's made in beach-holiday heaven. But how to find it, that's the trick. Start by asking yourself the questions shown on page 225 – although chances are you'll end up visiting the Greek islands over and over again, sampling a different one each time.

Santorini.

Corfu

Family appeal One of the greenest and most beautiful of the Greek islands, Corfu's hilly interior is draped with forests of olive and cypress trees. Gerald Durrell based *My Family and Other Animals* here, and you can still stumble upon wild, unspoilt corners of Corfu that inspired the author. There are resorts like Benítses where nightclubs, not cicadas, reverberate through the night, but there are also plenty of bolt holes where you'll find a more sympathetic balance between traditional Greek charm and tourist facilities.

Best beaches Most of the mass-market resorts are concentrated in the southeast. For something quieter look to the southwest (for sandy Maltas backed by thickly wooded hills), the northwest (for Palaiokastrítsa with its three coves clustered around a forested headland), the north (for long sweeping bays and interesting rock formations at Sidári) and the northeast (for

sandy Almíros or the lively resort at Kassiópi).

Best days out Older children will appreciate the elegant Venetian architecture, pavement cafés and shops of Corfu Town, and even littl'uns will enjoy exploring the maze of narrow streets in the old quarter – especially if you plonk them in a horse-drawn carriage. Also worthwhile is a day (or two) of island touring. Hire a car and dawdle inland, stopping for Durrell-style nature hunts (or more strenuous jaunts on Mount Pantokrátor). Alternatively, hire a motorboat and potter along the coast in search of hidden coves. And if you're seized by wanderlust, dont forget that Albania is just a ferry ride away.

Kefalloniá

Family appeal Kefalloniá has it in bucket loads. From mountains and caves to beach resorts and fishing villages, this large island is ideal for families seeking a bit

more than just a beach holiday.
Best beaches The liveliest resorts are at Lássi and nearby stretches of coast. Elsewhere you'll find a mixture of pebbly and sandy beaches, usually with a striking backdrop of mountains. Lourdas and Skála in the far south both have long stretches of white sand with safe swimming, while the north of Kefalloniá has mainly white-pebble beaches. Myrtou Bay, south of Asos, is considered the island's most beautiful.
Best days out Bus services are limited, so it's essential to hire a car. Allow plenty of time for getting around this large, rugged island. Highlights include Asos (with its nearby Venetian fortress), Fiskárdo (Kefalloniá's prettiest village), Mount Aínos (home to wild horses and native fir trees), Drogkaráti caves (the size of a large concert hall and dripping with stalactites) and the Melissaní Cave-Lake (a mysterious subterranean azure-blue lake). The island of

Ithaca – fabled as the home of Odysseus – is also worth a visit. Join a tour with a good guide who will bring to life the legends of Homer's epic, the Odyssey.

Kos

The sandy beaches in the southeast of Kos, as well as north-coast resorts like Tigkáki, make this a popular family destination. Inland, you'll find the remains of the Asklepieion, a fourth-century BC sanctuary dedicated to the god of healing. Kos Town, meanwhile, is the jumping-off point for boat trips to Kalymnos, renowned for its sponge-fishing industry.

Lésvos

Family appeal Once a favoured holiday haunt of the Romans, Lésvos still has what it takes to draw the crowds. A large island with a good scattering of sandy beaches and resorts, the so-called Garden of the Aegean has a rugged landscape rich in tradition.

Best beaches Skála Kallonis, a fishing village at the head of the Kallonis Gulf, has a gently shelving beach and warm shallow water that's ideal for small children. To the west, Skála Eresoú boasts one of the island's finest beaches – a 3-km stretch of dark sand.

Best days out There's a petrified forest and 12th-century

Sunset behind Kalymnos, viewed from Kos.

monastery at Mount Ordymnous – an extinct volcano in the west of the island. Birdwatchers should stake out the lagoons along the western coast, while culture vultures should descend on the atmospheric harbour town of Sykaminiá.

Límnos

Perfect for families in search of a traditional island with few other visitors, Límnos has plenty of sandy beaches for children, although teenagers may find it a little too quiet. The west coast has the pick of the beaches – try Avlónas, just to the north of Myrina with its cobbled streets, bazaar and Ottoman houses.

Rhodes

Family appeal Deservedly popular, this large sunny island has some excellent beaches, a fascinating historic town and a certain buzz that will appeal to families with teenagers.
Best beaches The east coast has a string of sandy beaches: from boisterous resorts like Faliráki, with watersports and nightlife, to quieter coves further south.
Best days out Base yourself on the east coast and it's a straightforward bus ride into Rhodes town. Kids will love exploring the walled Old Town where the Palace of the Grand Masters, a medieval citadel

built by the Knights of St John in the 1300s, is guaranteed to spark their imagination. Inside, challenge them to find the mosaic of the mythical Gorgon Medusa, with hair of writhing serpents. The nearby Street of the Knights, with its austere gateways and impressive coats of arms, is also worth a look. In the new town you can arrange diving and boat trips at Mandráki harbour where the 40-m statue of the Colossus of Rhodes is believed to have once stood. A popular boat excursion is to Líndos where an ancient acropolis looms over a village of whitewashed houses and cobbled streets. If you want shade and tranquillity, visit Petaloúdes, a wooded valley where thousands of Jersey tiger moths gather between June and September (get there before the tour buses arrive).

Santoríni

This famous island blew its top around 1450 BC, spewing clouds of molten debris over 30 km and unleashing a tsunami that devastated Minoan Crete. The volcanic eruption left a giant caldera, which subsequently flooded with seawater and inspired the legend of Atlantis. With whitewashed buildings perched on volcanic cliffs, the town of Firá is a port of call on just about every cruise ship operating in the Aegean Sea.

Paleokastrica Bay, Corfu.

Although there are black-sand beaches on Santoríni, families will find more inviting stretches of sand on other islands in the Cycaldes, such as Náxos and Páros. For independent-minded (ferry- or yacht-bound) families, this beautiful archipelago is ideal for island hopping.

Skiathos

Just 13 km long and with more than 50 sandy beaches, it's small

> **66 99** In the crumbling walls of the sunken garden lived dozens of little black scorpions, shining and polished as if they had been made out of bakelite; in the fig and lemon trees just below the garden were quantities of emerald-green tree-frogs, like delicious satiny sweets among the leaves; up on the hillside lived snakes of various sorts, brilliant lizards and tortoises.
>
> *From My Family and Other Animals by Gerald Durrell (Puffin Books, 2006)*

Pick the right Greek island

›› What do we want to do?

Relax on a beach, swim in the sea, sample a few tavernas… these are all pretty much Greek-island staples and won't help much in whittling down your shortlist. Instead, think of specifics. Do you want lots to do away from the beach? The larger islands – such as Crete, Evvia, Rhodes and Lésvos – have plenty to tempt you inland. Do you want to split your time between two or more islands? The Cyclades, for example, are well suited to island hopping by ferry, cruise ship or chartered yacht. What about activities? Do you need somewhere that offers good walking (Corfu, Crete, Lésvos, Naxos and Samos) or scuba-diving (Corfu, Kefalloniá and Zákynthos)?

›› How do we get there?

Some islands have direct international flights (ideal for younger kids who will want to hit the beach as soon as possible), while others require a ferry transfer, which older children might see as part of the adventure.

›› What kind of accommodation do we need?

You'll find something to suit most budgets, from luxury hotels and villas to self-catering apartments. Consider sharing a larger, pricier villa (which might have extra facilities like a pool) with the grandparents or another family. Lively resorts (like those on Kos and Corfu, for example) will suit families with teenagers, while anything with a kids' club and childcare facilities will appeal to parents with babies and toddlers.

wonder that package tourists overrun Skiathos during July and August. This exquisite little island is buzzing with resorts, watersports and nightlife, but combines well with much quieter Alónissos to the east.

Zákynthos

Although blighted in places by new development, Laganás Bay of Zákynthos has fine sandy beaches. Certain stretches are off-limits to tourists to enable endangered loggerhead turtles to lay their eggs in relative peace between May and August. The resorts of Tsiliví and Alykes are further north, along with the island's most popular boat-trip destinations – Shipwreck Beach and the Blue Caves. Meanwhile, at the tip of Vasilikós peninsula, Gerakí beach has clean, white sand and is gently shelving, making it ideal for children.

Crete Uncovering Minoan mysteries

This gnarled island of mountains and gorges, stubbled with olive groves and orchards, and fringed with superb sandy beaches, may lack the cutesy, intimate feel of smaller Greek islands, but you'll never be bored. As well as delving into ancient Minoan ruins, there are gorges to trek through, caves to visit and rare birds and flowers to spot.

Elafonisi.

Irákleio

Like Chanía in the west, Irákleio's instant appeal for kids is the old harbour and Venetian fortifications. Lure them beyond the uninspiring façade of the city's archaeological museum, however, and they will discover a treasure trove of Minoan artefacts. Star exhibits include the Phaestos Disc (a clay tablet inscribed with mysterious symbols), the black-stone Bull's Head (used for pouring ritual wines) and a pair of figurines depicting snake goddesses (serpents symbolized immortality for the Minoans). The museum provides a vivid insight into the highly sophisticated Minoan civilization that thrived on Crete some 3000

years ago – but don't overdo it; spend an hour or two checking out the highlights, then head out of town to Knosós.

Palace of Knosós

Many of the exhibits displayed in the Irákleio Archaeological Museum were found at these extraordinary ruins. The first palace was levelled during an earthquake in 1700 BC, so the Minoans knocked up a swanky new one – multi-storied and with grand courtyards, over 1000 rooms and an elaborate drainage system. The Royal Apartments even had an ensuite bathroom with what is believed to be the first-ever flush toilet (water was poured down by hand). The palace and some of its colourful

frescoes were partially restored in the early 1900s, so they're not quite as baffling as many other Greek ruins. And, of course, Knosós has the big advantage of a really juicy myth – there never was a labyrinth beneath the palace, but that won't stop kids pretending they're in the lair of the Minotaur.

Samariá Gorge

It's a long way (18 km to the coastal village of Agía Rouméli), but older kids and teens may well be up to the challenge of hiking through this dramatic gorge in western Crete. The well-trodden route takes at least five hours; it's mostly downhill,

◉ Inside info

▸▸ Crete is the largest, most southerly and most spectacular of the Greek islands.
▸▸ For flexibility (and somewhere for the kids to cool down) hire a car with air conditioning.
▸▸ Buses ply the north-coast highway, while ferries link villages along the southwest coast.
▸▸ Crete has ferry connections with Piraeus, the Peloponnese, Rhodes and the Cyclades.

Urns at Knosós.

but take plenty of water and snacks, wear good walking shoes and set off early in the morning. Keep an eye out for wild goats. You don't need to hike back up – boats depart from Agía Rouméli to Sfakií and Palaiochóra until around 1700.

Best beaches

Crete has no shortage of good family beaches, although some (particularly in the north where there is more development) tend to get very crowded at weekends and during peak summer months. The west-coast beaches are more remote and have fewer facilities. Elafonisi is a pink-sand beauty. Separated from an islet by a sheltered tidal lagoon of knee-deep water it's perfect for small children. Nearby, the laid-back resort of Paleochora also has a fine beach and is just a 90-minute bus ride to Chaniá with its old Venetian quarter, covered market and taverna-lined harbour.

Samariá Gorge.

Cyprus The divided island

Fabled as the birthplace of Aphrodite, goddess of beauty and love, Cyprus has legions of holidaymakers well and truly smitten by its beaches, climate and scenery. The southern part of Cyprus is by far the more developed with the kind of all-singing, all-dancing resorts that most teenagers will rave about. However, if you prefer something quieter and more off the beaten track, then North Cyprus (occupied by Turkey since 1974) couldn't be more of a contrast to its Greek Cypriot neighbour. Here, you will find sleepy harbour towns and rural villages, castles perched in the Kyrenia Mountains and beaches where turtles still dare to nest.

Lizard on the walls of Kolossi Castle.

South Cyprus

The fine sandy beaches along the south coast are what most families come here for. However, a few days in a rental car will put you in touch with the quieter, more authentic hinterland. It will also enable you to escape the heat by driving into the Troödos Massif (high and cold enough for skiing in winter). Walking in the mountains is superb, especially during spring when wild flowers are in bloom. A few kilometres outside Limassol, Kolossi Castle stands as testament to the rule of the Knights of St John in the 13th century, while the ancient port of Paphos in the southwest is famous both for its Roman mosaics and as the mythical birthplace of Aphrodite. If you want to find out more about the mysteries of the sea, check out the Museum of Marine Life and the Thalassa Municipal Museum of the Sea in Ayia Napa. Other favourites include the donkey sanctuary near Limassol (donkeycyprus.com) and the Mazotos Camel Park (camel-park.com). If go-karts are preferred, you'll find circuits at Erimi, Polis and Ayia Napa.

Inside info

»» The antithesis to the large resorts of Limassol, consider renting a traditional Cypriot house in the countryside (agrotourism.com.cy).
»» You'll bake in July and August, so try to visit Cyprus either side of this period; it often stays fine through to October.
»» Travel between the Greek and Turkish Cypriot regions is legal and straightforward.

North Cyprus

Although divided by the UN's Green Line, the city of Nicosia remains a friendly, laid-back place. However, kids will be far more interested in the harbour town of Kyrenia (Girne). Not only is there a great castle to explore, but inside you'll find the Shipwreck Museum where a 2300-year-old Greek trading vessel is on display along with its cargo of wine amphorae and some 9000 almonds that were salvaged from the seabed. Perched on a rocky crag in the mountains behind Kyrenia, St Hilarion Castle is a fairy-tale ruin of crenellated walls and watchtowers. Take extra care exploring this castle – some of the paths are steep and slippery, and there are no safety barriers. A little further inland, Bellapais Abbey, however lovely, may be one ruin too many. If that's the case, strike out along the Karpas Peninsula where you can run wild on long sandy beaches.

Splash zones

»» **Fasouri Watermania** (fasouri-watermania.com) Waterpark at Limassol with a kamikaze slide and wave pool.

»» **Waterworld** (waterworldwaterpark.com) Ayia Napa's splash zone, boasting the hair-raising waterslide, Fall of Icarus, and Poseidon's Wave Pool.

»» **Aphrodite** (aphroditewaterpark.com) Waterpark at Paphos with 26 rides, including a pirate ship slide.

🔍 **Riveting** ruins

What comes to mind when you look at the tumbled pillars of Ancient Olympia's Temple of Zeus? A classic example of Doric-style columns dating from the fifth century BC? Giant slices of chocolate Swiss roll? Rocks, rocks and more rocks? Let's face it – the average parent's grasp of ancient Greek history is going to be limited to distant recollections from the 1963 movie, *Jason & the Argonauts*. That's fine for starters, but you're going to need additional tactics if you want to avoid a mutiny with the kids at every ruin you visit. Here are eight tips for keeping them inspired:

▸▸ Try to view a model reconstruction beforehand so your kids have an idea of what the site looked like in its heyday.

▸▸ Give them a leaflet with an artist's impression of the reconstruction and let them play detectives – matching the drawing to the remains.

▸▸ Swat up on a few epic tales of Greek mythology.

▸▸ Play hide-and-seek – although make sure it's safe and that children are aware of roped-off no-go areas.

▸▸ Quiz them on what was good and what was bad about living in ancient Greek times.

▸▸ Role-play a Greek tragedy, an ancient procession or a sporting event.

▸▸ Touch the ancient marble and ask them to name anything they've touched that's older.

▸▸ Strike a deal – one ruin equals one day on the beach, a shopping trip or a boat ride.

Istanbul Where Europe meets Asia

With one foot in Europe and the other in Asia, Turkey is just that little bit more exciting and off the beaten track than Greece. Istanbul provides a distinctively Turkish workout for the senses, but don't feel bewildered. Istanbul is certainly crowded and noisy, but it's also a relatively straightforward place to explore. And what's more, you'll find that the Turks dote on children just as much as their Greek neighbours.

Two-day action plan

▶ **Day 1** Save the history lesson until later. On day one your main priority is to get to Aya Sofya early when morning light filters through the upper windows of this magnificent basilica. Any child who has ever attempted to create a design from tiny pieces of coloured paper will be enthralled by the exquisite artistry of Aya Sofya's mosaics. When Emperor Justinian opened his grand Byzantine design in AD 532, the interior was adorned with some 30 million gold mosaic tiles. But when the city fell to Islam in 1453, the great dome was converted to a mosque, four

minarets were added and the iconic mosaics (unacceptable to Muslim beliefs) were plastered over – inadvertently preserving them. Now a museum, with many of the mosaics restored, Aya Sofya is regarded as one of the world's most important artistic treasure troves. Take a long, close look at the Deësis (Prayer) mosaics depicting Jesus,

Mary and John the Baptist, and it's not hard to see why.

A short stroll from Aya Sofya, the Blue Mosque was constructed over 1000 years later as a rival to its Byzantine neighbour – and its six minarets and colossal 43-m-high dome still dominate the Sultanahmet district. The interior is decorated with some 20,000 exquisitely

◉ **Inside** info

▶ Most of the major sites (kultur. gov.tr) are located in the small district of Sultanahmet; the Grand Bazaar is just a 15-minute walk away, while the ferry dock for trips on the Bosphorus is located at the nearby Eminönü waterfront (tourist departures daily at 1035).
▶ Take a pair of binoculars to help children see the fine detail in the high domes.
▶ Mosques are closed Friday, from around 1300-1500.

painted tiles, shimmering in the light pouring through 260 windows. Each of the elephant foot pillars supporting the dome is 5 m wide.

With all the head spinning, neck craning and hushed reverence that goes on at Aya Sofya and the Blue Mosque, you would be asking a lot of your kids to take in the Topkapi Palace in the same day. Save this historical gem for your second day and instead head for the spooky (and blissfully cool) Basilica Cistern – a vast underground chamber with pillars supported by carved Medusa heads.

A few hundred metres away, you'll find the 650-year-old Grand Bazaar. A vaulted labyrinth of 4000 shops, this is the world's original shopping mall where you'll be able to buy anything from a gold trinket to a belly-dancing costume. Be prepared to haggle, to enter into friendly banter with stallholders and to get lost – it's all part of the fun. If your children are tired and fractious, however, the Grand Bazaar is almost guaranteed misery.

» **Day 2** Start with a boat trip on the Bosphorus, arriving at least an hour before departure to get a good seat. A typical four-hour tour takes you north along the famous straits that link the Sea of Marmara with the Black Sea. On your left is Europe, on your right is Asia. How cool is that! You'll pass the extravagant Dolmabahçe Palace, where Ottoman sultans were enthroned in rooms of gold leaf and alabaster. Then you'll sail under the Bosphorus Bridge and continue to the imposing fortress of Rumeli Hisari before returning to the Eminönü waterfront in Istanbul.

From there it's a short walk to the Topkapi Palace – once the powerhouse of the sultans and now a fine museum. Don't miss the treasury, which displays riches from the Ottoman Empire, including gold thrones, the emerald-encrusted Topkapi

Dagger and the 86-carat Kasikdi Diamond. The rooms in the palace are lavishly decorated with painted tiles and gold leaf, particularly in the harem, which functioned as a glorified prison for the sultans' wives, concubines and children.

Top left: Blue Mosque. Left: Spooky Cistern. Above: Interior of Aya Sofya.

Turkish coast Aegean, Turquoise & Med

There are plenty of family resorts and enticing beaches along Turkey's 8300-km coastline. On the Aegean Coast, ancient ruins like Ephesus are some of the finest in the Mediterranean, while the unspoilt Turquoise Coast (hemmed in by pine-covered mountains and stretching from Marmaris in the west to Antalya in the east) offers a wide range of activities – particularly if you like boat trips. Beach-lovers will find no shortage of long sandy bays and warm, sheltered sea on the Mediterranean Coast – and adventure addicts can take to the Taurus Mountains in search of hiking and rafting opportunities.

Library of Celsus, Ephesus.

Northern Aegean

Think hard before visiting the legendary city of Troy in the far north – it's a patchy, largely uninspiring ruin that children might struggle to marry with Homer's epic tale of the Trojan War. Having said that, the site does have a large wooden horse that children will enjoy clambering inside, just as Greek soldiers are said to have done when they besieged the city thousands of years ago. A better all-round family destination in the northern Aegean is the popular spa resort of Cesme.

Explore the 14th-century Genoese fortress overlooking the harbour, and take a trip on a *gület* (traditional schooner) to Donkey Island – a sanctuary for abandoned beasts of burden.

Southern Aegean

Ephesus
In complete contrast to Troy, above, Ephesus fires the imagination with its incredibly well-preserved gateways, columns and streets. The most complete ancient city in the eastern Mediterranean, the former Roman capital of

Asia Minor began life in the 11th century BC as a centre of worship to Artemis, goddess of fertility. Ephesus only floundered in the sixth century AD when its port silted up, effectively severing the city's lifeblood. Try to reach Ephesus early – there's little shade. The site also gets very crowded, but if anything that will help to recreate the atmosphere of this once-bustling city – especially when you stroll down Curetes Street. This colonnaded thoroughfare was the equivalent of London's Oxford Street or New York's Fifth Avenue. Get the kids to

Inside info

» Tourism is more established in the southern Aegean with a greater choice of resorts.
» Too packaged for some, but handy for visiting Ephesus, Kusadasi is a major cruise port, while boisterous Bodrum is a popular sailing and watersports centre.
» To reach the southern Aegean from Istanbul, one option is to take the overnight express train to Pamukkale, then head west to the coast.

Cool pools

Limestone deposits from a mineral-rich spring have created the travertine waterfall at **Pamukkale** in the southern Aegean, 220 km east of Kusadasi. The best viewpoint of these mysterious pools is from the north gate, but beware of steep, unfenced drops.

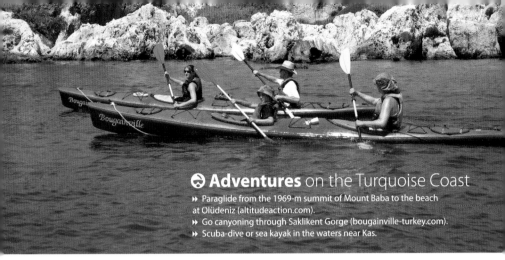

⊘ **Adventures** on the Turquoise Coast

▸▸ Paraglide from the 1969-m summit of Mount Baba to the beach at Olüdeniz (altitudeaction.com).
▸▸ Go canyoning through Saklikent Gorge (bougainville-turkey.com).
▸▸ Scuba-dive or sea kayak in the waters near Kas.

imagine they're Romans out for a morning's shopping. At the end of Curetes Street looms the grand, two-storey façade of the Library of Celsus, while the Marble Way (its surface etched with ancient cartwheel tracks) leads to a vast Roman theatre capable of seating no less than 24,000 people.

To put Ephesus into even greater focus, visit the museum at nearby Seçuk where a multi-breasted statue of fertility goddess Artemis will either bemuse or amuse your children, depending on their age. If the heat and dust begin to take their toll, retreat to the resort of Kusadasi where kids will find cool relief in the form of the Adaland Aquapark (adaland.com). The best beach, meanwhile, is Kadinlar Plaji.

Bodrum
Further south, Bodrum and its satellite resorts of Bitez and Gümbet are magnets to the bronze and booze crowd. However, the old part of Bodrum is definitely worth visiting for its medieval castle. When kids tire of firing imaginary arrows from the ramparts on to the yachts moored in the harbour below, entice them into the castle's fascinating Museum of Underwater Archaeology (bodrum-museum.com). As well as finding out about Roman shipwrecks and crusading knights they can venture into the dungeons and learn about ancient medicine in the spooky-sounding Snake Tower.

Turquoise Coast

Dalyan River
One of the region's most popular excursions, tour boats depart at 1030 and return to Dalyan around 1600. At the start of the cruise you'll see some of the perplexing Lycian tombs for which the Turquoise Coast is renowned. How stonemasons from the fourth century BC managed to chisel these elaborate graves in the middle of a cliff face is still something of a mystery. Remember to pack binoculars – you'll need them for scanning the tombs and spotting birds, terrapins and other river wildlife. After a stop at the ancient Roman trading centre of Kaunos (where you may also glimpse herons and storks in the nearby reed beds) you continue to Istuzu Beach, a 7-km sandy strip which is frequented by nesting turtles

⦿ **Inside** info

▸▸ There are several family resorts at centres such as Kas and Olüdeniz.
▸▸ Rent a car to explore the coast and the rugged hinterland.
▸▸ Rhodes (see page 224) is an easy day trip from Marmaris.

between May and July. Then it's back through the marshy waterways to Ilica for the tour's gooey highlight – a frolic in the natural mud pools.

Fethiye
For a sweet treat, stop at one of Fethiye's Turkish delight stores where you can see the sticky stuff being made and sample the bewildering range of flavours.

Kekova Island
Most boat trips to uninhabited Kekova leave from Andriake and involve a 40-minute boat journey across open water. A better option for families is to drive to the fishing village of Uçagiz from where it's only a 15-minute crossing. That way, you get more time for swimming, snorkelling and viewing the strange Sunken City – a Lycian town off the island's northern shore that was inundated by rising sea levels.

Myra
If the cliff tombs at Dalyan, above, sound intriguing, then the extraordinary Sea Necropolis at Myra will give you an opportunity to study more of these vertiginous graveyards. Get there early, though, because the site can feel like an oven by mid-morning.

Best beaches
Spectacular, some say overdeveloped, the teardrop beach and azure lagoon of Olüdeniz graces almost every other postcard along the Turquoise Coast. The shallow, sheltered waters are perfect for tots, while older children will enjoy the wide range of watersports. Further east, Patara is a complete contrast – a 19-km swathe of sand that has been spared the curse of the concrete mixer thanks to its popularity with nesting loggerhead turtles. Apart from a drinks and ice cream stall, there are no facilities here, but it's still a beach made in sandcastle-building heaven. Just inland there are some atmospheric Roman ruins, while canoe trips on the nearby Xanthos River include gentle rapids as well as wallowing in some natural mud pools.

Original Santa
At Demre, near Myra, you'll find a small church containing the tomb of Nicholas I, a local fourth-century bishop who was canonized after his death for performing a number of miracles and for his generous habit of dropping bags of gold down the chimneys of the poor. In the 17th century, Dutch immigrants brought tales of St Nicholas (or Sinterklaas) to America where the name was eventually corrupted to Santa Claus. Because the feast day of the Turkish-born saint was celebrated in December, people naturally began to envisage him in winter attire, riding a sleigh.

Mediterranean Coast

Best ruins
Crowned by a vaulted walkway, the magnificent Roman theatre at Aspendos is so well preserved that it's still used for opera, ballet and folk concerts during June and July. Perge, meanwhile, showcases more second-century remains, including a stadium measuring 234 m by 34 m that could hold 12,000 spectators. Statues found at the site are on display at Antalya Archaeological Museum.

Best adventures
Frothing and sloshing its way through a canyon in the Taurus Mountains, the Köprülü River is a popular rafting destination between May and October (minimum age eight). For something drier (but no less bouncy) book a 4WD safari into the mountains with any of the tour operators at Antalya, Side and Alanya. A typical tour climbs through forests on the slopes of the Taurus Mountains, visiting remote villages and picnicking beside a river.

◉ Inside info
▸▸ With its cafés, shops and marina, Antalya would suit teenagers.
▸▸ The popular resort of Alanya has 11 km of sandy beaches and a 13th-century citadel.
▸▸ The town of Side combines Roman ruins with a thriving holiday centre.

⚓ **Sail** away

Gület cruises are available from resorts along Turkey's coast, while Sunvil (sunvil.co.uk) operates sailing trips from Lefkas in the Ionian Islands. Families Worldwide (familiesworldwide.co.uk) offers eight-day family sailing holidays in the Greek Islands, suitable for all ages. So, what can you expect from a Greek island sailing holiday? Families Worldwide managing director and sailing enthusiast, Mark Wright and his 11-year-old daughter, Hannah share some nautical nuggets:

Is it better than a beach holiday?
Dad: Absolutely 100%.
Daughter: It's more adventurous.

Best thing about Aegean sailing?
Dad: Sailing on calm seas and arriving in a port like Hydra where there are no roads and the only way to travel is by donkey or on foot.
Daughter: It's very peaceful and I like having a go at steering the boat.

Top tip?
Dad: Go with a locally owned company which can introduce you to local life.
Daughter: Be prepared for some very different experiences.

Greece & Turkey Grown-ups' stuff

When to go

Spring and autumn are ideal times to visit **Athens**. The weather is not usually too hot and the city's attractions are less crowded. Summer lingers in this corner of the Mediterranean, so you might find decent weather as late as November. Temperatures in January reach an annual low of around 12°C, while summer highs soar well above 30°C.

The tourist season in the **Greek islands** begins during April and May, when you can expect few other tourists, warm sunny days and cool nights; the spring flowers are out, but not all facilities, shops and tavernas will be open. In June and early July temperatures start to reach 25°C and, although resorts remain uncrowded, most facilities will be open. Mid-July to late August is peak season (with prices to match). It's hot and busy with everything up and running. Crete, the Dodecanese and the Cyclades may be windy during this period. The weather in September is still good, although you can expect a few thunderstorms; tourist facilities start to close down towards the end of the month. October sees changeable weather, but it's often sunny, especially on southern islands like Crete.

In **Turkey**, the weather and tourist season follow a broadly similar pattern, with Istanbul becoming unbearably hot (35°C+) during July and August – a time when locals and holidaymakers make for the coast. Try to visit in spring or autumn when it's cooler and less busy.

Getting there

The majority of holidaymakers to Greece arrive by **charter flight** arranged through a package tour company. However, there are also numerous **scheduled flights** operated by various airlines. Olympic Airlines (olympicairlines.com) flies to Athens from several European cities, as well as from Montreal, Toronto, New York, Sydney and Johannesburg. Expect to pay around €200 return for a London–Athens ticket during August. British Airways (britishairways.com) has direct flights from London to Athens (around £175 return during August) and also flies to Thessaloníki. Transatlantic flights to Athens operate from Atlanta, Los Angeles and New York with Delta (delta.com) and from Montreal and Toronto with Air Transat (airtransat.ca).

Low-cost flights are available with easyJet (easyjet.com), with direct services from Luton and Gatwick to Athens. Thomsonfly (thomsonfly.com) has flights from over 20 UK airports to numerous destinations in the region, including Corfu, Zákynthos, Crete, Kos, Rhodes, Santoríni, Thessaloníki, Antalya, Dalaman and Cyprus.

Cyprus Airways (cyprus airways.com) has non-stop flights from all over Europe to Lárnaka, with a return fare from London costing around £450 during August.

Charter flights serve popular resort areas along the Turkish coast. Turkish Airlines (thy.com) offer scheduled flights to Istanbul from London, Manchester and Dublin, as well as numerous European and worldwide destinations, including New York Expect to pay around €400 for return London–Istanbul flights during August. Other airlines flying this route include British Airways, easyJet and GB Airways – the latter also flies to Dalaman on the Turquoise Coast.

Getting around

Following huge investment in the run-up to the 2004 Olympics, **Athens** is now the proud owner of a modern, fully integrated public-transport system. The Athens metro (ametro.gr) has three main lines converging on the city centre, while the Athens tram system (tramsa.org) provides a fast link between Syntagma and the southern (coastal) suburbs. The suburban railway (proastiakos.gr) connects Elefthérios Venizélos International Airport to central Athens, Corinth and Piraeus. Rent a car from one of the numerous agencies based at the airport and you can easily drive to western Attica via the smart new Attiki Odos motorway (aodos.gr) and onwards to the Peloponnese across the Rio-Andirrio Bridge, the longest cable-stayed suspension bridge in Europe. There are also numerous tour operators in Athens, such as Hop In Sightseeing (hopin.com) offering excursions to Cape Soúnion, Corinth, the Saronic Gulf Islands and further afield.

Most major towns and cities in **Greece** are connected by coach services operated by KTEL (ktel.org), while the Hellenic Railways Organisation (ose. gr) offers another reasonably priced means of getting around. A one-way fare from Athens to Thessaloníki, for example, costs around €20. Companies operating domestic flights in Greece include Olympic Airlines and Aegean Airlines (aegeanair. com). Not surprisingly, Greece has an extensive domestic ferry network, with the port of Piraeus acting as the main hub. There are around 25 operators, offering everything from high-speed catamarans and hydrofoils to slower and cheaper ferries. Schedules, timetables and online bookings are available at ferries.gr. A day trip from Piraeus to Hydra on a Blue Dolphin hydrofoil operated by Hellenic Seaways (hellenicseaways.gr) costs around €20 return per person. A return voyage between Piraeus and Irákleio (lasting 6½ hours each way) with Minoan Lines (ferries.gr/minoan) costs from around €170 for two adults and two children.

Like Athens, **Istanbul** has an excellent public transport system. To save money, time and stress at ticket booths get hold of a daily Akbil travel card, which you can charge with as much Turkish Lira as you like. Then it's simply a case of pressing the card into the fare machine on a bus, ferry, train or tram and the correct amount is deducted. Your Abkil card will come in useful on ferry trips to and from the Asian and European shores of the Bosphorus (the main docks are at Eminönü, Sirkeci and Karaköy at the mouth of the Golden Horn) and on the Light Rail Transit, which connects Atatürk Airport with Askaray, from where it's easy to connect with a tram to Sultanahmet and Eminönü.

Skip the flight

›› **Take a ferry** from the Italian port of Bari to Patras in the Peloponnese with Blue Star Ferries (bluestarferries.com) or Superfast Ferries (ferries.gr/sff). Alternatively, sail from Venice to Corfu and Patras with Minoan Lines (minoan.gr).

›› **Join a family-friendly cruise** in the eastern Mediterranean.

›› **Travel by train** using Europe's international rail network. You can travel from London to Greece in just 48 hours, either by train and ferry via Italy or solely by train via Budapest.

›› **Link mainland Greece and Turkey** by travelling on the air-conditioned Thessaloniki–Istanbul sleeper train.

ⓘ **Fact** file

Country	Time	Language	Currency	Exchange rate approximate	International dialling code	Tourist information
Greece	GMT+2	Greek	Euro €	£1 = €1.15	+30	gnto.gr
Cyprus	GMT+2	Greek, Turkish	Euro €	£1 = €1.15	+357	visitcyprus.org.cy
Turkey	GMT+2	Turkish	Turkish Lira	£1 = TRY2.5	+90	tourismturkey.org

Greece & Turkey Grown-ups' stuff

Turkish Airlines operates daily flights from Istanbul to Izmir, Antalya, Bodrum and Dalaman. If you have the time, a cheaper alternative is to catch a long-distance bus. You won't need to drive in Istanbul, but hiring a car is the most relaxing and flexible way of touring the coast. Allow around £400 for two weeks' rental in August for a Renault Clio or £750 for a Renault Laguna – both with that all-essential air conditioning.

Accommodation
In a country so heavily dependent on tourism, **Greece** has abundant accommodation – and much of it is good value compared with other European countries. Numerous package-holiday companies and specialist tour operators offer a bewildering range of hotels, resorts, villas and self-catering apartments. The Hellenic Chamber of Hotels (grhotels.gr) has an online search facility for 9000 properties, while a campsite directory is available from the Panhellenic Camping Association (panhellenic-camping-union.gr). Agrotravel (agrotravel.gr) has a list of rural lodgings.

Like Greece, **Cyprus** and coastal parts of Turkey have a great choice of family-friendly villas, hotels and resorts.

In **Istanbul** there are dozens of hotels to choose from, but an excellent alternative for families are the Istanbul Holiday Apartments (istanbulholidayapartments. com). Located near the tourist sights of Sultanahmet, these modern, well-equipped suites sleep up to six and cost from around £60 per night.

Food & drink
Eating out in **Greece** is often a family affair where it's not unusual for children to stay up late in restaurants. What makes it all the more fun and relaxed, though, is the food itself. A traditional Greek meal starts with a selection of *méze* dishes. These nibbles and tidbits are a great way to introduce your kids to a range of Greek cuisine and there's bound to be one or two dishes which find favour with juvenile taste buds, whether it's bread dipped in *tzatzíki* or *taramosaláta* or a handful of olives (especially the fat, juicy Kalamátas ones). Other must-try *méze* snacks include *souvláki* (grilled pork kebabs flavoured with lemon and herbs that kids will also enjoy as a main course), *melitzanosaláta* (grilled aubergine purée), *melitzánes* (aubergines stuffed with onions and tomatoes) and *choriátiki saláta* (the ubiquitous Greek salad made with feta cheese, tomatoes, cucumbers and onions).

The main course, if your children still have room, is usually a meat or fish dish. For visual impact, order *psária plakí*, a whole fish baked with potatoes and vegetables. Other seafood worth trying is grilled swordfish, fried calamari and, for the more adventurous, whitebait and octopus. For the carnivore in your family, order *stifádo* (braised beef and onion stew), *keftédes* (pork mince balls), *kotópoulo riganáto* (roast chicken) or *choriátiko choirinó* (pork chop marinated in olive oil and lemon juice).

When it comes to dessert, *giaoúrti kai méli* (Greek yoghurt and honey) always slips down a treat, or you could go the whole hog and order a platter of *loukoúmia* (doughnuts drenched in syrup). Parents will no doubt want to wash everything down with a bottle of local wine and a shot or two of aniseed-flavoured *ouzo*.

Food in **Cyprus** is a similarly daunting, yet pleasurable, affair with plenty of *méze* dishes to try, as well as lamb or fish cooked with olive oil, tomato and herbs.

In **Turkey**, the *méze* is more

of a social event than merely a meal course – something to be lingered over with friends and *raki* (a raisin and aniseed spirit). Dishes include garlic yoghurt, mashed broad bean salad, salted fish, olives, hummus and flat bread.

For a basic main course, few children will turn their noses up at a grilled meat kebab or *lahmacun* (Turkish pizza topped with ground meat or sausage). You'll also find many Greek-influenced foods, such as fried calamari and aubergine, while the more adventurous can grapple with local specialities like *hülüklü dügün çorbasi* (a thick soup of chopped tripe and meatballs). Those with a sweet tooth will find salvation in *lokum* (Turkish delight) and *baklava* (a layered pastry – see page 211 for details of how to make this at home yourself).

Health & safety

Greece is generally a very safe country with a low crime rate compared to other European nations. Tap water is generally safe to drink in Greece and Cyprus. The most obvious precaution to take while travelling in the region is to avoid overexposure to the sun: wear a hat and sunglasses, drink plenty of water, use a high-factor sunblock, seek shade during the middle part of the day and consider taking swimsuits with built-in sun protection for young children.

Other potential dangers in the region include road accidents – Greece has one of the highest crash rates in Europe. Take your time when driving anywhere and make sure that any children's seats you may have rented with your hire car are fit for the job. To avoid

travellers' diarrhoea steer clear of street food (particularly meat or fish snacks in Istanbul) and be wary of reheated *méze* dishes. If you are unlucky enough to suffer a bout of 'sultan's revenge' make sure you have some sachets of rehydration powder to hand. Think carefully before taking asthma-sufferers to Istanbul as Turks tend to smoke like chimneys.

66 99 Our favourite family destination has to be northeast Corfu in a decent CV Travel villa, plus a rented motor boat. If you've got teenagers, go for something near Kassiópi because then they can go to the (safe) discos.

David Wickers, Journalist

Greece & Turkey Family favourites

Palmiye

Where? Antalya, Turquoise Coast, Turkey.

Why? Fantastic family package with sports galore (sailing, waterskiing, wakeboarding, circus school, kayaking, football etc), two childrens pools, dedicated clubs for babes to teens, plus a spa and hammam (Turkish bath) for the grown-ups.

How much? Expect to pay around £3500 for a family of four during August, including flights, transfers, full-board accommodation, leisure activities, drinks and snacks.

Contact Club Med, T+44 (0)871-424 4044, clubmed.co.uk.

Thanos

Where? Kassiópi, Corfu.

Why? A spacious villa sleeping up to eight, Thanos has superb sea or mountain views from every room. Its quiet mountainside location is perfect for Durrell-style exploration, while Kassiópi (with watersports and boat hire) is just a 15-minute walk away. As well as an outdoor pool, Thanos has a spacious patio and outdoor eating area.

How much? From £480 to £915 per person per week including flights and transfers.

Contact CV Travel, T+44 (0)20-7401 1010, cvtravel.co.uk.

Eleftheria Hotel

Where? Agia Marina, western Crete.

Why? Just 8 km from the harbour town of Chainia and a short walk from the long, sandy beach, shops and tavernas of Agia Marina, this quiet, family-run hotel has lush gardens and a large pool with children's area. The family rooms are partitioned to divide a double bedroom from a twin bed area.

How much? Family rooms from £735 to £945 per week, including breakfast and car hire.

Contact Cretan Ambience, T+44 (0)20-7553 6959, cretanambience.co.uk).

Nautica Bay Hotel

Where? Porto Heli, Peloponnese.

Why? Inclusive tuition in dinghy sailing, windsurfing and mountain biking, plus a dive centre and on-site tennis coach make this a guaranteed hit with active families. Hotel facilities include family rooms, children's clubs, a large pool, beach bar and beautiful seafront gardens.

How much? From £486 to £810 per adult and £399 to £655 per child per week, including flights, transfers, half-board accommodation, sporting activities and tuition.

Contact Neilson Active Holidays, T+44 (0)844-879 8155, neilson.co.uk.

Kyprianos Apartments

Where? Limni Keri, Zákynthos.

Why? A short walk from the beach, this traditionally-styled group of 13 open-plan studios and six two-bedroom apartments are set in pretty gardens with a swimming pool. All have air-conditioning, shower room, kitchenette and a balcony or terrace – some with views of the sea. For a small extra charge, breakfast is available by the pool.

How much? Two-bedroom apartment around £440 to £600 per person per week, including flights.

Contact Sunvil Holidays, T+44 (0)20-879 8155 (sunvil.co.uk).

Tour operators

The Adventure Company
adventurecompany.co.uk

Anatolian Sky
anatolian-sky.co.uk

ClubMed
clubmed.com

Cretan Ambience
cretanambience.co.uk

Crystal Holidays
crystalholidays.co.uk

CV Travel Greek Islands
cvtravel.co.uk

Exodus
exodus.co.uk

Explore
explore.co.uk

Families Worldwide
familiesworldwide.co.uk

Greek Islands Club
greekislandsclub.com

Greek Options
greekoptions.co.uk

Greek Sun Holidays
greeksun.co.uk

Inntravel
inntravel.co.uk/Greece

Ionian Island Holidays
ionianislandholidays.com

Islands of Greece
islands-of-greece.co.uk

Mark Warner
markwarner.co.uk

Neilson Active Holidays
neilson.co.uk

Planos Holidays
planos.co.uk

Powder Byrne
powderbyrne.com

Sailing Holidays
sailingholidays.com

Sunvil Holidays
sunvil.co.uk

Island in the sun – Zákynthos.

Hiking in Triglav National Park, Slovenia.
Right: Ljubljana dragon.

Contents

245 Introduction

246 Kids' stuff

248 Tots to teens

250 Czech Republic
250 Prague

252 Poland
252 Kraków
252 Wieliczka Salt Mine

253 Slovakia

253 Hungary

254 Romania
254 Bran Castle
254 Carpathian
     Mountains
255 Danube Delta

255 Bulgaria

256 Slovenia
256 Ljubljana
256 Lake Bled
256 Lake Bohinj
257 Adriatic Sea

258 Croatia
258 Dubrovnik
259 Plitvice Lakes
     National Park

260 Grown-ups'
     stuff

Eastern Europe

LITHUANIA
VILNIUS

Baltic
Sea

Largest city
Warsaw,
population
2.2 million

BERLIN

Oder

Vistula

WARSAW

POLAND

Elbe

PRAGUE

CZECH REPUBLIC

Kraków

Danube

Tatra Mountains

Bieszczady Mountains

SLOVAKIA

VIENNA   BRATISLAVA

BUDAPEST

Lake Balaton   HUNGARY

SLOVENIA
LJUBLJANA

Venice

ZAGREB

CROATIA

ROMANIA

Carpathian Mountains

Transylvanian Alps

BUCHAREST

Longest river
Danube
2850 km

Danube

Adriatic
Sea

Dalmatian Coast

Korčula

Mljet   Dubrovnik

BULGARIA

Black
Sea

SOFIA

Balkan Peninsula

Musala

Rhodope Mountains

Highest mountain
Musala,
Bulgaria
2925 m

Mediterranean
Sea

❂ Did you know?

- The famous 13th-century traveller, Marco Polo, was born on the Croatian island of Korčula.
- Born in 1810, Polish composer, Frédéric Chopin gave his first public piano concert at the age of eight.
- Weighing 1.31 kg, the world's largest truffle was found in Istria, Croatia, in 1999 by Giancarlo Zigante and his dog, Diana.
- *King Ottokar's Sceptre*, one of the Adventures of Tintin, is based on the Czech crown jewels, which are kept under lock and key at Prague Castle.

metres
3000
2000
1000
500
200
0

N

100 km
100 miles

Introduction

1 Take a family-friendly break in Prague

▸▸ Czech Republic, page 250

2 Hike or ski in the Tatra Mountains

▸▸ Slovakia, page 253

3 Search for dragons

▸▸ Slovenia, page 256; Poland, page 252

4 Dare to enter Dracula's castle

▸▸ Romania, page 254

5 Swim in a mountain lake

▸▸ Slovenia, page 256

6 Explore a giant cavern

▸▸ Slovenia, page 256

7 Island hop along the Adriatic

▸▸ Croatia, page 258

When it comes to carefree holidays in Europe with the kids, traditional favourites like France and Spain will always reap the most beach towels. However, an increasing number of families are looking to the east for a holiday that not only gives them excellent value for money, but also has many of the facilities offered by resorts further west. Following the turbulent 1990s, Croatia's tourism is back in top gear with excellent hotels and holiday camps along the Adriatic coast. Adventurous families can kayak through the Dalmatian archipelago or explore inland national parks like Plitvice Lakes. Making a quieter splash, Croatia's northern neighbour, Slovenia, is slowly gaining popularity. It's small (about the size of Wales), but has everything from mountains and castles to alpine lakes and a dash of Adriatic coastline. Prague and Kraków are well-established city-break destinations, but families in the know will be able to find plenty to please children, from Prague Castle to the Wieliczka Salt Mine near Kraków. A cultural sojourn in either city combines well with an adventure- or wildlife-focused break in the Carpathian Mountains. There are wolves and bears to be spotted in Romania's wildwoods and if that doesn't have enough bite, try Dracula's Castle.

Eastern Europe Kids' stuff

Books to read

Little Dracula's First Bite
Walker Books, 2001
The inhabitants of Castle Dracula are a colourful bunch – not least Little Dracula who is small, bald and green. In this story Little Dracula tries to be just like Dad and has a 'fangtastic' time!
Ages 4-6

Stories of Dragons
Usborne Books, 2007
There's a dragon to match every mood in these myths and folklore tales gathered from around the world. Some are friendly, some fierce and there's even one which loves to dance.
Ages 8-12

Hidden Tales from Eastern Europe
Frances Lincoln, 2002
A collection of elegantly told and beautifully illustrated folk tales from Poland, Slovakia, Russia, Croatia, Serbia, Slovenia and Romania.
All ages

Dracula
Usborne Classics retold, 2007
Can eccentric Professor Van Helsing and his brave young friends take on the world's vilest vampire? A modern retelling of the classic Bram Stoker horror novel.
Ages 9+

Chopin and Romantic Music
Barrons Educational Series, 2000
Discover the accomplishments of Polish-born Frédéric Chopin, including his influence on the romantic movement of music.
Ages 12+

Surviving Auschwitz: Children of the Shoah
ibooks, 2005
The harrowing story of three young girls who survived Hitler's most notorious death camp. Intensely moving, these children's stories provide a remarkable insight into the Holocaust years and its implications. Ages 14+

Cool kayaking

Croatia's island-spattered Adriatic coastline is crying out for some serious sea kayaking. You must wear a lifejacket and be able to swim. Sea kayaks are quite stable, but try to avoid rough water. If you're a beginner it's a good idea to share a two-person kayak with an adult. Here's how to perfect your paddling:

1 Adjust your seat and foot pedals so that your knees are touching the inside of the hull. This will help your balance.

2 Sit upright and space your hands on the paddle about 50 cm apart.

3 Grip the paddle lightly, otherwise your forearms will quickly feel tired.

4 Don't dip the paddle too deeply into the water.

5 Imagine tracing a figure-of-eight with your hands as you paddle. Keep a smooth and steady rhythm.

6 Use the rudder only when necessary – oversteering will slow the kayak and make paddling much harder work.

Taste of Poland
apple baba

A popular dessert in Poland, apple baba is a light and delicious cake using tart apples and plenty of sugar.

What you need
- 4 tart apples (such as Granny Smiths), peeled, cored, quartered and thinly sliced crosswise
- 500 g of granulated sugar
- 1 tsp cinnamon
- 4 large eggs
- 150 ml vegetable oil
- 75 ml fresh orange juice
- 2 tsp vanilla extract
- 900 g plain flour
- 1 tsp baking powder
- confectioners' sugar for sprinkling

What to do
- Heat oven to 175°C and grease a 25-cm loaf tin.
- Place the apples in a bowl and sprinkle with 60 g sugar and the cinnamon.
- In another bowl, beat the eggs and the rest of the sugar until pale yellow and thick.
- Gradually beat in the oil, orange juice and vanilla extract.
- Sift the flour and baking powder and slowly add it to the egg mixture until it is like thick honey.
- Fold the apples evenly into the batter and pour into the tin.
- Bake for around 1½ hours until the top is well browned and splitting.
- Invert on to a wire rack to cool and sprinkle with sugar just before serving.

Paint 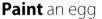 an egg

It is traditional to paint and decorate eggs in many parts of Eastern Europe. Here's how to create your own *pysanka*, or Ukranian Easter egg, using the written-wax batik method. It's fiddly but fun.

What you need
- smooth fresh eggs
- long straight pins stuck into corks (your writing tools)
- wax (equal amounts of beeswax and paraffin)
- wax warmer (candle-heated container)
- egg dyes in containers large enough to submerge eggs
- paper tissues
- candle
- varnish

What you need
- Ask an adult to help you blow your egg. Use a long pin to make a tiny hole at each end (slightly larger at the bottom). Pierce and break the yolk with the pin, shake to mix the contents. Blow gently through the smaller hole to empty the contents into a bowl. Rinse carefully and leave it to dry.
- Practise your design on paper.
- Dip your pinhead into melted wax and use it to draw your design on the egg.
- When you are happy with the

design, place the egg in the lightest-colour dye for 10 to 30 minutes. Blot dry with tissues.
- When completely dry add further designs with wax before submerging in the next colour of dye. Repeat with one more colour.
- An adult can complete the design by holding the egg, a small section at a time, against the side of a candle flame for no more than five seconds to remove the wax (by blotting with a tissue).
- Preserve the egg with two light coats of clear varnish.

Spot a bear

Bears still roam the dense forests of Eastern Europe, but they can be very elusive. One of the best places to catch a glimpse is Kingstone Mountain National Park in Slovenia. Poland's Bieszczady Mountains are still roamed by Europe's Big Five: wolf, bison, bear, lynx and red deer, while Croatia's Plitvice Lakes National Park is home to bears and wolves.

Eastern Europe Tots to teens

When it comes to family holidays there's no doubt that some parts of Eastern Europe, particularly rural areas, can be more of a challenge than elsewhere on the continent. You won't, for example, find as many theme parks here as you do in Scandinavia or France. And on more remote forays in Eastern Europe you might occasionally find yourself wondering whether you've strayed too far off the beaten track. However, all of the countries covered in this chapter have not only popular resort areas and fascinating cities but also a good range of family-friendly accommodation, activities and facilities.

Lake Bled.

Babies

If you've tried a Mediterranean holiday in France, Italy or Spain with tiny tots, you'll find that Croatia's Adriatic coast is just as warm, comfortable and friendly. True, it's further to fly – and there can't be many new parents willing to summon the energy required to drive 1600 km from the UK to Split. However, once you reach Croatia, there's a wide range of baby-friendly accommodation to choose from, including self-catering villas, holiday camps with crèches and hotels with paddling pools.

Now is also the time to snatch a weekend break in cities like Prague or Kraków while your little darling is still buggy-bound and hasn't yet found the voice to offer unwanted suggestions to your sightseeing plan. Avoid the crazy midsummer months, though, when you'll spend half your time apologizing for running your buggy over the feet of endless streams of other tourists.

Toddlers/pre-school

As with babies, travelling to Croatia with pre-school children means you can avoid the blisteringly hot month of August. It's cooler and less crowded in June and September. Be aware that many beaches along this stretch of Adriatic coast are either rocky or pebbly – a godsend to parents who abhor the prospect of sand finding its way into every nook and cranny, but a tad frustrating for a budding sandcastle-building three-year-old. It's

worth remembering to pack jelly shoes or wetsuit boots to help littl'uns negotiate pebbly coves with the minimum of fuss and scraped knees.

With its shallow waters and gently shelving shores, Lake Balaton in Hungary (page 253) is another good beach option for young children – and excellent value if you're on a tight budget. So too are the Baltic states (see box opposite).

Kids/school age

The Czech Republic, Slovakia, Romania and Slovenia all start to have more appeal around this age. Slovenia is a doddle to travel around and its compact size means you can give youngsters a taster of all things Eastern European, from spooky castles and mysterious forests to

66 99 Little Slovenia not only proved to be a big on boredom-busting, but it enabled our children to experience something new, from whitewater kayaking to sipping water straight from a mountain spring. It was less crowded and better value for money than its more popular European rivals, but ultimately its main draw was that it was somewhere just that little bit different. *Will*

Baltic break

Easily overlooked, but bursting with ideas for a family holiday, the Baltic states of Estonia, Latvia and Lithuania promise exceptional value for money. English is widely spoken, it's easy to get around and accommodation includes child-friendly guesthouses, farms and cottages.

Lithuania family holiday Start by exploring the narrow lanes and secret courtyards of Vilnius' Old Town, then delve into the countryside by kayak or cycle. Visit the island castle of Trakai on Lake Galvė, then relax on the Amber Coast.

Trakai Castle.

action-packed mountain resorts.

Usually, you will find that the minimum age for things like river rafting (with gentle rapids) is five or six. It's around this age (possibly earlier if they have older siblings) that kids start nurturing a fascination with all things gruesome – vampires included. Romania's Bran Castle, the legendary home of Dracula, will either titillate or terrify them. If it's likely to be the latter, opt instead for Kraków where the Royal Castle has an altogether less sinister dragon's lair.
The history of Eastern Europe doesn't feature as much on the school curriculum as other parts of the continent, but that's no reason to sidestep the beautiful Czech capital, Prague. Forget its reputation as a couples-only city break destination. With a little forward planning you can easily adapt it to suit children and adults alike.

Teenagers

One aspect of Eastern European history that older children will encounter in their studies is the rise and fall of Nazi Germany. However, prepare yourself for some difficult questions before taking teenagers to Auschwitz in Poland. Reading about it in school textbooks is one thing, but to actually visit the site of this notorious death camp is a harsh lesson for young minds.

Elsewhere in the region, teenagers will love the mix of nightlife and water-based activities along the Croatian coast. Plan a sea-kayaking expedition among the Dalmatian islands or opt for a centre-based holiday in which youngsters can dabble in a range of activities, from sailing to scuba-diving.

The Adventure Company (adventurecompany.co.uk),

Special needs

Certain attractions in Eastern Europe, such as Slovenia's Skocjan Caves, present obvious difficulties to wheelchair users. However, although facilities for the disabled are still somewhat limited throughout the region, most countries are making strong moves to improve access for all. Wheelchair-accessible monuments in Prague include St Vitus Cathedral, Old Royal Palace, St George's Basilica, Ballgame Hall and Prague Castle Gardens, while Wawel Royal Castle in Kraków can be reached (albeit with some effort) by its ramp-like approach road. Thanks to a million-dollar accessibility project, disabled travellers can tour most parts of the Wieliczka Salt Mine.

Single parents

The Adventure Company (adventurecompany.co.uk) offers single parent family departures on its Croatian sea kayaking and multi-activity holidays, as well as trips to the Czech Republic and Slovenia. Mango (mangokids. co.uk) specializes in group holidays for single-parent families and runs a Single Parent Family Ski Holiday to Romania each February half-term. For a gentle seaside break, Small Families (smallfamilies.co.uk) runs a trip to the Island of Lopud in Croatia.

Explore Worldwide (explore. co.uk) and Exodus (exodus.co.uk) offer teenage departures on trips to various Eastern European countries, including Croatia, the Czech Republic, Poland, Romania, Slovakia and Slovenia.

Czech Republic Prague for kids

The beautiful medieval capital of the Czech Republic, Prague has become one of Europe's most trendy city-break destinations – a magnet for couples in search of café culture, a spot of shopping and a lazy trawl around the historical sights. However, before you ship your brood off to the grandparents, you might want to know that Prague is also quite child-friendly. One or two carefully planned days will mean you can still see many of the city's highlights and keep the kids happy in the process. Of course, it would help if you promise them a week of fun in Slovakia's Tatra Mountains afterwards…

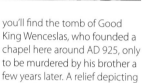
Statue on Charles Bridge.

Prague

➤ **Day 1** Take the funicular railway up 318-m Petřín Hill where you'll find an imitation Eiffel Tower built for the Jubilee Exhibition of 1891. Although it's only a quarter the height of the Parisian version, the 299 steps lead to a viewing platform with far-reaching views of the city and distant mountains. Next, head to the nearby maze, which

◉ **Inside** info

▸▸ Pick up a travel pass for the city's trams, metro and buses at the tourist office in Old Town Square (prague-info.cz). The Prague Card can also be used as a ticket to some 40 attractions, including Prague Castle and the zoo.
▸▸ The Nostalgic Tram 91 (Nostalgická Linka 91) departs from Vozovna Střešovice every hour from 1200 to 1800 at weekends and weaves through the Old Town.
▸▸ Certovka, a small park with a playground at the western end of Charles Bridge, and the Franciscan Garden near Wenceslas Square both offer space for kids to run about.

has walls lined with distorting mirrors, so you can get lost and laugh about it at the same time. Inside this bizarre labyrinth is a huge painting depicting the 1648 battle that ended the Thirty Years' War. On the way down from Petřín Hill, stop for a snack at the Nebozizek restaurant, which has an outdoor patio, fine views and a varied menu.

In the afternoon, tram route 22 or 23 will take you to Prague Castle (hrad.cz). Founded in the ninth century, the city's crowning glory contains churches, palaces, towers and convents within its fortified walls. As you enter, look out for the statue of the fighting giants above the castle gates. Beyond the president's office looms Prague's richly decorated Gothic icon, St Vitus's Cathedral. See if you can spot the gargoyles on the western façade. Inside,

Astronomical clock.

you'll find the tomb of Good King Wenceslas, who founded a chapel here around AD 925, only to be murdered by his brother a few years later. A relief depicting the brutal act can be seen on the west door.

If cultural fatigue starts to take its toll on your children, give them a quick boost at the Toy Museum (barbiemuseum.cz). This quirky collection has everything from tin soldiers, model aeroplanes and wooden farm animals to clockwork robots, teddy bears and several hundred Barbie dolls. While you're at this end of Prague Castle, take a wander down Golden Lane with its quaint 16th-century artisans' cottages, then backtrack towards the cathedral for one last cultural biggie. It's a difficult decision between the Royal Palace, with its massive vaulted halls and

The Vltava River

coats of arms, and St George's Convent with its national collection of Renaissance and Baroque art.

▶ **Day 2** Start in the Little Quarter where kids can play in the park on Kampa Island and feed the swans on Vltava River. Then cross Charles Bridge, admiring the famous statues of various saints, and walk the short distance to the Old Town Square. Traffic-free (unless you count the horse-drawn carriages) this wonderful public space, with cafés spilling out on to the cobbles, is framed by beautiful churches, palaces, town houses and arcades. The most eye-catching building is the Old Town Hall. Make sure you get a good position in front

of its astronomical clock, which strikes the hour accompanied by an elaborate charade of clockwork Apostles, and other moving figures.

In the afternoon, catch a tram to the Prístaviste Parníku landing stage (located between Palackého and Jiráskuv bridges) for a boat ride on the Vltava. Heading north, you'll pass riverside landmarks, like the National Theatre, before reaching Stromovka Park and the Výstaviste fairgrounds – site of a dancing fountain and the Sea World aquarium (morsky-svet.cz). On the opposite bank, Prague Zoo (zoopraha. cz) is renowned for its captive breeding programmes of endangered species, such as Przewalski's horse.

⛫ **Cool** castles

Karlstein (*pictured above*)
25 km southwest of Prague
Rises above woodland that has changed little since Charles IV hunted there in the 14th century.

Konopište
40 km southeast of Prague
Striking for its extravagant displays of stags' heads and other hunting trophies.

Krivoklát
45 km west of Prague
Dominated by a massive Great Tower, Krivoklát has a vaulted Gothic hall reminiscent of the one in Prague's Royal Palace.

Poland A pinch of salt with your city break

Like Prague in the Czech Republic (see page 250), Kraków in southern Poland is one of Eastern Europe's essential city-break destinations. Spared the ravages of the Second World War, its Old Town is a medieval marvel that could almost have been lifted straight from the pages of a child's storybook (there's even a dragon's den under the castle). Combine a day or two in Kraków with a visit to the nearby Wieliczka Salt Mine (not as dry and dull as you might imagine), then head south to the mountains.

Kraków Castle.

Kraków

Heart and soul of the city, Kraków's central square (Rynek Glowny) is a great place to start your sightseeing. Young children will be obsessed with feeding the pigeons, while teenagers can practise being cool at the pavement cafés. Either way, parents will be able to snatch admiring glances at the square's impressive buildings, including the Cloth Hall and the 14th-century St Mary's Church.

Kraków's Old Town is only 800 m wide by 1200 m in length, so it won't take you long

 Inside info

» Hire a horse-drawn carriage in the Old Town (krakow-info.com).
» For light relief, head for the IMAX cinema, puppet theatre or Park Wodny (parkwodny.pl) waterpark on the city's northern outskirts.
» Auschwitz concentration camp (auschwitz-muzeum.oswiecim. pl) is an hour's drive from Kraków. However, even if your kids have studied the barbarism of Nazi Germany at school, Auschwitz is not suitable for anyone under 14.

to walk to the Czartoryskich Museum (muzeum-czartoryskich.krakow.pl) with its exquisite portrait, *Lady with the Ermine*, by none other than Leonardo da Vinci. Next, it's off to Wawel Hill (wawel.krakow.pl), where Kraków's greatest urban myth lurks beneath the Royal Castle. Once upon a time there was a powerful prince called Krak who built a castle on a hill above the Vistula River. He founded a town named after himself and everyone lived happily ever after – or at least they would have done had it not been for the dastardly dragon living in the cave under the castle. This monstrous beast was a perfect nuisance, gobbling up cattle, sheep and people (it was particularly partial to pretty maidens). But wise Prince Krak had a cunning plan. One day, he ordered a sheep's hide to be stuffed with sulphur and tossed into the dragon's den. Of course, the repulsive reptile swallowed it in one gulp, only then feeling the sulphur burning its stomach. Rushing down to the river, the dragon drank and drank...

until it exploded. The end. Well, not quite – you can visit the Dragon's Cave for yourself by clambering down the steps inside one of the castle's towers, but be sure to explore the fine treasures in the fort beforehand.

Wieliczka Salt Mine

Wieliczka, T012-278 7302, kopalnia. pl. Apr-Oct, daily 0730-1930, Nov-Mar, daily 0800-1700, from PLN48/adult, PLN33/child (4-16), PLN129/family.
» Mainline train Kraków – Wieliczka Rynek

Caves made of salt? You may well have to pinch yourself when venturing into this extraordinary subterranean labyrinth, carved entirely from salt and extending to some 300 km of passages and more than 2000 caverns. Mined since the Middle Ages, when salt was as valuable as a commodity as oil is today, the Wieliczka Salt Mine is just 10 km from the city centre. Although excavations reach a depth of 327 m, the section accessible to visitors only goes down as far as 135 m.

The 2-km tour takes you through a surreal, almost fairytale, world of vast floodlit chambers some with underground lakes, others with salt carvings and murals left by Wieliczka's miners. There are chapels illuminated by chandeliers, great wooden stairways, displays of old mining equipment and even a subterranean restaurant, souvenir shop and post office.

Hiking in the Tatra Mountains.

Wieliczka Salt Mine.

Slovakia mountains and castles

Zuberec
Nestled beneath the Roháce range, the small village of Zuberec (rohace.sk) has become a thriving centre for winter and summer activities. As well as being the starting point for hiking trails to nearby lakes and waterfalls, Zuberec is within cycling distance (around 18 km) of Brestova's open-air museum (museum.sk) where traditional buildings – from sawmills to churches – evoke rural Slovakian life from the late 19th century. Hands-on activities allow children to take part in crafts, games and folk dancing. In winter, Zuberec is an ideal place for learning to ski or snowboard, with easy access to around 4 km of pistes. Cross-country trails, snowshoeing and dog sledging are also available.

Malá Fatra National Park
Cloaked in beech forests and home to bear, lynx and golden eagle, this beautiful mountain reserve (80 km from Zuberec) is also renowned for its whitewater rafting. Trips depart from Parnica, swooping you through grade II-III rapids in the Vratna Valley.

Oravice
More gentle float trips are possible here, drifting downstream on traditional wooden rafts to Orava Castle (oravamuzeum.sk), perched on a rocky bluff 100 m above the river. Oravice also has a thermal pool complex (meanderpark.com), which doubles as a ski park in winter.

Ski poles
Located in the Tatra Mountains about 100 km south of Kraków, Zakopane (zakopane.pl) is Poland's premier ski resort, with access to over 50 lifts and a wide variety of runs to suit all abilities.

Hungary for a holiday
Lake Balaton is the place to go. Central Europe's largest lake has an average depth of just 2-3 m. It warms quickly in the sun and has gently shelving beaches, making it ideal for young children. Sailing, windsurfing, canoeing and other watersports can be found on the southern shore, while the north has rugged scenery that will appeal to hikers, cyclists and horse riders. Thermal springs and spas, meanwhile, offer a spot of relaxation.

Get a package Vacansoleil (vacansoleil.co.uk) offers a week at Füred on the shores of Lake Balaton from around £275 to £580 per week for a fully equipped six-berth tent, including Dover–Calais ferry crossings. The campsite offers excursions to Budapest where kids will love exploring the 10-km labyrinth of passageways beneath Buda Castle (labirintus.com). Ryanair (ryanair.com) has flights to Budapest.

Further info Hungarian National Tourist Office (hungary.com).

Romania Walk in the woods… if you dare

The Carpathian Mountains sweep through Romania in a broad swathe of densely forested peaks, peppered with small villages and farming communities, while the River Danube scrawls a lazy outline along the country's southern border. Rural Romania feels remote and unspoilt – locals will tell you the country has more brown bears than British Columbia. But despite this image of tranquil wilderness, there's always something gnawing away at your mind – or rather your neck – when you contemplate Romania. Just the mere mention of the words 'Dracula's castle' will have your kids more riveted than any amount of spiel about the adventure, wildlife and cultural highlights in this land of Transylvanian vampires!

Fangs for the memory – Bran Castle.

Bran Castle

Nr Brasov, T0268-237 700, bran-castle.com (museum: T0268-238332, brancastlemuseum.ro). Year round, Mon 1200-1900, Tue-Sun 0900-1900, RON12/adult, RON6/child (6-18). Creepy courtyards, dingy passageways and an underground network of secret tunnels – if this austere, forbidding Gothic stronghold, perched on a rocky outcrop in the village of Bran, doesn't give you goose pimples, nothing will. After all, this was the lair of Dracula, wasn't it? Before you dash off to buy garlic cloves, wooden crosses and any other

 Inside info

» Rail travel is inexpensive, although a hire car will give you more freedom to roam.
» As well as the highlights on this page, try to fit in a visit to the medieval town of Sighisoara.
» Beach resorts are located along the Black Sea coast between Mangalia and Mamaia.

vampire repellents, let's be absolutely (and historically) clear about Bran Castle and its Dracula association. Dracula never existed. He was a character in Bram Stoker's 1897 classic novel. Vlad Tepes, on the other hand, did exist. Born in 1431, he was the son of a Transylvanian governor who happened to be a member of an anti-Turk secret society known as the Order of the Dragon. In folklore, the dragon was associated with the devil, so Vlad's father was known as Dracul ('Devil'), while Vlad himself became Dracula ('Son of the Devil'). What's this got to do with vampires? Well, that's where fact and fiction begin to blur. Tepes grew up to be a ruthless warlord, battling the hated Turks and picking up a few of their less salubrious habits, such as impaling prisoners on long stakes (earning him the jolly title of 'Vlad the Impaler'). So, more of a blood-letter than a bloodsucker,

but the whole Dracula vampire myth has somehow stuck to Bran Castle where Tepes briefly sought refuge in 1462. When it comes to the crunch, though, no kid is going to let a bit of history spoil a juicy excuse for a vampire hunt.

Carpathian Mountains

A three-hour drive north of Bucharest, Kingstone Mountain National Park has one of Europe's largest concentrations of brown bears, wolves and lynxes. Based in nearby Zarnesti, you can make forays into the reserve's primeval woods, tracking these elusive predators or even seeing them up-close from a hide. Elsewhere in the Carpathians there are plenty of opportunities for activities, including mountain biking and whitewater rafting in summer, and cross-country skiing and horse-sleigh rides in winter. The village of Lunca Bradului will lull you into a gentle pace of life,

Painted church, Bucovina.

where you can experience rural life while indulging in a spot of hiking, horse riding or fishing.

Painted churches

Located in Bucovina, northern Romania, this extraordinary cluster of medieval picture book churches are painted, inside and out, with elaborate murals depicting Biblical stories, ranging from Genesis to the Last Judgement.

Danube Delta

Sprawling over 5700 sq km, Europe's largest wetland is a watery wilderness of lakes, channels, reed beds, meadows and islands that's home to

Danube Delta.

lively nesting colonies of great white pelicans (pictured right), herons and terns, plus huge flocks of overwintering ducks, geese and waders. You can feast your eyes on this avian spectacle by taking the train to Tulcea and then hopping on a tour boat.

Bulgaria break

There's more to Bulgaria than Black Sea resorts and cheap skiing packages. Head for the Rhodope Mountains in summer for hiking, caving, rock climbing and horse riding. If a winter visit appeals, base yourself in one of the quieter resorts, like Chepelare, which offers dog sledging and snowmobiling as well as skiing.

Slovenia A little bit of what you fancy

Small, but perfectly formed, Slovenia is a medley of dramatic alpine peaks, beguiling lakes and bear-filled forests tucked away at the top of the Adriatic. It is often hailed as one of Europe's last genuinely unspoilt destinations. But if that translates in your mind as wild and uninviting, then think again. Slovenia is not only emerging as prime adventure territory, but its compact size, extraordinary diversity and well-established infrastructure makes it ideal for family holidays. With its modest 46-km coastline, there's not much in the way of sun-soaked beaches, but at least you can paddle your toes in the Adriatic at the lovely old town of Piran.

Rafting on the Sava Bohinjka.

Ljubljana

Slovenia's capital (Ljubljana-tourism.si) won't blow your mind, but it's pleasant enough for a day or two at either end of your itinerary. Climb up to the castle for views over the city's terracotta-tiled rooftops, and wander the old quarter's tangle of cobbled streets and squares. Tivoli Park has a children's playground, and there's a waterpark (atlantis-vodnomesto.si) on the city's outskirts. With its lovely town squares, riverside setting and hilltop castle, the nearby medieval town of Škofja Loka (skofjaloka.si) is a good excuse for a day trip.

 Inside info

» Head to Lake Bohinj (bohinj.si) for a no-frills, action-packed break. If you want more hotels, restaurants, nightlife (and tourists), opt for Lake Bled (bled.si) instead.
» Roads are well-maintained and uncrowded, making self-drive a breeze. A scenic train journey links Bohinj to Nova Gorica, within striking distance of the coast.

Lake Bled

With paved lakeside paths, picture-perfect Lake Bled is a godsend if you've got a baby or toddler in a stroller. There are also horse-and-cart rides, boat trips to the island and an excellent swimming area with waterslide and shady trees. Treat the kids to a cream cake at the Park Hotel.

Lake Bohinj

Far less manicured than Bled, Lake Bohinj is wild and woody. Pick up a map from the tourist office, pack a picnic and set off to explore Triglav National Park (sigov.si/tnp). Right on your doorstep there are easy, level trails around Lake Bohinj – or you could hire a bike, canoe or rowing boat. Mount Vogel cable car has stunning views over the lake and Julian Alps, while a 90-minute hike through beautiful beech woodland leads to the impressive 78-m-high Savica Falls. Children will love horse riding at Ranch Mrcina where

the ponies are small and docile. For adrenaline addicts there is canyoning, tandem paragliding, rock climbing, quad-biking and gentle whitewater rafting on the Sava Bohinjka. Swimming is also popular – but bring something for the kids' feet because the lakeside beaches are quite gritty and stony.

Caves and castles

A combo ticket will allow you to explore Postojna Caves (postojnska-jama.si) and lay siege to the nearby 700-year-old Predjama Castle, wedged dramatically in a 123-m-high cliff face. But if you go underground just once in Slovenia, make sure it's into the mighty Skocjan Caves (park-skocjanske-jame.si). You'll need jackets, torches and a head for heights. It's pitch black (surprise, surprise), so don't take kids who are afraid of the dark – or bats for that matter. After several smallish caverns that are drizzled with stalagmites and stalactites, you enter a vast chamber with plunging cliffs, a

Boulder-hopping in Triglav National Park.

subterranean river and Indiana Jones-style bridge. The guided tour lasts 90 minutes; there are hundreds of steps (slippery in places), but kids will emerge wide-eyed with wonder.

Adriatic Sea

With its cutesy harbour, Venetian architecture and restaurant-lined waterfront, Piran (piran.si) is a perfect little seaside retreat. Try to get Room 40A in Hotel Tartini – it's a family apartment with great views over the town square and harbour. For sandy beaches, nip around the coast to Portoroz (portoroz.si).

Predjama Castle.

Croatia Set sail for the Adriatic

Of all the countries in Eastern Europe, Croatia is the one that cries out 'family holiday'. Not only is its beautiful coast bathed in crystal-clear waters and warm sunshine, but it is also endowed with enough islands and cultural nuggets to turn a seaside holiday into an Adriatic adventure. Base yourself in Dubrovnik, for example, and the kids could be scaling the ramparts of the old city one day and paddling a sea kayak to a deserted cove the next. Rocked by war in the early 1990s, Croatia's tourism industry is back in top gear, whether you want to island hop along the Dalmatian coast or head inland to explore the freshwater wonder of the Plitvice Lakes National Park.

Blazing paddles – kayaking in Croatia.

Dubrovnik

Built between the 13th and 16th centuries, Dubrovnik's fortified walls encircle the Old Town in a curtain of stone 6 m thick and 25 m high, punctuated by 16 towers. You can walk right around the walls – an epic 2-km amble which offers spectacular views across Dubrovnik's terracotta-tiled rooftops and the Adriatic beyond. The access point for the one-hour circuit is

at Pile Gate; head clockwise to get the uphill bits over with first. Down at street level, most of the highlights are concentrated around the Old Port, including the Dominican Monastery and Rector's Palace. There's also an aquarium, but better to don mask and snorkel and head to one of the city's offshore islands.

Best islands

Just a stone's throw from the city walls, tiny Lokrum is a beauty, with its own subtropical gardens, an 11th-century monastery and a small lake linked to the open sea. You can join a half- or full-day sea-kayaking trip here, or take the less strenuous option of a boat tour. Lying further afield are the three, equally verdant isles of the Elaphite archipelago: Kolocep, Lopud and Šipan. All have small, picturesque villages with options for staying overnight, making them an excellent proposition for a multi-day, island-hopping

adventure, either by kayak or ferry. If you take the former option, you should be prepared to paddle up to 14 km a day, although in a double kayak you can at least share the workload. Be sure to visit Lopud's sandy Šunj Bay and explore the sea caves on Kolocep. Further north lies the large island of Mljet (mljet.hr) – possibly the most beautiful in the Adriatic, with emerald forests, turquoise seas

Dubrovnik.

Inside info

»» There's a small beach next to Dubrovnik's Old Town (tzdubrovnik.hr), with additional pebbly coves around the Lapad headland.

»» The Elaphite islands are connected by ferries, while Oldtimer motor cruisers (maestral.hr) can be chartered for voyages lasting from a few days to a week or more.

»» Local companies offering sea-kayaking trips include Adriatic Kayak Tours (adriatickayaktours.com) and Adriatic Sea Kayaking (adriatic-sea-kayak.com).

and saltwater lakes. That said, however, Korcula (korculainfo. com), further along the coast, is also pretty special – not to mention the hundreds of other islands dotted along the Dalmatian coast.

Plitvice Lakes

A beautiful mosaic of 16 lakes connected by waterfalls, the densely forested Plitvice Lakes National Park (np-plitvicka-jezera.hr) lies 140 km from Zagreb. You can take boat trips on the larger lakes or explore walking trails in the woods.

Plitvice Lakes National Park.

Croatian coast.

Eastern Europe Grown-ups' stuff

When to go

The climate varies widely across Eastern Europe. **Croatia**'s long hot Mediterranean summers, for example, might allow you to eke out a beach holiday in late October – a time when the Carpathian Mountains of **Poland**, **Slovakia** and **Romania** are bracing themselves for their first winter snowfalls. As you might expect, anywhere in the region away from the Adriatic coast can be bitterly cold during winter. The skiing season lasts from December to mid-April, while the peak summer months are July and August. Avoid the crowds (and the prospect of irritable, overheated children) by visiting popular cities like Prague and Kraków during spring or autumn.

Getting there

The proliferation of low-cost airlines has made Eastern Europe more accessible and forced national carriers to cut prices and improve their services. From the UK, Czech Airlines (czechairlines. com) flies from London and Manchester to Prague. There are also services from Dublin, Paris, Amsterdam and numerous other European cities. From the US, there are flights from New York, Montreal and Toronto. Allow around £180 (including taxes) for a return flight in June with British Airways (britishairways.

com) between London and Prague. Low-cost airlines serving the Czech Republic include easyJet (easyjet.com), Ryanair (ryanair.com), Flybe (flybe.com), BmiBaby (bmibaby.com) and Jet2 (jet2.com). The most useful of these is probably easyJet, which serves Prague from Gatwick, Stansted, Bristol, East Midlands and Newcastle. Ryanair only flies to Brno. Smartwings (smartwings.com), a Czech low-cost airline, has flights to destinations throughout Europe, but not the UK.

LOT Polish Airlines (lot. com) has flights from London and Manchester to Warsaw, but only serves Kraków from Frankfurt, Munich, Paris and Vienna. Ryanair is a better bet for reaching Kraków from Britain and Ireland, with direct services from Dublin, Shannon, East Midlands, Glasgow, Liverpool and Stansted.

Romania's national carrier, Tarom (tarom.ro), offers return flights London–Bucharest from around €250 plus taxes. Low-cost airline, Wizz (wizzair.com), also flies this route.

In Slovenia, national airline Adria (adria.si) has return flights London–Ljubljana from around €170. Also serving Ljubljana is easyJet, while Ryanair flies London–Maribor.

With August return flights London–Dubrovnik from around €250 return, including taxes, Croatia Airlines (croatiaairlines.

hr) also flies from London to Split and Zagreb. Budget airlines serving Croatia include Wizz, easyJet and Flybe.

Getting around

Trains and buses probe most corners of the **Czech Republic**, although you will find that buses have a reduced service at the weekends. For public transport timetables, visit vlak.cz.

Information on rail travel in **Poland** is available from PKP Intercity (intercity.com. pl), while international coach lines connect cities like Warsaw, Kraków and Gdansk. LOT Polish Airlines will whisk you from Warsaw to Kraków in just 55 minutes from around €60 return.

In **Slovakia**, Lod (lod.sk) upholds the long tradition of river travel on the Danube with regular cruises departing from Bratislavia, while major rail routes (slovakrail.sk) connect the capital with Kúty, Zilina, Košice and Štúrovo. Slovakia also has a good road network (some 300 km of new highways were constructed in 2004).

In **Romania**, domestic flights are operated by Tarom (see left) and Carpatair (carpatair.com). Getting around by bus and train is also straightforward and inexpensive. For details of rail services, log on to infofer.ro.

Small in size, but with an excellent road network, **Slovenia** is perfect for self-drive and you will find all the main car-rental companies in Ljubljana. Daily charges for a Volkswagon Polo during August with Europcar (europcar.si) are around €60 (including CDW and unlimited kilometres), while a Renault Laguna will cost nearer €80. For details of bus services in Slovenia, contact Avtobusna Postaja Ljubljana (ap-ljubljana.si). For trains, contact Slovenske zeleznice (slo-zeleznice.si).

In **Croatia**, buses operated by Autotrans (autotrans.hr)

connect main towns and cities, while Hrvatske zeljeznice (hznet.hr) runs trains to most major centres except Dubrovnik. If you have the time, rent a car and drive the scenic Adriatic Highway from Rijeka to Dubrovnik. Car and passenger ferries are operated by Jadrolinija (jadrolinija.hr) between islands as well as ports along the mainland.

Accommodation

You can pitch a tent in one of the **Czech Republic**'s 500 or so campsites for as little as €4 a night. At the other end of the scale, a room in a five-star hotel in Prague will easily relieve you of €225 or more. Cloister Inn (cloister-inn.com) is a good mid-range option in Prague's Old Town, just a few minutes' walk from Charles Bridge. An increasingly popular alternative for families is to rent a self-catering apartment.

Skip the flight

» **Skim across the Adriatic** from Venice to Piran (Slovenia) aboard a high-speed catamaran operated by Venezia Lines (venezialines.com) for around €90 return (€45 for children).

» **River-cruise companies** based in Austria ply the Danube River to Hungary. DDSG Blue Danube Shipping (ddsg-blue-danube.at) offers return trips by hydrofoil between Vienna and Budapest for around €110 (50% less for children aged two to 14). Alternatively, take the boat one way and return by night train.

» **Travelling by coach** to Eastern Europe inevitably means long journeys, but if you're feeling up to it Eurolines (eurolines.com) has services to Poland, Czech Republic, Hungary and Romania. Capital Express (capitalexpress.cz) has a London–Prague service.

Apartments.cz (apartments.cz) offers more than 80 furnished apartments in Prague, with rates

ⓘ **Fact** file

Country	Time	Language	Currency	Exchange rate approximate	International dialling code	Tourist information
Czech Republic	GMT+1	Czech	Czech Koruna	£1 = CZK30	+420	czechtourism.com
Poland	GMT+1	Polish	New Zloty	£1 = PLN4.50	+48	poland-tourism.com
Slovakia	GMT+1	Slovak	Euro	£1 = €1.15	+421	slovakiatourism.sk
Romania	GMT+2	Romanian	New Leu	£1 = RON4.75	+40	romaniatourism.com
Slovenia	GMT+1	Slovenian	Euro	£1 = €1.15	+386	slovenia.info
Croatia	GMT+1	Croatian	Croatia Kuna	£1 = HRK8.0	+385	croatia.hr

Eastern Europe Grown-ups' stuff

starting at just €25 per person per night.

A family apartment in Kraków's Old Town costs from around €85 per night with Stay Poland (staypoland. com), which also offers hotels in Warsaw and Kraków. For rural holiday accommodation (or *agroturystyka*) in **Poland**, try Polish Country Invites (agritourism.pl).

Apartments and hotels in **Slovakia**'s capital, Bratislava, are available from Bratislava Hotels (bratislavahotels.com), while ABC Slovakia (abcslovensko.sk) has links to a wide range of rural properties, from cottages and pensions to horse ranches. For information on where to stay in the Tatra Mountains, try tatry.sk.

In **Romania**, a good base for exploring Bran Castle and the Carpathian Mountains is Hotel Balada (balada.ro) in Suceava, which has doubles from around €60 and an apartment from €90 per night, including breakfast.

Accommodation in **Slovenia** ranges from campsites, farmstays and pensions to grand lakeside hotels. At Lake Bohinj, well-equipped campsites like Autokamp Zlatorog cost from €6 per person, while the four-star Hotel Bohinj has doubles from around €45 per person half-board. Both can be booked through Alpinum (alpinum.net). A good self-catering option is the Zdovc Apartments (bohinj. si/zdovc).

With its alluring Adriatic coastline, **Croatia** has the cream of Eastern Europe's family-friendly accommodation. Mainstream holiday-camp operators, such as Eurocamp and Keycamp, both feature northern Croatia, while villa and apartment specialists like Croatian Affair have properties throughout the country.

Food & drink

Hearty and non-spicy (though occasionally on the stodgy side), traditional Eastern European cuisine should appeal to most children. In the **Czech Republic** and **Slovakia**, expect plenty of fried or roast meat, usually pork or beef, accompanied by dumplings, potatoes or rice. Pot-roasted beef in a rich creamy sauce with cranberries and vegetables is delicious, as are fruit dumplings, strudels and pancakes. In the cities, you will find everything from pizzas to Chinese.

A typical meal in **Poland** consists of noodle soup followed by pork cutlet with red cabbage and potatoes and rounded off with cheesecake.

Traditional dishes in **Romania** include *ciorba de perisoare* (meatball soup), *scrumbie la gratar* (grilled herring), *sarmale* (pickled cabbage leaves stuffed with minced meat and rice) and *papanasi* (cottage cheese doughnuts). Parents will no doubt want to sample *tuica*, a potent plum brandy, as well as a few of Romania's best wines, such as Murfatlar and Jidvei.

In **Slovenia**, dishes range from Hungarian goulash, Austrian strudels and Italian risotto to more local fare, such as fresh lake trout and sweet pastries. Expect lots of cabbage and potatoes with everything and don't forget to try *potica*, a roll stuffed with walnuts, poppy seeds, raisins, herbs, cottage cheese or honey.

Not surprisingly, **Croatia** has excellent seafood, ranging from universal favourites like scampi to Dalmatian *brodet*, a mixed fish stew served with rice. You'll also find no shortage of Italian-inspired food along the coast.

Health & safety

No special inoculations are required for Eastern Europe. However, if you plan on walking in thickly forested areas, take precautions against tick-borne encephalitis by avoiding tick-infested areas from May to August, using insect repellent, tucking long trousers into socks and wearing a hat. On the whole, tap water is safe to drink. If in doubt, err on the cautious side and buy bottled water. Sunburn and dehydration can be a threat during summer, particularly along the Adriatic where you should also keep an eye out for spiny sea urchins.

Eastern Europe Family favourites

Camp Lanterna.

Camp Lanterna

Where? Porec, Croatia.

Why? Good value for money and excellent facilities, including three fabulous swimming pools, supermarket, pizzeria and watersports such as sailing and canoeing, make this large holiday park a safe bet for families. The resort of Porec is just 10 km away, while Brijuni Safari Park, Cave Baredine and Plitvice Lakes National Park are also within easy striking distance. Accommodation includes seven-berth mobile homes with air conditioning.

How much? Around £310 to £1650 for 12 nights in a two-bed Villanova mobile home.

Contact Keycamp Holidays, T+44 (0)844-844 1000, keycamp.co.uk.

Llubljana Resort

Where? Llubljana, Slovenia.

Why? Located alongside the River Sava, close to the centre of picturesque Llubljana, this park combines all the attractions of a holiday centre (including a superb water complex with pools, river ride and slides and onsite activities such as badminton, football and cycling) with the galleries, shops and sights of a small city. The Atlantis indoor water park (one of the largest in Europe) is nearby, while Lake Bled is just a 40-minute drive away.

How much? Around £435 to £1760 for 12 nights in a two-bed Superior mobile home.

Contact Eurocamp, T+44 (0)844-406 0402, eurocamp.co.uk.

Tour operators

In the UK
The Adventure Company
adventurecompany.co.uk

Bond Tours
bondtours.co.uk

Croatian Affair
croatianaffair.com

Crystal Holidays
crystalholidays.co.uk

Eurocamp
eurocamp.co.uk

Explore
explore.co.uk

Exodus
exodus.co.uk

Families Worldwide
familiesworldwide.co.uk

Holiday Options
holidayoptions.co.uk

Just Slovenia
justslovenia.co.uk

KE Adventure Travel
keadventure.com

Keycamp Holidays
keycamp.ie

Lakes and Mountains Holidays
lakes-mountains.co.uk

Romanian Affair
romanianaffair.com

In the USA
Adriatic Tours
adriatictours.com

Croatia Travel
croatiatravel.com

Slovenia Travel
sloveniatravel.com

Snow doubt about it – kids love a winter Lapland.

Contents

267 **Introduction**

268 **Kids' stuff**

270 **Tots to teens**

274 **Denmark**
274 Copenhagen

278 **Sweden**
278 Stockholm
278 Stockholm
    Archipelago
279 Gothenburg
279 Swedish Lapland

282 **Norway**
282 Oslo
283 Norwegian fjords
284 Svalbard

286 **Finland**
286 Helsinki
288 Finnish Lapland

290 **Iceland**
290 Southwest
    Iceland
292 North Iceland

294 **Grown-ups'
    stuff**

Scandinavia

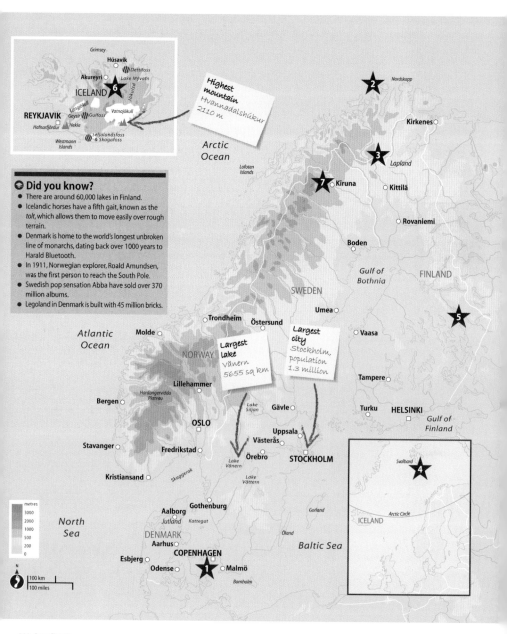

Grimsey

Húsavík

Dettifoss

Akureyri   Lake Mývatn

ICELAND **6**

Langjökull   Vatnajökull

REYKJAVIK   Geysir   Gulfoss

Hafnarfjörður   Hekla

Westmann   Seljalandsfoss
Islands   & Skogafoss

Highest mountain.
Hvannadalshúkur
2110 m

Nordkapp   **2**

Kirkenes

Arctic Ocean

Lofoten Islands

3   Lapland

Kiruna   Kittilä   **★**

Rovaniemi

Boden

Gulf of Bothnia   **FINLAND**

SWEDEN

Umea   **5**

○ Did you know?
- There are around 60,000 lakes in Finland.
- Icelandic horses have a fifth gait, known as the *tolt*, which allows them to move easily over rough terrain.
- Denmark is home to the world's longest unbroken line of monarchs, dating back over 1000 years to Harald Bluetooth.
- In 1911, Norwegian explorer, Roald Amundsen, was the first person to reach the South Pole.
- Swedish pop sensation Abba have sold over 370 million albums.
- Legoland in Denmark is built with 45 million bricks.

Trondheim   Östersund

Atlantic Ocean   Molde

Vaasa

Largest city
Stockholm,
population
1.3 million

NORWAY   **Largest lake**
Vänern
5655 sq km

Tampere

Lillehammer

Bergen   Hardangervidda Plateau

Lake Siljan   Gävle

Turku   **HELSINKI**

Gulf of Finland

OSLO

Uppsala

Stavanger   Västerås

Fredrikstad   Örebro   **STOCKHOLM**

Lake Vänern

Kristiansand   Skagerrak

Lake Vättern

Svalbard   **4**   **★**

metres
3000
2000
1000
500
200
0

Gothenburg

Aalborg   Gotland

Jutland   Kattegat

Arctic Circle

North Sea   **DENMARK**   Öland   **ICELAND**

Aarhus

Baltic Sea

Esbjerg   **COPENHAGEN**

Odense   **1**   Malmö

Bornholm

N

100 km
100 miles

Introduction

1 Board a Viking ship
▸▸ Denmark, page 276

2 See the midnight sun
▸▸ Lapland, page 279

3 Go husky sledging
▸▸ Lapland, page 280

4 Sail to the Arctic
▸▸ Svalbard, page 284

5 Learn how to cross-country ski
▸▸ Finland, page 288

6 Walk on lava
▸▸ Iceland, page 292

7 Stay in a hotel made of ice
▸▸ Swedish Lapland, page 299

When it comes to family holidays, there's more to Scandinavia than Santa Claus and Legoland although both will probably get a vigorous chorus of approval from your children. Cities like Copenhagen, Stockholm and Oslo may be on the pricey side, but they are also supremely kid-friendly with plenty of attractions, ranging from theme parks and gardens to museums and castles. Further afield you'll discover nature's very own theme park – a wilderness of lakes, forests and mountains where thrills and spills come in the form of rafting trips, husky sledging and a veritable smörgåsbord of other activities, depending on when you visit. Scandinavia is also an easily accessible place to introduce your children to some of the world's most extraordinary phenomena. Lapland has the Northern Lights and midnight sun, Iceland has volcanoes and ice caps and Finland has the Moomintrolls. If those endearing white hippo-like characters don't do it for your kids, however, Denmark's Viking legacy is sure to fire their imagination. Lapland's reindeer-herding Sami culture will also captivate most children, while the home of the big man himself, Mr S Claus, can be visited year round.

Scandinavia Kids' stuff

CHILDREN OF THE FOREST

Books to read

Children of the Forest
Floris Books, 1987
Elsa Beskow's exquisitely illustrated story of the little folk who live deep in the roots of an old pine tree. Ages 2-6

Fairy Tales of Hans Christian Andersen
Readers Digest, 2005
An illustrated collection of 40 captivating stories, including The Little Mermaid, The Princess and the Pea, The Tinderbox and The Emperor's New Clothes. Ages 1+

Viking
DK Publishing, 2005
Vivid photography and at-a-glance captions transport young readers into the world of the Vikings. Ages 9-12

Pippi Longstocking
Oxford University Press, 2007
Astrid Lindgren's classic tale about the feisty, unconventional nine-year-old who lives at Villa Villekulla with a horse, a monkey and a suitcase full of gold coins. Ages 8-11

The Vicious Vikings
Scholastic Hippo, 2007
Find out how to build a longboat and why some Vikings had names like Fat Thighs and Stinking. Ages 8+

Troll Blood
HarperCollins, 2007
The action-packed conclusion to Katherine Langrish's acclaimed trilogy describes a perilous journey to Vinland (North America). Ages 12+

Big six
How many of Sweden's 'big six' will you spot on a Scandinavian wildlife safari?

Moose
Wolverine
Brown bear

Lynx
Wolf
Musk ox

Hidden people
Up to 80% of Icelanders admit to believing in elves. In 2006, machinery failure interrupted an extension project at the Blue Lagoon when it became clear that the work was disturbing local elves. Staff lit 12 candles to make peace with the Hidden People and avoid further mishaps. Your best chance for spotting an elf is at Hafnarfjodur, near Reykjavík. Also look out for dwarves (moodier than elves), light-fairies (think Tinkerbell) and trolls (who live solitary lives inside mountains and glaciers and don't like being disturbed).

Wacky sports
World Wife-Carrying Championships Sonkajarvi, July.
World Cell Phone Throwing Championships Riihisaari, August.
Swamp Football World Championships Hyrynsalmi, July.
Other eccentric Finnish contests include snowshoe football, cattle calling, milking stool throwing, mosquito swatting and sitting on ants' nests.

See Santa

- Write a letter to Santa Claus a few weeks before your journey.
- Fly to Ivalo airport in Finnish Lapland where you will be met by one of Santa's elves and a reindeer with its Sami handler.
- Get kitted out in thermal bodysuits, boots, gloves and hats.
- Make a snowman, go tobogganing and try your hand (and feet) at snowshoeing.
- Take a reindeer sleigh ride, then learn how to mush a team of huskies.
- Receive a certificate celebrating your crossing of the Arctic Circle and listen to stories from a Sami guide.
- Ride a snowmobile through snowy forests, keeping an eye out for wild reindeer and a glimpse of Santa's cabin.
- Meet Santa in his secret hideaway and tell him how good you've been all year.

Build an igloo

What you need
- Saw
- Spade
- Several short sticks
- Hard snow

What you need
- Use the sticks to mark out a circle measuring no more than 2 m wide.
- Cut out blocks of snow around 20-30 cm thick.
- Arrange the first row of blocks, making sure they are angled slightly inwards (otherwise you will end up with a tower instead of a dome shape). Don't worry about gaps between blocks at this stage.

- Use vertically placed blocks for each side of the entrance with a solid block on top to form a small porch.
- Continue adding snow blocks to the igloo, removing any snow that piles up inside. You can also dig out the floor at this stage, increasing headroom.
- Slide the last few blocks through the entrance and push them up into the remaining gap in the roof to close the igloo.
- Fill in any cracks with snow.
- Smooth the inside of the igloo using your gloved hand.

Taste of Scandinavia madekeitto

A popular winter dish in Finland, *madekeitto* is a delicious creamy soup of fish and potatoes traditionally made using burbot, but salmon works just as well.

What you need
- 1 kg burbot or salmon
- 6 potatoes
- 2 onions
- ¼ tsp allspice
- 500 ml water
- 500 ml milk
- 250 ml double cream
- 2 tbsp flour
- Chopped dill and a pinch of salt

What to do
- Peel and dice the potatoes and onions; add to boiling water with salt and allspice and simmer for 10-15 minutes.
- Cut the fish into large chunks and add to the vegetables.
- Whisk the milk and flour together and pour into the soup; simmer for a further five minutes.

- Add the cream, sprinkle with chopped dill and serve with freshly baked bread.

Scandinavia Tots to teens

Scandinavia, as you might expect, is generally a very straightforward place to take children on holiday. It's the Volvo of the family travel world; safe, reliable and efficient. Everywhere you go you will find copious and clean facilities, whether you're looking for a city park playground, family accommodation or somewhere to change a nappy. The only potential downside is that travelling en famille in Scandinavia can wallop your wallet. Iceland, Norway, Sweden, Finland and Denmark are some of the world's most expensive travel destinations. But when you weigh this up against a reassuring level of child-friendliness and unique attractions (Santa Claus and Hans Christian Andersen to name a couple), the extra expense is usually more than justified.

Horse riding in Iceland.

Babies

Stick to the cities and you'll find supermarkets stocked with baby food, parks with playgrounds and restaurants with high chairs. Most Scandinavian cities are also compact (especially Copenhagen) with excellent public transport that is gentle on both your stroller and your nerves. Most people speak English and in summer there's a relaxed outdoor café culture that new parents will relish. If you're feeling slightly more adventurous, head for the countryside or coast where you'll find plenty of options for renting cottages or staying at a holiday park. Just be wary of the fact that the further north you go, the more severe the landscape and climate become, and the less you'll find in the way of facilities.

66 99 Tom and eight-year-old Niko are grinning like mad things. So is their 74-year-old granny. We hurtle into the wide avenue of Sogne Fjord before the helicopter pilot presses the up button. We shoot skywards, the horizon tilts at a silly angle, the fjords seem miles below as we clear the plateau and are in a revealed new world of gashed hanging valleys, snow fields and sparkling tarns. The pilot asks if we are up for some fun and gets a resounding affirmation from the back. He puts the chopper into a sharp left-hand bank stomachs churn as we speed at head height over an ice field before screaming over the edge, an endless drop opens up below, Niko and granny screeching in unison.

Sanka Guha, TV presenter

Toddlers/pre-school

It's every child's dream to visit the home of Santa Claus high above the Arctic Circle in Finnish Lapland and it's surprisingly easy to make it come true (see page 287). Arrange a package trip through a reputable operator and you can avoid the slightly tacky, over-commercialized aspects of a Santa pilgrimage and instead experience something far more intimate and magical. Santa is at home all year (except during a certain night in December, of course) so you can pop up and see him during the long balmy days of summer if you like. However, it's much more fun when Lapland is transformed into a winter wonderland and you can ride in a reindeer-pulled sleigh and perhaps even glimpse the Northern Lights. Remember that Jack Frost will definitely be nipping at the toes, nose and other extremities of your toddler at this time of year (temperatures can plunge to -30°C during a Lapland winter). Be sure to pack plenty of warm clothing, including spare sets of essential items like gloves, hats and goggles. It's amazing how these things tend to go missing when your children are this age.

Another obsession for pre-schoolers is Lego, and the original home of building-block heaven can be found at Legoland in Denmark. Piece together a day in the theme park with a couple of days in Copenhagen and a few more at the coast and you'll make most three- and four-year-olds very happy indeed. Denmark is also ideal for family cycling.

Kids/school age

Legoland and Santa Claus still appeal to this age range, as do many Scandinavian cities. All seem to have more than their fair share of theme parks and child-friendly museums, with enough attractions to satisfy toddlers through to teenagers. Visit Santa with a three-year-old, for example, and they will probably be content with a sleigh ride; take kids aged seven or eight, however, and they'll want to ride a team of huskies to St Nick's door. Similarly, Legoland and other theme parks are more than capable of meeting the hyped-up adrenaline demands of older children. Just don't let the slick

marketing of these contrived pleasurelands divert you from Scandinavia's real adventure hotspot – its wilderness.

The woody, watery hinterland of countries like Sweden and Finland is prime territory for hiking and canoeing in summer, and snowmobiling, cross-country skiing, ice fishing and husky sledging in winter. Iceland, too, offers plenty in the way of outdoor activities, from scouring the north Atlantic for minke whales to riding Icelandic ponies across glacial valleys. Several family tour operators offer winter or summer multi-activity packages to Scandinavia where, in just a week or 10 days, you can sample a variety of adventure pursuits, all under expert guidance and in the company of other families. Alternatively, strike out alone on a self-drive tour. With its coastal ring road and laid-back farmstays, Iceland is particularly well suited to this form of travel.

Educationally, Scandinavia scores highly on the national curriculum. When your children start to learn about Vikings at school, plan a visit to Denmark where they will be able to witness this vibrant culture through restored longships, hands-on museums and even themed parks where actors role-play characters from the period. A visit to the spectacular Viking ship museum on Oslo's Bygdøynes Peninsula is also

Special needs

Tourist boards can advise on hotels, restaurants and attractions that are wheelchair-friendly, while many forms of public transport have facilities for travellers with mobility, sight or hearing impairment. In Denmark, many restaurants, hotels, campsites and attractions provide facilities for the disabled; ferries have special cabins and wide elevators for wheelchair users and intercity trains have toilets for the disabled as well as special lifts and ramps. Sweden has launched Tourism For All – Accessible Equality (turismforalla.se), which features an online database of accessible facilities. In Finland check out travel4all.fi). In Iceland, several hotels in Reykjavík and Akureyri have rooms specially designed for guests with disabilities. The coastal ferries, *Baldur* and *Herjólfur*, are also wheelchair-friendly. A list of fully accessible tourist attractions can be found at sjalfsbjorg.is. One of the best options for disabled travellers in Norway is to book a voyage on a wheelchair-friendly cruise ship. Try Accessible Travel & Leisure (accessibletravel.co.uk).

Single parents

Small Families (smallfamilies.co.uk) offers hosted group holidays for single-parent families. They have a number of Lapland itineraries, including a visit to Santa in his log cabin, husky sledging and a trip to a reindeer farm. The Adventure Company (adventurecompany.co.uk) offers single parent family departures on its Winter Wonderland trip to Finland.

Scandinavia Tots to teens

Teenagers

Image-conscious teenagers will find suitably trendy shops and cafés in cities like Copenhagen, Bergen, Stockholm and Oslo, though prices may hamper their style somewhat. Big thrill rides can be found at amusement parks like Liseberg near Gothenburg and Oslo's Tusenfryd. For adventure, Iceland has challenging horse riding and whitewater rafting journeys, while Sweden and Finland offer all kinds of epic undertakings from week-long husky-sledging expeditions to wilderness survival and multi-activity breaks. Various family adventure tour operators offer teenage departures on their Scandinavian itineraries, including The Adventure Company, Explore Worldwide, Exodus and Families Worldwide.

worthwhile – as are the nearby Maritime Museum and Kon-Tiki Museum. In fact, if your kids have an interest in boats there is probably no better place in the world to take them.

Another aspect of Scandinavian culture that will appeal to school-age children (and impress their teachers) is the Sami culture. You can visit these reindeer-herding people in the remote reaches of Lapland or get a taster of their lifestyle at the open-air museum of Skansen in Stockholm.

Animal lovers may find Scandinavia slightly frustrating. The prospect of seeing wolves, bears and lynx is guaranteed to prick the ears of most children, but arctic wildlife is notoriously elusive. Your best bet is to visit a wildlife park specializing in native species or focus instead on coastal critters, like puffins, whales and dolphins, which can often be seen on ferry trips and cruises in Norway and Iceland. That said, a quiet rafting or canoeing trip along a river in

Sweden or Finland may well reward you with sightings of beaver and otter.

Scandinavia's strong literary tradition is a great excuse to get your kids' noses in some excellent reading books. Hans Christian Andersen's *Little Mermaid*, Tove Jansson's *Moominland* and Astrid Lindgren's *Pippi Longstocking* are all from here – and chances are you'll also find a theme park or hands-on museum where they can see the characters brought to life.

Blue Lagoon, Iceland.

66 99 Iceland was fantastic; the children loved the scenery. Highlights included Gulfoss Falls, which silenced them for a good 10 minutes. A visit to the Blue Lagoon is a must, although I would recommend going later in the afternoon when it's less busy. The best thing was driving into the mountains between Reykjavík and Hverageroi in the middle of the night. It was freezing, but we sat there for over an hour watching the Northern Lights and occasionally jumping into the car to run the heater. The itinerary we received from Discover the World was outstanding; it took away all the stress from the trip and allowed us to make the most of our time. Our 13-year-old wants to know when were going back. She wants to go horse trekking next, but we would also like to explore the glaciers.

The Mason family, Discover the World

Light relief

Head to northern Scandinavia to witness the midnight sun. A celebration of the longest day, midsummer here is as popular as Christmas. Flower-wreathed women dance around maypoles in Sweden, while in Finland and Norway bonfires are lit to ward off evil spirits.

Denmark Land of Vikings & Lego

Denmark might not strike you as an obvious choice for a family holiday, but few European countries can match its combination of compact size, efficient, family-friendly infrastructure and range of attractions. You've probably heard of Legoland and Tivoli Gardens – two of the country's family favourites, but there's a lot more to Denmark than rollercoasters and brightly coloured bits of plastic. Copenhagen is a laid-back city endowed with parks, museums, palaces and the rich legacy of storyteller-supreme, Hans Christian Anderson. Further afield, you will find long sandy beaches, holiday centres and a veritable treasure trail of Viking sites. Denmark's real trump card – particularly with young families – is that it just seems that little bit less remote than other parts of Scandinavia.

Tivoli Gardens.

Copenhagen

The Little Mermaid
If your four- to seven-year-old daughter has any say in the matter, a pilgrimage to The Little Mermaid statue will top your sightseeing list. Hans Christian Andersen's 1837 fairy tale about the mermaid who falls in love with a prince she saves from drowning has enchanted just about every girl who has seen the feature cartoon and bought the Disney merchandise. Break it to them gently, but a 165-cm tall bronze figure perched on the edge of Copenhagen's harbour might be a bit of an anticlimax.

Rosenborg Slot
Ample compensation for any disappointment over The Little Mermaid, this 17th-century castle (rosenborg-slot.dk) not only has a fairy-tale moat and gardens, but holds glittering displays of the crown jewels.

Amalienborg Slot
Although Queen Margrethe II lives here, visitors can peek into a wing of her palace where rooms have been reconstructed to show what royal life was like from 1863 to 1947.

Christiansborg Slot
The Royal Reception Rooms (ses.dk) in this impressive palace (home to the Parliament and Prime Minister's Office) contain colourful tapestries depicting the history of Denmark and the world.

Rundetårn
A spiral staircase leads to the top of the Round Tower (rundetaarn.dk), from where there are great views across the Copenhagen's red-tiled rooftops.

The Little Mermaid.

✪ Beach days

Copenhagen Just 5 km from the city, Amager Strandpark (amager-strand.dk) is an artificial beach park with white sand and lots of facilities.

West Jutland Long, wide sandy beaches backed by dunes and often raked by surf.

East Jutland Gentle sandy beaches and wonderful swimming can be found at Kattegat, Lolland, Falster and Bornholm.

Nyhavn

Lined by colourful townhouses and trendy cafés and filled with wooden sailing ships, historic Nyhavn canal is an atmospheric place for a drink or ice-cream.

Strøget

Thronging with street performers this mile-long pedestrianized shopping strip is an essential stomping ground for teenagers or anyone in search of retail therapy.

Tivoli Gardens

Easily worth a day on its own, Tivoli Gardens (tivoli.dk) combines simple pleasures with high-octane thrills. Dating from 1843, it is a nostalgic mishmash of flower gardens, amusement park rides, open-air stage shows, restaurants, cafés and a boating lake. The rides range from a train journey through a land of pixies to the Demon rollercoaster with its triple loop-the-loop. Not to be missed is The Flying Trunk, where you are transported into puppet scenes from Hans Christian Anderson stories.

Best museums

Pick of the bunch is the interactive Experimentarium (experimentarium.dk), a science museum with over 260 hands-on exhibits ranging from an earthquake simulator to a special area for three- to six-year-olds. Also highly recommended are the Guinness World of Records Museum and the Louis Tussauds Wax Museum.

Best parks

Most of Copenhagen's parks have great playgrounds. From June to August there are free puppet shows in Kongens Have.

✪ Natural cycle

You can cycle just about anywhere in Denmark. The country has a 4000-km cycle network linking most major towns. Routes follow traffic-scarce roads, forest tracks, cycle lanes and disused railway lines. There are 11 long-distance routes, or you can simply pedal about in Copenhagen on the well-marked cycle paths.

Kids' top 10 Viking Denmark

① **Dress** like a Viking warlord and board a 7-m replica longboat at the Children's Museum in Copenhagen's Nationalmuseet (natmus.dk).

② **Eat** like a Viking at Valhal restaurant in Tivoli Gardens (vegetarians may go hungry).

③ **Sail** a replica longboat (or man one of the oars) at Roskilde where five Viking ships have been reconstructed from wrecks dragged from the fiord at Vikingeskibsmuseet (vikingeskibsmuseet.dk).

④ **Imagine** the formidable Harold Bluetooth presiding over Trelleborg, a Viking fortress built around AD 980 and excavated near Slagelse.

⑤ **Discover** the treasures found at Ladbyskibet, the burial ground of a Viking chief unearthed near Kerteminde on the island of Funen.

⑥ **Learn** how Vikings lived at Ribe Viking Centre (ribevc.dynamicweb.dk) where costumed actors bring the period to life. Join in with activities, from baking to archery.

⑦ **Marvel** at Jellings runic stones (standing stones with ancient inscriptions) – one erected more than 1000 years ago by King Gorm the Old and containing the first written mention of Denmark; the other erected by Harold Bluetooth recording the arrival of Christianity and the end of the Vikings.

⑧ **Celebrate** the ancient feast day of St Olaf at the Viking Moot held during the last weekend in July at Moesgård Museum (moesmus.dk) near Århus. As well as traditional craft stalls and spit-roasts galore, faux-Vikings stage ferocious battles on foot and horseback. While you're at the museum don't forget to gawp at Grauballe Man – a 2000-year-old body found almost perfectly preserved in a peat bog.

⑨ **Investigate** the mysterious Viking graveyard at Lindholm Høje near Nørresundby where stone circles are arranged in the outline of longboats.

⑩ **Ride** the Vikings River Splash at Legoland. Located in Billund, central Jutland, Legoland (legoland.dk) has eight main lands, including the signature Miniland – a miniature masterpiece of famous world locations constructed from over 20 million Lego bricks. In Adventure Land, you will find the X-Treme Racers rollercoaster (minimum height 120 cm) and the Robot Power Builder where you programme all the twists and turns yourself. Smaller kids will get a buzz from the Dragon Coaster (minimum height 100 cm), the Jungle Rally electric cars, the Dive to Atlantis aquarium and the Falck Fire Brigade where you race other teams to douse a burning building. Don't miss the Spellbreaker 4D movie in the Imagination Zone a riveting romp with medieval knights where you will be clutching at the characters that appear to leap from the screen.

Sweden Call of the Arctic

Parents in Sweden get some of Europe's best deals in maternity and paternity rights, so you can expect no shortage of child-friendly facilities when you head there on holiday. The two major cities, Stockholm and Gothenburg, have plenty to keep all ages entertained during a short break, but sooner or later youll feel the lure of the Arctic Circle. Head north in winter for a fairy-tale night at the Icehotel and to learn the art of husky mushing, or enjoy long summer days in Sweden's great outdoors.

Stockholm Archipelago.

Stockholm

The Venice of the North, Stockholm is a beautiful city spread over 14 islands. Get your bearings by taking a boat trip through the capital's waterways, then focus your attention on the parkland island of Kungliga Djurgården. You'll find several family-friendly attractions here, including Skansen (skansen.se), the oldest open-air museum in the world. Children will love

◉ Inside info

›› A Stockholm Card (available online at stockholmtown.com) entitles you to free admission to 75 museums and sites, unlimited travel on buses and trains, plus a sightseeing boat trip. Children under seven travel free.
›› An extensive ferry network (waxholmsbolaget.se) links the Stockholm Archipelago.
›› If you need to get from Gothenburg to Stockholm, break the journey at the Sommarland waterpark (sommarland.se) near Skara or take a longer loop via Lake Siljan (siljan.se), a popular holiday centre with everything from Santaworld to a summer toboggan track.

stepping back in time as they explore Skansen's 150 historic buildings, ranging from a traditional Swedish farmstead to a Sami camp – each one inhabited by staff in period costumes. There's even a zoo where you can learn about Scandinavian wildlife, such as wolves, brown bears and lynx. Djurgården is also the home of Junibacken (junibacken. se), a treat for anyone who has enjoyed Astrid Lindgren's children's books. This indoor attraction (perfect for a rainy day) brings the adventures of Pippi Longstocking to life through theatre shows, craft activities, a playhouse based on Villa Villekulla and a fantasy train ride through some of Lindgren's best-loved stories. Other children's highlights on Djurgården include the shark tunnel at Aquaria (aquaria.se) and the *Vasa* – an impressive, but ill-fated, triple-masted warship that sank within minutes of being launched

A snow leopard – one of the endangered species being bred at Norden's Ark.

in 1625. You can find out why at the National Maritime Museum (vasamuseet.com).

Stockholm Archipelago

A liberal scattering of 24,000 or so islands fringing the Gulf of Bothnia, the Stockholm Archipelago is a popular playground for urbanites. For a taster you can simply join a cruise from the capital, but you'll find it far more satisfying to spend a few days staying on one or more of the islands. The best ones for kids are Vaxholm with its historic fortress, Sandhamn, a popular seaside resort with lots of watersports, and Utö – a three-hour ferry ride from Stockholm, but well worth the trip for its beautiful walking trails and fine

swimming. You'll find shops, restaurants, and accommodation (including family-friendly cabins and camping) on many of the islands. Operators on Utö, Grinda and Sandön can arrange sailing trips with an experienced skipper or rent kayaks by the hour or longer.

Gothenburg

Though not as pretty as Stockholm, Sweden's second biggest city still has plenty to offer children. Top of their list will be Liseberg (liseberg. com), Scandinavia's largest amusement park. With 35 rides there's everything from a pony carousel to the hair-raising Balder, a mighty wooden roller coaster that inflicts passengers with no less than 10 doses of negative G-force. The new Uppswinget, meanwhile, does just that – swings you up and around at 80 kph. Replenish your children's brain cells at Gothenburg's interactive science museum, Universeum (universeum.se) before striking out north along Sweden's dramatic, rocky west coast. There are plenty of simple pleasures to be found here, such as crab-fishing from jetties or exploring the offshore islands on a boat trip. Other natural diversions include Havets Hus aquarium (havetshus. se) at Lysekil and Nordens Ark (nordensark.se), a captive-

breeding programme for endangered species like snow leopard and great grey owl.

Swedish Lapland

With its positively balmy temperatures and 24-hour daylight, summer might seem the obvious time to take your kids to Lapland. Unleash them on Europe's Great Outdoors and they'll be more than happy fishing, kayaking, hiking and getting away with later bedtimes thanks to the midnight sun. The big question is whether winter is even more fun. Yes, the days are ridiculously short and you'll have to wear snowsuits that feel like wrap-around duvets, but the fact remains that a week of winter activities in Lapland makes a superb break at Christmas, Easter or the February half-term.

Several family adventure operators (see page 299) offer guided activity breaks to either Finnish or Swedish Lapland. Typically, they include a mixture of dog sledging, snowmobiling, snowshoeing, cross-country skiing, ice fishing and reindeer sleigh rides. If you're lucky they may also feature traditional storytelling where you can learn about the culture of the indigenous Sami people.

More of a polar pot-pourri than a full-blown Arctic expedition, these trips are designed to give you a gentle

introduction to everything, which means they're suitable for children as young as five. And, of course, the added bonus of a winter visit to Lapland is that you may glimpse the Northern Lights. See page 288 for a first-hand account of a winter activity break in Finland.

Sami woman herding reindeer.

◉ **Inside** info

▸▸ A 90-minute flight from Stockholm, Kiruna makes an ideal base for exploring Lapland.
▸▸ Nearby Jukkasjärvi offers many winter activities, plus the not-to-be-missed Icehotel.
▸▸ Further south, Åre doubles as a winter skiing Mecca and summer activity centre.
▸▸ Temperatures range from -30ºC in winter to +30ºC in summer.
▸▸ Want to visit Santa Claus? See page 287.

To mush or not to mush

In addition to Lapland, you can mush in Greenland, Iceland and Alaska. Arctic specialists, Discover the World (discover-the-world.co.uk) cover all four destinations. Don't worry if the closest you've come to dog sledging is grappling with a trolley down the frozen foods section of your local supermarket. With expert tuition you'll quickly get the hang of it and don't forget that the sledges do have brakes. Older children can join dedicated husky safaris, controlling their own sledge, looking after their team of dogs and staying overnight in cosy wilderness cabins. Young children can ride in the sledge, but make sure they are very well wrapped up, with goggles to protect their eyes from bits of ice kicked up by the huskies. Remember that huskies are excitable, bouncy and noisy, and a lot of them look like they've stepped straight from the local wolf pack. If your children are the slightest bit nervous of dogs, take them to see Santa instead. He's a lot less frisky.

❝❞ All morning we sweep through a wintry landscape of silent forests and frozen lakes. At times all you can hear is the panting of the dogs and the tinkle of their collar chains. Twice we spot reindeer browsing among the lichen-clad fir trees and the huskies ears prick alert. But the team has settled into a steady, exhilarating, rhythm. They have only one thing on their minds: to run.

Will

Norway Plain sailing for mini cruisers

A maritime theme quickly emerges when you contemplate a family holiday to Norway. The fjords are perfect for a voyage on a child-friendly cruise liner, while Oslo's trio of nautical museums showcases a wonderful array of historical ships. More adventurous families can set sail for the arctic wilderness of Svalbard, while adrenaline addicts can experience the watery thrills and spills of theme parks like Bø Sommarland.

Bergen.

Oslo

Bygdøynes Peninsula

With a coastline as famous as Norway's, it's hardly surprising that the nation has a strong seafaring tradition, and nowhere is this more vividly portrayed than in the four nautically themed museums on Oslo's Bygdøynes Peninsula. Start with Vikingskiphuset (khm.uio.no), where three Viking funerary ships are displayed, along with treasures and practical objects that accompanied the deceased into the afterlife. The Oseberg is the most exquisite of the trio. Built in 820 AD and measuring around 22 m in length, this richly ornamented oak vessel was exhumed from a large burial mound in 1904. Two skeletons were discovered on board, one of whom may have been a queen or priestess – study the grave goods on display and decide for yourself. The Norsk Sjøfartsmuseum or Norwegian Maritime Museum (norsk-sjofartsmuseum.no) chronicles the entire history of Norwegian seafaring, from a 2200-year-old Bronze Age log boat to a panoramic film depicting a cruise through the fjords. Next door, Frammuseet (fram.museum.no) contains the famous exploration ship, Fram, and recounts the epic voyages of Roald Amundsen and other great polar explorers. Finally, the Kon-Tiki Museum (kon-tiki. no) houses the original 14-m-long balsa raft that Norwegian scientist Thor Heyerdahl sailed 6880 km across the Pacific in 1947 – a voyage that lasted an incredible 101 days.

Ski central

Tryvann Winter Park (tryvann. no) is just 20 minutes from downtown Oslo and boasts 14 slopes, seven lifts, cross-country skiing, a snowboarding park and half-pipe, plus a special area for children and beginners. The longest ski run is 1400 m. Snow cannons ensure snow from December to April, while floodlighting enables evening skiing throughout the week.

◉ Inside info

» The Oslo Pass (visitoslo.com) provides unlimited travel by bus, tram, underground, boat and local trains, free entry to numerous museums and discounted admission to Tusenfryd amusement park.
» Take your pick of dozens of lakeside and coastal beaches.
» To reach the Bygdøynes Peninsula with its popular museums, ferries operate from the city hall quayside May-October.

Theme parks

Tusenfryd
Around 20 km from Oslo, Tusenfryd (tusenfryd.no) is home to one of Scandinavia's most extreme rides, Speed Monster, which takes you to 90 kph in two seconds and inflicts seven bouts of weightlessness.

Hunderfossen
Located 13 km from Lillehammer, Hunderfossen (hunderfossen.no) is a fairy-tale land with 50 attractions, including a troll park, high ropes course, 4D films and an adventure ship that swings through 70° to a height of 14 m.

Bø Sommarland
Norway's biggest waterpark, Bø Sommarland (sommarland.no) has one of the world's largest artificial waves for surfing as well as Europe's first roller-coaster flume – an enormous water chute with tight bends and stomach-churning drops.

The Kon-Tiki on display in Oslo.
Below: Cruise ship in Geirangerfjord.

Norwegian fjords

If you thought Norwegian cruising was the kind of thing only the grandparents would be interested in, think again. Just imagine the thrill your kids would get from living on a ship bound for the Arctic! Calling at remote fishing communities to drop off cargo or to collect local passengers, the Norwegian Coastal Voyage vessels are more entwined with daily life than your average cruise ship. There will also be times when you feel you can almost stretch out your arms and touch both walls of a fjord; youll be able to spot dolphins, orca whales, puffins and sea eagles from on deck and notch up a few geographical milestones – crossing the Arctic Circle, visiting Honingsvåg (the world's northernmost village) and witnessing the midnight sun. Not bad for a week's comfortable cruising. Other highlights include stopovers at Trondheim (Norway's first capital with its well-preserved medieval district), Geiranger (nuzzled in the head-spinning grandeur of Geirangerfjord) and the Lofoten Islands (a fascinating, weather-beaten archipelago of jagged mountains, U-shaped glacial valleys and brightly coloured fishing settlements dotted with wooden cod-drying racks). Ultimately, though, your compass is set for Honingsvåg where the Midnight Sun Road dips and turns across Nordskapp plateau to reach the top of Europe and an unforgettable view over the Arctic Ocean.

◉ **Inside** info

▸▸ To reach Bergen from Oslo (or vice versa) take the spectacular train journey (nsb.no) across the Hardangervidda plateau.
▸▸ Norwegian Coastal Voyage (hurtigruten.com) operates a fleet of stylish ferries calling at 34 ports between Bergen and Kirkenes.
▸▸ Spare time in Bergen before your cruise? Visit the aquarium (akvariet.no), ride the Fløibanen funicular railway (floibanen.no) or explore the fish market and the old wooden buildings alongside Bryggen Wharf.

It is midnight and broad daylight when we drop anchor near the northern tip of 20 m of the walruses. There are at least 150 of them lounging about the pebbles, snoring, we have other privileged encounters with arctic wildlife. Following a hike through the At Alkhornet, the skies are peppered with a blizzard of guillemots and little auks, an arctic fox the haunting siren calls of belugas pulsing mysteriously through the ship's hull. We never see however, that such a subtle sound can prove so captivating. Along with the cooing of eider

Svalbard magnetic north

Despite being squashed by converging lines of longitude and barely clinging to the top of a world map, Svalbard (svalbard.net) is served by scheduled flights from Norway, making it the most accessible high arctic region in the world. Visit between June and September when retreating pack ice frees the spectacular coastline of this mountainous archipelago. Expedition ships range from ice-breakers capable of holding 100 passengers to the 20-berth, steel-hulled schooner, Nooderlicht. Arctic cruises are by no means a cheap family-holiday option, and the style of travel is only suitable for older children. A cheaper option is to base yourself in the capital, Longyearbyen, and arrange day trips and activities such as kayaking and hiking.

Prins Karls Forland in Svalbard. Shuttled ashore in the ships dinghies, we walk to within belching and breaking wind, completely oblivious to our presence. In the days that follow crystal-maze icescape of a giant glacier, we spot a polar bear loping across distant pack ice. tiptoeing beneath the seabird city on the lookout for eggs. And at Magdalena Fjord we hear the white whales – apparently their song can carry for miles. It is a sign of true wilderness, ducks and the creaking of ancient glaciers, it embodies the very essence of the Arctic.

Will

Finland Lapping it up in the Arctic

Finland has plenty to keep kids entertained, whatever time of year you visit. Give them a choice of where and when to go, however, and they will invariably choose Lapland in winter. And who can blame them? Whether it's a sleigh ride in search of Santa or a white-knuckle ride with a team of boisterous huskies, Finland's northern extremity is the ultimate winter wonderland.

Lapland winter fun.

Helsinki

Suomenlinna
Constructed in the 1700s and now a UNESCO World Heritage Site, Suomenlinna (suomenlinna.fi) is one of the world's largest maritime fortresses. Built on several islands off the coast of Helsinki, it's a fun place to explore by boat and on foot. There are several museums and cafés, plus special events during the summer.

Heureka
Helsinkis interactive science centre, Heureka (heureka.fi) challenges young minds with a smörgåsbord of high-tech activities. The adjacent outdoor Galilei Science Park (open

May to September) has lots of water-themed experiments and contraptions – a kind of waterpark for budding Einsteins.

Linnanmäki
A perennial summer favourite for Finnish children, Linnanmäki (linnanmaki.fi) has been providing thrills and squeals since 1950. In addition to old favourites like the wooden roller coaster, there are numerous modern rides, as well as a Sea Life Aquarium (sealife.fi) where you can get dizzy by walking inside a ring-shaped aquarium full of shoaling herring.

Further afield
To the west of Helsinki, the cities of Tampere and Turku have no shortage of quirky family attractions. For example, there's Moominworld (muumimaailma.fi), a theme park 16 km from Turku dedicated to those loveable, white hippo-looking creatures (pictured right) created by Finnish author Tove Jansson. Yes, that's right – you can actually meet Moominmamma,

❝❞ So, you just sit on that bench and get all hot and sweaty?
A typical six-year-old's reaction to the prospect of a sauna

Moominpappa, Sniff, Snufkin and the Snork Maiden. Older children (though not necessarily their parents) will prefer Tampere Spy Museum (vakoilumuseo.fi) where aspiring secret agents can learn how to decipher hidden messages, change their voice and conceal a sword inside a walking stick.

◉ Inside info
➠ Get a feel for the city by hopping on the T3 tram.
➠ Helsinki has several parks, while the islands are perfect for a picnic and a swim. In winter you can skate on dozens of ice rinks throughout the city.
➠ A Helsinki Card gives unlimited travel on public transport and free entry to major sights and over 50 museums, including Suomenlinna sea fortress and Helsinki Zoo.

⊘ **Where** can we see Santa?

The best way to meet Santa is to book an all-inclusive trip with a specialist operator. Esprit (esprit-holidays.co.uk) offers packages to Finnish Lapland lasting from one to four days. Further south, near Rovaniemi, Santa's Village (santaclausvillage.info) has Santa's Post Office (where elves stamp letters) and Santa House (which describes how various nations celebrate Christmas).

Finnish Lapland The white stuff

❝❞ In Finland there's no better place for a winter activity holiday than Pielinen, a 900-sq-km lake in the province of North Koraelia. Our first morning was bright and chilly, sunlight sparking through the fresh powder snow that had fallen overnight. Due to the unusually mild winter, however, the lake hadn't frozen sufficiently to safely support the weight of seven hyperactive children (aged five to eleven). Ice fishing would have to wait.

Instead, we drove to a nearby farm where wild boar and reindeer looked on bemused as our children cavorted through the snow like a pack of highly-wired wolf cubs. There were calming moments, like the wonderful views over pine-stubbled hills to the Russian border, or the traditional lunch huddled around an open fire clutching steaming bowls of salmon and potato broth.

Next up was cross-country skiing where the children were briefly reduced to penguin-shuffling mode. However, with their low centres of gravity and amply padded snowsuits, they quickly learnt not to be afraid of falling over. Inevitably, the first session deteriorated into a hysterical tangle of limbs, skis and poles; but they quickly picked up the technique over the following days. Like all the activities on this week-long trip, it was best done in quick bursts before tiredness or cold set in.

Talking of speed, nothing could match the pace of our next icy pursuit. No sooner had we stepped from our minibus into a forest clearing somewhere near Russia than we were assailed by the canine cacophony of dozens of huskies. They whipped themselves into a frenzy of leaping, slavering, wild-eyed excitement that was only unleashed when they were allowed to run. Each child sat huddled on a reindeer skin in the sledge, while a parent stood on the back runners, operating the spiky foot brake, leaning into corners and generally keeping things running smoothly. That, at least, was the theory. In fact, once the dogs started bounding though the forest it was more a case of hang on and try not to let your shoulders become dislocated.

After the exhilaration of husky sledging, there were more high-speed thrills with a snowmobiling safari and an adrenaline-charged tobogganing session in the mountains of Koli National Park.

The lake never did freeze sufficiently for ice fishing, but it hardly mattered. Besides, the children would probably have been far too busy making snow angels, cross-country skiing or pelting each other with snowballs…

Will

⬤ Inside info

▸▸ Pielinen can be reached via Joensuu, a 45-minute flight from Helsinki.

▸▸ Accommodation around the lake is mainly in rustic farmhouses or country inns.

▸▸ If you plan to squeeze several activities into a week you're better off booking a guided tour with a specialist family operator like the Adventure Company (adventurecompany.co.uk) who can take care of all the logistics.

Iceland Nature's own theme park

Iceland puts the wild in wilderness. It's an austere land riddled with suppurating mud pits, sulphurous steam vents and lava flows that resemble vast swathes of burned apple crumble. Waterfalls bloated with glacial silt retch into canyons, while fully grown trees cower inches above ground to shelter from scything Arctic winds. It's hardly your typical image of a family holiday paradise and yet Iceland, for all its austerity, is a superb destination for kids who have a sense of adventure. More back of beyond than back to the beach, the Land of Ice and Fire is Europe's ultimate – though admittedly quite pricey – adventure playground, where you can search for whales one day and skidoo across an ice cap the next.

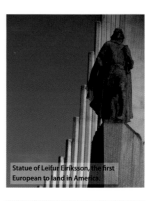
Statue of Leifur Eiríksson, the first European to land in America.

Southwest Iceland

Reykjavík

Chances are you'll be out and about most of the time, but Reykjavík (visitreykjavik.is) has enough to keep you occupied for any spare mornings or afternoons. Littl'uns will enjoy feeding the ducks at the city's central lake, while Reykjavík Zoo (husdyragardur.is) makes a fun outing to see reindeer and seals. There's also an aquarium here, plus a park for pony rides. For a dose of culture, head to the Saga Museum (sagamuseum.is) where your kids can go Viking, or the open-air Reykjavík City Museum (reykjavikmuseum.is) with its nostalgic village and farm recreations.

● Inside info

Blue Lagoon

Located between the airport and Reykjavík, the Blue Lagoon (bluelagoon.com) is about as weird and wonderful as swimming pools get. Surrounded by a barren lava landscape, the milky-blue, geothermal waters of this open-air pool steam away at 35-40°C. Wading into the waist-deep water your toes squidge into a layer of silica sludge that you can slap on your face for a therapeutic mud mask. Gently poaching yourself in the Blue Lagoon is without doubt Iceland's balmiest – and most barmy – pastime. Other thermal

Round trip

With at least a couple of weeks to spare, you could easily tour Iceland's ring road, either in a rental car or by using the long-distance bus network (bsi.is).

pools in Reykjavík include the Laugar Spa (laugarspa.is), which has the added attraction of a water slide.

The Golden Circle

Iceland's definitive day trip, this geologically supercharged tour visits Thingvellir (a UNESCO World Heritage Site of lava flows, deep ravines and the site of Iceland's original parliament), Geysir (a hotspot of geothermal vents, including the Stokkur geyser, which erupts 20 m every five minutes) and Gullfoss or Golden Falls (a beautiful waterfall plunging around 33 m into a 2.5-km-long gorge).

Seljalandsfoss & Skogafoss

This gushing duo is accessible from Road 1. Be prepared for a good soaking from the falls'

Seljalandsfoss.

Great outdoors

Horse riding
Located near Hafnarfjörður, about 10 minutes' drive from Reykjavík, Ishestar Riding Tours (ishestar.is) offers horse-riding options (for first-timers to experts) using sure-footed Icelandic ponies.

Whale watching
Available from March to October, three-hour boat trips off the Reykjavík coast are often rewarded with sightings of white-beaked dolphins, minke whales and even humpbacks and orcas.

Whitewater rafting
For gentle to moderate rapids, paddle on the Hvítá River, about an hour from Reykjavík. The River Fun trip offered by Arctic Rafting (arcticrafting.com) is suitable for children aged 10 and above.

spray, and watch your step on the slippery, uneven terrain.

Mount Hekla
You can take a jeep tour to the foot of Iceland's most active volcano. It's a long and bumpy ride, but the scenery is amazing.

Westman Islands
Unless it's dead calm (in which case the three-hour ferry trip is just about bearable), hop on a flight to this cluster of 15 volcanic islands off the south coast – made famous in 1973 when a volcano on Heimaey erupted and destroyed much of the main town. From May to early August you'll be able to see thousands of puffins.

Where can I ride in one of these?

With their giant tyres, 4WD and raised suspension, superjeeps are, quite simply, unstoppable. Join a safari from Reykjavík or the Lake Myvatn region to explore Iceland's interior in one of these monster machines and you'll spend the day driving up and down mountains, pummelling snowdrifts and treating glacial rivers like car washes. From Reykjavík it's possible to drive to the Langjökull Icecap where you can trade superjeep for an equally exhilarating snowmobile.

North Iceland

Lake Myvatn

Nowhere is Iceland's volatile character more evident than near Lake Myvatn. At Hverarönd, for example, kids will be captivated by (and no doubt keen to impersonate) the belching, foul-smelling mud pits, while at Krafla they can scurry across lava fields contorted into swirls, coils and honeycombs. Hverfjall, meanwhile, is a squat, kilometre-wide crater with a rough path stamped in its flank of loose rock. The scramble to the rim at 312 m provides dramatic views of Lake Myvatn.

⊙ Inside info

>> It's a 45-minute flight from Reykjavík to Akureyri, followed by a scenic drive to Lake Myvatn.
>> Myvatn is named after the midges that can swarm during midsummer. Local shops sell repellents and head nets.
>> In Húsavík don't miss the superb Whale Museum (icewhale.is), open May-September.

At Dimmuborgir, a walking trail probes a bizarre maze of tortured basalt, sculptured into spires, caves, arches and a disconcerting number of trolls. Driving (or cycling) around the lake, you will also encounter pseudocraters (mini-volcanoes created by steam exploding from water trapped beneath lava) and lava pillars (formed during a fissure eruption). Don't worry if the technical interpretations are beyond you or your kids; the gawp factor of the scenery far outweighs the need to grapple with too much in the way of geophysics.

Dettifoss

The central highlands of Iceland are smothered in ice caps. Thousands of years ago, volcanic activity under one of the largest, Vatnajökull, unleashed a catastrophic flood that chiselled out the Jökulsá Canyon (an hour's drive east of Lake Myvatn and a lovely location for easy walks), and laid the foundation for a series of impressive waterfalls. Dettifoss is one of Europe's most powerful – a bloated cataract spewing between terraced cliffs of lava. Every second, 200 cubic metres of dirty water is hurled 45 m to the canyon floor where it roars and froths like a gigantic cappuccino machine. It's a spectacular sight – just keep a firm hand-hold of children.

Main photo: Dettifoss.
Above left: Lake Myvatn.
Below: Humpback whale
breaching in Skjátfandi Bay.

Húsavík

Setting out several times a day into Skjátfandi Bay from the fishing town of Húsavík, a small fleet of beautifully restored, oak-hulled herring trawlers (northsailing.is) have found a new lease of life as whale-watching boats. Fulmars and arctic terns swirling above the surface are often your best clues as to the cetaceans' whereabouts. Minke whales are seen on well over 90% of outings, while harbour porpoises and pods of leaping white-beaked dolphins are also fairly common. Humpback whales and orcas are regular visitors and there have even been close encounters with blue whales.

Scandinavia Grown-ups' stuff

When to go

Milder than other parts of Scandinavia, **Denmark** has a climate more like that of London or Amsterdam. July and August are the busiest months for heading to the beach or countryside, while Copenhagen receives a burst of visitors in the run-up to Christmas when Tivoli Gardens has a festive fair and ice rink. Expect snow in the Lapland region of **Sweden** and **Finland** from November to April, with temperatures plunging to -30°C and no proper sunrise during December and January. This is the best time of year to witness the Aurora borealis, usually seen at least one night in three. Further south, cities like Stockholm and Helsinki don't get so cold or dark, and everywhere warms and brightens up in summer. Bring mozzie repellent if venturing into the wilds between June and August. The lowest temperature recorded in **Norway** is -51°C in Kárásjohka-Karasjok in the far north. However, average annual temperatures along the western coast are around 8°C with the warmest month being July. Norway's mountains protect much of the eastern part of the country from precipitation, with as little as 300 mm falling annually in some areas. Expect up to ten times this along parts of the coast. Despite its lofty latitude, **Iceland** benefits from the Gulf Stream to enjoy a temperate climate with cool summers and fairly mild winters. Average January temperatures in Reykjavík are actually higher than those in New York. Come prepared, however, for changeable weather. During mid-June you can see the midnight sun from the island of Grímsey.

Getting there

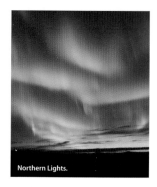

Northern Lights.

The most extensive flight network in the region is from Scandinavian Airlines (flysas.com), which serves Copenhagen daily from London Heathrow, Aberdeen, Birmingham, Dublin, and Manchester. SAS also flies daily to Stockholm and Gothenburg from Heathrow, with less frequent flights to Stockholm from Birmingham, Dublin, Edinburgh and Manchester. Oslo, Bergen and Stavanger have daily direct flights from London, with Stavanger also being served by Aberdeen and Newcastle. A non-stop service from Newark and Chicago to Stockholm is operated by SAS in partnership with United Airlines and other members of Star Alliance, while flights via Copenhagen depart from Seattle and Washington.

Finnair (finnair.com) flies from Heathrow, Bangor, Dublin and Manchester to Helsinki, as well as from Heathrow to Stockholm. Icelandair (icelandair.net) has regular scheduled flights to Iceland all year from London, Glasgow, Manchester, Amsterdam, Copenhagen, Frankfurt, Oslo, Paris, Stockholm, Boston, New York, Orlando and Washington. Additional destinations during summer include Barcelona, Berlin, Helsinki and Milan. British Airways (britishairways.com) has regular flights to Copenhagen, Billund, Stockholm, Oslo, Keflavík and Helsinki.

Ryanair (ryanair.com) flies daily from London Stansted to Stockholm, Gothenburg and Malmö, from where there is a connecting coach service to Copenhagen. Additional routes include Dublin to Malmö and Billund and Stansted to Oslo and Tampere. Other low-cost airlines with flights to the region are Bmi (flybmi.com), easyJet (easyjet.com), Iceland Express (icelandexpress.com) and Norwegian (norwegian.no).

During August, expect to pay around £85-100 for a return London-Copenhagen flight with SAS. A return flight with

Ryanair between London and Stockholm during August costs from as little as £20, plus taxes.

Getting around

In Denmark, the national train network is operated by Danish Rail (dsb. dk), coach services are offered by Abildskous Busser (abildskou. dk) and ferries are run by Scandlines (scandlines.dk). Car rental outlets are widespread expect to pay from around £50 per day. Internal flights in Sweden are served by SAS (see above) and Flynordic (flynordic. com), both of which fly from Stockholm to Kiruna in the far north. Travel on the country's sophisticated rail network can be booked through Sweden Booking (swedenbooking. com). The X-2000 train travels at up to 200 kph on all major routes, including Stockholm-Malmö-Copenhagen (via the Öresund bridge) and

Stockholm-Gothenburg. Some train services in Sweden offer family carriages with children's play corners. Express coach service is provided by Swebus (swebusexpress.se). In Norway, internal flights are available from SAS Braathens (sasbraathens. no) and Widerøe (wideroe.no). The Norwegian State Railway (nsb.no) has a well-developed network stretching from the southwest coast to Nordland. Norway Buss Express (nor-way. no) also covers most of the country, while car rental is offered by Rent a Wreck (rent-a-wreck.no), Hertz (hertz.no) and Avis (avis.no). Numerous ferries ply the fjords, including the long-established Norwegian Coastal Voyage (hurtigruten. com) which sails between Bergen and Kirkenes. The trip takes around 11 days with frequent stops along the coast. There are daily departures and the ships can carry cars.

Covering over 90% of public roads and with more than

Skip the flight

» **Drive or take the train** across the 16-km Öresund Bridge linking Denmark's capital, Copenhagen, with Malmö in Sweden.

» **Catch a ferry** with DFDS Seaways (dfds.co.uk) from Harwich to Esbjerg in Denmark. The crossing time is 17 hours and the service operates every other day.

» **Cruise with Smyril Line** (smyril-line.com) which operates a weekly passenger/car-ferry service between Bergen (Norway), Hanstholm (Denmark), Lerwick (Shetland Islands), the Faroe Islands and Seyðisfjörður (Iceland).

» **Hop on a Eurolines** (eurolines. com) coach bound for Denmark, Sweden or Norway.

» **Travel by Eurostar** (eurostar. com) from London St Pancras International to Brussels, with connecting trains to major cities in Denmark via Cologne and Hamburg.

40,000 daily bus departures, Finland has one of Europe's most comprehensive coach networks (matkahuolto.fi).

ⓘ **Fact** file

Country	Time	Language	Currency	Exchange rate approximate	International dialling code	Tourist information
Denmark	GMT+1	Danish	Danish Krona DKK	£1 = DKK8.5	+45	visitdenmark.com
Sweden	GMT+1	Swedish	Swedish Krona SEK	£1 = SEK12	+46	visitsweden.com
Norway	GMT+1	Norwegian	Norwegian Kroner NOK	£1 = NOK9.5	+47	visitnorway.com
Finland	GMT+2	Finnish, Swedish	Euro €	£1 = €1.15	+358	visitfinland.com
Iceland	GMT	Icelandic	Icelandic Kroner ISK	£1 = ISK200	+354	visiticeland.com

* English is widely spoken in each of the listed countries.

Scandinavia Grown-ups' stuff

You can also get around using high-speed trains (vr.fi) and internal flights (blue1.com). Finland's maze of interconnected lakes can be navigated on ferries operated by companies such as Silverline (finnishsilverline.com) and Karelia Lines (karelialines.fi). Silja Line (silja.com) and Viking Line (vikingline.fi) offer luxury cruises between Helsinki and Stockholm with activities and entertainment laid on for kids and teenagers. In Iceland, Air Iceland (airiceland.is) runs scheduled flights between Reykjavík and domestic airports throughout the country. Buses are operated by Trex (trex.is), Austurleid (austurleid.is) and SBK (sbk.is). Cars and campervans can be rented through several agencies, including Budget (budget.is).

Accommodation

Check out tourist board websites for online booking facilities. In Denmark, popular family choices include rental cottages, holiday villages, farmstays, campsites and hostels. Novasol Cottages (novasol.co.uk) offer weekly rentals throughout the country. Standard cottages (modern homes with accommodation for up to six people) cost from around £300 per week during peak season, while top-end properties (sleeping up to 12 people and with luxury touches

like swimming pools) start at around £1000 per week. Also try Dansommer (dansommer.com). Denmark's holiday villages are well equipped for self-catering holidays. Weekly peak-season rates range from £350-900, depending on the type of accommodation. Try Lalandia (lalandia.com) near Rødby which has its own waterpark; Strandhotellerne (strandhotellerne.dk) which has four beachside resorts around Denmark; Skallerup Klit (skallerup.dk) with its indoor Atlantis Waterland and Silkeborg (danparcs.com) which boasts an artificial ski slope. You can book farmstays in Denmark at bondegaardsferie.dk and ecoholiday.dk, while family hostels are available through Danhostels (danhostel.dk). Denmark's campsites have excellent facilities and are very popular with Danish families.

In Sweden, camping is the most popular form of accommodation during summer months. SCR (camping.se) publishes an extensive directory of campsites, as well as some 12,000 rental cottages. Also offering excellent facilities for inexpensive self-catering holidays, the Swedish Tourist Association (svenskaturistforeningen.se) has a network of about 300 youth hostels (known as vandrarhem). Hotel accommodation in Stockholm is expensive,

but you can save money by staying in a holiday cottage on the coast, 30-minutes' drive from the city. Destination Stockholms Skärgård (dess.se) lists properties throughout the region (including the Stockholm Archipelago) with peak-season rates from around £350 per week. Two hours north of Gothenburg, TanumStrand (tanumstrand.se) is a popular family-friendly resort with waterslides and a mini-zoo, while Isaberg (isaberg.com), 120 km east of Gothenburg, has 70 chalets in a holiday village setting, plus a plethora of year-round activities, from canoeing to skiing.

Norway's Fjord Pass (fjord-pass.com) offers discounts on accommodation at 150 hotels, guesthouses and cabins throughout the country. It costs around £10 and is valid for two adults and any children under the age of 15. With the pass, you will find cabins and apartments from as little as £40 per night. Also good value, Hostelling International Norway (vandrerhjem.no) operates 110 youth and family hostels.

In Finland you will find a wide range of cottages and farmstays at Lomarengas (lomarengas.fi), while Destination Lapland (yllas-travel-service.fi) specializes in log cabins in Lapland. Camping in Finland (camping.fi) provides access to 330 campsites across the country. Expect to pay between £10-20 per family pitch. Located mainly in the central lakeland area, Finland has about 200 holiday villages, with prices from £100-350 per week per cottage.

Iceland has a wide range of hotels and guesthouses, many of which offer children's discounts. Expect to pay anything from £35-120 for a double room with breakfast. For hands-on rural stays, try Icelandic Farm Holidays (farmholidays.is). There are also 26 hostels around Iceland which can be booked through Hostelling International (hostel. is). Campsites in Iceland are usually open from the beginning of June until the end of August and are free of charge for children under 16.

Food & drink

Seafood features predominantly in Scandinavian cuisine. Local specialities like pickled fish and black bread may demand an acquired taste, but you will also find basics like meat and potatoes. The *smörgåsbord* buffet-style of dining will appeal to picky children, while fast-food outlets and pizzerias are widespread. In Denmark try herring in various guises (from raw and pickled to cooked in a rich cream sauce). *Smørrebrød*, the Danish open sandwich, is available in umpteen varieties.

❝❞ Unlike the British salad bar, where you get one shot at loading and no chance of a refill, the thing about all Swedish buffets is that there is no stigma attached to shuttling back to the trough as many times as you fancy. For children this free-range approach to feeding comes close to heaven.

David Wickers, journalist and director, Bridge & Wickers

Fresh, pickled and smoked seafood (particularly herring, crayfish, salmon and eel) are popular dishes in Sweden, but you should also try game dishes such as stir-fried reindeer. *Dagens rätt* (dish of the day), consisting of a main course with salad, bread and a drink, is available from many restaurants for around £6. Expect to pay anything from £20 upwards for a three-course meal in a mid-priced restaurant. In northern Norway there is a long tradition of drying cod on wooden racks. To eat this local delicacy, first beat the dried fillets with a wooden mallet, soak them in water and douse in mustard or butter. Other specialities include roast pork ribs, cured mutton and sheep's heads, with ears, eyes and all. *Fårikål*, a stew of lamb, cabbage and whole peppercorns is a traditional autumn dish. Finland's traditional cuisine is closely tied to the seasons. In summer new potatoes, fresh vegetables, salmon, whitefish and Baltic herring dominate menus, with crayfish in season from late July to September.

Game meats, mushrooms, cloudberries, blueberries and lingonberries figure prominently in the autumn, while fish, such as burbot, are hauled from ice-covered lakes during winter. The seafood in Iceland is of outstanding quality. Try Icelandic Fish and Chips in the old harbour area of Reykjavík, where plaice, cod and haddock are served with vegetables and homemade lemonade.

Health & safety

Scandinavia is generally very safe and there is no need to take any special vaccination precautions. Mosquitoes can be a nuisance during summer months, particularly in Sweden and Finland. Potentially more dangerous are severe winter temperatures in the far north. Be sure to take warm clothing and be especially alert to the threat of frostbite or hyperthermia in young children. Other safety issues to be aware of include unfenced natural hazards, like waterfalls and volcanic areas in Iceland and frozen lakes in Finland and Sweden.

Scandinavia Family favourites

Lapland specialist **Discover the World** (T+44 (0)1737-214250, discover-the-world.co.uk) offers several unusual winter breaks in Lapland suitable for families. The three-night Sami Experience (available November to April, from around £680 per person based on a family of four) promises a fascinating insight into the lives of the indigenous Sami of Swedish Lapland, including a stay in a wooden *lavvu*. Three nights at Kakslauttanen Cabins in Finnish Lapland, where you have a chance to spend a night in an igloo (made of ice or glass) and explore the surrounding forest by reindeer sleigh, husky sledge or snowmobile, costs from £890 per person. Alternatively, stay at Finland's Lainio Snow Village with its ice rooms and gentle ski slopes.

Inntravel (T+44 (0)1653-617001, inntravel.co.uk) offers an original winter experience in Norway for keen skiers with babies. Wrapped in furs and securely strapped into mini-sledges, under-fours can glide along behind their parents on easy cross-country ski trails. One week half board at Bardola Hotel in Geilo, including return flights to Oslo, rail and hotel transfers, costs from around £980/adult and £370/child (aged two to three). Children under two travel free.

Tour operators

The Adventure Company
adventurecompany.co.uk

Discover the World
discover-the-world.co.uk

Esprit Holidays
esprit-holidays.co.uk

Exodus
exodus.co.uk

Explore Worldwide
explore.co.uk

Families Worldwide
familiesworldwide.co.uk

Headwater
headwater.com

Inntravel
inntravel.co.uk

Specialised Tours
specialisedtours.com

Expect a frosty reception at the **Icehotel** (icehotel.com) in Swedish Lapland. The thermometer behind the check-in counter usually reads around -6°C. The counter is, naturally, made of ice, along with everything else in this fairy-tale hotel located in Jukkasjärvi, a small village 200 km north of the Arctic Circle. From the outside, the hotel resembles a giant, featureless igloo. But inside there are ice chandeliers sparkling with fibre optics, candles burning in carved recesses and intricately chiselled pillars. It feels like you've arrived on Planet Krypton. Each room has its own ice bed strewn with reindeer furs, but guests are also given Arctic-grade sleeping bags. Hotel staff provide a full briefing on what to wear (thermal everything) and how to breathe (preferably through your nose). In the morning you're awoken with a hot cup of lingonberry juice. Rooms cost from around £100 per person per night.

Index

accommodation 18
air travel 16
Alberobello 170
Algarve 135
Alpes 100
Alps, French 96
Alps ski guide 98
Amalfi Coast 173
Amsterdam 192
Andalucía 126
Arctic Circle 72
Assisi 168
Athens 214
Austria 200
Azores 136

Balearic Islands 128
Barcelona 122
Bari 170
Bath 35
Belgium 190
Berlin 194
Bernese Oberland 198
Birmingham 36
Black Forest 195
Blackpool 38
Blue Lagoon 290
bottle-feeding 20
breastfeeding 20
Bristol 35
Britain 22-47
Brittany 91
Brussels 190
Bulgaria 255

camping 19
Canary Islands 130
Cantabria 120
car travel 17
Cardiff 40
Carinthia 201
Carpathian Mountains 254
Catalonia 122
Central Europe 182-205
Chamonix 96
Channel Islands 29

Co Clare 68
Co Cork 70
Co Kerry 71
Co Wicklow 58
coach travel 17
Copenhagen 274
Corfu 222
Cornwall 35
Corsica 103
Costa Blanca 125
Costa Brava 124
Costa Daurada 124
Costa del Sol 127
Côte d'Azur 100
Coto Doñana 127
Cotswolds 37
Crete 226
Croatia 258
Cyprus 228
Czech Republic 230

Danube Delta 255
Denmark 274
Derbyshire 36
Dettifoss 292
Devon 34
Disneyland Resort, Paris 88
documents 14
Dordogne 92
Dorset, Jurassic Coast 34
drinking 20
Dublin 56
Dubrovnik 258

East Anglia 33
Eastern Europe 242-263
Edinburgh 42
England, central 36
England, north 38
England, northeast 39
England, southeast 32
England, southwest 34
Extremadura 119

farmstays 18
ferry travel 17

Finland 286
Flanders 190
Florence 160
food 19
Formentera 128
France 76-109
France, Atlantic coast 92
France, south 100
French Alps 96
French Pyrenees 93
Fuerteventura 131

Galicia 121
Galway 67
Germany 194
Giant's Causeway 60
Glasgow 43
Gothenburg 279
Gower Peninsula 40
Gran Canaria 130
Granada 126
Graubunden 198
Greece & Turkey 206-241
Greek islands 222

Halkidikí 219
Helsinki 286
hotels 18
Hungary 253
Húsavík 293

Ibiza 128
Iceland 290
Irákleio 226
Ireland 48-75
Isle of Wight 32
Istanbul 230
Italy 146-181
Italian Lakes 166

Kefalloniá 222
Kos 223
Kraków 252

L

Lake Bled 256
Lake Bohinj 256
Lake District 39
Lake Garda 166
Lakes, Italy 166
Languedoc-Rousillon 102
Lanzarote 131
Lapland 279, 288
Le Marche 168
Lecce 170
Leicestershire 36
Lésvos 223
Límnos 224
Lisbon 134
Liverpool 38
Ljubljana 256
Loire Valley 94
London 30
Lucca 158
Lucerne 199
Luxembourg 193

M

Madeira 136
Madrid 118
Mallorca 128
Manchester 38
Mayo 66
Menorca 128
Milan 167
motorhomes 19
Mount Etna 174

N

Nafplio 219
Naples 172
Netherlands 192
Newcastle 39
New Forest 32
Norfolk 33
Normandy 90
Norway 282
Norwegian fjords 283
Nottinghamshire 36

O

Oslo 282

Otranto 170

P

packing 14
Parc Astérix 89
Paris 84
Peloponnese 218
Pembrokeshire 41
Perugia 168
Pisa 158
Poland 252
Pompeii 172
Portugal 134
Prague 250
Provence 100
Puglia 170
Pyrenees, French 93
Pyrenees, Spanish 125

R

Reykjavík 290
Rhodes 224
road travel 16
Romania 254
Rome 154
Ronda 126
Roscommon 66

S

Salzburg 200
Santoríni 224
Sardinia 175
Scandinavia 264-299
Scotland 42
Scotland, Highlands 43
Scotland, Islands 43
Seville 126
Shannon 68
Shropshire 36
Sicily 174
Siena 158
Sierra Nevada 127
ski guide, Alps 98
Skiathos 224
Slovakia 253
Slovenia 256
snacks 20
Snowdonia 40
Somerset 35

Sorrento 173
Spain & Portugal 110-145
Spain, central 118
Spain, northern 120
Staffordshire 36
Stockholm 278
Styria 201
Sweden 278
Switzerland 198

T

Tenerife 132
Tignes-le-Lac 97
tour operators 12
train 17
Trani 170
Turkey 230
Turkey, Aegean coast 232
Turkey, Mediterranean Coast 234
Turkey, Turquoise Coast 233
Tuscany 158
Tyrol 201

U

Umbria 168

V

Valais 199
Venice 162
Vienna 200
villas 18
Vizcayan Coast 120

W

Wales 40
Wallonia 190
Warwickshire 37
Worcestershire 37

Y

Yorkshire 38

Z

Zákynthos 225

Picture credits

William Gray
pg 1, 2, 4, 5, 6-7, 8, 22, 23, 25, 26, 28, 30-31, 32, 33, 34, 35, 36, 37, 38, 39, 40, 41, 42, 43, 46, 47, 76-77, 78, 81 (chef), 83, 84, 85, 90, 91, 92, 94, 95 (châteaux), 96, 97, 103, 146-147,149 (Venice and Lake Garda), 153, 162, 163, 165, 166, 170, 171 (fisherman), 172, 177, 180-181, 185 (Amsterdam), 193, 198 (boat), 205, 207, 208 (Athens and Ancient Olympia), 211 (statue), 214, 217, 218, 219 (Epídaurus), 220-221, 223, 229, 242-243, 245 (dragon, lake and cave), 248, 256, 257, 260, 264-265, 267 (all except ship), 272 (snow angels), 273 (midnight sun), 280-281, 282, 284-285, 286 (sledging), 287, 289, 290, 291 (jeep), 292, 293 (waterfall), 298, 299, 303

Shutterstock
Aznym Adam: pg 51 (castle); **Danilo Ascione:** pg 155 (statue), 162 (mask), 173 (Positano); **Denis Babenko:** pg 157 (St Peter's Square); **Veronika Bakos:** pg 171 (oil); **Can Balcioglu:** pg 209 (boat); **John de la Bastide:** pg 196 (gnome); **Mauro Bighin:** pg 158; **Graham Bloomfield:** pg 228; **W H Chow:** pg 251 (Prague); **David Romero Corral:** pg 230-231; **Paul Cowan:** pg 53 (bread); **Nathan B Dappen:** pg 171 (Gargano); **Antonio Ovejero Diaz:** pg 251 (castle); **Marc Dietrich:** pg 187 (pretzel); **Willem Dijkstra:** pg 174 (temple); **Z Dreamer:** pg 61; **Brian Dunne:** pg 51 (Connemara); **Dushenina:** pg 219 (coast); **Holger Ehlers:** pg 278 (snow leopard); **Gianni Fantauzzi:** pg 149 (hill town); **Stephen Finn:** pg 100 (Pont du Gard); **Gabriel GS:** pg 201;**Vladislav Garfinkel:** pg 87; **Joe Gough:** pg 55, 60; **Jaroslaw Grudzinski:** pg 269 (igloo); **Agnieszka Guzowska:** pg 70-71; **Jeanne Hatch:** pg 51 (wakeboarder); **Fred Hendriks:** pg 291 (waterfall); **John Hua:** pg 173 (Pompeii); **Wojciech Jaskowski:** pg 226 (beach); **Kameel:** pg 81 (petanque); **Azmil Khazali:** pg 211 (baklava); **Falk Kienas:** pg 255 (church); **Igor XIII:** pg 253 (mountains); **Eric Isselée:** pg 198 (marmot); **Sarah Johnson:** pg 187 (Toblerone); **L Kelly:** pg 57 (Trinity College); **Julius Kielaitis:** pg 249 (castle); **Irina Korshunova:**

pg 226-227; **Patryk Kosmider:** pg 68; **Koster:** pg 208 (Knossos); **Jan Kranendonk:** pg 192 (bike); **Roman Krochuk:** pg 294; **Emilia Kun:** pg 196 (Heidelberg); **Philip Lange:** pg 197 (Pied Piper); **Luri:** pg 169; **Elisa Locci:** pg 259 (Plitvice); **Franco Mantegani:** pg 171 (Lecce); **Milan Markovic:** pg 240-241; **Vladimir Melnik:** pg 209 (bazaar); **Galina Mikhalishina:** pg 216; **Mik Lav:** pg 102; **Lukasz Misiek:** pg58; **Eugene Mogilnikov:** pg 156 (Pieta); **Morgan Lane Photography:** pg 53 (leprechaun); **Clara Natoli:** pg 151 (mosaic), 232; **Mikhail Nekrasov:** pg 149 (Pompeii); **Anna Nemkovich:** pg 167 (Milan); **Netfalls:** pg 219 (boat), 235; **Ioan Nicolae:** pg 245 (castle); **Govert Nieuwland:** pg 174 (Etna); **Niserin:** pg 253 (hikers); **Michael Onisiforou:** pg 208 (castle); **Wikus Otto:** pg 200 (horse); **Regien Paassen:** pg 186 (tulips); **Bruno Pagnanelli:** pg 175; **PaintedLens:** pg 147 (Constantine); **Panaspics:** pg 62 (castle); **Amra Pasic:** pg 157 (St Peter's); **Catalin Plesa:** pg 255 (Danube); **Martin Pohlack:** pg 149 (Etna); **Vova Pomortzeff:** pg 250 (clock); **Viktor Pryymachuk:** pg 185 (castle); **Puchan:** pg 252, 253 (mine); **Radu Razvan:** pg 247 (egg); **Rebvt:** pg 238; **Styve Reineck:** pg 192 (windmills); **Steeve Roche:** pg 66-67; **Salamanderman:** pg 194-195; **Marcel Schauer:** pg 51 (eagle); **Nailia Schwarz:** pg 197 (mountains); **Elena Schweitzer:** pg 196 (puppets); **Andrea Seemann:** pg 69 (Clonmacnoise), pg 201; **David H Seymour:** pg 215; **Iryna Shpulak:** pg 194; **Marek Slusarczyk:** pg 154 (Trevi Fountain); **Ronald Sumners:** pg 191 (Mannekin Pis); **N A Switzerland:** pg 255 (pelican); **Tatonka:** pg 293 (whale); **Trykster:** pg 227 (gorge); **Tsonis:** pg 208 (yacht), 222; **Vinicius Tupinamba:** pg 157 (St Peter's dome); **Rui Vale de Sousa:** pg 250 (statue); **Valeria73:** pg 168; **Jeffrey Van Daele:** pg 187 (snowboarder); **Asier Villafranca:** pg 160-161; **Vladiwelt:** pg 197 (castle); **Walsh Photos:** pg 59, 64 (Mullaghmore); **Pippa West:** pg 149 (Roman Forum), 154 (Colosseum); **Brent Wong:** pg 232 (temple); **Andy Z:** pg 93; **Zalka:** pg 283 (cruise ship);

Jarno Gonzalez Zarraonandia: pg 230, 231; **Zurijeta:** pg 51 (chocolate)

BI-TC
pg 185 (Tintin)

Baby Friendly Boltholes
pg 108

Bushmills Inn
pg 74

Center Parcs
pg 108

Club Med
pg 109, 179

Corsican Places
pg 107

Croatia National Tourist Board
pg 259 (Dubrovnik)

Discover the World
pg 270, 272 (rafting), 273 (Blue Lagoon), 279, 291 (horses, whale and rafting)

Disney
pg 88, 107

Esprit Holidays
pg 78 (skiers), 98, 99, 109

Eurocamp
pg 104 (beach), 106

Europa Park
pg 185, 195

Exodus
pg 206-207, 233, 258 (boys)

French Affair
pg 108

Futuroscope
pg 100

Gardaland
pg 167

Jennifer Gray
pg 159

Jason Hobbins
pg 152

Inntravel
pg 179

Jersey Tourism
pg 29

Kelly's Resort Hotel
pg 75

Keycamp Holidays
pg 106, 180, 263

Kon-Tiki Museum
pg 283

London Eye
pg 25

Moominworld
pg 286

Nausicaa
C Alexis Rosenfield: pg 91

Powder Byrne
pg 180

Siblu
pg 106

swiss-image.ch
pg 182-183, 185 (hiking and cycling),
188-189, 199

Ally Thompson
pg 51 (Tramore Strand and folk
museum)

Tourism Ireland
pg 48-49, 54, 56, 57 (Croke Park), 62
(trout), 63, 64 (surfers), 65, 67, 69,
70, 72

Visit Denmark
pg 267 (Viking ship), 274, 275, 276-277

Walibi Belgium
pg 190-191

waterloo1815.be
pg 191

Mark Wright
pg 212

Footprint credits

Project Editor: Jo Williams
Text Editor: William Gray
Picture Editor: William Gray
Proofreader: Ria Gane
Layout & production: William Gray,
Angus Dawson
Maps: Kevin Feeney

Managing Director: Andy Riddle
Commercial Director: Patrick Dawson
Publisher: Alan Murphy
Publishing managers: Felicity Laughton,
Jo Williams
Digital Editor: Alice Jell
Design: Rob Lunn
Marketing: Liz Harper, Hannah Bonnell
Sales: Jeremy Parr
Advertising: Renu Sibal
Finance & administration: Elizabeth Taylor

Print

Manufactured in India by Nutech.

Footprint Feedback

We try as hard as we can to make each Footprint
guide as up to date as possibie but, of course,
things always change. If you want to let us know
about your experiences – good, bad or ugly
– then don't delay, go to footprinttravelguides.
com and send in your comments.

Publishing information

Footprint Europe with Kids, 1st edition
© Footprint Handbooks Ltd, May 2010

ISBN 978-1-907263-02-6
CIP DATA: A catalogue record for this book is
available from the British Library.

® Footprint Handbooks and the Footprint
mark are a registered trademark of Footprint
Handbooks Ltd.

Published by Footprint

6 Riverside Court
Lower Bristol Road
Bath BA2 3DZ, UK
T +44 (0)1225 469141
F +44 (0)1225 469461
discover@footprinttravelguides.com
footprinttravelguides.com

Distributed in North America by

Globe Pequot Press, Guilford, Connecticut

Ordnance Survey® This product includes
mapping data licensed from
Ordnance Survey® with the permission of the
Controller of Her Majesty's Stationery Office.
© Crown Copyright. All rights reserved. Licence
No. 100027877.

Acknowledgements

Europe with Kids has been very much a family effort. It wouldn't have been possible without the
tremendous support of my wife, Sally, who is not only a brilliant mother to our twins, Joseph and Eleanor,
but has also been the super-efficient mastermind behind the extensive family trips we've undertaken
for this book. As for Joe and Ellie, they have responded superbly to every weird and wonderful travel
experience their parents have hauled them off on. They are fantastic little travellers, and I hope this book
will be the inspiration for many more trips with them throughout Europe.
Special thanks to Ally Thompson for contributing the chapter on Ireland.